Presented

To

Aileen Aderholdt, Librarian
For

Carl A. Rudisill Library
of
Lenoir Rhyne College
by the Author

E.M. Coulter
September 3
1973

WILLIAM
MONTAGUE
BROWNE

Versatile Anglo-Irish American
1823-1883

WILLIAM MONTAGUE BROWNE
Courtesy of Sara Cobb Baxter of Athens, Georgia

MRS. WILLIAM M. (ELIZA JANE) BROWNE
Courtesy of Sara Cobb Baxter of Athens, Georgia

WILLIAM MONTAGUE BROWNE

Versatile Anglo-Irish American
1823-1883

By E. MERTON COULTER

UNIVERSITY OF GEORGIA PRESS   •   ATHENS

To
DEAN J. ALTON HOSCH
Teacher, Soldier, Friend
Who Helped Me Discover
General William Montague Browne

❧ *Contents* ❧

Illustrations

≥ *Preface* ≥

THOSE WHO write history from the records (and who should not!) must stick to them within the proper limits of their meaning. Unfortunately but inevitably, on almost any subject complete records were never made, and not all of those which were made have generally been preserved. As a result, some parts of almost any story cannot be fully presented. This is especially true in writing a biography of William Montague Browne who, before coming to America, spent the first half of his life in Europe—principally in England and Ireland. This part of his career is almost a blank except for snatches of information which were published incidentally during his lifetime, much of which must have come from him or have had his approval. But he never left a connected story or reminiscences of this part of his life; and howsoever much curiosity might make one yearn for more information, his life in America was a unit within itself and it is all this biography purports to be; and certainly it was a remarkable career, entirely detached from what went before.

Information on Browne's life in America begins with his position on the editorial board of the *New York Journal of Commerce;* unfortunately his contributions to this newspaper cannot be definitely determined since they were not signed, though it is known that he was concerned mostly with foreign affairs. When in 1859 he arrived in Washington to become associate editor of the *Constitution,* and a little later when he bought the paper, his position on public issues was more apparent. He now became an important force in the Buchanan administration, using his newspaper always in support of the President's policies, and making it a powerful factor in promoting the Democratic party. The editorials in the *Constitution* give a complete picture of Browne politically and mark him as one of the most outspoken secessionists in Washington.

He went with the Confederacy, where records of his services link him closely with Jefferson Davis in diplomatic and military affairs;

but not until the close of the war does it become possible to present him fully in the flesh and blood. Of special value in this respect is the correspondence that passed between him and his New York friend Samuel L. M. Barlow, which began in 1860, was interrupted by the war, and afterwards continued into the late 1870's. The fuller treatment of his life after the war is justified by the importance of his contributions to agriculture, journalism, and education.

Much of what Browne was can be captured only by frequent quotations of what he said about men, issues, and the pestilences of the times—especially by correspondence resulting from his close association with the Howell Cobb family and with the Jefferson Davises and other important people of the day. It should not be considered wasted words to give in detail a glimpse into the personal life of an expatriate Anglo-Irishman and his Yorkshire wife, who came to America for a new life, joined wholeheartedly the South in its fight for independence, lost all in that struggle never regretting that decision, and at last mingled their dust in Southern soil.

As usual no one writes a book wholly by himself, and as usual in my experience John W. Bonner, Special Collections Librarian, and Mrs. William Tate of the same Department, University of Georgia Library, have been alert in finding fugitive facts. Also, special mention must be made of the help Col. H. B. Fant of the National Archives gave in locating material which would never have come to my attention, in collections in the Library of Congress as well as in the National Archives.

Ezra J. Warner of LaJolla, California, author of the biographies of the Union and Confederate generals, became especially interested in the European background of Browne and used every effort and device to ferret him out, but with little success. Further reference is made to Warner in the appendix. It should be superfluous to add in this age of enlightment that librarians and directors of historical societies have been uniformly eager to help; but a special accolade must be handed to Mattie Russell, Custodian of Manuscripts in the Duke University Library.

E. M. C

PRESIDENT BUCHANAN AND HIS CABINET IN 1859
From the Collections of the Library of Congress

HOWELL COBB, SPECIAL FRIEND OF BROWNE
From a photograph taken when he was Secretary of the United States
Treasury, in Samuel Boykin, *A Memorial of the Hon. Howell Cobb
of Georgia,* frontispiece

MRS. HOWELL COBB

UNIVERSITY OF GEORGIA IN ANTE-BELLUM TIMES
From *Gleason's Pictorial* (Boston), May 13, 1854

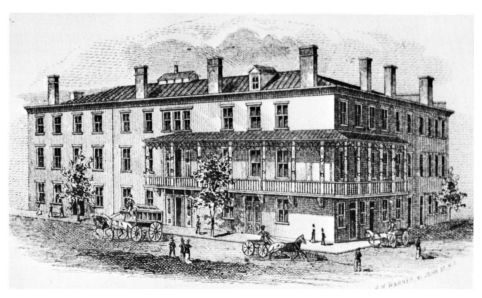

COMMERCIAL HOTEL, ATHENS, GEORGIA, WHERE BROWNE OCCASIONALLY DINED
From a hotel letterhead in the Office of the Ordinary, Clarke County, Athens

SAMUEL LATHAM MITCHILL BARLOW OF NEW
YORK, LONG-TIME FRIEND OF BROWNE
From a photo by Kurtz, in *Harper's Weekly*, July 27, 1889

ROCK COLLEGE, ATHENS, GEORGIA, WHERE BROWNE
LIVED DURING HIS LAST YEARS
From *Souvenir of the State Normal School, Athens, Ga.*, about 1900

The Southern Farm & Home

WM. M. BROWNE, EDITOR.

J. W. BURKE & CO., PUBLISHERS.

TERMS: $2 per Annum.

Athens, ~~Macon~~, Ga., April 8 1870

Dear Colonel,

I learned from Col. Yancey in Atlanta that our friend Lewis has resigned his place as Sec'y of the G.S.A.S. & that Col. Yancey has nominated me for the vacancy in a circular letter to the members of the Executive Committee.

I would not under any circumstances run against Col. Lewis, but if as I understand his resignation is definite and irrevocable I should like to be elected. I do not want to be beaten if I can help it, and write to you as a friend in whom I can confide to do all you can for me. I would go there for but I have no house to devise.

Yr. friend

Yr. colleagues of the 6th Dist.,
Messrs. Montgomery & (I believe)
Howard, can no doubt be influenced by a line from you.

Wm. M. Browne

HOLOGRAPH LETTER BY WILLIAM MONTAGUE BROWNE.
(IN THE POSSESSION OF E. M. COULTER.)

MONOGRAM OF WILLIAM MONTAGUE BROWNE

❧ I ❧

William Montague Browne Settles in America and Becomes a Journalist

WILLIAM MONTAGUE BROWNE, Anglo-Irish-American, must have considered that part of his life before he came to America as of little or no importance, for he left no authentic record of it, and little such from other sources seems to exist. Yet there were during his lifetime widespread rumors and statements purporting to be facts concerning his ancestry, education, and career in Ireland, England, and on the Continent. It is not known how this information or misinformation originated, but it may be suspected that some of it must have come from Browne himself. Certainly, however, he could not have spread the report that he had fought in the Crimean War, for he was at that time in the United States.

There seems to be no doubt that Browne was born in County Mayo, Ireland, on July 7, 1823, for he celebrated that day as his birthday, and there is supporting evidence as to the year and place of his birth. He was of English ancestry transplanted to Ireland probably as early as the reign of King James I. Information retailed about him was specific enough to hold that he was a son of D. Geoffrey Browne, who was for many years a member of the British Parliament, representing County Mayo, holding the title of Lord Oranmore and Browne, and for a time a Privy Councillor. Also, it was frequently stated that William Montague Browne was a graduate of Trinity College, University of Dublin, and that he had been prepared for college at Rugby while the famous Dr. Thomas Arnold was headmaster. Persistent research in England and Ireland failed to substantiate these statements, although he could have been an "unrecorded" son of D. Geoffrey Browne; and whether or not he attended Rugby and Trinity College, Dublin, he received a highly polished and thorough education somewhere. There can be no doubt that he was widely traveled over Europe—Poland, Italy, France, and elsewhere—and that he was

1

well versed in international relations and probably held a place in the diplomatic service of England for some years before he came to America.[1]

The mystery of Browne's early life does not end with his arrival in America, which was probably in 1851 or 1852. What he did for the next three or four years is unknown. William H. Russell, a reporter for *The Times* of London, who came to America in the spring of 1861 and who visited Montgomery, Alabama, while the Confederate government was still located there, had an interview with Browne and reported that he had "lost his money in land speculation,"[2] which Browne or someone well acquainted with him must have told Russell. Browne's liking for travel, which he had displayed in Europe, may have set him on the go when he first came to America, for there is reason to believe that he may have visited some of the islands of the West Indies, because in a statement supposedly made by him he referred to an intimate knowledge of conditions in Haiti and Jamaica, which was "derived from actual observation."[3] As for his land speculation, he might have carried it on in the West or possibly in New York City, which he probably made his headquarters, as he had landed in America there.

At any rate, when he had lost whatever fortune he had brought with him, as his fellow countryman Russell said, Browne "turned his pen to good account as a journalist."[4] He joined the editorial department of the *New York Journal of Commerce* "three or four years" ago, as noted by the management of that newspaper in 1859. He would, therefore, have begun his newspaper career in 1855 or 1856, in time to play some part in the presidential campaign of 1856; but in recognition of his international background, the *Journal* noted that with "foreign affairs, and especially with European topics" he was "very familiar" and that it was "with this branch of service" to which he had chiefly devoted himself.[5]

Browne gave much attention to Napoleon III and his ambitions, the rumblings of unification of the Italian states around Sardinia, and the developments in Prussia, Russia, Austria, Serbia, with the Chinese treaty, and affairs in India. He also had something to say about Cuba, Mexico, and the ambitions of England and the United States in Central America. On the last-named subject he took occasion to praise Queen Victoria and her England: "Her Majesty can truly announce that which every friend of liberty must rejoice to learn, that free England and free America are on terms of the most cordial amity and good will," and he predicted that the "long disputed Central American question will be finally and satisfactorily settled."[6]

Browne could not forego commenting on affairs in his native Ireland, especially on some of the revolutionary lawlessness carried out by their so-called Ribbon Societies. Their chief aim and object, he said, was "to assert the indefeasible right of the occupiers [of land] to perpetuate possession, and to aid in assassinating any landlord or land agent" who might "venture to dispute the claim."[7]

Although Browne's chief duty was to comment on foreign relations and international developments around the world, he did not deny himself the pleasure of giving his opinions on domestic subjects. Since the editors of the *Journal* were friends of James Buchanan— and Hallock, one of the editors, was especially close—the paper took a decided though not a very active part in the presidential election of 1856, and Browne was in the forefront. Browne was to profit from Buchanan's election in the course of time. When some of the British newspapers attacked some of President Buchanan's policies, Browne accused them of "editorial comments which betray more solicitude for us and our institutions than is exactly the rules of that truly benevolent association founded in England some years ago, namely, 'the Never-poke-your-nose-into-other-people's-business Society'." He added, "We have an idea, arrogant perhaps, that we are able to mind our own affairs, and so not need counsel from interested outsiders."[8]

Browne early took a position on abolitionism and the slavery question out of line with that held by many Englishmen. In 1859, in castigating the Earl of Carlisle (Lord Morpeth) for his abolition speech, Browne noted that we were "a very practical people in this country. We are also a really philanthropic people," he added, "but we are bitterly opposed to wild theories and bogus philanthropy. With the example of Jamaica and Hayti before our eyes; with a knowledge derived from actual observation of the practical effects of Abolitionism in those two islands, namely,—utter debasement of the negro population, untilled sugar plantations, and deserted cotton fields," Americans would oppose such a catastrophe for their own country.[9]

Certainly since the days of President Andrew Jackson, if not before, presidents had rewarded their friends and party workers with positions in the government; Buchanan did so, and, of course, the practice was not to end with him. His New York friends were variously taken care of: John A. Dix to be postmaster of New York City; Augustus Schell, Collector of Customs of New York City—and William Montague Browne, a clerk in the customs house.

Browne had worked both with tongue and pen, equally fluent with both, for Buchanan and the Democratic nominees in New York in

1856, and he was to continue his party service on into the campaign of 1860. By 1856, having been in this country for only four or five years, Browne had already become an intense practicing Democrat, and his zeal for the party had recommended him to the New York State Democratic Central Committee, which invited him to "make addresses in counties surrounding the city of New York." He did so "with ability and effect."[10] His efforts were expended in getting John B. Haskin elected to Congress. During the next two years Haskin strayed from the strict Buchanan Democrats on the Kansas slavery issue and went off with the anti-Lecompton wing of the party.

This was too much for Browne and the regular Democrats. When Haskin came up for re-election in 1858, he was denied the regular Democratic nomination, and Browne was asked by the Democratic Central Committee "to address the democracy of the State" both in Haskin's district and elsewhere. Browne confined his campaign largely to Westchester County, where the speech he made at Morrisania denouncing Haskin attracted much attention. Haskin naturally received some Republican votes as well as the support of the disgruntled anti-Lecompton Democrats and, consequently, was re-elected by a small majority over the regular Democratic nominee, Gouverneur Kemble.[11]

By this time Browne had established himself as a man of influence in the New York Democratic party, and President Buchanan was coming to look upon him as a party force not to be neglected, to now and then use him as a trouble-shooter in the criss-cross of Empire State politics. In 1859 Buchanan suggested that he checkmate the attempts of the Republicans to seduce the Irish voters, feeling that Irishman Browne would have special influence with other Irishmen.[12]

With this party service in mind, it was, therefore, not surprising that Browne should be given a clerkship in the New York City customs house—the surprise should be at its insignificance. Collector Schell in appointing Browne seemed to be moved as much by some complimentary editorials Browne had written about him in the *Journal of Commerce* as by Browne's party service. But, after all, the position was a sinecure, some days requiring no work, although Browne scrupulously went to his desk every day to see what there was to do. The annual salary was about a thousand dollars, and Browne held the position for only three or four months, during which time he was out six or seven weeks on account of sickness.[13]

On April 30, 1859, the editorial board of the *Journal of Commerce* announced that the news had gone out to the press that their colleague Browne had "been invited to take the responsible position of chief

editor of the Washington Constitution (later the Washington Union)."
There then followed this editorial tribute to Browne:

We have no doubt of the fact that he has been so invited, with the full approbation of President BUCHANAN, and that he has accepted the invitation, and will soon enter upon his duties.

While we regret to part with Mr. Browne, whose amiable character and unassuming manners have endeared him to us all, we congratulate the readers of the Washington Constitution, and especially the persons immediately concerned in it and with it, that they are to have the benefit of his valuable services.

Mr. Browne, although a foreigner by birth, is a great admirer of American institutions, and by diligent study during the eight years of his residence in this country, has made himself better acquainted with them, and with the principles on which they are founded, than are most native born Americans of equally fine talents and education, and of mature age. He is a Democrat of the first water, although belonging to a noble family in Ireland, and liable at a future day to inherit its distinctions. He however regards these things at a very low rate, and only desires to act well his part as an American citizen, to which honor he attained some two years ago.

With foreign affairs, and especially with European topics, he is very familiar, and it is this branch of service to which he has chiefly devoted himself in connection with the Journal of Commerce. Qualifications still more important in the responsible position in which he is to be placed, and which he possesses in an eminent degree, are sound judgment, steadiness of purpose, integrity, faithfulness, and true patriotism. We have great confidence that, under his direction, the Constitution will possess a character not uncongenial to that of the excellent Administration of which it is, in a sense, the mouth-piece. And we confess to a little pride that a gentleman deemed worthy of such a position, should be found in the office of the Journal of Commerce. Success to him.[14]

As noted by the *Journal* editors, Browne had been naturalized two years previously,[15] but his enemies and ill-wishers were long to enjoy calling him an "unnaturalized Englishman,"[16] a "renegade Englishman,"[17] or worse. He arrived in Washington on May 1, and during his residence there for the next year and nine months he played an important part in the Buchanan administration and kept the journalistic atmosphere in a state of agitation.

Who brought Browne to Washington? This soon became a question frequently asked. Certainly he came with the full approval of President Buchanan, as was stated in the *Journal of Commerce* announcement; but there is no evidence that the President issued a personal invitation, though subsequently, for a long time, it was so stated. Samuel F. Butterworth, Superintendent of the Assay Office in New York, in an appearance before a committee of the House of Representatives of Congress, was asked by a hostile questioner whether he had not had a part in putting Browne on the *Constitution* or had introduced him to President Buchanan. Butterworth answered, "No. None in the world." He said further, however, "I have frequently recommended Mr. Browne to gentlemen in Washington as a man of eminent ability, a ready writer, and one whose capacity could be very well employed upon the government organ." He added that he did not think that Browne had been employed on account of anything he had said but because Browne "showed very great ability" as an editor, and it was "simply on that account" that Browne was brought to the *Constitution*.[18]

Many years later, after Browne's death, there was going the rounds another explanation, supposedly put out by that ubiquitous lobbyist, promoter, and revolutionist George N. Sanders, "about as follows:" in a letter to President Buchanan, Sanders wrote: "There is a young Irishman over here by the name of Browne. He is in some way connected with the Sligo family, but he is as poor as a rat, doing penny-a-line for the Journal of Commerce. He has good manners and a ready pen, no alliances and no principles, and in my judgment, he is just the man you need to edit the Constitution." The President thereupon gave Browne the position. Although it seems that this letter, if not spurious, was at least a joke, it was taken seriously enough by an intimate friend of Browne's to produce this reply: "There never lived a more high-toned, chivalrous gentleman than Gen. Browne, and he would have resented any such recommendation."[19]

When Browne himself was asked before a Congressional committee how he got to be editor of the *Constitution* and whether he came "at the instigation of Mr. Bowman," Browne answered: "Yes, sir; at the invitation, rather than at the instigation."[20] George W. Bowman was at this time the editor and proprietor of the *Constitution*. And although he had "paragraphists and reporters," he needed editorial assistance, and he now gave Browne the title of "associate editor." He did not, however, make an announcement of Browne's coming to the paper and did not even include his name as Associate Editor until the edition of November 23, 1859, almost seven months later. Whatever Bowman's reason was for not adding Browne's name earlier, it was, of course, not lack of faith in Browne's responsibility as an editor, for Bowman put Browne in complete charge of the editorial page, and Browne said that he and Bowman were very close and on "intimate terms, and in confidential relations."[21] Bowman himself said Browne had his confidence "to the fullest extent."[22] In fact, so completely were the *Constitution* and Browne one and the same in sentiment and principles that Browne came to be familiarly referred to as "Constitution" Browne.[23]

Bowman was a practical printer and newspaperman, having worked with Duff Green when the latter was printer to Congress under President Andrew Jackson, and later he was an editor of a paper in Bedford, Pennsylvania, for a quarter-century before going to Washington. In the meantime he had become a major general of Pennsylvania troops in the Mexican War and then adjutant general of Pennsylvania.[24] Being a close friend of Buchanan, he had come to Washington as Superintendent of Public Printing, and there came in contact with Cornelius Wendell, who had migrated to Washington some years previously from Albany, New York, and was making a fortune in the government printing business. It was from Wendell that Bowman secured the *Constitution,* which had been previously known as the *Washington Union.*

Government printing had from early times been tied into party patronage and was used to promote the party's interests and especially to sustain a newspaper in Washington as the party organ. As Jefferson Davis said in 1860, "No great party paper yet has ever been expected to sustain itself by its own circulation, in this city."[25]

On August 26, 1852, Congress had repealed all former laws and resolutions relating to government printing and had set up the Office of Superintendent of Public Printing, which was given general oversight of all printing ordered by the House, the Senate, and by the Executive departments. There should be two public printers, one elected by the House and one by the Senate, each to have control of the printing of the respective houses, either to do the printing himself or to let it out by contract. The heads of the Executive departments controlled their printing requirements, but as they were in reality extensions of presidential authority, they were alert to suggestions by the President. The law required all printing to be done in Washington, except for forms needed for use outside of the city, when it could be done as cheaply. The most lucrative of this kind of printing was the post office forms, which, of course, were used all over the country.[26]

The system grew up whereby all the government printing was sublet by the respective authorities to practical printers, who took the printing contracts at a certain percentage of what the government appropriated. The amount that remained in the hands of the respective authorities was used to support the administration organ. For the Thirty-Fifth Congress (1857-1859), the Senate Printer was William

A. Harris, a former Representative from Virginia; and the House Printer was James B. Steadman (Steedman), an arrival from Ohio. For "certain fixed sums" they contracted with Wendell to do the printing for both houses. William Rice, proprietor of the *Pennsylvanian* of Philadelphia, got the contract for the post office forms, but he sub-let the actual printing of them to Wendell, who agreed to do the work for 57 per cent of the government appropriation, leaving 43 per cent to Rice. Wendell diverted some of the 43 per cent without Rice's knowledge or assent to the Philadelphia *Argus*. Wendell, now with a monopoly of the government printing, was making about $100,000 annually.[27]

Harris was at the time of his election as Senate Printer the editor and proprietor of the *Washington Union,* the Buchanan administration paper, and it was this fact that secured his election. When he allotted the printing to Wendell, he transferred the *Union* to Wendell for $10,000 annually and with the understanding that Wendell must continue the paper as an administration organ and let Assistant Secretary of State John Appleton look after the editorial management.[28] Wendell was glad to do this since he admitted that he was no editor: "No, sir; I was never a writing man."[29] But very soon Wendell wanted to rid himself of the burden of the *Union,* for he asserted that he was losing from $18,000 to $20,000 annually on the paper. He tried to unload the paper on Appleton, who declined to have it.

Now, in looking around for somebody to take the *Union* off his hands, Wendell hit upon Bowman, who was at the time Superintendent of Public Printing. Wendell felt that it would be a happy outcome if Bowman could be induced to take the paper, for as Superintendent of Public Printing Bowman had held a stiff rein over Wendell's printing activities, and if Bowman took the paper he would have to resign as Superintendent. Efforts were made to have Buchanan advise Bowman to accept, but the President refused, saying that Bowman's little savings might be lost in the venture. An agreement was finally reached on March 26, 1859, whereby Wendell transferred ("do hereby give, grant, bargain, sell, and convey") the *Union* to Bowman and promised him $20,000 annually as long as he held the printing contracts he then enjoyed. Included were "the name, good will, press, and printing and other material belonging to and used in the establishment."[30] On March 29 Wendell announced in the *Washington Union* that Bowman had "become the sole proprietor" and that he would take possession on April 11. On April 13 the first issue under Bowman appeared, and apparently the "good will" of the *Washington Union* he considered worth nothing, for he gave the paper now the new name, the *Constitution.*

Bowman announced that he was the sole owner of the newspaper and that he alone was responsible for what went into its columns; but naturally he would support the Democratic party throughout and very particularly the Buchanan administration. To be untrammeled in the minutest detail, he divested himself of all obligations to the administration by resigning his position of Superintendent of Public Printing, saying: "That he might be entirely free from the imputation which malice would be swift to suggest, of a selfish or slavish interest in upholding the present administration at Washington, he was voluntarily resigned an office of trust and emolument under the government, and is bound to its support this day by no tie, other than that honest faith in its policy, which links it to the hearts of the Democracy all over the land."[31]

Before Bowman took over the *Washington Union* and made it into the *Constitution,* he was probably negotiating with Browne in New York to come to Washington and assume chief editorial control, for seventeen days after the first issue Browne was at work on the paper; and when people thought of the *Constitution* or read it they thought of Browne.[32] But some people, especially the opponents of the Democratic party, chose to think of Buchanan, charging him with using Browne and Bowman as his mouthpiece. It came to be firmly fixed in history that the *Constitution* was the Buchanan administration organ; but all evidence indicates that it was not an administrative organ, not in the sense that Buchanan saw the editorials before they were published or dictated the publication of any. The *National Intelligencer,* the best known of the Washington newspapers except the *Constitution,* always referred to it as "the Government paper," "the official journal," or "the administration organ." Other contemporary newspapers in Washington and outside, and subsequent historians, did likewise.

The *Constitution* in several instances took occasion to deny the charges. Before the end of its first year, answering those who were insisting that Buchanan and his cabinet decided on its editorials, it said: "While it is true that our opinions on all political questions are in harmony with those of the Administration, and while we give the President and his Cabinet our unqualified support, the editors of this paper are alone responsible for what appears in its columns. Anybody who, after this notice, charges that there is any editor of the *Constitution* but those whose names appear at the head of this column, states that which he knows to be untrue."[33] The *New York Times,* which had a low opinion of the *Constitution,* refused to be convinced. In attacking "its morals and its manners," it insisted that the paper was echoing Buchanan and that it was " 'conducted under his direct supervision.' " The *Constitution* answered: "They knew that the President of the United States had no more to do with the editorial management of this paper than they have, and that for what we think proper to say, or leave unsaid, no human being is responsible but ourselves." It then reprinted its disclaimer.[34]

The *Constitution* had a neat attractive format, six columns, and four pages. The first and fourth pages were almost entirely advertisements and much of the third page was so. In unrestrained praise of itself the paper bragged that it was "an admitted fact that the *mechanical execution of the Constitution* is superior to that of any other political journal in the United States."[35] There were three editions, daily (except Monday), semi-weekly, and weekly, at the yearly price of $6.00, $4.00, and $2.00, respectively, with the announcement that the price scarcely covered the cost of the paper. For a few months there was a Sunday issue; but it was dropped because the public might think that work was being done on it on Sunday, which was not so.[36] Instead of continuing the Sunday edition two issues were got out on Saturday, one being the evening edition.

The *Constitution* became famous (and infamous), depending on the point of view, for its sharp and incisive editorials; but it also served its readers with the news of the day, quoting copiously from its contemporaries, but always giving credit. It was doubly careful in this regard, for it was often copied without credit, a fact which led to this "Gentle Hint: Honesty, not to speak of editorial courtesy, demands that the 'credit' should always be given where it is due."[37] Now and then long documents and letters and, especially when Congress was in session, excerpts from its debates were the order of the day. It published Augustus Baldwin Longstreet's long letter in defense of slavery as an economic institution, in answer to Lord Brougham's slurring attack on the United States.[38] Also it published in full Benjamin M. Palmer's Thanksgiving Sermon of November 29, 1860, in New Orleans, which was to become an important document in the secession movement.[39] Browne liked to drop back and give the historical background of important movements and politicians, either to praise or to embarrass. And he was not slow in publishing speeches of Democratic statesmen. He announced in January, 1860: "We intend from time to time to continue the publication of some speeches, delivered by the champions of democracy, as may be most eminent for ability and forcible presentation of principles fundamental to the party."[40]

The Democratic press over the nation looked to the *Constitution* for inspiration, instruction, and guidance—not all the time and not all the press, of course, but sufficiently to lead the *Constitution* to modestly publish some of the praise that came its way. According to an Ohio paper, " 'it is the best edited democratic sheet in the Union. On every point it is fearless, able, and sound, and we never open it without expecting to be instructed by its editorials, and have never been disappointed.' "[41] And an Iowa paper commended its editorials as " 'able, pungent, and logical, . . . contending with the factions and seditious heresies that labor for the anarchizing and prostration of our political being.' " [42]

Browne liked to swap compliments with those members of the press with whom he was on good terms. One of his favorites, which might well have been so since he had at one time been on its staff, which he frequently quoted, was the *New York Journal of Commerce*. He said that there was "no journal in the Union for whose opinion we entertain a higher respect." Without being a party paper, he declared, it always advocated "sound, conservative, democratic doctrine, and on all questions on which the interests of the country are involved it is always found on the right side."[43] Another of Browne's favorites was the Albany *Argus*. With his neighbor, the rather staid sedate *National Intelligencer*, Browne found no occasion to engage in any feuds until the heat of the secession movement was at the boiling point, and the *Intelligencer* never crossed Browne except on preferences within the Democratic party.[44] When Joseph Gales, who was one of its editors and who like Browne was born an English subject, died in 1860, Browne said it was "a sorrowful shock to the wide circle of friends and acquaintances, by whom he was respected and esteemed for his many virtues, high character, intellectual capacity, and long and faithful service as a high-toned, reliable journalist."[45]

The newspapers which were most constantly hostile to the *Constitution* were the three New York publications, the *Times, Tribune,* and *Herald*. Browne always answered them in kind.

❧ II ❧

Browne, Bowman, and Congressional Investigations

BROWNE AND BOWMAN, with their *Constitution*, were stalwart Democrats, and intense Buchanan Democrats at that. In the late 1850's the party ran into trouble over admitting as a state the Territory of Kansas, slavery being the disturbing issue. Buchanan's attempt to bring Kansas into statehood under a pro-slavery constitution written at Lecompton led to a split in his party, with Stephen A. Douglas, a Senator from Illinois, heading the opposition. Some Democrats with extreme views against slavery joined the Republicans; others who insisted on remaining in the party came to be called anti-Lecompton Democrats, and many others less extreme made up a wing of the party known as simply Douglas Democrats. The Buchanan Democrats were, of course, in control of the administration in Washington.

In the Congressional election of 1858, as has already been noted, Browne campaigned in New York against John B. Haskin, one of the anti-Lecompton Democrats, whom he chose to call "a black republican." Haskin won, and this was wormwood and gall to Browne, who had in 1856 supported Haskin as a regular Democrat. After his two terms in Congress, the Thirty-Fifth (1857-1859) and Thirty-Sixth (1859-1861), Haskin retired from office-holding and resumed his law practice, living on until 1895; but before leaving Congress he and Browne were to have some bitter exchanges of uncomplimentary remarks about each other.

In this Thirty-Sixth Congress, meeting on December 5, 1859, the Republicans held a plurality of the membership in the House, which led to a contest for the speakership, not finally settled until February 1, 1860. For almost two months the House was paralyzed in any effective work it could do, and acrimonious and angry speeches ruled the day, as vote after vote was taken in the effort to elect a speaker.

12

The chief contenders were Thomas S. Bocock, of Virginia, for the Democrats, and John Sherman, of Ohio, for the Republicans. Sherman ruined his chances when he endorsed Hinton Rowan Helper's *Impending Crisis* without ever having read it. This book attacked slavery as being an incubus on the South and, according to Browne, it was "a book written by a renegade criminal, containing the most treasonable, incendiary, and villainous doctrines, at variance not only with the laws of the land and the interests of the Union, but with every principle of divine and human justice and the very existence of civilized society."[1]

When Sherman realized that his endorsement of the book had raised a furor endangering his election as speaker, he admitted that he had never read the book, though it had become a Republican campaign document. This admission led Browne to remark: "So long as he could hope, by a sneaking assertion of ignorance of the contents of the book when he recommended its circulation, to escape the consequences of his act, he was quite ready to appear as a fool, if he could only wiggle out of the responsibility attaching to his act which he could not deny."[2]

So hot was the *Constitution* in pursuing all Congressmen who had endorsed the *Impending Crisis* (calling them traitors), that Schuyler Colfax, a Representative from Indiana, advocated excluding from the House gallery the editors and reporters of that paper. This attempt brought forth the reply: "We consider that all men who commend treason are traitors, that all men who connive at the commission of murder are murderers; and that all men who recommend robbery are robbers."[3]

When the balloting for the speakership began, Haskin refused to vote for the Democratic nominee, but engaging in a little strategy with two other anti-Lecompton Democrats, John Hickman and John Schwartz, both from Pennsylvania, Haskin voted for Hickman and Hickman and Schwartz voted for Haskin. But on the fifth ballot all three showed their hand by voting for Sherman amidst "applause and hisses from the galleries."[4]

Browne observed that he did not know how many anti-Lecompton Democrats had their price but he did know that "Pylades Hickman and Orestes Haskin not only will take, but have taken, the black-republican shilling,"[5] and he devoted a biting editorial attack on Haskin alone: "It has long been a matter of notoriety that Mr. Haskin was 'independent.' When, though elected by a democratic constituency, pledged by every promise which a man of honor would hold sacred to support the democratic party and the democratic Administration, and to oppose the black-republican enemies of that party,—he turned against his party, took counsel and acted in concert with the black-republicans, he gave the most striking proof that he was entirely 'independent' of those obligations which honorable men are in the habit of holding sacred." Pursuing Haskin further, Browne sarcastically observed that since becoming independent Haskin had made himself "a very sleuth-hound on the track of corruption and extravagance, the detector of every moral and political delinquency, the ruthless avenger of even the most trifling peccadillio."[6] Browne was here alluding to Haskin's campaign to saddle the Buchanan administration with corruption and polite bribery by the use of public funds, a campaign which Haskin would intensify within a month or two.

On December 12, 1859, Haskin made a long bitter speech in which he attacked Browne and Buchanan. Rising to "a personal explanation," he said that he had not intended to enter the debate relating to the election of a speaker but "for a grossly libelous attack upon me in the home organ of the President on Saturday last." It was not his custom, he said, "upon this floor or away from it, to notice *little* things, but, as rumor has accorded to the President and his Attorney General [Jeremiah S.] Black the editorial management of the Constitution, concealing themselves by the temporary employment of a hireling writer named Browne—not a relative of Ossawatomie Brown [who had recently been hanged for his Harpers Ferry raid], for, though a madman, a fanatic, and a traitor, yet he was a truthful and brave man, I feel that the high authority which supervised and justified the attack made, in the article to which I have alluded upon the eight anti-Lecompton Democrats of this House, including myself, warrant me in noticing it at this time and in this place."

He then began to pay special attention to Browne: "It is unnecessary for me to allude to the character of President Buchanan or Attorney General Black, as their character is well known to the country; but let me say in relation to this man Browne, who is, I am informed, an alien originally from England, but lately imported into this city by Mr. Buchanan to grind the music from his dolorous organ, that he was previously employed as a penny-a-liner in the city of New York upon the Journal of Commerce."[7]

Browne replied that Haskin's "vulgar denunciation neither frightens nor disturbs us. . . . Mr. Browne feels that he can afford to despise any comments that Mr. Haskin may utter on his course, past, present, or future, as a journalist and a gentleman, and feels assured that where honor, the usages of gentlemen's society, integrity and truth are understood and practiced, he need not defend himself against anything which Mr. Haskin can say or read against him."[8] And since Haskin fancied himself a gentleman, there "must be merit in a capacity capable of such a daring thought."[9]

Turning attention to Haskin's reference to Browne's being a foreigner, Browne replied, "Our orator and statesman is no foreigner; he boasts a nativity in the Empire State; and his friends can claim for him an emulation of two of her most notorious sons—Arnold and Ossawatomie [Brown]— . . . who shall say that, fulfilling the promise of his youth, either of his 'illustrious predecessors' shall outshine him in their deeds, or eclipse him in their end?"[10]

As for defending Buchanan and his administration against Haskin's attacks, Browne said, "We respect that great Statesman and his advisers too highly, and we have too much contempt for Mr. Haskin and his libels, to allow ourselves to be led into the commission of any such act."[11] Browne asked Haskin for proof of his charges of extravagance and corruption leveled against Buchanan's administration, and since Haskin had produced none, "he stands before the country now as a columniator and a slanderer." And since Hickman had been equally a slanderer of Buchanan's administration, Browne pronounced against him "the same opinion as we have already expressed in regard to Mr. Haskin."[12]

As for an assertion Haskin had made that his position on the Buchanan administration was the same as that of John Van Buren ("Prince John"), who stood well in New York, Browne said that he had heard Van Buren "comment on Mr. Haskin's notorious harangue at Tarrytown, in the fall of 1858, and compare the author of that harangue to Benedict Arnold, another character whom history has branded as a traitor, and whose treachery was perpetrated at the same beautiful village on the banks of the Hudson."[13]

As the voting for the speakership continued, Browne entitled one of his editorials "The Three Traitors," referring to the three anti-Lecompton Democrats who had joined "the black republican Helper abolitionists" and were voting for Sherman. "It is hardly necessary," he said, "to inform our readers that the names of the three renegades who committed this act of the deepest political perfidy which the history of our country records" were Haskin, Hickman, and Schwartz. "For ourselves," he continued, "we only rejoice that the great democratic party is no longer disgraced by even the nominal association of such men. They are now in the ranks to which they belong, and where they will find congenial spirits. Among honest men and patriots they had no place. That which they once occupied they obtained by false pretences. They were found out and branded as they deserve; and, henceforth, whenever the few American names are mentioned to which the infamous epithet of Traitor is appended,— whenever Benedict Arnold and Ossawatomie Brown are spoken of,— the name of Haskin, Hickman, and Schwartz will also be repeated." And Browne could not refrain from adding, "Like Judas Iscariot, they were chosen and trusted; like Judas, they betrayed their trust; but, unlike that paragon of treachery, they have not had the decency to hang themselves."[14]

The speakership fight became so bitter that Representatives began carrying pistols, and Haskin became quite embarrassed one day when his pistol fell from his pocket while he was excitedly making a speech. He explained that he lived on the outskirts of Washington and that a number of outrages had taken place in the neighborhood recently; he was carrying a pistol for protection out there and not for use against any member of the House unless he were assaulted. And he added, "I say now, that when this House is organized, I hope every gentleman here will pledge his honor to the country not to have any fire-arms within this Hall where the business of legislation is to be conducted."[15] Finally, on the forty-fourth ballot the speakership was filled by the election of William Pennington, a Whig-Republican from New Jersey, by a majority of one vote.

To discredit the Buchanan administration, the Republicans, aided by disgruntled Democrats, soon set going three Congressional investigations, one by the Senate and two by the House. Both groups were looking forward to the presidential election of that year (1860). The anti-Buchanan Democrats were hoping to nominate Douglas; the Republicans wanted to tarnish all factions of the Democrats in their forthcoming campaign to elect their candidate, whoever he might be.

Browne was to be involved in all of these hearings because of his editorship of the *Constitution,* and the *Constitution* was dragged in because of Bowman's interest in the public printing, where the Republicans were sure that they smelled corruption. In fact, before any of the investigations had been ordered, the election of the printer for the Senate produced a squabble among the Democratic Senators, much to the satisfaction of the Republicans. The squabble followed a circuitous route; its starting point was Jackson, Mississippi. On November 7, 1859, Albert Gallatin Brown, one of Mississippi's United States Senators, spoke before the Mississippi legislature, making some extreme statements and criticizing the *Constitution.* Brown was a radical Southern Nationalist who wanted slavery protected in the territories by a Congressional slave code (a position Jefferson Davis, the other Mississippi Senator, was later to take) and was ready for secession from the National Democratic Convention (which was to meet in Charleston), if that plank was not put into the platform.[16] He distrusted the Northern Democrats and intimated that he would prefer William H. Seward, Republican United States Senator from New York, over Buchanan. Brown hit a tender spot in the *Constitution* in this reference to Buchanan, and without printing Brown's speech, one of the editors wrote a stinging editorial on Brown (whether Bowman or Browne wrote the editorial, they were in agreement). In it the editor said that if Brown should stand for re-election on his Buchanan statement "he would not receive five votes within the limits of the State of Mississippi, and that there are not five democrats within the limits of this broad Union who do not feel astonishment not unmixed with disgust at the avowal of any man who is not a black-republican in his heart or a traitor to the democratic party, of so monstrous a sentiment."[17]

Brown had expressed resentment at this criticism, especially since the *Constitution* had not published his speech. In a private letter, but not to Brown, Bowman wrote that neither he nor "my colleague, Mr. W. M. Browne" meant to offer any indignity to the Mississippi Senator, but, he added, "We reserve to ourselves the right to publish or omit to publish what we please, while we always desire to do justice to everybody."[18]

One of the conditions under which Bowman took the *Constitution* from Wendell was the assumption from the "Democratic Establishment" that the Senate would elect Bowman to be the Senate Printer, for in that position he could let out the Senate printing on a percentage basis, and from his part he would be able to protect himself against loss in running the *Constitution*. On the very day the vote was to be taken, January 17, 1860, Albert Gallatin Brown made an explosive speech in the Senate in which he noted five reasons why he would not support Bowman. Of course, the *Constitution*'s criticism of his speech and its refusal to publish it was one of his reasons, supplemented by the charge that there were bargain and corruption in the stipulation that Bowman was to receive $20,000 annually for taking over the *Constitution*, for this was in reality money siphoned out of the United States Treasury,[19] to be paid "to sustain his miserable, rickety, corrupt concern called the Washington *Constitution*."[20]

But what was particularly galling to Senator Brown was the fact that Bowman had associated with him a man "I have heard, and believe it to be true of foreign birth, who never has been naturalized; that he has not been in our country one-third as long as I have been battling in defense of Democratic principles; and yet he is put up to teach me what is Democracy, and what is my duty to the principles and the old democratic faith of the fathers. I know nothing of this person." Not deigning to mention Browne by name throughout his whole speech, Brown admitted, however, that he thought that "upon one occasion, I did meet him."

Assuming that Browne was a foreigner unnaturalized, the Mississippi Senator asked "if he is a proper man to edit the national Democratic organ; to write essays denunciatory of men who have served the party twenty years before he ever put his foot upon American soil." Brown emphasized that he understood that this person had not been naturalized, "that he is the heir to an estate and title; that he is in prospective the Marquis of Sligo." With mounting indignation, Brown exclaimed, "Sir, I would rather learn my democracy from a native-born American; I am an American to that extent; but if I must take it from a foreigner at all, he must be a man who has sworn allegiance to my country, and not one who might take up arms against it to-morrow without committing treason."

At this point William Bigler, a Senator from Pennsylvania who had been defending his fellow Pennsylvanian, Bowman, entered the fray and remarked that the Mississippi Senator's reason for not voting for Bowman because of his association with Browne was "a far-fetched objection; but I have the authority of Mr. Browne for saying that Mr. Brown is mistaken; and I here, in my place, tell Mr. Brown that Mr. Browne is a naturalized citizen—has been naturalized for years." When Senator Brown expressed doubt and wanted to know more about Browne's naturalization papers, in what court Browne was naturalized, Bigler replied that he did not carry Browne's naturalization papers with him, saying, "I am not in possession of his naturalization papers. If I supposed for one moment that the word of this gentleman was not good, I would not vote for Mr. Bowman if he would associate with any man capable of any such an imposition." Bigler then produced a letter which Browne had written giving the details of his naturalization and asked the clerk to read it. There were crys of "Oh, no!" and Bigler then said that he would not take up the time of the Senate to have it read. He then offered it to Brown to read but he objected, saying that he wanted the "evidence of the paper of naturalization to show in what court he was naturalized."

Senator Brown now calmed down and remarked, "If Mr. Browne says he has been naturalized, of course, I must take it." And bringing the Brown-Bigler tussle to an end, Bigler said, "If he were not a naturalized citizen, I could very well excuse the prejudices of the Senator. But, sir, if naturalized, as I believe, he is a citizen of the United States, equal in every particular to the Senator from Mississippi or myself; entitled to vote and entitled to hold an office; entitled to the protection of the Government, and, I doubt not, ready to serve it against its enemies." Before the vote was taken which (27 to 21) made Bowman the Senate Printer for the Thirty-Sixth Congress, Jefferson Davis remarked that he was glad to have confirmed that Browne "under the operation of our beneficent laws [had] been promoted to the rank of a sovereign in his own right." He added, "But whether it had been true, as was first erroneously supposed by my colleague, that the associate editor of the Constitution was an unnaturalized citizen and heir apparent to the title of Marquis of Sligo or not, what has that to do with Mr. Bowman's fitness to be Printer to the Senate?" In defense of Browne, Davis said, "I was gratified at the acquisition to the editorial corps of the Constitution, of this gentleman of classical learning and accomplishment; of extensive observation by travel, and the varied knowledge which such opportunity has enabled him to acquire."[21]

The Senate had had so much to say about Browne, Bowman, and the *Constitution,* that the editors of the paper decided to have their little say with special reference to Browne: "So much alarm has been expressed that the source of the democracy which flows through the columns of this paper is rendered impure by contact with 'foreign aristocracy,' and that the 'heir to a marquisate' is one of its editors," the answer should be made "that neither of the editors who control this paper is heir presumptive, apparent or remote, to any foreign title of nobility." It was then stated that Browne was born in Ireland. "He was born a gentleman. That may be his misfortune, but it is certainly not his fault; and if it operates prejudicially to his interests or advancement as an American citizen (which he became upwards of two years ago) he has yet to learn it." It was now hoped that "this piece of vulgar gossip" would cease with this explanation.[22]

The first of the three Congressional investigations was ordered in a Senate resolution of January 24, 1860, directed specifically to investigate the payment of monies to the *Constitution* and other newspapers, and especially about the $20,000 Bowman was supposed to receive annually.[23] When Bowman originally took over the *Constitution* from Wendell, he was led to do so not only by Wendell's promise of $20,000 annually (in reality only $10,000 to Bowman, with the remainder going to the *Pennsylvanian*) but also by a general understanding with Senate leaders that he would be elected Senate Printer for the Thirty-

Sixth Congress. In the event of Bowman's election, Wendell understood that Bowman would award him the Senate printing for a certain percentage of the government appropriation.

It was brought out in the investigation that Bowman very definitely and properly told Wendell that he could not sign a contract or make a commitment in any fashion before his election—it would be illogical and illegal. But nevertheless, with or without Bowman's knowledge, conversations were held by representatives of Bowman and Wendell as to certain details of a prospective agreement, especially the percentage that Wendell should receive. These representatives were Browne for Bowman and John Appleton for Wendell. Certainly Wendell knew that the conference was to take place, for he appointed Appleton as his agent; and although Bowman was hesitant about making a firm statement as to foreknowledge of the conference, he did say that he had confidence in Browne "to the fullest extent," but that Browne had "no authority to hold a conversation that would bind me to anything at all." Browne was in complete agreement with Bowman, that his talks with Appleton were purely exploratory and binding in no way; but in the conversations 20 to 22 per cent was mentioned as what Wendell might expect.

All of this was brought out by the fact that after Bowman was elected Senate Printer (January 17, 1860), instead of giving the contract for the Senate printing to Wendell, he made a contract with John C. Rives to do it in his plant for two-thirds of the government appropriation—the other third remaining in Bowman's hands to keep the *Constitution* going. Wendell was bitter at this outcome, and this marks the beginning of the end of the reign of Wendell in the domain of government printing in Washington.[24] The Majority Report and the Minority Report led to little more than party bickering, filling almost four hundred pages of testimony.

During the long-drawn-out speakership contest, John Haskin had taken occasion to charge the Buchanan administration with extravagance and corruption, as has been previously noted. Then on February 9 and 13 the House passed resolutions directing the Committee on Public Expenditures to inquire into the price of public printing and to suggest modifications of both prices and laws relating to the subject. The first House investigation, which ran from March 3 to March 23, was conducted by a committee of seven, directed by Haskin. He now had full rein to pursue his pet project of proving how corrupt the Buchanan administration was. It would be his special delight to summon before his committee the detested William Montague Browne and George W. Bowman to show how they were siphoning money out of the United States Treasury to support their miserable sheet, the *Constitution.*

"The Three Traitors" editorial, which had been published in the *Constitution* on December 16, 1859, was still rankling with Haskin, and he was determined to find out whether it was Browne or Bowman who had written it. On March 15, 1860, Browne appeared before the committee, and Haskin began by first asking that question, which he thought might still be loaded, although he knew full well the answer: "Are you a native or naturalized citizen of this country?" Browne answered, "I am a naturalized citizen," before Thomas C. Hindman could object. Hindman, a Democratic member of the committee from Arkansas and later to be a major general in the Confederate army, was throughout the hearing (March 3-23) to prove a nettle to Haskin and, with David Clopton, a Representative from Alabama on the committee, was to sign a minority report.

Hindman said that he objected to the question because the committee had no right to ask it, not because he thought Browne had any objection to answering it. Hindman thought the question was irrelevant, unless, adding sarcastically, Haskin "desired to base another question upon it as to the knowledge of the witness about printing in foreign countries, and then there could be no objection to it."

This thought led Haskin to ask Browne whether he was "acquainted with any abuses connected with the existing system of public printing," to which question Browne answered, "I know nothing of the details of the public printing at all."[25] Haskin then wanted to know whether Browne had any "interest, directly or indirectly, in the proceeds arising from the Senate printing or the printing of the executive departments." Browne answered, "Not to the extent of one cent."

Now Haskin showed Browne a copy of the *Constitution* of December 16, 1859, containing "The Three Traitors" editorial and asked whether he or Bowman had written it. Hindman objected to Browne's answering and announced that he would "not submit to any such questions in the committee." They should neither be asked nor answered.[26] And Hindman later added, "I will not agree that this committee shall be made a mere partisan machine, or a personal machine, to be wielded by the chairman or any one else for resenting personal wrongs or punishing political opponents."[27]

For the next several hours, the Committee wrangled over the right of anyone to ask such questions, during which time Browne sat still, listening to Hindman and Clopton defend him against answering the question, which undoubtedly he would have been glad to answer affirmatively, for all evidence points to his having written the editorial.

Hindman and Clopton argued that the question had no relation to public printing and was purely a personal matter, but Haskin and other members of the committee argued that since Bowman owned the *Constitution,* he paid its costs from the surplus money he got from being the Senate Printer, and since Browne was on the payroll of the *Constitution,* the question was germane to the investigation.[28] Daniel E. Somes, a Representative from Maine on the committee, remarked, "I have not discovered any reluctance on the part of the witness to answer the question, and I presume that he feels none."[29] Defending his right to try to find out the authorship of the editorial, Haskin said that "representatives of the people have been villified, abused, and libelled in this home organ of Mr. Buchanan, supported by the profits made out of appropriations voted by the body of which we are members."[30]

Hindman's championship of Browne was so intense that he made a remark which might have been a challenge to a duel. Suggesting that there might be a way to meet the difficulty of finding out who wrote the editorial, he said, "There is a mode known to all honorable men by which matters of this sort can be determined; and, without having had any former acquaintance with the witness, I constitute myself his friend, if he will accept my services, and, as such, I am ready to receive any inquiries the chairman may wish to propound to him. In this way the chairman can ascertain at once whether or not he is the author of the communication referred to, and can then take such steps as he may deem proper under the circumstances. Besides, the whole country will also ascertain who wrote it and where the *onus* rests."[31] The Majority Report of the Committee condemned the Buchanan administration, with the Minority Report, of course, dissenting.

The best known of the three Congressional investigations into the Buchanan administration was the third and last one. It was ordered by the House, March 5, 1860, on motion of John Covode, a Representative from Pennsylvania. The hearings continued for almost three months (March 20-June 16), and the testimony and accompanying documents filled 835 pages in the printed report. The resolution called for the appointment of a committee of five "for the purpose of investigating whether the President of the United States, or any other officer of the government, has, by money, patronage, or other improper means, sought to influence the action of Congress, or any committees thereof, for or against the passage of any law appertaining to the rights of any State or Territory," to ascertain whether the President had not enforced any laws, and to investigate post office and other abuses. Covode was appointed chairman of the committee.[32]

Buchanan declared that the committee was set up "to render the existing Democratic administration odious in the eyes of the people, and thereby to promote the election of any Republican candidate who might be nominated."[33] And the *Constitution* seconded that sentiment, saying, "We repeat—and we deliberately weigh our words, because we know what we say—that the President and his Cabinet repel with scorn and contempt any and every accusation, from whatever quarter it may emanate, which affects in the minutest particular their official or personal honor and integrity."[34]

Browne, who was to be brought into the investigation, made a stinging attack on Covode, in which he said that Covode "was what might be termed an obscure man. Nature had denied him the possession of any one quality which could raise him above the level of the most mediocre of the human race. By the few who had the opportunity of knowing him he was regarded as one of the most essentially stupid men in existence, but animated by an insane desire to be distinguished, or rather, we should say, to be conspicuous, just as we see physical cowards anxious to be considered men of valor, and habituated liars profess to be earnest admirers of the truth." [35]

Like John Haskin, Abram Baldwin Olin, a Representative from New York on the committee, wanted to know of Bowman who had written certain editorials in the *Constitution*. Bowman replied that Browne "writes the leading editorials," but in the case of the editorials inquired about, Browne had not written them as he was out of Washington at the time they appeared.[36] Charles Russell Train, a Massachusetts representative on the committee, asked Sam Butterworth if he had sent Browne into Haskin's district to attempt to defeat him in the Congressional election of 1858. Butterworth replied that "no doubt I did advise him to go into Mr. Haskin's district. I advised every man who could make a good democratic speech to go there, and he was a good speaker."[37]

In an attempt to involve Browne and Schell, the Collector of Customs of New York, in raiding the public treasury, Covode sought to prove that in return for friendly editorials by Browne in the *Journal of Commerce,* Schell had appointed him to a position in the New York customs house without any duties to perform—was it "a mere sinecure, in order to give you a salary?" Was not one of those friendly editorials a defense of Schell against certain charges made against him? Covode wanted to know. Browne made a rather inconclusive reply: "I do not recollect any occasion particularly when a charge was brought against him. If I had seen a charge made against him that I deemed unfounded, I believe I should have defended him; but I know there was no special reason of that sort for giving me this place, and I think if I had defended him on any special occasion I should have recollected it."[38] Browne had appeared before the committee on May 15, exactly two months after his session with the Haskin committee.

Covode's attempt to smear Browne increased his contempt for Covode, whom he characterized anew as a "man to whom nature had denied the means of being famous, but whose disregard for honor, truth, and morality afforded him ample means of becoming notorious . . . [and made] the proper person to direct so dastardly inquisition, and the proceedings of the last four months afford the most conclusive evidence of the entire fitness of the choice."[39]

The whole investigation seemed to have resulted in much sound and fury but nothing in particular. The Majority Report ended with the statement that the testimony was thereby submitted, "and your commitee have no further suggesions to make thereon."[40] The Minority Report, signed by Warren Winslow, Representative from North Carolina on the committee, observed that the Majority Report recommended neither impeachment nor censure of the President and ended with the statement. "At all events, the failure to take such action is a clear indication on the part of the majority that none was justified by the evidence, in which opinion the undersigned fully concurs."[41] According to the *Constitution*, the House ordered 100,000 copies of the testimony to be printed "so that the black republicans have not labored altogether in vain in collecting the rotten material out of which they have manufactured this book."[42]

Characterizing the whole hearing in the *Constitution*, Browne said that a "drag net was spread over the entire continent to catch every reprobate who was willing to swear to any calumny against the Administration; and every anonymous letter-writer and forger who would suggest an infamous charge or insinuation found no difficulty in having his suggestions and insinuations adopted, acted on, and published through the columns of infamous presses, as *proofs* against the Chief Magistrate and democrats of the highest standing and most unsullied integrity."[43] And Buchanan, who was upset all along by this investigation and had sent a message to the House about it, when the hearings were completed, wrote James Gordon Bennett, of the hostile *New York Herald*, that the "committee were engaged in secret conclave for nearly three months in examining every man, *ex parte,* who from disappointment or personal malignity, would cast a shadow upon the Executive. If this dragooning can exist, the Presidential office would be unworthy of the acceptance of a gentleman."[44]

Browne, Bowman, and the *Constitution* had been dragged into all three of these Congressional investigations, and Bowman was getting tired of this constant harassment; but Browne, being an intrepid fighter with his pen, was enjoying the opportunity to castigate the enemies of the Buchanan administration and of the Democratic party. Furthermore, Bowman had not received the $20,000 which Wendell had promised him—really only $10,000, for the *Constitution* itself. Wendell asserted that he had paid Bowman $5,000,[45] but conflicting testimony reveals that Bowman received only about $3,000. And according to a letter that Browne wrote to a New York friend on June 29, 1860, the *Constitution* was "in the last stage of a galloping consumption. There is no mistake about it." He said that Congress had cut off 40 per cent of "printing prices & placed us *below* zero. Old Buck's gratitude which you know is abundant is now the only reliance in the future of your very faithful friend."[46]

At this very time, and for some time previously, Browne had been negotiating with Bowman on terms for the transfer of ownership of the *Constitution* to Browne. On July 3, Browne wrote his New York friend: "I believe I go under this week. I am damned wretched, & forlorn, God knows what I am to do. I have spent my income and relied on its [*Constitution's*] continuance from now till March at least [1861, when a new administration would probably come in]."[47] Three days later he wrote his same friend that he needed $5,000 and that $3,000 of it had been subscribed. "If I can get the other $2,000," he added, "I shall go it and win. If not I shall go as U.S. Minister to Guatemala and die of yellow fever I suppose like my two predecessors."[48]

It is not known whether Browne needed the $5,000 as a purchase price for the *Constitution* or for some special promotion of the Breckinridge and Lane ticket, as the presidential campaign for 1860 election was now on. Since the administration paper for years previously had been subsidized by the public printing, it seems illogical that Bowman could expect payment for a paper which he had received as a gift and had been promised $20,000 (part to go to other papers) to keep it going. The printing establishment (at E Street between 11th and 12th streets) consisted of two presses "and an engine; the type in the office is barely sufficient for the execution of the paper."[49] When in early 1860 Bowman had been asked what the *Constitution* equipment might be worth, he said he would not have taken it as a present if he were obligated to carry on the paper, but depending on circumstances as to time and a person desiring newspaper equipment it might bring any price from $3,000 to $10,000, and on the other hand it "might be offered at a time when you could not find anybody" who cared about buying it.[50] So, it seems very probable that Bowman offered the *Constitution* to Browne for nothing; and it is known that whatever income Bowman had from the public printing he kept, a fact which placed Browne under no obligation to keep the *Constitution* going any longer than he pleased.

Whatever the arrangements for the transfer were, they were completed on July 6, 1860, and on the masthead of the issue for the following day and thereafter Bowman's name did not appear. In announcing that the paper now belonged to Browne, "my esteemed friend and associate," Bowman said, "I resign it to one eminently qualified to fill it, in whose ability, zeal, and devotion to his party, the democracy of the nation can have full confidence, and with whom the readers of the *Constitution* are already acquainted."

In announcing his ownership, Browne promised a continuance of the policy he had already been carrying out: To maintain the government "upon the principles of the Constitution"; to aid in "perpetuating the Union on the basis on which the patriot heroes of the revolution founded it"; and to promote the election of Breckinridge and Lane.[51]

Politics was already boiling, even inside the Democratic party. On July 6, the day before Bowman gave up the paper, an editorial appeared in the *Constitution* attacking a Douglas supporter, by name Ellis B. Schnabel: "This individual has earned a wide-spread notoriety. The Governors of at least two States of the Union are anxiously endeavoring to find him within their jurisdiction, with the desire of providing him with board and lodging at the expense of their respective commonwealths."[52] The next day Schnabel, assuming that Bowman had written the editorial, entered the *Constitution* office and, finding Bowman at his desk before he had cleared it and moved out, attacked him with a loaded cane, breaking it in his assault. Schnabel was arrested and bound over for grand jury action; and Browne wrote that it was a reflection on the administration of justice "that a person so steeped in infamy as this man, has not heretofore been lodged in the penitentiary, to serve out the accumulated sentences from which he has escaped."[53]

Browne was now to do in part what Jefferson Davis had said no administration newspaper in Washington could ever do: He was to conduct for the next six months a paper that was not a party organ, though it did support the Buchanan administration, receiving no percentage of the government printing costs—only advertisements of the executive departments. Six-sevenths of the advertisements were of this kind—generally all of the first and fourth pages and all but a column or two of the third page. The second page was always devoted to editorials and news.

The "black-republican" papers delighted in imagining and stating as a fact that Bowman paid out of his Senate printing profits the bills of the *Constitution*. Browne became weary of denying these allegations, saying that Bowman did not pay a dime: "We pay our own bills, and are happy to assure our black republican friends that we are abundantly able to do so without aid from any body"; and on another occasion, "neither the Senate Printer nor anybody else has contributed in any shape or manner to the payment of its bills."[54] But the most amazing of all these fabrications was the statement by the *New York Express* that Philip F. Thomas before he resigned from his short term as Secretary of the Treasury (December 12, 1859-January 11, 1860) " 'ordered to be paid $60,000, said to be due the *Constitution* newspaper for printing.' " Browne replied that this falsehood was "stupid or mendacious." The statement had "not a shadow of truth."[55]

For some time there had been a substantial feeling in Congress, heightened by the three Congressional investigations, that the system of government printing was in great need of reorganization and that a government-owned printing establishment should be set up. Naturally, the beneficiaries of the prevailing system were opposed; so were some of the Democratic newspapers, on the basis of principle. While Browne was on the editorial board of the *New York Journal of Commerce*, an editorial was published, probably written by him, strongly opposing the government's entry into the printing business.[56] Browne now republished, slightly amended, this editorial in the *Constitution*: "We have not yet seen any notice of a bill for the creation of a Government blacksmith shop, a Government carpenter-shop, or other mechanical establishments under Government control, but these will doubtless follow in good time after the Printing Department is once in operation." Next would be a paper mill, a tape factory, an ink factory, a cutlery establishment, a sealing-wax shop, and so on. Washington would soon be transformed into a government manufacturing city.[57]

By a joint resolution of Congress, signed by President Buchanan on June 23, 1860, the government was to enter the printing business after March 4, 1861. All printing would be done through the Superintendent of Printing, who was ordered immediately to make arrangements for a printing establishment. Negotiations resulted in the purchase for $135,000 of the Wendell establishment. The resolution specifically forbade the Superintendent of Printing or any other person connected with government printing to have "any interest, direct or indirect, in the publication of any newspaper or periodical."[58] And thus came to an end the era of administration organs subsidized by the operations of government printing. The exact time and circumstance of this end may be stated to have been on July 6, 1860, when Bowman gave up the *Constitution* to Browne.

≥ III ≤

Browne and His Friends in Washington and New York

WILLIAM MONTAGUE BROWNE was of commanding appearance; he was six feet tall, a man whose splendid physique would be noticed in any crowd. He had a genial face and large head, though it was not out of proportion to his body. If by the time he reached Washington he did not wear a beard, he would soon develop one, which with the years became iron gray, making him patriarchal in appearance. His lustrous gray eyes seemed to have a touch of wistful sadness or weakness or a wildish look—intriguing, whatever it was.[1]

Ever-observant Mary Boykin Chesnut, the famout diarist, was attracted by "his fine English accent, so pleasant to the ear."[2] Browne spoke several foreign languages, French and German undoubtedly, and Italian probably. He had courtly manners and was at ease in any group; people felt at ease in his presence. He was always unostentatious and respectful of those above him in public life as well as those below. He had the qualities and characteristics which made up the gentleman, and he admitted that he was born to that rank.

He had a wide knowledge of public affairs, national and international, and wherever it was that he obtained his formal education, it was broad and deep, always being enlarged by the avidity with which he read books on American and foreign history, English classics, and fiction in general. He had a remarkably facile pen and was a fluent speaker, with a style which might be classed as oratorical though at times severely factual.

He was tenacious of his opinions and principles, upholding them in language which, on occasion when he was properly provoked, might border on the extreme. He defended his friends and stood by them loyally; he found it difficult to give one up even for cause. And he defied his enemies, who felt his verbal lash unsparingly. When he made a decision or took a course of action based on his fixed principles, though it might bring about his financial ruin, he never expressed a regret at having done so.

Browne's health was never good; he was frequently sick, and in his later life his ill health was a constant worry. For six or seven weeks during the year before going to Washington he was unable to do any work at all either on the *Journal of Commerce* or in his custom house position.[3] In the summer of 1860 he wrote that he was suffering from "a violent attack of bronchitis" and that his throat inside and out felt as though it were on fire.[4] Early the next year he was laid up for some days with rheumatism.[5]

Browne was a *bon vivant*, enjoying good wine, good cigars, and intelligent conversation. Just as he was taking over the *Constitution*, he wrote a New York friend: "Find out for me where I can get some good cigars at a moderate price—such a price as will suit the man who was rich enough to edit the Constitution on his own hook."[6] And again he wrote for 250 cigars, the kind that had been sent to Senator Gwin.[7]

There was a Mrs. Browne, Eliza Jane, whom he affectionately called Lizzie. Undoubtedly they were married before coming to America, and probably not long before coming, for in 1851 (which was likely the year they arrived), she would have been twenty-one and he, twenty-eight. She was a Yorkshire lady, not particularly handsome, but as "handsome is that handsome does," she well qualified. She was sensitive, refined, cultured, and it might not be going too far to say that she was vivacious, judging from some of her correspondence. One of her Washington friends wrote in 1859, "I found her a very pleasant person—an English woman—a voice & pronunciation like Lady Napier's [wife of the British minister to the United States]— *not quite so soft & sweet* but more natural."[8] Mrs. Browne, like her husband, was never very well and at times severely sick—she preceded him to the grave by ten years. She was much on his mind, and he could scarcely write a letter, even official, without saying that Mrs. Browne sent her regards.

In the summer of 1860 Mrs. Browne made a visit to England, and when she was due to return to New York, Browne hurried there to meet the *Fulton*, "with her precious freight."[9] Some of Mrs. Browne's friends in England teased her, " 'Oh, you are a Yankee girl.' " Mrs. Browne, who considered herself a Southerner in Washington, answered, " 'The Southern people hate Yankee girls worse than you do.' "[10]

Browne was well prepared with wife, position, and all requisite personal qualifications to take his place in Washington society; Mrs.

Browne was equally well endowed personally. Washington society had long been dominated by Southerners, not only because it was a slave city surrounded by slave states, but also because the Democratic party had been in power nationally for most of the time since the city was founded. Southerners generally controlled that party, particularly during the Buchanan administration.

Browne became a Democrat through having read much American history and having studied the American Constitution and system of government. His position on the strongly Democratic *New York Journal of Commerce* confirmed his party faith, which doubtless in the first place got him that position.

One of his most constant and long-standing New York friends was Samuel Latham Mitchill Barlow, who was in many respects a kindred spirit. Born of a French emigré mother in Massachusetts in 1826, he moved to New York City when he was sixteen. There he became a lawyer for large corporations and handled only the most lucrative cases, frequently compromising them without going to trial. He was a bibliophile with special interests in American history; he was a connoisseur of art, old wines, and liquors; he was a fancier of blooded stock and dogs; he liked to entertain; and he was an expert whist player. He had an outstanding art and autograph collection and a large library, the latter bring published in a preliminary listing in 1885 and the former in 1890, the year after his death. He had a country estate at Glen Cove, Long Island.[11] Barlow was a strong Democrat, never giving up that political faith and never deserting Buchanan, whom he had first learned to know in London, when Buchanan was minister to England. Barlow was an indispensable factor in securing Buchanan's nomination in Cincinnati in 1856.[12]

Browne, in Washington, and Barlow, in New York, corresponded frequently, and Browne often acted as Barlow's honest broker with the Buchanan administration. Barlow was, of course, a close acquaintance of Howell Cobb, Buchanan's Secretary of the Treasury, and this fact made it easy for Browne, who was an even closer acquaintance of Cobb, to get special favors for Barlow. Wherever a fee might be involved in any transactions in Washington, Barlow always promised to divide it with Browne. Browne helped Barlow get certain of his friends appointed to consulships and other positions. Such were, of course, favors by Browne without fees; and in thanking him in one instance Barlow reminded him, "you must remember that if you are never repaid in this world you will be in that better one" where all good Democrats were sent to be rewarded.[13]

There were other services than political which Browne performed in

Washington for Barlow. He helped Barlow in hunting up books and autographs and especially in attending on one occasion a sale of a collection of George Washington autographs. Barlow wanted Browne to look out also for autographs of John Adams, Jefferson, and other presidents, as well as of John Hancock and a variety of early Americans. Barlow was at this time illustrating his copy of Joel Barlow's *The Columbiad* and he needed Browne's aid in that, too.[14]

Their kindred interests led to a good deal of visiting back and forth, particularly with Browne's visiting Barlow in New York. In September, 1860, Browne was able to get a season's ticket over the Philadelphia, Wilmington and Baltimore Railroad, good until the following January, for $30, payable in an advertisement to be run in the *Constitution*. He found it difficult to induce a few other railroads, such as the Camden and Amboy and the New Jersey Railroad to give him similar treatment, and he now called on Barlow to lend his help.[15]

"I long to get a rest, a stretch, a smoke, and a chat with a friend," wrote Browne to Barlow in July, 1860. "The counterfeit article is very abundant here, the reality very scarce."[16] And a few days later, when he said that the thermometer in Washington was "25,000" degrees, he told Barlow that he had "lots to say to you on all sorts of subjects, political, moral, social & religious."[17] A month later he was still longing for the hospitality of Barlow's home: "I remember with delight the agreeable evenings I spent with you. They are oases in the desert of a political editor's life."[18] Then in October he informed Barlow that he was about to visit him. "If the Fates are propitious," he wrote, "my valise packed, and the cars keep on the track, I shall leave this city of desolation and sin at 6 A.M. tomorrow (Saturday) morning and reach 229 Fifth Avenue, that bode of happiness, peace and virtue at about 7 oclock, or rather when the Sun has passed the Meridian seven hours."[19]

Then in mid-December he wrote Barlow that he had planned to attend the South Carolina secession convention, scheduled to meet in Columbia, but that he had been dissuaded from doing so; instead, he intended to visit him in New York. But it turned out after all that he changed his mind and decided to remain in Washington, where events were happening thick and fast.[20] Lizzie Browne now and then accompanied her husband on these visits to the Barlows; but this time she had decided not to go because of the cold weather and of her poor health.

Sam Butterworth, the superintendent of the New York Assay Office, was a friend of Barlow's as, indeed, he was of Browne's, and as likely as not when Browne visited Barlow he would find Butterworth there.

In one of his whimsical mock-serious announcements to Barlow that he was about to visit him, Browne said, "Were my association to be with you and him [Butterworth] alone I should recoil from the revolting duty; but as I know I shall have the pleasure of seeing & conversing with the excellent lady who has the misfortune to be linked to you, & with the dear children who are afflicted with you as a father, I have resolved to make the experiment."[21]

William H. Russell, the London *Times* correspondent, wrote in his diary that when Browne went from New York to Washington, "he became intimate with the Southern gentlemen, with whom he naturally associated in preference to the Northern members."[22] He used the word "naturally" advisedly, for to many Englishmen before him, Southerners seemed much more like Englishmen than did the active, hard-pushing, money-making Northerners. And Browne's natural social proclivities made it logical for him to become a part of that Southern group, who set the tone and made up largely the content of Washington society. Browne's intense Democracy coupled with his emotional defense of it fitted in well with the proverbial Southern impetuosity.

The Brownes were well able to play their part in Washington society. Both were socially inclined and skilled in witty and intellectual conversation. They were in the prime of life; William Montague told the census-taker on June 7, 1860, that he was thirty-eight years old and that his wife was thirty. He reported the value of his real estate at $1,000 and his personal estate at $2,500. If his real estate consisted of his newspaper quarters, it would, therefore, follow that the home he lived in was rented property. At any rate, he was handsomely prepared to entertain guests in his home, for he had three servants: Bridget Parkinson (aged thirty), Rose Cloonon (aged twenty), and John Kelly (aged fourteen). As their names indicate, all were Irish and all were born in Ireland. The fact that there were three servants for a family of only two indicates that the Brownes were quite active in their entertaining. By comparison, Howell Cobb, high in government service and in the confidence and affection of President Buchanan, with a family of a wife and seven children (three not living in Washington), had only three servants, two colored manservants and an Irish nurse.[23]

Buchanan's cabinet was largely dominated by its Southern members: Howell Cobb of Georgia, Secretary of the Treasury; Jacob Thompson of Mississippi, Secretary of the Interior; and John Floyd of Virginia, Secretary of War. Cobb was more influential with the President than any other member of the cabinet, and Mrs. Cobb was next to Harriet

Lane, the President's niece and hostess (Buchanan being a bachelor), in setting White House social affairs. In vivacity and clever conversation Mrs. Jacob Thompson had few if any equals—Kati she was to all her friends and acquaintances. Then there were the dozens of Southern Senators and Representatives with their wives, few of whom, however, could reach the social heights occupied by Mary Boykin Chesnut, the wife of Senator James Chesnut, Jr., one of the South Carolina senators.

The Brownes were of the inner circle of Washington's Southern society and very close to the Cobbs. Before Browne had come to Washington, he had no doubt become acquainted with Cobb and had developed a great affection for him, which never grew dim as long as Cobb lived. The Brownes had been in Washington only a short time before Kati Thompson was calling on them; and one evening she spent two hours talking with Lizzie Browne in the front reception room, while in the dining room Howell Cobb, Montague Browne, and a select group of politicians were smoking and talking politics.[24] Browne's *Constitution* was not given to reporting social news, but it noted that Kati after spending four weeks in her Mississippi home had returned "in excellent health and spirits."[25] After the election of Lincoln, Browne wrote his friend Barlow that there would probably be a caucus at his house, to be attended by Senators John Slidell of Louisiana, Jefferson Davis of Mississippi, James M. Mason of Virginia, Jesse D. Bright of Indiana, and Clement C. Clay of Alabama.[26] This meeting was, of course, if held, more political than social.

Meetings and gatherings were only infrequently purely social, for where the men were present and even their ladies, it was hard to keep politics out of the conversations. If it was only a ladies' party, and there were many of them, it would be the same. In the summer of 1860 Browne invited Barlow to a picnic which was to be held at the Great Falls of the Potomac. The men would provide the boats in which to get there, and the ladies would take care to fill the baskets. The group was to consist of Howell Cobb and his wife Mary Ann, Jacob Thompson and Kati, Browne and Lizzie, the John Floyds, the William Henry Trescotts (of the State Department), George W. Riggs, Treasurer of the Democratic National Executive Committee, and Barlow, if he should come.[27] Postmaster General Joseph Holt, though from Kentucky, did not qualify completely as a dyed-in-the-wool Southerner, especially after Buchanan's cabinet began to crumble, but he ran more with the Southerners than with the Northerners. Now and then he invited Browne to dinner parties, and Browne reciprocated. On February 9, 1860, Holt held a dinner party to which he invited

Browne; Robert Toombs; James H. Hammond, one of the South
Carolina Senators; Judah P. Benjamin, Senator from Louisiana; and
Andrew Johnson, a Tennessee Senator. Only Browne and Toombs
attended. Hammond declined, and Benjamin and Johnson accepted
but did not come.[28]

It must not be understood that the Southerners were an exclusive
set and admitted no Northern ladies and politicians. Browne would
see that Barlow always had a place when he came to Washington;
and Northern Democrats such as Senator William Bigler of Pennsylvania, Jesse Bright of Indiana, and George W. Bowman of Pennsylvania were welcomed in conclaves, social or political. But there were
some Southerners like Albert Gallatin Brown of Mississippi who distrusted all Northern Democrats and knew that Northern Democrats
would stand in the way of Southern nationalism.

Browne's greatest Washington friend was the President himself,
whom he privately and affectionately called Old Buck, the Public
Functionary, the Tycoon, and other names, but never in derision.
Buchanan made Browne not only a social friend to be entertained in
the White House, and an assistant to help entertain important visitors,
but also a political adviser and trouble-shooter. In this last capacity
Browne as editor of the *Constitution* was always ready to come to the
President's aid. When in December, 1859, Buchanan was chided by
Governor Henry A. Wise for failing to notice a military group of
Virginians who marched by the White House, Browne came to his
rescue by saying that the President would have welcomed them "however pressing might have been his official, social, or personal engage-
ments" had he been informed that they were coming.[29]

The President's receptions always received flattering notices in
Browne's *Constitution*, for he and Lizzie could be depended upon to
attend them. In announcing a New Year reception, Browne stated
that he was authorized to inform the public that the gates would be
opened at noon and would be closed at 2 P.M. Carriages should "approach the President's House by the east gate."[30]

Browne almost taxed his customary flow of fine language in describing the President's reception near the end of January, 1860: "Seldom,
within the recollection of the oldest habitue of levees and drawing
rooms, has the Executive Mansion been so densely thronged as it was
on Tuesday evening. It was exceedingly interesting and inspiring to
see the tide of distinction in every walk of life—as well as of fashion
and beauty, and elegance—pouring in alongside of the simplest, yet
well-attired and easy-mannered, persons of different classes, to pay
their respects to the Chief Magistrate. Such a spectacle cannot be

witnessed in any other land beneath the sun. . . . The President, it is universally acknowledged, receives his visitors with the cordiality and social tact which bespeak the gentleman of the olden time. He forgets no one. He makes no mistake of names; and the tide passes on with the agreeable impression that each one has met with kind looks and pleasant words from the Head of the Nation." Harriet Lane, Buchanan's niece and White House hostess, deepened "that impression by her admirable and inimitable manners and address." Ladies familiar with presidential receptions as far back as John Quincy Adams declared that Miss Lane was "without a parallel as the lady of the Executive mansion."[31]

At his Washington Birthday reception the same year Buchanan "received, with his usual dignified urbanity; and his lovely relative, Miss Lane, surrounded by a constellation of stars of the first magnitude, shown supreme in the firmament of beauty." Browne knew all this, for undoubtedly he was there to see—and his Lizzie would have had to be there, too.[32]

Mrs. Browne was of the inner circle of White House society and would likely have been in parties accompanying Buchanan to Bedford Springs, a famous Pennsylvania resort, which he visited frequently. In July of 1859 he with his party of ladies spent a two-week vacation there. In the party was, of course, Miss Lane, but she would hardly have considered the group complete without Lizzie Browne and Kati Thompson; and, indeed, there would be other Washington ladies. Writing about this particular party, Browne, of course, out of modesty and tact could not include by name his wife in this praise: "It need scarcely be added that Miss Lane and Mrs. Thompson, by their admirable social tact and the mingled grace and affability of their address, impart a charm to the presidential circle that leaves nothing to be desired."[33] The party returned on August 2.[34]

Browne's distinguished look and cultured address made him especially useful in welcoming, accompanying, and otherwise entertaining important people to whom protocol demanded that the President devote special attention. In May, 1860, a group of more than seventy Japanese officials and their retainers visited Washington to exchange ratifications of a treaty of amity and commerce which Townsend Harris had made in 1858 in Yeddo, Japan. How Browne towered above these "little men" from the Far East can easily be imagined. They created as much excitement as a circus and developed as much curiosity, which led Browne causticly to remark: "We do not propose to comment in detail on the exhibition which so much disgusted us, but we lament to admit that the spirit of flunkyism displayed itself in a form to be found most luxuriant in a corrupt stage of civilization, while it was here combined with a degree of uncivilized curiosity worthy of the most uncouth natives."

And Browne could not entirely exonerate the women. When one of the Japanese was asked what he thought of the American women, he was reported to have said, " 'American women very beautiful, but very bold.' " Browne observed, "We confess with grief that much of what the Japanese saw of American women justifies the sentence."[35]

On August 10, 1860, Browne wrote Barlow: "I went yesterday with the old public functionary to see the Great Eastern. We had a very good time if it was not so damned hot."[36] This great steamship was the pride of England, and in the words of the *Illustrated London News*, "we are the fortunate creators and possessors of a vessel such as the world never yet saw, and which is not to be considered as a gigantic toy, but as an emblem and a type of advancing civilization."[37] After making the port of New York, before returning to England, it proceeded to Annapolis, and it was there that President Buchanan with a party including the Brownes, Mrs. Howell Cobb, Harriet Lane, Secretary of the Navy Isaac Toucey, and others went to view this marvel of the ship-building industry of England. The captain paid his respects with a twenty-one gun salute and entertained the party on board the ship.[38] England had another attraction for Americans, even greater than the *Great Eastern,* in the person of Queen Victoria's son, The Prince of Wales, the future King Edward VII, who traveled under the title of Lord Renfrew. After visiting the Canadian provinces, he crossed into the United States at Detroit and proceeded to Washington, visiting various cities on the way. He reached Washington in early October, 1860, and his prospective arrival led Browne to say in his *Constitution,* "While we shall welcome him with cordiality and courtesy wherever he goes, we will carefully abstain from any manifestation which would be inconsistent with the character in which the distinguished stranger desires to be regarded during his sojourn in the United States."[39]

Browne's English-American background made him an appropriate choice to help entertain the English prince, the future sovereign of Browne's former country. Soon Buchanan, Browne, and a distinguished party were on their way aboard the *Harriet Lane,* going down the Potomac to visit Mount Vernon. Browne gave a minute description of the trip in his *Constitution.*[40] Browne was part of the small gatherings at the White House (as well as of the formal receptions held in honor of the Prince) and, being a smoker of good cigars, just as the Prince himself was, he presented the Prince with some. While they were sitting on the piazza of the White House enjoying a good smoke the Prince commented on the fine cigars which Browne had given him, whereupon Buchanan remarked to the Prince, " 'I was keeping some excellent ones for you, but Browne has got ahead of me.' "[41]

When the Prince was ready to leave Washington to continue his visit to Richmond, Buchanan assigned Browne "to go with *H. R. H.* to Acquia [Aquia] Creek in the *Harriet Lane*." "I was forced to do this," Browne reported to Barlow, explaining why he could not accept an invitation of Barlow's.[42] At Aquia Creek the Prince boarded the Richmond, Fredericksburg and Potomac Railroad train and there Browne left him in the hands of the Virginia authorities. Browne was much attracted to the Prince and commented that he had "won golden opinions by his amiable disposition and graceful manner."[43]

❧ IV ❧

In the Campaign and Election of 1860

THE YEAR 1860 was the most portentous in American history; it was equally so in the life of Browne. The winds of sectional hate had been blowing for more than a quarter of a century; now they were to increase into a whirlwind of emotionalism which would soon develop into bloody fighting. Browne would be in the midst of it all. With his *Constitution* he would hope to save his adopted country, and he was to make decisions that would completely change his life; but rather than give up fixed principles he would willingly undergo any personal sacrifice.

Had he accepted an offer that Frederick Law Olmsted made him a few years previously, he would, indeed, have had a life vastly different from the one the choice he did make gave him. Olmsted, best remembered for his travels in the South in 1853 resulting in the publication of his *Journey in the Seaboard Slave States* and his travels in England published under the title *Walks and Talks of an American Farmer in England,* but also well remembered for having designed Central Park in New York City, had offered Browne a position in developing the park.

In answering a letter from Olmsted in which Olmsted had asked a favor of Browne in securing the appointment of a friend to a Federal position, Browne said that he feared the position had already been promised but added: "Your success in the Park affords me sincere pleasure. Although in point of money, influence and position I have done better, I often regret the quiet I might have had, if I had accepted yr. offer of employment under you. I have achieved, I believe, great political success, but comfort, home enjoyment, & time to read and *enjoy* myself are utterly lost to me. I am in the vortex, & am spinning around with every eddy."[1]

Browne had come to know Olmsted about the time he accepted the position with the *New York Journal of Commerce,* but Olmsted could

not have made Browne the offer at that time, for Olmsted was not
appointed to the superintendency of Central Park until 1857. Their
acquaintance and long-time friendship probably grew out of the fact
that Olmsted had visited England and written his book about his
walks there; Browne, now an American citizen, never divested himself of his English ways.

This was the year of a presidential election, and some of the people
had not yet decided which party they would support; and if neither
party appealed to them, they would form a new one. The two great
contending parties were the Democrats and the Republicans. The
Democrats were divided over the issue of the protection of slavery
in the territories. The Republicans were a conglomeration of dissatis-
fied Democrats and remnants of former Whigs, Know Nothings, and
Free Soilers, held together by varying and conflicting principles,
mainly that of containing slavery within its present bounds and working for its extinction, immediately or ultimately.

As if anxious for the fray, the party national conventions met early;
all had met and nominated their candidates before the end of June.
The Democrats, dominated by the Southerners, met first and in the
most fiery of the Southern states—South Carolina—in Charleston,
on April 23. Browne attended and wrote back dispatches for the
Constitution. He also wrote a long letter to Buchanan the day before
the convention met, giving descriptions of delegates and his views and
predictions. He said that he had communicated with "nearly all the
delegations" from the Northern and Southern states and found that
R. M. T. Hunter of Virginia was being widely and favorably mentioned for the presidency. He found also that Douglas was bitterly
opposed in the South and that many delegates said they would as
soon have the New York Republican William H. Seward. Browne
predicted that if Douglas should be nominated there would be six
Southern states that would bolt and form a convention of their own.[2]
Buchanan was doubtless much interested in this information, for he
was opposed to Douglas; he himself had refused to be considered for
a second term.

Browne was vastly impressed with the importance of this convention, for he believed that out of its deliberations would come either
the salvation or the destruction of the nation. He declared that it was
more important "than a dozen European congresses charged with
the destiny of ever so many provinces like Savoy and Nice."[3] He was
haunted by the fear that the convention might break up, and to
prevent it he advocated that at all hazards the nominees must be

accepted and supported by all. Some months before the convention met, he had said, "We express no preferences and no dislikes. As we have already said, we have confidence in the wisdom of the Charleston Convention."[4] He could say this in the face of his strong opposition to Douglas, for at this time he would accept Douglas in preference to disunion, which he believed would follow the disruption of the Democratic party.

Browne's worst fears came true. In setting up its order of business, the convention decided to frame the platform before making its nominations. The Committee on Platform was made up of one representative from each state, which thereby threw the majority into the hands of the South. The platform presented to the convention embodied the South's contentions that slavery in the territories should be protected by Congress against hostile territorial legislation or none at all, according to resolutions which Jefferson Davis had introduced in the Senate providing for a Congressional slave code. Douglas and his followers had objected to this action, for it cut the ground from under his position on popular sovereignty and the Freeport Doctrine, which held that by a territory's refusal to pass laws to protect slavery, it could thereby smother it out.

When this platform was presented to the convention it was voted down, for each delegate to the convention had a vote and the populous Northern and Western states had a majority of the delegates. The minority on the Platform Committee had written their platform, which embraced the Douglas point of view, and when it was submitted to the convention it was adopted. Browne in his dispatch of April 30 described the intense drama of the occasion. He had a seat on the platform, where he had a full view of the hall and galleries.

He wrote: "There are few men who could have witnessed this day's proceedings in the National Democratic Convention without deep and solemn emotion, and a due appreciation of the momentous consequences, both immediate and prospective, which will result therefrom. I have never seen anything which impressed me so gravely." When the final vote on the minority report was taken and it was adopted, "the dropping of a pin might have been heard in the Convention. Every man, woman and child within the vast hall in which the delegates assembled seemed aware that a great crisis had arrived and that events were about to occur in which the dearest interests of American citizens were involved. . . . That great and hitherto tumultuous assembly seemed awed into silence and intent suspense." Then delegation after delegation withdrew from the hall. As one followed the other in quick succession, one could see the entire crowd quiver as under a heavy blow." And Browne observed that down "many a manly cheek did I see flow tears of heartfelt sorrow."

Browne sternly blamed the Douglas men for this catastrophe, men who were determined to follow a man rather than a constitutional principle, uncompromisingly. "When all the seceding delegations had retired," Browne noted, it was "impossible to portray the dismay of those by whose insolent and factious conduct that grave event had been occasioned, and when a motion to adjourn was made it was readily assented to." He defended the South by saying that it "asked for no intervention of Congress to establish slavery in any Territory." The South wanted only protection of its property by Congress if by "non-action or unfriendly legislation" by a territory such protection should be needed.[5]

Browne's friend Barlow attended this convention and their friendship was deepened by their association there. A few days after the convention had adjourned, broken into fragments with no nominations made, when Browne was back in Washington and Barlow in New York, Barlow wrote, "My dear Browne, I intended to write you a long and abusive letter for not writing me all the news as you promised," but he would refrain this time.[6] Barlow was interested in the undercurrents in Washington.

There was, indeed, much news in Washington and out that interested Browne no less than Barlow. The seceding Southern delegations went back home and some of the delegates prepared for a convention of their own, to meet in Richmond; and the Douglas Democrats, unable to make a nomination in Charleston for want of the required two-thirds majority, adjourned to meet in Baltimore in June. As it turned out, that part of the Southern Democrats who met in Richmond on June 11, ineffective in their proceedings, adjourned to June 21 and finally adopted the nominations of John C. Breckinridge of Kentucky and Joseph Lane of Oregon for president and vice president respectively. Breckinridge and Lane had been nominated in a convention in Baltimore made up of Southern seceders from the Douglas convention there. A few days before the Richmond convention met, Browne dropped a note to Buchanan saying, "I have some idea of going to Richmond to watch the proceedings there, unless you wish me to stay or think I can in any way be useful to you."[7] No evidence has been found to indicate that Browne went.

As Baltimore was much nearer Washington than Richmond was, Browne attended the convention which the Douglas Democrats held beginning on June 18. Sending back to the *Constitution* his first report on the opening day, he noted that the city was thronged with people from every state. They stood "in knots on all the hotel steps and corners of streets" discussing the questions of the day, "with zeal rendered much more ardent by frequent visits to those saloons where sherry cobbler and mint juleps are dispensed by thousands to the delight of enterprising Bonifaces."[8] He noted that a mass meeting held in Monument Square to boost Douglas was a failure.[9] When some of the Southern delegates were refused seats in this convention, Browne almost exploded with wrath at such chicanery: "Never in the history of politics in this or any other country, is there to be found a parallel for this shameless disregard of justice and honesty, to subserve the lowest partisan purposes."[10] Having purged the convention of the undesirable delegates, the Douglas managers found it easy to nominate their leader for the presidency; but the man they nominated for the vice presidency refused to accept, and after the convention had adjourned Herschel V. Johnson of Georgia was selected by the National Committee.

Soon after the disruption of the Charleston convention, remnants of old Whigs and Know Nothings who pronounced a plague on both factions of the Democrats and could not think of joining the Republicans held a convention on May 9 in Baltimore and nominated John Bell of Tennessee for president and Edward Everett of Massachusetts for vice president.

The Republicans met in Chicago on May 16, and in their deliberations they nominated Abraham Lincoln of Illinois for president and Hannibal Hamlin of Maine for vice president.

There were now four sets of candidates in the field, and, of course, it was not difficult for Browne to decide which set he would support. Having become as much a Southerner as any person ever born in the South, he worked hard for Breckinridge and Lane; but having a special knack at opposing those whom he did not like, he devoted more attention to them by way of supporting those whom he did like.

His damnation of Lincoln was about equal to his damnation of Douglas. He paid no attention to Everett, for whom he had doubtless some admiration, and he was more sarcastic toward Bell than bitter; but for that nondescript John Minor Botts of Virginia, who tried to get the nomination for the presidency at the Constitutional Union convention, which nominated Bell, and who then flirted with the Republicans, Browne had no respect whatever.

It is not clear why Browne noticed Botts at all, unless it was because of his slur on foreign-born citizens, as when he said that they might enjoy the franchise "only after they have acquired sufficient knowledge of our institutions to understand and value them."[11] "Everybody has heard of Botts—John Minor Botts we mean," began one of Browne's attacks. "Botts, who would like to be President but won't be. . . . Botts, who boasts of his valor but never fights. . . . Botts, who is a great man away from home and nobody at home. Botts, who talks as if he were master of Virginia, but couldn't be elected constable in any town in the state."[12]

As for Bell, he belied his name—he didn't ring. Browne headed one of his editorials "The Bell without a Tongue." "Ordinarily garrulous, he is now dumb." Was it not because his slogan, "the Union, the Constitution, and the Enforcement of the Laws," was "a clumsy piece of deception, which cannot bear examination or defence? For once in his life, Mr. Bell is afraid to speak."[13]

Browne made no personal attacks on Douglas, but he condemned his disruption of the Democratic party and his claims that he was the regular Democratic nominee. "Mr. Douglas has not the remotest pretense to be called the regular nominee," Browne declared. At no time did he get a two-thirds majority in the Baltimore convention, or even a majority when all expulsions and withdrawal of delegates were taken into account.[14] Time and again did Browne strike this note. The Douglas ticket was a nuisance as well as a threat to the success of the Breckinridge ticket. He could not possibly be elected: "With regard to the DOUGLAS and JOHNSON, and BELL and EVERETT tickets, no man in his senses can honestly believe that either has the semblance of a chance of carrying the electoral vote of any one State, much less, therefore, of obtaining a majority in the electoral college."[15]

Squatter sovereignty was the keystone to the Douglas arch, the doctrine which bracketed with Douglas' Freeport Doctrine would permit a territory to destroy slavery within its limits by refusing to pass laws that would protect it. Browne declared that for the past three years Douglas had been antagonistic to the doctrines and principles of the Democratic party and had "advanced and advocated the dogma of squatter sovereignty which fifteen States of the union regard as destructive of their constitutional rights, hostile to their interests, and insulting to their honor and dignity."[16] So far as the rights of the Southern States in the territories were concerned, Browne said that "we do not see much difference between the squatter-sovereignty doctrine of the 'Douglas party' and the direct intervention to prohibit slavery of the black-republicans."[17]

Pursuing this charge further, Browne hammered on the point that the kinship of the Douglas Democrats and the Republicans was quite evident, reinforced by the fact that there had been a fusion of the two parties in the election of an Oregon senator. Although some of the Douglas followers denounced Lincoln, "we find others who are equally earnest in his advocacy who do not hesitate to recommend an alliance with LINCOLN and all other opposition elements to secure the defeat of BRECKINRIDGE and the democratic party."[18] After the example of this Oregon fusion, would "there be a voice for Douglas in the South?" Browne asked.[19] Answering, he said: "The black-republicans tender the issue—'THE ELECTION OF LINCOLN IS THE DOWNFALL OF SLAVERY.' The South must meet it—there is no escape; if they falter by supporting Mr. Douglas, they have only postponed the evil."[20] If Lincoln should be elected, Douglas would be responsible, for "his whole course, and that of his friends, prove, beyond dispute, that he and they prefer the election of Lincoln to that of a thorough democrat."[21]

As a last reminder to the Douglas Democrats and the Constitutional Unionists, too, Browne on the eve of the election wrote: "With to-day two of the parties in the presidential contest pass away forever. The Bell-Everett party and the Douglas party, the products of mere partisan trickery and personal ambition, will be known only as incidents of a campaign whose result, whatever it be, will terminate their existence. . . . On whichever side victory rests, the two distinctive parties will now be, the democracy, the embodiment of national sentiment and patriotic aspiration, and the black-republicans, the aggregate representation of insolent fanaticism, and sectionalism utterly incompatible with permanent existence of the Union."[22]

Although Browne held that Douglas could not carry a single Southern state, he found it necessary to notice Alexander H. Stephens of Georgia, who was somewhat "a darling" of the Georgians and who was hoping to carry the state for Douglas. Knowing Stephens' honorable past, Browne was much disappointed in his Augusta speech, for Stephens showed "that in his zeal for Mr. Douglas his mind has undergone a complete change in every respect."[23] And, as the election approached, Browne said that he had long ago made up his mind "to fight the battles of the Constitution without Mr. Stephens's aid."[24]

Having obliterated Douglas and Bell, and thereby in a negative way promoted Breckinridge, Browne at the same time was carrying on in a positive way a campaign for Breckinridge. He placed the Breckinridge and Lane ticket at the head of his editorial page in the *Constitution,* and on July 19 he published the first issue of the *Campaign Constitution,* devoted to the "Democracy of the Union." It was to continue until after the presidential election in November; it was a weekly, and a single subscription cost fifty cents. He announced that it was "unnecessary to tell our brother democrats that if they would conquer in the great contest in November next, they should exert themselves to circulate papers which sustain their principles and support their candidates. We hope that every friend of BRECKIN-RIDGE and LANE will assist us in giving the widest circulation to the Campaign Constitution." The National Democratic Executive Committee recommended it "to the patronage and confidence of our friends throughout the Union."[25] It carried no advertisements and thereby escaped criticism as being subsidized by the Buchanan administration; but, of course, Buchanan supported the Breckinridge and Lane ticket.

Browne sent a copy of his first issue to Barlow and could not refrain from remarking in a bantering vein, "If you do not compliment me on my campaign paper I shall challenge you to mortal combat. I am really proud of it."[26] Knowing that his New York friend was wealthy and influential, a few weeks later Browne wrote him: "Can you not find any enthusiastic democrats who will help a poor editor by ordering a couple of hundred 'Campaign Constitutions' at $40 per 100. They are 'the best democratic documents extant' says J. Slidell."[27]

Browne said he had no favorite candidate at the time of the Charleston convention; but he supported Breckinridge and Lane because he had the fixed determination to support only the one who stood for the fundamental principles of the Democratic party and the Constitution. Douglas did not qualify; Breckinridge did. "Nobody can regret more deeply than we do," said Browne, "the unfortunate division which exists in the ranks of the democratic party. Nobody would have been willing to go further than we to avert that calamity and restore union, harmony, and zealous community of thought and action among all who profess allegiance to the democratic faith, and desire the defeat of the black-republican fanatics who are endeavoring to sap the foundations of our Government."[28]

Browne thought the Breckinridge campaign was slow in getting started. He was impatient. Only a few days after Breckinridge's nomination, he wrote Barlow, "I am almost crazy at the shilly shally, dilly dally policy being pursued." He was all for making "a holocaust of the Douglas men."[29] A few days later it did his heart good to report a great mass meeting in Washington for Breckinridge, where Jefferson Davis, Howell Cobb, and others spoke. There were between eight and ten thousand present; the outer fringe could not hear the speakers. After the speeches they marched to the White House to pay their respects to the President, who came to the balcony and congratulated them on the nomination of Breckinridge and Lane. Many banners were displayed by the crowd, one of which bore the couplet:

> Let millions join the loud refrain,
> Hurrah for Breckinridge and Lane![30]

It was soon after this that Browne set up his *Campaign Constitution*.

Browne never wearied in stating what Breckinridge and the Democrats stood for: "Our creed is that of justice, truth, honor, liberty, and patriotism. It contends for a strict construction of the Constitution, a faithful observance of all the provisions and guarantees of that sacred instrument, the sovereignty of the several States, the inviolability of their domestic institutions, and their perfect equality under the Constitution."[31] Its simplicity and justice commanded "for it the support and sympathy of all but the factious, the treacherous, and the traitorous."[32]

Dismissing Douglas as important in the campaign only by taking votes away from Breckinridge and bringing about the danger of electing Lincoln, Browne said that there were only two candidates in the race having any chance of election. They were Breckinridge and Lincoln. "For one or other of them the people must vote," said Browne, "since for whomever they vote, if it be against BRECKINRIDGE, they really vote for LINCOLN and black-republican rule. There is one issue, and that is between the party of the Constitution and the Union of which BRECKINRIDGE is the standard-bearer, and that of violence and treason of which LINCOLN is the accidental champion."[33]

In describing the Republican party, Browne said that the country had been "deluged by the falsehoods of this odious organization, composed of all the cast-off shreds and patches of every political party that has ever existed. Every dodge, every trick fraud that could possibly mislead the people and distract attention from their real purpose has been resorted to by these political jugglers."[34] The Republicans were a sectional party, held together by hatred of the South and its institutions, said Browne: "It is very generally believed that the political organization which is confined exclusively to the Northern States, and is familiarly known as the black-republican party, is entirely sectional, hostile to the interests and institutions of the Southern States, hostile to the Constitution, hostile to the perpetuity of the Union, and very decidedly in favor of investing the geographical, sectional majority of the North with power to crush out the rights of the fifteen slaveholding States."[35]

Browne held that the Republicans were a disunion party, for if they should win, as they expected, their announced hostility to the South would force it to leave the Union. Yet, in their electioneering propaganda they discounted this danger and "all attempts to convince the Northern aggressionists of the danger to which their agitation must inevitably lead have been treated with manifest disdain."[36] The party could not be trusted, and Browne declared that the "South does not and ought not to believe in any pledges that the dominant party at the North might give of their conservative intentions or resolution to act justly. There is no oath, however solemn, by which they can bind themselves to renounce their past course of aggression and insult which ought to satisfy or give confidence to the South. The South cannot trust them."[37]

In language like that applied to the Communist party a hundred years later, Browne said: "No party, like the so-called republicans ever before existed in this country. . . . In fact, the republician is not a legitimate political party at all. Its only principles are antagonism to slavery with which it has no more legitimate right to interfere than it has with the English window tax."[38]

In the hierarchy of the Republicans, Lincoln came in for most of Browne's attention, but Charles Sumner could not be entirely neglected, largely because Preston S. Brooks, a South Carolina Representative, in 1856 had give him a caning for his insult to a fellow South Carolinian. Sumner took a long vacation in Europe to recuperate, a much longer one than seemed necessary, in order to draw attention to his vacant seat in the Senate, mute evidence of the assault by that barbarous Brooks. Said Browne, "For nearly four years the Hon. Charles Sumner, one of the senators in Congress from the State of Massachusetts, has given no sign of political existence. Were it not for the pusillanimous appeals for sympathy under the bodily suffering inflicted on him as a just punishment for his slanders and insolence, which he and his friends have published from time to time in the public press, we had no evidence that he still existed in the flesh." But recently he had "again ventured to malign, slander and misrepresent half the States" of the Union and was again spouting "that seditious venom which has made him odious and despicable among honorable men."

The occasion for this verbal attack by Browne was Sumner's recent condemnation of the South and slavery and his assertion that he had discovered in England an article on the evils of slavery which the great historian Thomas Babington Macaulay had written when a youth and represented the first time he had appeared in print. Browne asserted that Macaulay was not the author of the article and that Macaulay had published something before this article had appeared.[39]

Lincoln did not appear of sufficient importance for Browne to notice until about two months before his nomination, when Browne associated him with Seward's "irrepressible conflict" doctrine.[40] Browne then began to look up Lincoln's "short and simple annals of the poor" and soon hit on his Mexican War record; he announced: "While Abraham Lincoln and his traitorous confederates were aiding the cause of the enemy in Mexico, by traducing and reviling that of their own country;—while they were endeavoring by their votes to prevent the supplies to carry on the war, and were encouraging the truculent hordes of Santa Anna to greet our noble army with *'bloody hands and hospitable graves,'* BRECKINRIDGE and LANE were engaged in fighting the enemies of our country, upholding its cause, its honor and its glory."[41]

Personally the Republican "candidate for the first office is a mere obscure partisan, utterly unknown in the higher annals of American politics," and Hamlin, the vice-presidential candidate, was "distinguished for little else than for a mediocricy of abilities which would render him harmless were the principles of which he is one of the representatives less dangerous in themselves." And his Mexican War record was no better than Lincoln's.[42]

As early as August, 1860, some of Lincoln's supporters were assuming that he was "as good as already elected," and now the question was whether he would take another term. The improbabilities reminded Browne of the story "told of a young girl who began to cry violently when a pot of boiling water fell off the fire and was overturned, and who, when asked why she cried, said sobbingly that she was thinking, if she was married and had a baby, and the pot of water had fallen on the baby, and the baby had been scalded to death, what a terrible thing it would be." And Browne was also reminded that the recipe "for hare soup—'first catch the hare'—contains a vast amount of practical sense."[43]

In the event that Lincoln should be elected, it would "be but the beginning of contention, of sectional alienation, and probably of ruinous and bloody conflict." [44]

As the election approached, Republican leaders kept saying that Lincoln was conservative, which led Browne to describe something which about a century later became one of Adolph Hitler's tricks, "that a lie if persistently adhered to, and plausibly told, answers all the purposes of truth." [45]

Browne felt that if Breckinridge did not carry New York, he would

probably fail of election. Also Browne's residence in that state for some
years gave him a special interest in New York state politics. He went
there frequently from Washington to visit Barlow and talk politics and
to plan the campaign. "The great State of New York—the Empire
State of the Union—will render the decision," Browne wrote; and
if Lincoln should be elected New York City would collapse, for the
Union would be broken and the city's Southern trade would disappear.[46] A few weeks before the election, Browne wrote Barlow that
their mutual friend Howell Cobb, Secretary of the Treasury, would
come to New York soon and would "try for 24 hours to save the
Union."[47]

Browne's worst fears were realized, and his prediction that New
York was the pivotal state proved true. Lincoln received 180 electoral
votes and was elected, but without New York's 35, the election would
have been thrown into the House of Representatives, where Lincoln
could not have won. Though elected through the electoral college,
Lincoln failed by almost a million votes of being the choice of the
American people. Breckinridge received 72 electoral votes, Bell, 39,
and Douglas, 12.

The die was now cast as far as Browne was concerned. "We can
understand the effect," he wrote in his *Constitution*, "that will be
produced in every Southern mind when he reads the news this morning—that he is now called on to decide for himself, his children, and
his children's children" whether he would submit to the rule of a hostile
government or "defend his rights, his inheritance, and his honor."
Continuing he said, "The people of the Northern States, by an apparently overwhelming majority, have rendered their verdict on an
issue fully made up, and after full deliberation, and their verdict says
that they deny that fifteen States of the Union are entitled to equality
in the Union; and that the future policy of the Federal Government
shall be based on active deadly hostility to the South and her institutions." [48]

Horatio King, First Assistant Postmaster General, was greatly disturbed by the reaction of officials high in Buchanan's administration.
He wrote the President the day after the election, saying that they
"were parading the streets here this morning with disunion cockades
on their hats!" And what was more, "the leading article of the
'*Constitution*' to-day can have no other effect than to encourage and
fan the flame of disunion, both here and at the South."[49]

In the light of his editorial to which King objected, Browne was
stretching a point when a few days later he said, "Whoever charges
us with recommending disunion states what he knows to be infamous

slander." Not directly but by implication he was recommending disunion. But he now added, "We have no ambition to find favor in the sight of Mr. Lincoln. We announce now our determination to earn his disfavor, and thus leave the field open to others who are less foolish and are endowed with more common sense than ourselves."[50]

The next month, when John Bell wrote his letter stating that all the South's grievances could be redressed in the Union, Browne replied that "hundreds, thousands, as good as Mr. Bell have said the same scores of times already. The South has heard the saying even unto weariness. What is wanted is, a statement of the specific means by which the wrongs of the South may be redressed, and its rights guaranteed 'in the Union.' " "Mr. Bell will, we trust," continued Browne, "pardon our inability to treat his letter with more formal reverence. But really these dreary echoes of the same purposeless story are sickening. Mr. Bell should leave this sort of thing to Botts. A man who talks only for the sake of hearing his own sweet voice, and who writes that he may see himself in print, may be excused for the endless iteration of the cant and commonplaces of a by-gone stage of the controversy."[51]

Instead of supporting Lincoln, Browne held him up to ridicule. He said that according to one of "Uncle Abe's confidants" the rail-splitter received about a dozen letters a day which threatened him "with flaying alive, assassination, mayhem, fire and brimstone, and getting his nose pulled. And, Uncle Abe smiles at all this, we are told, and throws the missives aside, to illustrate in the future the humorous side of his Administration."[52]

On noting a meeting of Lincoln and Hamlin after the election, Browne took occasion to pass a comment on each. Browne said that little had been heard of Hamlin during the past few weeks, but a friend who had visited him "found him engaged in storing material for pumpkin pies." As for Lincoln, on hearing of his election, "he was elated, buoyant, and disposed to crow; rather after the fashion of a rail-splitter whose game rooster comes out conqueror from a hard-fought main, than of a statesman solemnly alive to the responsibilities of his position. . . . Panic and impending revolution seem to him as nothing. He laughs and jokes, gulps down the largest doses of adulation that a village crowd can manufacture. . . . The latest narratives exhibit him, with legs crossed, reading aloud Henry Ward Beecher's rant from the columns of the *Independent;* and anon, with arms akimbo, serenely smiling at the ominous tidings that rush over the wires from the cotton-growing States."[53] This whole editorial greatly amused Browne's friend Barlow, who wrote him: "By the way your last, on the meeting between Lincoln and Hamlin was a *stunner*."⁵⁴

Like many other people, Browne was anxious to have President-elect Lincoln say something to reassure the Southerners, as well as many Northerners, that he would treat the South fairly, but his silence along this line was as profound as that of the sphinx. However, he was garrulous enough under the trees and on the streets of Springfield, where a newspaper correspondent pictured him as "in the centre of a promiscuous group of hangers-on, telling broad stories and laughing most loudly at them himself."⁵⁵ Commenting on Lincoln's silence on national policies, Browne said that the "world has heard of over-wise, over-cautious, and over-cunning people. We begin to believe that Mr. Abraham Lincoln is one of them." He had "steadily refused to comply with the request to expound his principles and purposes as President elect. He has been mum in the presence of a great emergency."⁵⁶ Reports of his cabinet-making indicated his "prolonged juvenility or premature senility." One day it was "Thingumbob" to be Secretary of State, and the next it was "Senator Skinflint" to be Secretary of the Treasury.⁵⁷

As editor of the *Constitution,* it was incumbent on Browne to have something to say for Thanksgiving Day, but the best he could do was to write: "The prosperity in which we have rejoiced has been in a large degree the product of mutual forbearance between the different sections of the country. And if this policy is to be discarded in our internal relations, we fear that Fasts will be more frequent than Thanksgiving days for many years to come."⁵⁸

Browne was sternly opposed to any coercion of the South. The day after the election he said that the crisis had come, yet there might still be time to save the Union; and if adjustment were possible, it would "not be in force, nor in precipitate acts of hostility," but in statesmanship, patriotism, and the sagacity of the American people. Reiterating his disclaimer that he was favoring the break-up of the Union, he said that the "attempt to distort our remarks into a recommendation of disunion is as unjustified as the efforts to hold others responsible for our language is disreputable." Knowing that the *Constitution* was regarded by many as Buchanan's mouthpiece, he was here divesting the President of any agreement or blame for what Browne said. Wrestling with his sentimental attachment to the Union and his determination to uphold the South, he said further, "In the silent of the night we gave expression to the honest impulses of a heartfull of sympathy with a section of our country threatened with wrong and danger."⁵⁹

Lincoln was apparently letting the New York newspapers speak for him on the subject of coercion, thought Browne: "Coercion, coercion,

coercion is all their cry. It is advocated piously by the *World,* respectably by the *Post,* jesuitically by the *Tribune,* and ferociously by the heroes of the *Times* and the *Courier.*"[60] At one time the *Post* was reassuring the country that there would be no coercion, but the latest news Browne had, held that "the *Post* was on the opposite tack, and had actually found a precedent for coercion — where think you! Why, in the 'Whiskey War of Pennsylvania.' "[61]

The apologists for coercion were saying that no one intended to coerce the South, that Lincoln would only enforce the laws, but that there would be no invasion by armies. To all of this, Browne replied, "It is high time that the absurdity of enforcing the laws without coercion should be exposed and understood. It is time that the people of the North should know that coercing a State to remain in the Union, and compelling its citizens to obey laws which they have renounced, are in effect one and the same thing, and that neither can be accomplished without war."[62] Browne said that those coercionists "would like to preserve this Government because it 'pays' "; but would coercion pay when it came to paying for a war, with the government borrowing money to fight it? Browne reminded them that capitalists "do not like to lend to men who are about to visit faro banks, patronize fast horses and women, and make fools of themselves generally."[63]

✣ V ✣

Browne Travels the Road to Secession

THE ROAD to secession lay open and wide. How could Southerners live under the same roof with Northerners who reviled and prayed against them? The chaplain of the House of Representatives prayed on one occasion, "Oh Lord, Thou knowest that there are traitors in the land who want to destroy this glorious Union." The *New York Tribune* reported that the disunionists in the House "seemed to be thrown into perfect confusion." Browne, always ready to cross swords with the *Tribune* and with such clerics as the House chaplain, wanted to know what right the chaplain had "to plant himself between representatives of the people and the Almighty, and to deal out damnation to those, whose political principles are at variance with his?"[1]

So completely had Browne Americanized himself and steeled himself against Republican doctrines that he never hesitated to draw comparisons to the disadvantage of the British, as for example bracketing the Republicans with the Tories of the American Revolution: "Whoever will take the trouble to compare the writing and speaking of English Tories in America during the war of Independence with the language of the black-republican leaders and journals of the present day will perceive an identity of venom and falsehood, only to be accounted for by the identity of motives that actuates them."[2]

Though Browne a few days after the election had denied that he was recommending disunion, very soon he was slanting his editorials toward secession, and when it actually occurred, with South Carolina's secession, he advocated secession for every Southern state — all fifteen of the slave states. By the end of January, 1861, he could say, "I advocated secession. I hoped, and still hope, that all the Souhern States will secede."[3] A week after the election Mrs. Jefferson Davis, commenting on the uncertain attitude of some of the Southern leaders, wrote to her husband, then in Mississippi, "No one rings like the true metal so much as Constitution Browne, who is enthusiastic and thoroughgoing, repudiates Mr. Buchanan openly, assuming secession responsibility."[4]

54

Browne had frequent quarrels with the *New York Times,* provoked by that newspaper, on various subjects. The *Times'* constant claim to being an independent journal led Browne on one occasion to comment: "It has frequently been found that those who most loudly boast of their 'independence' are the most ready to be purchased, mollified, or silenced."[5] So it was when the subject of secession came up. The *Times* bitterly condemned Browne's *Constitution* as a secessionist organ that was trying to destroy the Republican party: "It prefers secession, disunion, anarchy — anything rather than the instalment of a republican administration over the Government of the United States." It was advocating hatred of the North and was "utterly incapable of any but the most bitter partisan views of this or any other subject, and its steady aim now is, not to save the Union, but to defeat and destroy the republican party."[6]

Browne replied that the *Constitution* had labored to save the Union by trying to defeat Lincoln, whereas the *Times* had actually sought to destroy it by advocating his election. It had tried "to coax the South to have its hands tied, its mouth gaged, its eyes bandaged, that it might be the unresisting prey of black-republican policy. . . . The abuse and misrepresentation heaped by black-republican papers upon the *Constitution* is the best tribute to its fidelity to conservative principles in this crisis. And we beg the *Times* to take notice, that as we have been, so we shall be until these difficulties be disposed of satisfactorily, one way or another. We will not cry peace when there is no peace. We will not talk of safety when none is to be found. We will not recommend the South to confide in black-republican professions, when facts abundantly prove that these professions are deceptive, and are only intended to throw the Southern people off their guard."[7]

Browne was no pacifist when war seemed to be called for, but to his thinking, the assumption that secession could not be peaceably carried out defied normal human intelligence and ordinary common sense. "To suppose that States cannot separate without becoming mortal enemies —," he declared, "that they cannot pursue different lines, whether of industry or government, without first determining their relative strength upon scores of battle-fields — that their business relations cannot be readjusted save at the cost of civil war — is virtually to confess that the intelligence of the American people is mere sounding brass, and their moral principles and religion simply tingling cymbal."[8]

Without, of course, knowing it, Browne was making an answer to Lincoln's Gettysburg Address, of almost three years yet to come, when in December, 1860, he pointed out "the folly of attempting to perpetuate the unity of a democratic compact by force," — that democracy might not perish from the earth if the United States were not reunited. "Who that understands the nature of the compact," he declared, "and its bearings upon political institutions, imagines that the severance of States implies aught akin to what is called 'the failure of the republican experiment'?" Congress should come to terms with the new nation that was about to be set up in the South.[9]

It was long known that South Carolina would lead off the secession movement, and when its sovereign convention was about to meet in December, Browne intended to be there to observe this historic occasion; but he finally decided to remain in Washington, where equally important events were in the making.[10] On December 20 the convention voted to secede, and Browne published in the *Constitution* its "Address of the People of South Carolina, . . . to the People of the Slaveholding States of the United States."[11]

It was a solemn moment for Browne when South Carolina seceded, but one in which he rejoiced; for had not the secession of the South come about, he would have been disconsolate, even to the extent of abjuring his own claim to being a Southerner and then returning to England. But it was otherwise, and now it was futile "to discuss the abstract principle of secession." South Carolina's withdrawal from the Union, he declared "has changed the contest from one of theory to one of stern reality. It is no longer a question of right or policy, to be dealt with leisurely and with comparative indifference, but a question of fact, involving new and momentous issues, and demanding both promptitude and prudence on the part of all in authority, whether of the seceding State or of the Federal Government as it remains." The central government, he said, "presuming upon its strength, may be disposed to view the secession of a single State as less serious than it really is; forgetting that the traditional glory of the Union is for the time bedimmed, that its strength is for the time impaired; and ignoring the crowd of probabilities, we might almost say the certainties which indicate South Carolina as the leader of a mighty movement rather than the isolated actor in a scene speedily to be reversed."[12]

The states as they seceded expected to come to terms with the national government in some formal treaty or arrangement whereby they would settle all points arising from their establishment of a new government. Although Browne had talked about civil war if the North forced it on the South, there was a general feeling in both sections that peace would be maintained. So it was, then, that immediately after South Carolina had seceded and declared herself another republic, she sent a commission to Washington to treat with the Federal government. Browne thought that they should be received by Congress and listened to. "Spurn them from your door haughtily, defiantly, and you will in effect apply the lighted match to a magazine of powder. No human agency can then prevent an explosion." "You must recognize secession," he warned, "when ordained by a people of a State; or, dreaming of coercion, you must prepare for civil war." [13] Browne would use no such language in reference to the President, and Buchanan did see the Commissioners on December 28, but nothing came of the meeting since Federal troops already occupied Fort Sumter. Buchanan had determined that if war should come he would do nothing to bring it on and would let Lincoln wrestle with the secession movement and the Southern Confederacy, which was organized a month before Lincoln took office. The South Carolina Commissioners went back empty-handed.

Browne pounded away time and again on the point that secession was a fact. When three states were already out of the Union, Browne wrote, "Recognize secession, as you would any other incontrovertable fact. Acknowledge that the Union is broken. And then seek to mitigate the misfortune which you have no longer power to avert. Since secession is inevitable let care be taken to render it peaceful. One calamity is enough."[14] He felt that one of the important causes of the secession movement was the "obstinate, unaccountable, unreasonable, and unreasoning incredulity of Northern people" that the South meant what it had been saying.[15]

Why could the North not see that the secession movement was the application of democracy in its purest form? As glorious as the old Union in its pristine form had been, it was not sacred; it had not been decreed by the Supreme Being and handed down on Mount Sinai. Browne quoted the *London Star* as having said that the Union had been " 'rather an imposing spectacle than an indispensable structure.' " Reiterating his answer to the doctrine in Lincoln's Gettysburg Address, yet three years in the future, Browne said, "Instead of lamenting the severance of the Union, then, as an injury to the democratic idea of government, we may point to the capacity which seceded States have shown for assuming the attributes of sovereignty, as an illustration of the skill and wisdom that dictated the maintainance of 'independent rights and separate interests.' " "The continent," he declared, "is large enough for two great powers. There is scope for two Unions, each as truly great as that which events have destroyed."[16]

Being a former English subject, Browne could point with pride to the policy adopted by England in allowing her colonies independence if they so desired: "Surely the States of the American Union are entitled to the rights which the government of England accords to her colonies. Why should South Carolina be less free than Canada 'to decide its own future?' " "South Carolina," he continued, "merely claims the right of doing what Canada may do any day." [17]

As much as Barlow admired and respected his friend Browne, he could not agree with him on secession. Barlow considered himself a friend of the South, but not to the extent of supporting it in breaking up the Union. The South ought not be ungrateful for the aid and friendship of the great mass of Democrats in the North, who would go to any lengths in standing by the South, short of agreeing with secession. Browne was under great nervous tension in viewing the course of events and on November 18, 1860, he wrote Barlow, "I shall lay violent hands on some of your whiskey. We need some soothing beverages now, to calm our excited nerves, and save ourselves from despair." As much as he disliked the pestilences of the times, he saw the only escape for the South in secession and the organization of another government. "I do not entertain much doubt now that Georgia, Mississippi, and Alabama will follow South Carolina [which he assumed would certainly be the first to go]. I should add Florida also." He would have liked to include Texas, but he was fearful that Sam Houston would make it difficult for that state to secede.[18]

Barlow wrote Browne a month before South Carolina seceded a strong appeal to stay his present course and work for a convention that might save the Union. Appealing both to his intellect and to his purse, Barlow wrote, "If any Southern party will in advance enable you to continue your paper as the representative of extreme Southern views & you think this is a wise policy of course you may do so though it seems to me that you are to a considerable extent bound body and soul to the views of the Govt. in this great crisis and that to support those views you can win a name and position which will be valuable to you and your paper in the future & in addition be of real service to the Country. Of course if you adopt this course your support must be thorough and earnest. You must bring to bear on this momentous question, in which the best interests of the country are involved the good sense & unusual ability with which you are blessed and take my word for it you will never regret the course you pursue. There is in no event, any future for you in the South. Here in Washington there is unless you destroy your position. . . ." Barlow implored him to "calm the excitement. Speak and write in favor of a Convention."[19]

Barlow's various arguments made a deep impression on Browne and "set me to thinking before acting, and has so entirely convinced

Mrs. Browne that you are right, that if I follow it not, I shall hear of it occasionally." This last rather cryptic expression could hardly mean that if hard times came to the Brownes in their Southern home, Lizzie would chide her husband and say "I told you so." Mrs. Browne was, in fact, entirely above such nagging, but being less concerned with political principles she might have been wondering how difficult it might be to get a new bonnet. But Browne, holding his fixed principles above purse or price, wrote Barlow, "Whatever course I might take as a public man, my intimate conviction is that were I a citizen of a Southern state I should suffer anything rather than submit to Lincoln's election, — not because it is the defeat of my party, but because it is the concentrated expression of the deadly hate of a majority to me and all value." He believed that apart from the honor involved, separation would be economically profitable, and that it could be carried out peacably. "I believe," he wrote, "in the absolute right of each state to secede when she pleases, and why she pleases" and that the Federal government could not prevent it. "That as a citizen of *the United States,* not influenced by pride of section [never having lived in the slave South, and having been in America for less than ten years], I can see very plainly the incalculable ills of dissolution," how the power of the United States would be reduced, and he hoped that a convention could be called to consider the situation, "but I cannot go to the length of saying that a state is to be no judge of her own wrongs, or the measure of her redress, and that if she is oppressed & has no other means of relief but secession, she cannot resort to it without permission of the federal govt." Browne said that he had read the documents on the formation of the constitution, including Elliot's *Debates* on its ratification by the states.[20]

Barlow, who had a wholesome respect for money, for he was a wealthy man, still argued with Browne on the financial ruin he would suffer by going with the South. He said that a new Democratic newspaper was being planned for New York City. "Will it not be possible," he inquired, "for you to sell our your present interest in Washington and take part in this new enterprise[?] I think it can be sustained liberally."[21]

Seeing that Browne could not be moved from his position by financial arguments, Barlow began emphasizing the possibility of a compromise between the two sections as a possibility of saving the Union and hoped that Browne would choose with greater enthusiasm that solution. There was no end of compromise measures and conventions being suggested by Union Democrats, by Border State leaders especially. On December 10, with Congress now in session and compromise being much in the air, Browne wrote Barlow a long letter arguing that the policy of the South was correct and that no Republican was suggesting any compromise that the South could accept. And in a spirit of finality he said, "The South will never bend the knee again and beg for her rights. Her rights are known. Why are they withheld?" In any argument with Barlow, Browne could never grow emotional, and he ended this letter, "In any event, My Dear Barlow, come war or peace, believe me that I am and ever shall be your friend." And to add a little levity to the somberness, he appended the postscript, "Are you so damned full of politics that you cannot tell a fellow how your dear little daughter is[?]"[22]

Another one of Browne's friends, Olmsted, tried to convince him that he should give up his Southern convictions and use his talents and influence in combating secession. In answer to Olmsted, Browne wrote in a letter to him on December 10, 1860: "I thank you for your interest in me. I know it is sincere. I have had abundant proof of it for the five years we have known each other. I respect your opinion because I *know* your honesty and singleness of purpose. But I cannot agree with you. I cannot plead guilty to the indictment that I am 'wrong,' 'unjust,' 'insolent,' in the political course which I have pursued in the responsible position to which I have been called. I feel as honestly convinced that I am right and fully justified before God, & in my conscience as I am of my life. The South has not asked, and does not ask, anything more than her rights, her equality & that which the Constitution gives her. . . ." He then argued for the protection which the Constitution gave slavery.

Is there a day or an hour that efforts are not made to rob her of her slaves, & induce them to rise against their masters?

Is she not told from every rostrum, pulpit, lecture room, & newspaper, of the Republican party, that she is barbarous, unholy, criminal, because she preserves an institution which the Constitution recognized, & which she is resolved to maintain as essential to her prosperity & comfort? And yet we are told that she is not wronged, insulted, & outraged; that she has no right to complain, & no ground for remonstrance against Lincoln's election . . . .

No, my dear Olmsted, I am not a disunionist. I regret as deeply as anybody, the present troubles, but I think the South is right, and if she cannot get justice in the Union I am in favor of her securing it by separation. I do not see why there should be either war or even reluctance on the part of the North. By separation the *consciences* of the philanthropists will be made easy as they will no longer be responsible for slavery. By fair and liberal treaties they can secure commercial relations of a satisfactory & prosperous character, and as two independent nations they need have no cause of quarrel. I cannot agree with you as to the sufferings of the South. Possessing three fourths of the basis of exchange of the whole country, she cannot be ruined if she is wise & united, & if there is no war. If there is war, of course, ruin & desolation must ensue; but why should there be war?

You may rely on it as a fixed fact that before the 4th of March twelve of the fifteen states of the South will be out of the Union, & the only thing to be done is to prevent bloodshed. This can be done, & I shall labor earnestly for it.

It is madness to talk of subduing the South. It is infamous to attempt to excite [incite?] servile insurrection. Justice, humanity, Christianity & self interest demand peace. By negotiation the separation will be peaceful, & perhaps, but *temporary*. Coercion is death, & reunion is impossible.

Browne wrote this letter without heat or passion. He sent his "kindest remembrances to Mrs. Olmsted," and he closed with: "Let me hear from you often."[23]

Two compromise plans which were introduced in Congress gained great public interest, but both failed of adoption. Thomas Corwin of Ohio presented to the House a proposal to amend the Constitution to the effect that no future amendment should ever be adopted allowing Congress to interfere with slavery in a state. This resolution passed both House and Senate, but in each chamber it was opposed by a majority of the Republicans. It was never ratified by the states; the coming war intervened. In the Senate, John J. Crittenden of Kentucky introduced a set of resolutions known as the "Crittenden Compromise," which was referred to a committee of thirteen, on which there were five Republicans. As Lincoln refused to agree to it, all Republicans on the committee voted against it, and it was never brought to the floor of the Senate until too late, every Republican in the Senate voting against allowing it to be brought out of committee.

These events convinced Browne that compromise was a delusion and a snare. In December he remarked that Corwin had "hoisted the flag of truce in Congress, and his friends have dragged it through the dirt ever since. Mr. Crittenden presented terms of peace, and not a solitary black-republican has opened his mouth, save to disclaim them."[24] And he observed in a letter to Barlow that Lincoln would "not recede one inch from the Chicago platforms & his party sustain him in his obstinancy." [25]

By the end of the year Browne had come to the conclusion that come what may, if any compromise should ever be discussed, it would have to be between an organized Southern confederacy and what was left of the old Union. He wrote Barlow early in the new year, 1861, that the South would not accept "any milk and water compromise which the Republicans will fraudulently offer; that the separation of the 15 Southern States is a necessary condition to reconstruction."[26] A few days later he wrote in his *Constitution* that the hopelessness of compromise must now be evident to everybody who did not want to be deceived. The Republicans would not give what the South demanded, "and the South will not take anything less."[27]

After the Republicans in the Senate refused to let the Crittenden Compromise come to a vote on January 16, Browne pronounced its death and wrote its epitaph: "The Crittenden Compromise is no more. The black-republicans in the Senate yesterday ruthlessly slaughtered it, and now it sleeps the sleep of death. What shall be its epitaph. 'Here rests the Last of the Compromises: Conceived in good intentions, and brought forth in hope, it lingered only to prove its weakness, and died unchristened, choked in its swaddling clothes.' Peace to its manes!"[28]

Compromises had failed; the South had determined to secede and with South Carolina's secession on December 20 the movement was on. The Republicans were adamant against recognizing secession or treating with Southern commissioners but were resolved to enforce the laws everywhere — what was left was war. Browne disconsolately observed in a letter to Barlow on January 10, 1861, that he could "see no hope of avoiding a collision. God knows I have labored to arrest it, & so have our friends. But what can honest men do against imbicility, treachery, and mad impulsiveness?"[29] And he wrote in his *Constitution* five days later that whatever might happen in the meantime, "two months hence President Lincoln will commission General Scott to subjugate 'the rebellious States,' and flog them 'back into the Union.' Two months hence, therefore, there will be war."[30] In answer to Horace Greeley's recent demand that England recognize the independence of Ireland in deference to the will of the people, Browne asked him: "Why shriek for freedom in Ireland, then, and howl for the punishment for 'rebels' in the seceding States? The British government is more just toward Ireland, than are the black-republicans, who have elected a President, toward the South."[31]

Browne rather forlornly hoped that the Northern Democrats would stand by the South against "these traitors, who with the Union on their lips, but the Constitution under their feet, are plunging our country into the horrors of civil war."[32]

There was a wild campaign sweeping through the North building up military ardor among the deluded people. "The military ardor," Browne wrote, "which costs no greater sacrifice for its display than the time and labor spent in writing letters to the newspapers has grown into a mania. There is scarcely a village in the Northern States that does not contain some major general or brigadier who pants (on paper) for an opportunity to annihilate the South, and whose love for the Union is so passionate that the only means that he can recommend for its preservation is to devastate half of it by fire and sword."[33] The war that was inevitably in the making would be "the most calamitous, the most unholy, the most infamous that was ever declared since the world began."[34]

And that was just what the war-makers in the North were predicting — calamitous to the South, and its "humiliation and ruin,"[35] if it persisted in its course. Had Browne been as good a prophet as he was a writer, he would have seen that this prediction was to come true. And in a New Year's message to the readers of his *Constitution* he described the Union as already in ruins: "The New Year dawns upon a broken Union — upon hostile sections of a common country — upon public credit blasted, enterprise paralyzed, all commerce at a standstill. It comes laden with danger — pregnant with promises of strife and ruin. It brings us face to face with the stern reality, that we are no longer a peaceful and prosperous people; and that if peace and prosperity are ever to return, they must travel by a road yet concealed from mortal vision. A new year and a new era, dark and dreary meet us together.

"And all this gloom is man's devising. Providence smiled bounteously in the year gone by. The great granaries are bursting with food. But for abolition madness, this had been a Happy New Year's Day."[36]

The only bright side of this picture of inevitable war was that it could not be believed "by any sane man that the Southern States can be conquered and subdued by a Northern army."[37] Had people forgotten "the history of the Revolution of their fathers, when only a handful, as it were, kept old England at defiance for seven years and upwards." The whole South would be in the fight, and any orders that might be given to the army and navy to invade it would be disobeyed. "Do any sensible men think that the ties of birth, nature, home, State, country, and all the relations incident to social existence, will be subject to an army or navy order? What influence will a commission exert when, by virtue of it, you order a man to take the life of his father or mother? Can it be obeyed? It is impossible and worse than madness that men should be indulging in any such false folly."[38] Browne was mostly right in this prediction as far as men in the army who were of Southern birth were concerned, for very few of such officers failed to resign their commissions in 1861. George H. Thomas and old Winfield Scott, both Virginians, were shining exceptions.

Browne found consolation also in his conviction that foreign countries would recognize a Southern government. Whatever sympathy there might be for the Negro in slavery and support of the Northern program to get rid of slavery in England and France would soon be forgotten in case of war. "Commercial interests," Browne argued, "the absolute existence of a vast industry, the peace of densely-populated districts are considerations not to be overborne by the maudlin story of Uncle Tom."[39] Browne and many others believed that the South's cotton crop would be the determining factor in winning the war for the South. Near the end of January, 1861, he said that word had come out of Toronto, Canada, that it would be English policy to recognize the South —"Their independence will be on record; their new government will stand, legitimate and regular; and England will inquire no further," said Browne.[40]

❧ VI ❧

Browne and Buchanan Part Company

PRESIDENT BUCHANAN was truly a friend of the South, but he denied the right of secession. He started out by appointing a majority of his cabinet members from the South; however, Postmaster General Aaron V. Brown of Tennessee died before the secession crisis arose, but he was replaced by Joseph Holt, a Kentuckian. The first secession casualty was Howell Cobb, Secretary of the Treasury, who resigned on December 8, 1860, though he had a deep feeling of friendship for the President and much regretted the necessity of this action.

Browne often said that Cobb was the greatest and truest friend he ever had. Undoubtedly Cobb exerted a deep influence over Browne and was responsible for making him a Georgian. They were in close association both socially and politically. On one occasion when Cobb was ailing, Browne sent him a bottle of wine with this "get well" note: "In order to render the cure perfect I take leave to send you a bottle of pure old port, a few glasses of which after your dinner will have a most salutary effect."[1]

Browne in his *Constitution* was always ready to come to Cobb's defense when attacked, as well as to praise him without any occasion to do so. Browne said that Cobb came to his cabinet position "with an exalted character as an orator, a patriot and a statesman," and that he had "given triumphant evidence that he is a practical business man, fully acquainted with the management of complicated figures, and the intricate commercial and financial questions constantly arising in the multifarious duties committed to his charge."[2]

Commenting on Cobb's Treasury Report for 1859, which had not met with universal praise, Browne said that for all who were "capable of understanding and appreciating a clear, lucid statement such as is essential in a State paper of this kind, it would be superfluous to comment or epitomize; to such as have the capacity and will not understand, (if any such exist,) it would be worse than idle to enlighten them."[3]

Although Cobb had been a Unionist in the Crisis of 1850, much had happened since then, and ten years later, on December 6, he issued his famous address "To the People of Georgia," which Browne described as "the most scathing, the most complete, and the most powerful exposure of the crimes of the black-republican party which is now extant in a compact form."[4] A week later he published in his *Constitution* this long document in its entirety and called for "that attentive persual to which that distinguished gentleman is so eminently entitled."[5]

Two days after issuing his Letter, Cobb handed in his resignation to Buchanan. Browne was loath to see Cobb depart Washington, but he could not think of blaming him: "Hosts of friends who, like ourselves, have learned to know his worth, to value his many high qualities of head and heart, to admire his great talents, and to appreciate his frank, genial manners, will miss him from among us regretfully as we shall." Continuing his praise of Cobb, Browne said, "We know that the same high and honorable motives which have ever guided him in his present course, and are sure that even those who differ most widely from him in opinion, must honor and respect his convictions of duty."[6]

John B. Floyd, Secretary of War, was next to go. Sick and in trouble over the financial management of his Department, he resigned on December 29. An additional reason for resigning was that he seemed no longer to have any direction over the army; for without his knowledge or consent, Major Robert Anderson, in command of troops in Fort Moultrie, had moved them into Fort Sumter on December 26. Browne wrote Barlow that Floyd had resigned "on the ground that he was pledged to S. Car. that the *status quo* should be preserved." However much others might condemn Floyd's management of his Department, the Southern element in Washington gave him their full support. Browne remarked that Floyd's house was "like a fair green. Everybody with a clean face has called to congratulate him & express their approval of his conduct." Continuing, Browne said that the South would not let "herself be led by the nose into the meshes of submission to Lincoln. She will be out by the day he assumes the rotten sceptre which awaits his grasp."[7]

Jacob Thompson, Secretary of the Interior, lasted into the new year; he went out on January 8. The occasion of his leaving was the dispatch of the *Star of the West* with reinforcements to Fort Sumter. As the expedition had been organized in great secrecy, Thompson felt that he had been deceived.

As delegation after delegation in Congress from the seceding states withdrew and made their farewell speeches, Browne followed them closely and commented with resounding praise on some of their addresses, a few of which were made several days before the Congressman actually left. For instance, Robert Toombs made his last speech in Congress on January 7. Browne was present to hear Toombs; the next day he wrote Barlow, "I wish you had heard Toombs. He was magnificent."[8] In his *Constitution* Browne wrote:

If any member of the black-republican party, entertained an honest doubt as to the nature, amount, and effect of the grievances which have driven the South to assume her present attitude, we think that Mr. Toombs dispelled that doubt in his speech of yesterday.

We have never listened to a more crushing bill of indictment, sustained in every count by irrefragable proof of the guilt of those whom it arraigned at the bar of the civilized world.

To say that Mr. Toombs was eloquent, powerful, bold, and convincing, is only to attrabute to him qualities which every body knows he possesses in as great a degree as any public man in America since the days of Patrick Henry.[9]

Three days later Jefferson Davis made his last speech in Congress, in which he held out a friendly hand to the North and hoped that there might be peace and uninterrupted friendly relations thereafter between the North and South. Browne said that he had heard this speech called "the most eloquent production of this gallant soldier and able statesman's life."[10] But Northern newspapers would not have it so; and in answering the sneering attack on it by the *New York Evening Post,* Browne said, "If any speech delivered in the Senate during the present session merited kindly regard at the hands of the North, it was Mr. Jefferson Davis's. In tone, in manner, in argument, it was as frank and generous overture as any Southern man could make without transgressing the limits of self-respect."[11]

Senator Alfred Iverson of Georgia spoke his farewell in a tone different from Davis's. He defied the North to conquer the South, if war must come; but he showed a courteous regard for the Senators, "wishing them each and all long life, prosperity, and happiness." Browne, who apparently was present, said that the speech was received "with derisive cheers and laughter." No honest man could have heard it "without feeling a deep sense of shame and disgust that men occupying such high and dignified positions could be guilty of such unseemly levity on so solemn and impressive an occasion."[12]

Long before Buchanan's cabinet began to break up and Southern congressmen to leave Washington, Browne had been a consistent defender of the President and his administration, and he would be among the last to desert the President. Ever since coming to Washington he had served the President and the President had relied much on Browne. Assessing Buchanan's message to Congress in December, 1859, he said that it would be "justly esteemed one of the most interesting, most able, and most important State papers which have been communicated to Congress." He especially liked Buchanan's call in this message for peace and fraternal feeling between the North and South. "Who is there within the limits of this vast continent whose soul is not dead to all sense of patriotic duty, and who is not totally bereft of feeling for the welfare and happiness of his country, who will turn a deaf ear to the appeal which the President addresses to his countrymen, North and South."[13]

Early in 1860 W. O. Bartlett, a New Yorker and an ardent Buchanan supporter, had heard Buchanan reminisce on his boyhood days, and he was so entranced by the account, feeling that it would be an inspiration to old and young alike, that he begged the President to write down these reminiscences for publication.[14] Browne dropped a note to Buchanan with the hope that he would comply with Bartlett's request. "You would furnish a paper," he told him, "which every man, woman & child in America would read with interest & instruction." [15] Buchanan promised to do so.[16]

Always at the beck and call of Buchanan, Browne seldom left Washington without communicating his intention. In June, 1860, he told the President that he was thinking of going to Richmond to attend the Democratic convention "unless you wish me to stay, or think I can in any way be useful to you,"[17] and in October he had to postpone a trip to New York because Buchanan needed him in connection with preparing his annual message to Congress.[18]

As December approached when Congress would meet, Browne declared that this session would be "the most exciting since the days of the Continental Congress," [19] and when Congress met and Buchanan's message was read on December 3, he wrote in his *Constitution,* "We indulge in no exaggeration when we pronounce the Message . . . the most important document emanating from the President of the United States since the formation of the Government." It was "a calm, dispassionate, and patriotic exposition of the case upon whose satisfactory solution depends the perpetuity of the Union." Though Buchanan said that there was no right of secession, yet there was no right to coerce a state back into the Union. Browne was especially pleased with this pronouncement on coercion.[20]

When a few days later the editor of the *New York Times* called on Buchanan to resign because he dilly-dallied and did nothing to scotch the secession movement, Browne replied that the President did not think that "he ought to usurp power in order to involve his country in years of bloodshed and confusion. How intolerably slow and hum-drum! No wonder that the Chevalier Bayard of newspapers should be disgusted, and ask the offender to 'go home.' "[21] And writing further in the same vein, he said, "Rave and abuse and falsify as they may, Mr. Buchanan's assailants will not succeed in persuading the country that he has acted in a manner inimical to its interests." [22]

As Browne read some of the extreme Republican journalists, he noted that they first began abusing Buchanan, "then they threatened impeachment, next they impugned his sanity," and finally, "as a last resort, they hold over him the terrors of assassination."[23] Answering the charges leveled against the President that he knew of the defalcations of the postmaster in New York City which led to his ousting and disgrace, "We shall not insult the President, or disgrace ourselves by any effort to vindicate him against a charge which is so transparently, stupidly, [and] false as it is infamous."[24]

The members of Buchanan's administration and his Democratic supporters did not object, of course, to Browne's forthright and heroic defense of the President; but some of them were becoming fearful that Browne's extreme pro-Southern position on the issues of secession and coercion was injuring Buchanan in the eyes of Northerners generally, since they looked upon the *Constitution* as representing the President.

The Assistant Postmaster General Horatio King felt especially concerned, and, as previously noted, he wrote Buchanan that the *Constitution's* leading editorial the day after Lincoln's election fanned the flames of disunion. The same day he wrote to John A. Dix, former United States Senator from New York and future major general in the Federal army and governor of New York, that the editorial would "do infinite mischief, and I am not certain that the writer of it ought not to be stretched up as a traitor." [25]

King took it upon himself to start a campaign of denunciation against the *Constitution*, not only because he loved the Union and hated secession, but more particularly because he felt that he might lose his property in Washington if secession was carried out. In mid-November he made a visit to New England and found the feeling there rising against Buchanan because he did not denounce secession. King addressed a note to the President telling him so, charging that "one or more of your official advisers favors the secession movement" and that "you are responsible for the course of the Constitution newspaper on that subject." King showed the letter to Joseph Holt, Postmaster General at this time, and Holt advised him not to send it, as it might cause offense.[26]

King hoped to enlist Dix in his campaign against the *Constitution,* writing him on November 23 that the friends of the President were determined to find out whether he was "responsible for the infamous course of the *Constitution.*"[27] Two days later he wrote to Dix again, saying that the course of the *Constitution* was infamous, "but the President, I presume, has no means of controlling it." He wanted Dix to write to Buchanan and tell him how much the paper was injuring him and to get "the papers to come out and denounce the 'Constitution.' " He now thought that Browne's secession editorials were "directly against the feelings of the President."[28] Dix replied that at one time he had decided that it would do no good, and he believed that Browne could not be "influenced from this quarter. At all events, those who might influence him, think as he does." Dix added, "I am in a quiet way doing all I can to promote a better feeling at the South."[29]

Not being able to make Dix as excited as he was, King sought to influence Attorney General Jeremiah S. Black. On December 14 he addressed a long letter to Black, in part of which he said, "I am amazed that some decided action is not taken by the government to cut itself entirely loose from disunion and disunionists. Look at the Constitution newspaper of today, and indeed, I may say of every issue, since the Presidential election. *Its whole bearing is for disunion,* and say what you will, the government is held and will be held, in a great degree, responsible for it. It was the organ to which the Message [Annual Message to Congress] was confidentially entrusted, and its columns are daily filled with advertisements, which it receives and can receive *only by the favor of the President,* for its circulation would not secure them to it by law." He repeated what he had told the President and others, that "every person of observation must have seen the very day after the election, that its influence was directed toward secession." King said that he was willing that the President listen to the secessionists on any measures to secure the rights of the South within the Union "and consign to infamy the leaders of the Black Republicans at the North." And he asked whether it was "not possible to relieve the Administration from the *infamy* which must attach to it for all time so far as it is made responsible for the course of the 'Constitution' and for keeping men in responsible positions, who are known and avowed disunionists."[30] King believed that one of the reasons why Lewis Cass resigned as Secretary of State was the course Browne was taking in his paper.[31] On December 20 King wrote to the Boston postmaster that the true friends of the Union were beginning more generally "to denounce the disunion *Constitution*."[32]

After Lincoln's election, Buchanan probably winced every time he opened the *Constitution* to the editorial page and read what Browne had to say on secession; for it was the President's passion to save the Union as well as to guarantee the rights of the South. Browne was his close friend and constant supporter, and although he disliked Browne's secession editorials he did not complain since he wanted to keep his own record clear that he did not in any way dictate the policy of the *Constitution*. So it must have been one of the most difficult letters Buchanan ever wrote, when on Christmas Day he informed Browne: "I have defended you as long as I can against numerous complaints. You have a perfect right to be in favor of secession, and for this I have no just reason to complain. The difficulty is that the 'Constitution' is considered my organ, and its articles subject me to the charge of insincerity and double dealing. I am deeply sorry to say that I must in some authentic form declare that the 'Constitution' is not the organ of the administration."[33]

Browne decided that the best way to get the President out of his difficulty was to assert, as he had already done several times, that he alone was responsible for the editorials in the *Constitution*. Taking no personal offense at Buchanan's note, Browne two days later wrote in his *Constitution* that it was being daily charged by the President's enemies that he dictated the editorials or that Browne submited them to the President for his approval, "and that to all intents and purposes," the *Constitution* was "the organ through which he and his Cabinet express their opinions." Browne declared again, "and for the last time," that "the assertion that the President, or anybody on earth, but the editor and proprietor of this paper, is responsible for its opinions, to be a deliberate falsehood." Although he gave Buchanan his "hearty and zealous support" he would always express his own views, however much they might differ from "those of our best friends." He had differed with Buchanan in the past and might do so in the future "without any diminution of the profound respect and regard which we feel for him."

"We speak for ourselves," Browne continued, "and for ourselves alone; and if the black-republican enemies of the country desire to denounce our doctrines, they can do so as bitterly and as often as they please; but they shall not include in their denunciations persons who are in no way responsible for what we think or write."[34]

Among the Washington papers that had been charging the *Constitution* with echoing the President was the *National Intelligencer,* which now said that in the light of the *Constitution's* disclaimer, "Those who have marked its recent course, under the erroneous impression (in which we shared) that it was the 'official organ,' will we are sure receive this announcement with satisfaction." [35]

But there was at least one newspaper that did not choose to be satisfied and exemplified the old adage that there are none so blind as will not see. The *New York Times* continued to say that what Browne wrote was what Buchanan wanted him to write. Wearily Browne again denied the charge and said that "we express our own opinions only; that we differed from the President, and, while we felt the highest respect for him, claimed the right to entertain and express our own sentiments, no matter how widely they might differ from his." Answering the *Times's* assertion that the *Constitution* was kept going by Presidential favors, Browne said, "We have labored under the delusion for the past six months that the 'Executive patronage' which we received did not pay one-tenth of our expenses; but will be more than happy to discover that the *Times* is better informed than we have been," and he said further that he was pleased and flattered to learn from the *Times* that he owed his position as editor of the *Constitution* to the kindness of the President. In answer to the *Times's* accusation that he favored secession, naturally Browne did not deny it but parried the blow by saying that "we have the good fortune to be the advocate of everything that the *Times* condemns, and that we denounce everything that the *Times* approves. We regard this as cause for gratulation." Browne dismissed the argument by saying that the *Times* was a nimble paper, advocating every side of every question: "It can be the organ of Seward one week, of Douglas the next, can oppose both the third, abuse Douglas the fourth, hint at the excellencies of Breckinridge the fifth, and become the flatterer of Lincoln the sixth, without even seeming to be aware that it has deviated in the least from the path of consistent journalism." [36]

Whether Browne was reflecting Buchanan or not, the *Albany* (New York) *Daily Knickerbocker* declared on January 12, 1861, that he had "been writing treason for some weeks," and that he "should meet with his reward." [37] And George Templeton Strong of New York City, an intense Lincoln Republican who wanted to meet the Southerners with fire and brimstone and who was willing to include in this treatment August Belmont, Barlow, and Fernando Wood, wrote in his diary, January 15, that many rumors were going the rounds that there was a secret organization in the city bent on raising a mob to seize the armories, break into banks, and sack the houses "of conspicuous Republicans." Putting aside rumors, he wrote, "I know . . . that the editor of the Washington *Constitution* (a renegade Englishman) is privy to this plot. . . ."[38]

Horatio King considered Browne a traitor and declared that it was folly for him "to issue his pronunciamentoes that he alone" was responsible for what went into the *Constitution, "so long as it is supported and kept alive by Government advertisements which it receives solely through the favor of the administration, for it is not entitled to them by law."*[39] And, he asked, "Can the Government give such a paper patronage and escape the charge of treason?"[40]

Buchanan's Christmas letter to Browne did not seem to have hurt his feelings, but an order issued and communicated to him by Secretary of State Black, January 10, 1861, was designed to hurt his purse. At last King was getting somewhere in his campaign against Browne. Black wrote, "The order heretofore given by the President of the United States designating the 'Constitution' as one of the papers in which the advertisements of the Execuive Department of the Government shall be published, has been revoked and annulled. All such advertisements therefore published in the Constitution after this date will be regarded by the Several Departments as unauthorized."[41] The departments concerned were the Treasury, Navy, Interior, War, and Post Office. On January 12 Black enclosed this order to Browne in a communication to Attorney General Edwin M. Stanton, asking him whether Browne was "entitled to be paid for any advertisement at all published after the date thereof."[42] Of course, Browne got no further pay for these advertisements, but he continued to carry them on to the bitter end. Probably he did so because they were in type and filled up half of the *Constitution,* and to have removed them would have left space which no advertiser in Washington would have bought and to have set type anew every day for news or documents would have been a greater expense. Buchanan gave to the *National Intelligencer* the advertisements taken away from the *Constitution.*[43]

In a plaintive mood, Browne wrote his friend Barlow, "I have been greatly harassed and worried, and am now persecuted by an administration which I sustained as long as it was possible to do so without flagrant dishonor."[44] King was greatly pleased, and now he had praise for Buchanan.[45]

Up until the time when the advertisements were taken away from Browne he supported Buchanan openly (whatever he might have written about him privately), and personally he was on friendly terms with the President, and even thereafter, he never attacked

Buchanan in the *Constitution.* Browne was now busying himself in trying to bring about an understanding between Buchanan and the South Carolina Commissioners. In January he reported to the President, "I have been working hard, and am sure that I have done good. . . . I know you will not regard my thus advising as a liberty, but attribute it to the sincere regard to your faithful friend and servt, Wm. M. Browne.' "[46]

The Brownes attended the New Year's levee at the White House, which Browne described as larger than ever, and he approvingly commented that "not one person failed in respect or the most scrupulous propriety toward the President." [47] But by the middle of January, 1861, most of the Southern element had left Washington or for other reasons good and sufficient failed to attend Presidential receptions. Mrs. Browne was "cut by President Buchanan," and so was Browne personally, because both agreed with Jacob Thompson, when he resigned, that he had been deceived (if not lied to by Buchanan) in the matter of sending troops to reinforce Fort Sumter.[48] However friendly Browne may always have felt toward Buchanan, the President seems never to have noticed Browne thereafter, and in his book, *Mr. Buchanan's Administration on the Eve of the Revolution,* which he wrote soon after leaving Washington, he never mentioned Browne's name, nor did his biographer George Ticknor Curtis, in his *Life of James Buchanan, Fifteenth President of the United States,* published in 1883.

Browne came to detest Joseph Holt, whom Buchanan had appointed ad interim Secretary of War on January 1, 1861, and held him responsible for sneaking the order to reinforce Fort Sumter, thus compromising the President. He much regretted that Buchanan would be held responsible for this order, and he had "but one course left, if he will escape the odium which will attach to all those who took part in the issue of the fatal order, and that is to dismiss Mr. Holt from a place to which he should never have been called."[49]

After this mild criticism of Buchanan, Browne was much further put out by the President's appointment of Holt to the permanent position. "We regret this nomination and confirmation because it will be considered by the South as an avowal by the present administration of a coercion policy," said Browne, "and because it will certainly encourage the black-republicans to anticipate by six weeks their career of lawless aggression."[50]

Browne correctly assessed Buchanan's policy to be the preservation of peace at all hazards until Lincoln should come in, and, therefore, to make no offensive military moves against the South; but he feared that the President was being dominated by his reconstructed cabinet, now free from its Southern members, and being pushed toward war, with Holt at the head. On January 11, 1861, he wrote Cobb, now in Georgia, that "great and lamentable changes have taken place since you left us. I have not had the heart to write to you concerning them, and waited from day to day on the hope that I might be able to inform you that justice, sound policy, and good faith had resumed their sway in the Executive Councils." As for Holt, "I lashed the traitor as he deserved. . . . This city is now a great military camp. . . . My future is more than perilous. Is there any opening in your State? I am utterly destroyed here. Black has deprived me of every shred of patronage I used to have."[51]

"Old Fuss and Feathers" Winfield Scott was as great a menace to the South as was Holt. He was making an armed camp out of Washington, and some extreme Republicans were advocating the expulsion of Buchanan and making Scott military dictator. Browne said that they wanted "as the Executive somebody who will assert the supremacy of the sword over the Constitution, and over the Southern States that have resolved 'to dare, and again to dare, and without end to dare,' in defence of their rights and honor."[52]

On January 14, 1861, Browne wrote Barlow, "This city is fast assuming the aspect of a military camp. Artillery barracks in G Street, a camp near the President's House, a camp on Capitol Hill, and a camp behind the City Hall. General Scott is President, Secretary of War, Congress, & commander in chief, all rolled into one; & doing his best to make 'the way straight' for Lincoln. I could not play the part of such a John the Baptist. . . . Go in for peaceable [*sic*] dissolution. Set your face against coercion, and before a year we shall have a reconstructed Union that will last." The Senators from Mississippi, Alabama, and Florida were leaving immediately, which would "then give the blacks a majority." He wrote, "The feeling here is intensely bitter. God grant that we may have no collision. Once begun nobody can calculate where it will end."[53]

"Ignorant of statesmanship, but with an inordinate vanity," Scott was bringing in troops and guns and fortifying Washington, Browne said. "We should feel no wonder if a battery of artillery were placed within the Senate Chamber to silence the few Southern Senators that remain—or if a company of riflemen were stationed in the other Chamber to shoot down members daring to defend the South—or if sappers and miners were employed to blow into the air every congregation that refused to pray for the restoration of the dead Union to life. . . . Well, perhaps it is desirable that General Scott should push this Mexican method of inaugurating a President to its furtherest limits."[54]

Scott was scattering companies of troops all over Washington and dared "to plant an artillery force at the very gates of the capitol," and Browne declared that "an authority as great and as sacred as that of the President is to be exercised before the muzzles of General Scott's guns." Why were all these troops quartered in the city, he wanted to know. Could not the city put down any riots and govern itself? The real reason, Browne said, was not only to make sure of Lincoln's inauguration, but also to intimidate Virginia and Maryland and to prevent them from going out of the Union.[55] The slumbers of Washingtonians were interrupted by "the roll of artillery carriages, the prancing of horses, the clanking of sabers, & the sounds of trumpets."[56]

Treason to Browne was not the act of leaving the Union and advocating that others do likewise, but it would be in the name of expediency, to abandon his principles and desert his friends. He intended to uphold both fearlessly in his *Constitution*, as long as he remained in Washington, where he had for some time decided that his days in that city were numbered. He wrote Cobb on January 15, 1861, that the Executive advertising had been taken away from him and given to the *National Intelligencer,* which one day praises Lincoln, and the next Buchanan. "In a few days," he said, "I must die out of Newspaper existence. . . . I go South immediately I close up here. My machinery is valueless now; but better times may come, and then I shall rise from my ashes, and get my revenge on Holt & his friends. I think I deserved more consideration at the hands of Mr. Buchanan."[57]

On the eve of his departure, defiant to the last, Browne wrote in his *Constitution* on January 30 that on Lincoln's election he felt that the South should insist on perfect equality in the Union or declare its independence. "When it became evident to all that she could not obtain the former," Browne wrote, "I hoped that she would promptly secure the latter, and I have faithfully used every exertion of which I was capable to aid her in striking the blow which was to free her from a partnership which had been diverted from the pious purposes of its founders, and made an instrument of oppression and insult."[58]

In this same issue of the *Constitution* he announced the imminent suspension of his paper. "Circumstances of recent occurrence," he said, "both of a public and private nature have made it expedient for me to suspend for a short time the publication of the *Constitution,* until I can complete arrangements, now in progress, for its reissue elsewhere under better and more favorable auspices." He hoped that his friends and patrons would pardon this temporary suspension "and continue to me in the more congenial atmosphere that generous support which they gave me in the capital of the Late United States." He would refund subscriptions to those who did not want to continue the paper.[59] He was leaving Washington with no bitterness in his heart and with a welcomed relief from an atmosphere surcharged with military threats against the South. In the last issue of his paper, he carried a news item on the further arrival late at night of a company of about ninety men, with their "artillery, horses, guns, gun-carriages, caissons, etc., . . . [who] immediately proceeded to the quarters allotted them by the Government, corner of Eighteen and G streets."[60] This was not many blocks away from where the *Constitution* was published—E Street beween 11th and 12th.

"I go hence with well-grounded hope of success;" he said, "but not without regrets. I am indebted to friends whom I leave behind for many acts of courtesy and kindness. To all such I bid a respectful and cordial farewell."[61] There were others he was undoubtedly glad to get away from. By his forthright defense of the South he had incurred the displeasure,

and, I may say, the hostility of those whose private interests are affected by secession [for instance, Horatio King], and who are, therefore, for the Union no matter at what sacrifice of principle or consistency; and I have been visited with the most vindictive animosity by certain members of the President's Cabinet, who never held an office of popular trust, and know nothing of the popular heart, because I did not permit their irresponsible and unwarranted conduct, exposing the country to war, and implicating the honor of their chief, to pass unrebuked. Having deceived the President—informing him of orders issued when it was too late for him to recall them, and knowing that those orders were opposed to the President's policy and in violation of his assurances to others [for instance, to Jacob Thompson]—those men, elevated by chance, and to the country's misfortune, to the high offices they now hold, are the fit originators and executors of the petty vengeance which, in the abused name of the President, they have wreaked upon me. I regret that the President did not punish their treachery; but my knowledge of his character will never suffer me to believe otherwise than that his kindness yielded what his judgment condemned, and that if he had been previously consulted as to General Scott's and Mr. Holt's strategical dodges, he would never have permitted the Star of the West to have been chartered and sent to Fort Sumter. It was very unfortunate that the President should have permitted such men to complicate him by acting in the most vital matters without previous consultation with him, since he must know that the world and posterity will hold him responsible for their proceedings."[62]

Commenting further on his going South, he said that he was not being driven away by "official persecution." If his punishment had been greater than the withdrawal of Executive patronage, he would have considered that "as the most signal tribute to my consistency and fidelity to the principles I have always advocated"; but it was the fact that most of his friends had left, now that an administration "not only foreign, but hostile to those with whom I am bound by every tie of sympathy" was about to establish itself in Washington. Therefore, he had "resolved to adopt the counsel of those in whom I place most confidence to publish my paper within the limits of the Southern Confederacy as at present constituted"; but he hoped "most fervently that in a short time Washington, and the state to which she belongs, may be included within those limits."[63]

In the last issue of the *Constitution,* January 31, 1861, appeared this "Parting Word": "The wish cannot be repressed that within every household and at every fireside where the CONSTITUTION has ever been a welcome guest, peace may still sit smiling and prosperity and happiness abide together, until the last great change upon the stage of Life shall be—EXEUNT OMNES."[64]

Most of the "newspaper fraternity" noted the passing of the *Constitution,* with merely a statement of the fact, as for instance the *National Intelligencer* and the *New-York Daily Tribune;*[65] but there was one paper that did not let it go at that, the insignificant *Confederation* of Washington. Its spleen against Browne and his *Constitution* needs to be quoted in full:

The *Constitution* is *dead!* not that glorious instrument which our fathers formed, and under which we have lived and flourished for nearly a century, but that paper which flaunted and polluted the sacred name of Constitution. We have no reproach for the persons of different sections who strongly advocate their different views; but this ingrate, bound to no part of the country, a desperate adventurer, does all he can to stir up hatred and strife and promote disunion. Rebellion and strife are in the blood of some animals, and in some races. They are never at rest unless they are fighting: never content unless they are destroyed or destroying somebody. This miserable sheet for weeks and months has abused and vilified some of the best men and the purest patriots in the land. The faithful and honest discharge of painful public duties has been the occasion and the provocation for assault and defamation.

That eminent statesman and pure patriot, Secretary Holt, has shared largely in its denunciation. It assumed to be the assistant organ of the President, while it denounced all his measures. The President went to the outer verge of the Constitution for the sake of peace, and yet indirectly he was accused of seeking war. It shows an improved atmosphere in

Washington that this traitorous sheet could not longer breath [breathe]. So may all the enemies of our beloved country perish and fall as untimely figs.

The *Constitution* issues its last number tomorrow, and then hopes for a resurrection in some other latitude. We trust there is no spot on the soil of America that will foster his efforts to blacken the reputation of our best and purest statesmen, engender strife among the American people, and destroy our glorious Union.[66]

❧ VII ❧

"Constitution" Browne Becomes
Confederate Browne

WHEN BROWNE abandoned his *Constitution* newspaper and set
out for the South, six states had already left the Union and another,
Texas, was in the throes of going out. Plans were being made for
delegates from these states to meet in Montgomery, Alabama, to
organize a new government. Browne was deep in this "conspiracy"
and was prepared to play his part in it.

He lost no time in leaving Washington; he moved out on the last
day his newspaper appeared, January 31, bound for Macon, Georgia,
and then on to Montgomery. A few days before departing he wrote
Cobb, who had long been away from Washington, busily preparing
for a Southern confederacy, that he would publish an address in his
newspaper, "noticing without too much asperity the persecution of the past," and that he would re-establish his paper "in a better and more congenial atmosphere." He would not call on Cobb
for any pecuniary aid in the venture (although apparently he had
lost everything in Washington) but added, "Your recommendation is
worth more than money to me."[1]

Browne was, of course, well known and highly respected by the
Southern newspaper editors, who were overjoyed at his casting his lot
with the South. In announcing the end of Browne's "able and fearless
journal," the editor of the Athens, Georgia, *Southern Banner* said,
"Since Mr. Browne's connection with the *Constitution*, the South
has had no more vigorous and uncompromising advocate anywhere,
and his manly and indignant protests against the coercive policy of
Scott and Holt, has brought down upon him the black looks, and
bitter words, and mean vindictiveness of a now imbecile and a treacherous Administration." He had battled nobly for the South, and it
was now time to repay him according to his merits "and in such wise
as will redound to his and our advantage." As he was a "polished,

80

vigorous, and profound writer, we hail with pleasure the prospect of his early enlistment in the editorial corps of the Southern Confederacy; and we extend to him, in the name of our people, a cordial welcome to their hospitalities and kind offices."[2]

Browne was soon in Montgomery investigating newspaper possibilities there and elsewhere in the heart of the Lower South—the upper South had not yet seceded. By February 4 the Southern Confederacy was in the process of being established with its capital, for the time being, in Montgomery. The editor of the *Montgomery Weekly Advertiser* was pleased to meet him and welcome him to the city and to pay him this compliment: "Although in imminent danger of Administration displeasure he never flinched or faltered in the prosecution of his work, and some of the severest, and at the same time most dignified castigations, which we have ever read from the pen of any man were administered by him upon Lieutenant General Scott and Secretary Holt for their base treachery and ingratitude to the South." The editor added that Browne would continue his newspaper at some city in the South "as occasion may render his efforts most available."[3]

When Jefferson Davis arrived in Montgomery to be inaugurated president of the Confederate States of America on February 18 and to be welcomed by William L. Yancey in a speech in which appeared this famous expression, "The man and the hour have met,"[4] Davis was accompanied on his trip from Mississippi by Ethelbert Barksdale. Barksdale was a powerful force in Mississippi politics as editor of the Jackson *Mississippian,* which was the official journal of the state; and it was only logical that he and Browne should meet here, if they were not already acquainted, and discuss their journalistic careers and prospects for the future. Within a few days the news was out that Browne had "associated himself with E. Barksdale, Esq., of the Jackson *Mississippian*"; and one editor in complimenting them said that this journal should not "monopolize so much talent." "Either of its editors," he remarked, "is sufficient, intellectually, for at least two first class papers."[5]

The rumor was soon going the rounds that the *Mississippian* would be brought to Montgomery to be the administration organ of President Davis; but Barksdale issued a denial that the paper would transfer its publication from Jackson to Montgomery or that it would act as the administration organ or, furthermore, even that Browne would be one of the editors, for Davis had determined to bring him into his official family and had made him Assistant Secretary of State—"a post for which his high attainments and thorough knowledge of international relations eminently qualify him." Barksdale added that although the *Mississippian* would not be the organ of the Davis administration, it would support the President in his every act.[6] Thus, Browne's Civil War career was not to be in journalism; but to clear his obligations to the subscribers of his *Constitution,* he now transferred his subscription list and good will to the *Montgomery Advertiser* without assuming any of the obligations of the editorship—his time would be taken up completely otherwise.

In completing his cabinet, Davis induced Robert Toombs to accept the position of Secretary of State. He was sworn in on February 21; and five days later the Confederate Congress authorized the appointment of an Assistant Secretary of State,[7] which was immediately conferred on Browne. Both Toombs and Davis were agreed that Browne was a happy choice. Toombs, who was none too interested in the position, expected Browne to do most of the work, for he knew that Browne was well versed in several foreign languages and, as a former Englishman with international experiences, Browne could relieve him of troublesome details and even of making important decisions. In announcing Browne's appointment, the *Weekly Montgomery Confederation* pronounced him "a gentleman of enlarged and comprehensive views."[8]

But all were not happy to see Browne in this position. He was another one of Davis' foreign pets; there were Judah P. Benjamin, born on St. Croix, in the Danish West Indies, who lived out the war, in succession, as Attorney General, Secretary of War, and Secretary of State; Stephen R. Mallory, a native of Trinidad, British West Indies, Secretary of the Navy; and Christopher G. Memminger, born in Wurttemberg, Germany, Secretary of the Treasury. John Beauchamp Jones, who was to become well known as the acrid author of *A Rebel War Clerk's Diary at the Confederate Capital,* had a special dislike for Browne, and on his appointment Jones said that "the Southern gorge rises at it."[9] Some of the women, ambitious for their husbands, resented Browne's appointment, as did one who disapprovingly referred to him as a foreigner, an adventurer in it for the money he could make, and a self-seeker who would turn against his friends.[10]

Full of restless energy in an atmosphere crying for action against the Yankees on the field of battle, Toombs could not be content to sit behind a desk and write letters. He was determined from the beginning to seize the first opportunity to resign and march to glory. But perforce he must be discreet and bide his time, for he could not desert his post at the crucial moment when the Confederacy was seeking to come to some friendly and peaceable understanding with the government in Washington.

It was in furtherance of this move that Browne now made a trip back to Washington to form an estimate of the situation when Lincoln should be inaugurated and take control of the government. Relations between the few-weeks-old Confederacy and the United States had hardly crystallized out sufficiently to make Browne appear as a spy; but when he left, about February 27, Mrs. Chesnut, who saw all and knew all and wrote it down in her diary, was a little apprehensive that he might be taken up as a traitor, and she guessed that if he were, he might "cause a civil war." She warned him not "to make himself a bone of contention." But even in the most serious situations the eternal feminine popped out in her; Mrs. Browne was going along, and Mrs. Chesnut wanted her to bring back some bonnet ribbons.[11] The Brownes attended the inaugural, and Lizzie reported that Buchanan's "farewell was far more imposing than Lincoln's inaugural."[12] It was Browne's feeling that Washington was not reconciled to the Yankee regime. He could not extend his visit to see his friend Barlow in New York, as he wrote him on March 6, for he must return immediately to Montgomery to take charge of the office in the absence of Toombs, who had business in Savannah.[13]

On February 27 President Davis appointed three commissioners to go to Washington and treat with the Federal government for a friendly settlement of all points at issue between the two governments, and Browne delivered to them that day "Instructions of the Department of State to Hons. Martin J. Crawford, John Forsyth, and A. B. Roman, Commissioners of the Confederate States of America to the Government of the United States." These instructions were written in the hand of Browne and were signed by him and have every indication of being basically his work, with, of course, the over-all direction of Davis and incidentally of Toombs. After explaining the historic policy of the United States in recognizing new governments, and giving examples, Browne instructed the Commissioners to say that the Confederate States of America was in every respect an organized and functioning government and should be dealt with and recognized as an independent nation. The Commissioners were instructed further that if they were not received officially they should continue any negotiations possible unofficially.

The Commissioners arrived in Washington soon after Lincoln's inauguration. They were not received by the Lincoln government, but for the next month they went through a tortuous course of negotiations with intermediaries, in which Secretary of State Seward played a back-stair part, either with or without Lincoln's knowledge. On March 14 Browne wrote a long letter to Crawford and Forsyth, which

Roman, who had returned to Montgomery, took back to Washington. This letter dealt largely with the principal forts in the Confederacy still occupied by the United States—Sumter, Pickens, and Taylor. They must be evacuated; but as for Fort Jefferson on Dry Tortugas, some seventy miles west of Key West, negotiations on it could wait. The Commissioners were to negotiate also tariff arrangements.

On March 28 a letter signed by Browne as "Acting Secretary of State" was sent to the Commissioners approving their course of negotiations but warning them against trusting the United States in any promises respecting the status quo at Fort Sumter. The evacuation of all forts on Confederate soil was called for, and the Commissioners were to ask why the United States was assembling its ships and bringing them back from foreign stations.[14]

Undoubtedly Toombs was irked by all this haggling that was going on in Washington. The Confederate Commissioners were given promises unkept and were finally double-crossed, resulting in the Confederate reduction of Fort Sumter on April 12-13 and the Federal preparation for civil war. Both sides began raising their troops and in Northern Virginia on the fields of Manassas or Bull Run, the first big battle took place on July 20-21. Toombs was now unable to endure his desk any longer and resigned on July 24 to enter the army; the next day R. M. T. Hunter, of Virginia, was nominated and confirmed as Secretary of State. Browne remained as Assistant Secretary of State.

Hunter continued until February 17, 1862, when he resigned; but in the meantime Browne had served as "Secretary of State ad interim" or "Acting Secretary of State" on several occasions when Hunter found it necessary to be absent. Had it not been that there were already three "foreigners" in his cabinet, Davis might well have appointed Browne, for he had a high regard for his qualifications. While Davis was making up his mind on Hunter's successor, Browne served as "Secretary of State ad interim" from February 17 to March 18, when Davis advanced Benjamin from the War Department to the Secretaryship of State; but for the next few days before Benjamin was prepared to take control, Browne ran the Department. Browne continued as Assistant Secretary of State until he resigned a month later (April 22).[15]

Browne played a much more important part in the State Department (especially during the Toombs regime) than has generally been known; and, in fact, it was Browne, who, during the various changes in the Secretaryship, gave continuity to that Department. He was not simply a head clerk to take dictation and write letters. He carried on a great deal of business which brought into play his wide knowledge of international law and foreign affairs; in addition, he directed the activities of agencies in Europe and Mexico charged with supplying the Confederacy with military supplies and carrying on propaganda abroad.

In the beginning the matter of the most immediate importance for the State Department was to seek recognition of the Confederacy by foreign governments; and in pursuance of this object President Davis soon appointed a mission to European countries consisting of William L. Yancey, Pierre A. Rost, and A. Dudley Mann. A little later James M. Mason and John Slidell were sent as commissioners to England and France respectively. One of Browne's specific duties was to keep the Confederate agents informed of all happenings that would aid them in presenting their country in the best light to Europeans. Victories on land and sea were to be played up to their fullest extent, and Browne stood ready to aid in this propaganda. After the big victory at Manassas in July, there followed in October the not inconsequential engagement at Leesburg, where the Confederates drove the Federals back across the Potomac. Browne immediately plyed Secretary of War Benjamin for full information that he might dispatch it to the Confederate agents in Europe. And in March, 1862, when the Confederate warship *Virginia* destroyed the Federal fleet at Hampton Roads, Browne wrote Mason, "It becomes my pleasant duty to announce to you . . . that a great naval battle was fought at Hampton Roads. . . . The loss on the Federal side in killed and wounded can not be less than 600."[16]

It was also necessary that Browne keep Yancey, Rost, Mann, and the other agents reinforced with information in their efforts to induce England and France to declare the Federal blockade of Confederate ports illegal. On August 24, 1861, he sent information on the number of ships that had entered and cleared the ports of Charleston, Savannah, Wilmington, and Pensacola and stated that it furnished "conclusive evidence that the blockade of the coast of the Confederate States is nominal, not real."[17]

It was of equal importance that the Confederacy defend its cruiser warfare against Federal shipping and its right to issue letters of marque, which would allow private vessels to take prizes on the high seas. When Russell of the London *Times* was in Montgomery in May, 1861, Browne sought to get any information from him which he might care to give on the most approved form for these letters.[18] There were other points of international law which Browne had to bring to bear on the problems of the State Department such as related to blockade, in particular, in the case of withholding clearance of two British ships, laden with naval stores in Wilmington, which might be seized by Federal ships off the port.[19] Also, Browne had to convince the House of the Confederate Congress that two French vessels in Chesapeake Bay were not there surreptitiously to take on cargoes of cotton and tobacco, the exportation of which at this time was prohibited.[20] The nationals of foreign countries, especially of England, came into the picture when they found themselves in the Confederate army and wanted out. This made frequent dealings with resident foreign consuls necessary. Also, Browne kept the consuls supplied with Confederate proclamations, laws, and other documents.[21] Keeping track of suspicious characters gave Browne concern, and now and then he had problems of this nature to investigate and settle, as for instance in the case of a person by the name of W. M. Cochrane, who said that he was a British subject. He had a passport from the War Department to go to Charleston, but Browne on investigation found that the British consul knew nothing about him; and, thereupon, Browne asked Secretary of War Benjamin to revoke the passport until Cochrane could prove his identity.[22]

In dealing with foreign countries relative to bringing in military supplies, the State Department naturally was much involved. Apart from running the blockade from European countries, the greatest source of war materials was from Mexico. It was, therefore, much to the interest of the Confederacy to establish proper connections with the Mexican government in Mexico City, but more particularly with the practically independent State of Nueva Leon and Coahuila, on the northern border, ruled over by Santiago Vidaurri. John T. Pickett, who was sent to Mexico City, made a fiasco of his mission; but Juan A. Quintero was much more successful in carrying out the mission with which he was entrusted. Quintero was a native Cuban who had lived in Mexico and was now a citizen of Texas. On August 29, 1861, Browne wrote Josiah Gorgas, Chief of the Confederate Ordnance Department, that the State Department could get "unlimited supplies of copper and lead" and also "large quantities of powder" in "new Leon" and wanted to know if Gorgas was interested.[23]

And now there was to begin that fruitful trade across the Rio Grande which was to be of great aid to the Confederacy. In the following September, Browne notified Quintero of his appointment as "confidential agent and special messenger" at $200 a month to the government "in northeastern Mexico." At the same time, Browne gave him minute instructions on what he was to do and how he was to do it, with the admonition to strict secrecy. His first assignment was to get 500 tons of lead, 200,000 pounds of powder, and to look out for saltpeter. He was always to keep an eye open for information on political conditions in Mexico and to see if there was anything to the rumor that the Mexican government was about to let United States troops land on its soil and march to attack the Confederacy.[24] In February, 1862, Quintero informed Browne that a "train of carts" with powder, sulphur, saltpeter, and other war materials was leaving Monterey for San Antonio; and, of course, previously and thereafter similar sights might be seen by onlookers who would not know their significance.[25]

Of course, there were many minor details of the State Department that Browne looked after, and now and then something unusual came up, as when a stranger appeared at Browne's office saying that he had a device for sending long dispatches to Europe quickly. Browne was impressed enough to ask Secretary of War LeRoy P. Walker whether the State Department should investigate.[26] Of course, nothing came of it, as was true of many other "remarkable inventions" which were offered both to the Confederacy and to the Union.

The firing on Fort Sumter and the outbreak of war drove the Upper South out of the Union, and with the accession of these new states to the Confederacy the capital was moved to Richmond. Just as it had been true in Washington, it was so in Montgomery, and would be in Richmond, that the social instincts of women never change: men may run the government, but women run society. The Southern ladies, the arbiters of society in Buchanan's Washington, were the same ladies who moved on to Montgomery and set up their little kingdom there. The First Lady was, of course, Varina Howell Davis, the President's lady; however, more interesting and vivacious were Mary Boykin Chesnut, Kati Thompson, Mary Ann Cobb, and Lizzie Browne; but all the others, both great and small, played their part. However, Mrs. Cobb generally stayed in Athens, Georgia. It would not have been a woman's kingdom without men, and, of course, the men were there. In the midst were the Brownes, Lizzie and William Montague (it is not known what the latter's household name was, but after he became a general, he was always "General" to Lizzie.) On moving to Montgomery, the Brownes took an apartment in the Exchange Hotel,[27] as Lizzie wrote the Chesnut lady, now absent in Charleston, "in preference to embarking on the unknown sea of troubles called Montgomery housekeeping." Seasoning her account with some little sarcasm, Lizzie continued, "At any moment that you have nothing better to do, think of me in that brilliant saloon, with tiny dishes of every sort before me, covered with all imaginable species of parboiled viands, and all called by courtesy eatables. Or you can see me in the luxurious chamber of the second floor with the asthmatic hair cloth sofa and the little painted rocking chair. And yet I am quite content, much preferring the 'Hall' to the misery of keeping house with the servants of other people."[28]

Lizzie Browne and Mary Boykin Chesnut were close and confidant friends. Mary Boykin recorded some of their thoughts and conversations in her hungry diary. She did Lizzie a favor with the Montgomery ladies by informing some of them that Lizzie was "childless now, but that she had lost three children." She added, "Women have such a contempt for a childless wife."[29]

Kati Thompson, spending some time in her home in Oxford, Mississippi, in a letter to Mary Ann Cobb in Athens, put in a word about the feminine atmosphere in Montgomery: "I am glad to think it will take many years to make that city like Washington, as regards married belles. There are enough *righteous* women to save the place for many years at least." Then, about Lizzie, "I hear from Mrs. Browne occasionally—she writes about marching in triumph back to dear old Washington which I can't exactly understand."[30] Lizzie probably had in mind the addition of Maryland and the District of Columbia to the Confederacy, rather than compromising with the old Union.

Undoubtedly it was "dear old Washington" to Lizzie, for it was much on her mind. As has been noted, she made the trip back there with her husband in February and March of 1861 and remarked that she liked Buchanan's farewell much better than Lincoln's inaugural. And reporting what Lizzie said about Lincoln's entrance into Washington, Mary Boykin wrote, "Lincoln came through Baltimore locked up in an Adams Express car. A noble entrance into the government of a free people! He wore a Scotch cap."[31] Mary Todd Lincoln, Abraham's lady, did not escape the comments of Lizzie and Mary Boykin. While on a stroll in Montgomery they aired their "indignation against Mrs. Lincoln and her shabby economy."[32]

Some of the Southern ladies who were left in Washington kept their friends in Montgomery informed on the sadly changed atmosphere there. Lizzie told Mary Boykin that she had recently had a letter from the Senator William M. Gwins, who were still in Washington, and they reported that the place was "like Goldsmith's Deserted Village."[33]

Montgomery's official society could hardly take root before the government moved on to Richmond. But, of course, while still in Montgomery, the First Lady held her receptions at the first White House of the Confederacy, and the Brownes were in the center of them, with Lizzie showing *"great graciousness* of manner to others around."[34] Browne was handy in keeping things and people moving with his easy courtly bearing. When Russell of the London *Times* was visiting in Montgomery in May, 1861, he attended one of the White House receptions and was presented to the First Lady by Browne. [35] After spending a few days in the Confederate capital and being warmly entertained, Russell "had a little farewell levee," attended by Browne, Toombs, Benjamin, Walker, and others. He departed on an Alabama River boat, with no very great regret at leaving the city and its natives, "but of my friends there, I must always retain pleasant memories, and, indeed, I hope some day I shall be able to keep my promise to return and see more of the Confederate ministers and their chief."[36]

Although Browne was high up socially with Southern women, he realized that he had keen competition from the other men, as he remarked one day to Mary Boykin Chesnut, " 'These Southern men have an awfully flattering way with women.' " His explanation was that many were descended from Irishmen, and that " 'some blarney remains yet, even in spite of their grey hairs.' " To this, Mary Boykin replied, " 'Yes, blarney as well as bravery comes in with the Irish.' "[37]

Browne was looked upon as a sort of authority on etiquette, especially when it related to titles of nobility. He liked to tell a funny story, as Mary Boykin repeated it, about the awkwardness of a "raw statesman" who asked Browne how to address Lord Morpeth, one of the party accompanying the Prince of Wales on the trip down the Potomac to Mount Vernon, back in "the good old Buchanan days." He wanted to know whether it should be "My Lord," "The Lord," or "Oh Lord." And as it turned out, "Coming back, the American had been made so easy in his mind by mint juleps that he slapped the noble stranger on the back and called him Moppy."[38]

Casting his lot with the South, Browne hoped, would not alienate his Northern friends. In a matter of deep conscience and profound principle there should be nothing personal. Communications between the two sections soon became so difficult that only by devious ways could letters pass back and forth; as a result, Browne soon lost contact with his friends to the north, with some because they did not choose to continue relationship with "rebels." But loyal and unterrified Barlow held out until communications became too difficult, then he was silent until after the war. However, during the first few months of the Confederacy, the Browne-Barlow entente continued to thrive.

On returning from his quick trip to Washington at the time of the inauguration of Lincoln, Browne found no time to continue to New York to see Barlow, for which he offered his explanation in a letter written in Washington on March 6, the day he left for Montgomery. He reminded Barlow of what he had long been telling him: "Depend on it, My dear Barlow, (you know that my prophecies have been finally fulfilled) that the Con.[federate] States are a success, and reconstruction is the most foolish of dreams. If the North acknowledges the independence of the Con. States, and resolves to live with them in peace, they can be two great and friendly nations, beneficial to themselves and the world."[39]

Browne waited almost two weeks to hear from Barlow without results, and he wrote him again, on March 18: "Is it the excess of your loyalty to the U. S. that has prevented your writing a line to an old friend; or is it forgetfulness? I have been looking anxiously for a letter from either yourself or Butterworth, but hitherto have looked in vain." He could not refrain from again singing the praises of the new Conferedate States of America, of which he was the Assistant Secretary of State (good taste preventing his mentioning it, though he wrote on "Confederate States of America, Department of State" stationery) : "I hope that by this time you are convinced that the C. S. A. are in earnest, and capable of sustaining their government either in peace or war. The most scrupulous or sensative Northern man cannot, I think, be offended at our attitude or language; nor can he doubt that while we are prepared to fight in defense of what we believe to be our rights, we desire peace, and friendly relations of society, trade, and commerce with our late Confederates. I have great hopes that there will be no war."

If as was believed in Montgomery, the United States would evacuate Fort Pickens and Fort Sumter, the obstacles to peace would be removed. The commercial interests in New York could play a great part in preserving peace, which would be as much to their welfare as to that of the Confederacy. Browne said flatly, "The Confederate States are gone. They will not return on any terms. You cannot force them to do so. They will be good neighbors, friends, allies, and customers, if let alone. Is it not plain, therefore, that to attempt to whip them must result disastrously?" Browne gave this assurance: "You may depend on one thing,—that the Government here will keep in the right, and will not foolishly provoke war. If they open fire it will be in defence of the soil of the Con. States, or in vindication of their honor and independence." The government was based on the solid foundation of the people: "I never saw such unanimity as that with which the people sanction the govt. and approve its acts."[40]

Browne in his first letter (of March 6) had warned Barlow to answer by the Adams Express Company and not by the United States Post Office, which would probably seize mail for the Confederacy. Barlow's first letter to reach Browne was written on March 16 and was received on March 22, by some "grapevine" route. In those uncertain times, six days passage from New York to Montgomery was quick service. Browne let State Department business wait and answered immediately.[41] Then on April 12, Federal duplicity led the Confederates to fire on Fort Sumter and seize it, and Lincoln issued his war proclamation; Browne wrote Barlow on April 16 (in answer to a letter no longer extant) to express his horror at Lincoln's proclamation: "I'll swear that Cromwell ought to rise from his grave and sue you for damages, for comparing him to the idiotic savage whom an adverse destiny has placed in a position to rule and ruin you. By a shameless fraud of which a penitentiary thief would be ashamed, he has involved you and us in a war the end of which nobody can see." The Confederacy would seize the gauntlet and declare war; and Browne promised that if the means of communication were not cut off, Barlow would hear from him continually.[42]

It was not Browne's intention to argue with Barlow or take a hostile attitude toward him in this stepped-up correspondence, for they both agreed that Lincoln was a tyrant, completely dominated by the Black Republicans. It was only that Barlow could never agree to the destruction of the American Union. What the contents of the correspondence from April to July, if any, were, is unknown; but on July 9 Barlow wrote a letter which Browne received on July 15, "by the hand of our friend." Browne replied the next day, saying "Though short I was delighted to receive it, as a proof that I have not been entirely obliterated from your friendly recollection." Barlow had done him a favor in paying the premium on his insurance policy, and now Browne was hard put to find a way to send the money across the frontier to repay Barlow. "Those I would trust refuse to take it," he wrote, "and those who would take it would certainly not pay it over." He hoped that Barlow would "see that the policy is kept alive [and] I shall be forever indebted to you. It is for the benefit of my wife."[43] And thus ended, as far as is known, all wartime correspondence between these two inveterate friends.

❧ VIII ❧

Browne in Richmond

LATE IN May the Confederate government prepared to break camp in Montgomery and move to Richmond, if not as an act of defiance to the enemy, at least to be nearer the field of operations and to please the Virginians. Charged with boxing up the State Department for the move, Browne closed its activities on May 25, to be ready to open for business in Richmond on June 5. On May 28 he received a telegram from Richmond to proceed "without delay." He was a little puzzled by the urgency and suggested, probably facetiously, to Howell Cobb, President of the Confederate Congress, "I do not suppose my military experience" was needed.[1] (This comment raises the question as to whether Browne in his European career might not have been in the English army for some little time.)

Additional weight is lent to the possibility of Browne's having had military experience by the fact that on April 19, 1862, President Davis nominated him to be an aide-de-camp on his military staff, with the rank of colonel of cavalry. Browne was confirmed the same day, and three days later he resigned his position in the State Department.[2] Including Browne, there were nine members of the President's Military Family, at one time or another, all holding the rank of colonel of cavalry.[3]

In Richmond, the new capital of the Confederacy, the society in which the Brownes circulated, although government- and city-wide, centered more particularly on the Cobbs, as it had done in the Buchanan days in Washington. The Cobbs were quite a contingent in Richmond, politically, militarily, and socially. Howell Cobb was President of the Provisional Congress of the Confederacy, and his brother Thomas R. R. was a member. Both were appointed colonels in the Provisional Army of the Confederate States in August, 1861, and advanced to brigadier generals the next year. In 1863 Howell was advanced to a major generalship, Thomas R. R. having been killed in December, 1862, at the Battle of Fredericksburg. Howell's three sons, Howell, Jr., John Addison, and Lamar were in the army in Virginia, and Howell's bachelor brother-in-law John B. Lamar was on his military staff. Mary Ann Lamar Cobb, his wife, maintained the home in Athens, Georgia, but was in Richmond now and then, whereas Marion Lumpkin Cobb, Thomas R. R. Cobb's wife, seldom if ever left Athens.

Browne was on closer terms with Howell Cobb than with his ascetic brother Thomas R. R., but he had soon become well acquainted with the latter when the Confederacy had been set up. Browne first met him as far back as the summer of 1859, when he published in the *Constitution* an address which Thomas R. R. made to a public school meeting in Washington.[4]

Although the Brownes had lived in a hotel in Montgomery, they set up housekeeping in Richmond and soon had as house guests the two Cobb brothers, and also for a time Secretary of the Treasury Memminger. On July 25, 1861, Thomas R. R. Cobb wrote his wife that he was "completely housed under the hospitable roof of my friend W. M. Browne" and that "the difference between this and the noisy hotel, with its uncourteous waiters and clerks is very marked."[5]

Something quite different from what prevailed in Montgomery was the military atmosphere that enveloped Richmond. When Congress was not in session, the Cobbs were out in the field at their respective camps training their troops; and now the ladies could visit them and get a little taste of what army life was like. In September, 1861, Mrs. Browne, Mrs. Toombs, Mrs. Memminger, and Mrs. Dudley M. Dubose (the wife of Toombs' adjutant) visited Thomas R. R. Cobb at his camp outside Richmond.[6]

As the winter months of 1861-1862 set in, Mrs. Browne must have noticed that Thomas R. R. Cobb was not properly protected from the cold weather; at any rate, she presented him with a great military coat, which had cost $50.00 in New Orleans.[7] Now and then on his rounds of the military camps, in the capacity of Davis' aide-de-camp, Colonel Browne visited Cobb, as in November, 1862, when on business with General Lee in Northern Virginia he spent the day at Cobb's "Camp Marian" (named for his wife).[8] General Cobb thus had good reason to feel socially obligated to Browne, and when in the fall of 1862 Browne had occasion to be in Athens, Georgia, Cobb wrote his wife "to extend every courtesy and hospitality to him, for I feel that his kindness to me in the past will claim this at your hands. You will find him a perfect gentleman, and though a good deal of a 'courtier' I believe he is sincerely my friend." [9]

When Howell Cobb, his sons, and his brother Thomas R. R. went into military service on the Peninsula below Richmond in the fall of 1861, Browne felt much apprehension for their safety and wrote Howell an affectionate letter, adding: "Mrs. Browne whose prayers are worth far more than mine prays fervently" for them, "and we both look with painful anxiety for news from the Peninsula." [10] Now in the field and moving about, Howell Cobb asked his wife to direct her letters to him care of Browne, who kept in close touch with him and could see that the letters reached him more speedily.

The Richmond ladies found many opportunities to show their social graces and hospitalities in entertaining the celebrities who had come into the city with the Confederate government. As an example, a Mrs. Stanard gave a dinner party of considerable proportions in February, 1862. Present were Prince de Polignac (the Frenchman who cast his lot with the Confederacy, became a major general, and was to be the last survivor of the Confederate generals of that rank), General Robert Toombs and his lady, Colonel William Montague Browne and his Eliza Jane, General Howell Cobb, General Thomas R. R. Cobb, General William C. Rives and his lady, and several others of sufficient rank to merit inclusion in this distinguished company. As reported by Thomas R. R. Cobb to his wife, in Athens, the fare included, "stewed oysters, beef hash, beefsteak, cold ham, big hominy, omelet biscuit, light bread, cornbread, batter cakes and a *profusion of silver.*" [11]

At the festivities around one of Mrs. Jefferson Davis' dinner parties, Prince de Polignac for the moment mistook Mrs. Browne for the President's wife, as the all-seeing eye of Mary Boykin Chesnut observed. [12]

Colonel Browne, as Davis' aide-de-camp, was always a prominent and distinguished-looking figure at the President's receptions. At the New Year levee in 1864, as reported by Mrs. Chesnut, "Colonels Browne and [Joseph C.] Ives, in full rig of swords and sashes, received as gentlemen ushers." [13]

Mrs. Browne was in the inner circle of the Chesnuts, and Mary Boykin liked to record what Lizzie had to say and to write. In 1862 they were on a visit to Mrs. Chesnut's native South Carolina, and while stopping in Columbia, Mrs. Browne, on hearing someone say that the war was lost, remarked, " 'I call him a Yankee spy. Why is he not taken up? In the North, Seward's little bell would tingle, a guard would come, and the Grand Inquisition of America would order that man to be put under arrest in the twinkling of an eye.' " [14] Mrs. Chesnut could not get out of the habit which she had formed in the Buchanan days in Washington, of calling her formally "Mrs. 'Constitution' Browne." [15]

Browne's urbanity and ease of manner in dealing with people led some to consider him as less than genuine, in fact, of being guilty of toadyism. Mrs. Philip Clayton, wife of a minor Georgia official in Cobb's Department of the Treasury in the Buchanan administration and later in Confederate service, had little respect for either of the Brownes, despite the fact that Browne had helped her son to a position in the Confederate State Department. She called both "toadies" and charged that Browne was "deceitful and treacherous." As proof, she said that Browne had called Judah P. Benjamin "little Jerusalem," but that when Benjamin became Secretary of State and, thereby, had authority over Browne, he gave Benjamin a big party.[16]

Even Howell Cobb had his doubtful moments (but soon to be forgotten and never recalled) as to how genuine Browne was and had said in the summer of 1862 that he believed that Browne's English education was "the weak point in his character. Have myself felt annoyed at his course with both Davis & Benjamin & am free to say he has lost much of my regard for [on account of] it." [17]

Browne never wearied in doing whatever favors he could for Cobb, and Cobb found occasion to call on Browne for little services and, sometimes, big ones. At Cobb's disastrous clash with the Yankees at Crampton's Gap, in September, 1862, his brother-in-law John B. Lamar was killed. Cobb wrote Browne asking him to do whatever he could to secure the release from the army of John A. Cobb, who was on his way back to Georgia with Lamar's body and who would need to take charge of certain Cobb plantations in that state. Howell Cobb told Browne that this was the first favor he had ever asked of the Confederate government, and he hoped that Browne could secure appropriate action from Secretary of War George W. Randolph.[18] Browne was successful in fulfilling this request.

Browne was soon able to do a greater service for Cobb, who now wanted to leave the field of operations in Virginia and be transferred to the Georgia-Florida arena. Browne saw Lee and was able to secure the change and, on informing Cobb of it, he said, "You may depend my dear General that no interest of yours that is confided to my care shall ever suffer from lukewarmness or neglect of mine. I remember too gratefully your many kindnesses to me, and am too anxious to prove to you the sincerity of my friendship to let pass an opportunity of doing you a service. Were my powers commensurate with my will, you would have very few unsatisfied desires." [19]

Another disaster struck the Cobb family when General Thomas R. R. Cobb was killed at the Battle of Fredericksburg in December, 1862. Browne had spent three days at Cobb's Culpeper camp, just before the battle, and now the tragedy was particularly distressing. In trying to console Howell Cobb, Browne wrote him, "My friend I can give you no comfort because I can find none myself from any earthly source. It seems so hard that among the few who fell at Fredericksburg, so shining a mark, so valuable a life should have been taken." [20]

Holding the rank of colonel of cavalry, Browne was placed in command of the local defense of Richmond. His military duties were not pressing all the time, and his position as aide-de-camp, as Davis regarded it, included many other activities—in fact, almost anything the President wanted him to do. He became, probably, as close to Davis as anyone in Richmond and was deep in his confidence. Davis' high regard for Browne's manifold abilities led him to make Browne a sort of assistant president; but the President never divested himself of any of his highly-cherished prerogatives, and Browne, of course, never sought to assume them. However, he did send Browne on important missions to iron out troublesome problems.

The ravages of war led the Confederacy to adopt a policy of conscription of soldiers in April, 1862, amended in the following September and again in February, 1864. Although some states had heretofore raised troops by this method, the United States government had never done so; and this movement by the Confederate government aroused great opposition in some regions—and nowhere more than in Georgia, where Governor Joseph E. Brown had already been feuding with Confederate authorities. Governor Brown declared conscription unconstitutional and he opposed as much as he could the work of Confederate conscription agents in the state. Here was a trouble zone that needed expert attention, and President Davis could think of no one but Colonel Browne, who with his diplomatic skill might tame the Georgia Governor. On November 28, 1862, he appointed Browne to be a special emissary to go to Georgia.

As there was some need to build up enthusiasm and material support for the war and to invigorate the conscription campaign, Davis issued a letter to that effect, addressed to the governors of the states of the Confederacy. After mentioning the many victories of Confederate arms and redoubling assurances of ultimate independence, Davis mentioned the unholy attempt of the Lincoln government to enlist slaves against the South and inflict on the civilian population "all the horrors of a servile war." To repel this barbarous campaign, he appealed to the governors to give all aid possible, specifically along these lines: (a) enrolling conscripts and sending them to camp for training; (b) speeding the return of all officers and men absent without leave; and (c) using every effort in providing supplies for the Confederate armies and "to suppress the shameful extortions now practiced upon the people by men who can be reached by no moral influence, and who are worse enemies of the Confederacy than if found in arms among the invading forces." [21]

On the same day of Browne's appointment (November 28), Davis addressed a letter of instructions to him, asking him to present to Governor Brown personally the circular letter and "to represent to him the existing necessity to send forward the recruits to fill the thinned ranks" of the Georgia regiments then in the field and to express to the Governor the hope of his acceptance of the recent decision of the Georgia Supreme Court holding that the conscription laws were constitutional and to "assure him of the pleasure it will afford me to have his co-operation." Davis further instructed Browne to visit the various Georgia camps of enrollment and to make inquiries concerning additional war supplies which the state might provide.[22] The next day Davis addressed a letter to Governor Brown informing him that Colonel Browne would hand him the circular letter to the governors "in the hope that by personal interview time may be gained in effecting the object mentioned in the letter." [23]

Browne left immediately (November 28) for Milledgeville, the Georgia capital, but did not arrive until December 5 "owing to detentions on the road." On that day he had an interview with the Governor which lasted three hours, and he had a second visit the next day. Browne reported that the Governor "indicated a better disposition and a more friendly spirit" than he had shown heretofore. But the discussions were frank and pointed to the issues in dispute. Governor Brown thought that he was not being treated with proper respect by the Confederate conscription agents, and he showed little disposition to co-operate with the Confederacy in enforcing its conscription laws. In discussing conscription Colonel Browne reminded the Governor that he himself had raised troops by the draft. The legislature was in session while Browne was in Milledgeville, which made it possible for him to interview several members of that body. In carrying out his mission Colonel Browne visited Augusta, Macon, Atlanta, Columbus, and other Georgia towns.[24]

Before returning to Richmond, Browne could not refrain from accepting the invitation of Mrs. Howell Cobb to spend a few days in her home in Athens. Always a favorite with the Cobb children, young ones as well as soldiers, Browne spent a day and two nights. The youngsters liked to refer to him as the "good Browne." [25]

On December 22, Browne was back in Richmond, and on that day he made his report personally to President Davis. He was able to bring back valuable information on conditions in Georgia, but as for pacifying Governor Brown, he could not report much progress. As he remarked some weeks later, "I am afraid I can do nothing with Joe B. He is a slippery gentleman too much for me to hold. I trust that the State of Ga. will rid us of him this fall." [26] Browne was referring to the gubernatorial election of 1863; his hopes were dashed, and the Confederacy was forced to endure Joseph E. Brown to the bitter end.

Serving the President as his aide-de-camp, Browne had many routine duties to perform as well as petty assigned tasks. If any citizen of the Confederacy felt the urge to write the President he did so, generally to ask a favor or to make some complaint. Any of these letters falling into the province of the military service Davis generally turned over to Browne for disposition, seldom making any recommendations. A lady in Tennessee wrote Davis, explaining that she had three sons, all of whom had joined the Confederate army; two had been killed, and now she wanted the third one to be discharged that he might come home to take care of her. Davis referred the letter to Browne, who passed it on to the Secretary of War.[27] A father wanted his son to be relieved of further military service; a person wanted to be detailed as superintendent of a sawmill; another wanted to be detailed as overseer of a plantation; and so the story went. Davis turned all these letters over to Browne, who passed them on to the Secretary of War.[28] Sometimes Browne made suggestions, but the final decision lay with the Secretary.

It fell to the Secretary of War to issue passports to persons wishing to go abroad. Such requests were frequently made to Davis or directly to Browne; and in all such instances Browne forwarded the letter to the War Department, often with comments and recommendations. An Irish family by the name of Decie wanted to return to Ireland, and Browne recommended it on the ground that the family had done good service in the Confederacy but was now in ill circumstances—the wife was sick and several children had died. In 1864 D. H. Wilcox of Augusta, Georgia, wanted a passport to go to England; Browne recommended that it be issued.[29]

More in line with military duties, Browne was often detailed by the President to visit the commanders of armies in the field, and now and then he and President Davis would ride out of Richmond on tours of inspection. On one well-known occasion, in July, 1862, when General George B. McClellan's armies were besieging Richmond, Davis and Browne were giving too close an inspection to the Federal lines when General Lee ordered Davis to go back out of danger, saying, according to Mrs. Chesnut, " 'Any exposure of a life like yours is wrong, and this is useless exposure. You must go back.' " Davis complied.[30]

But after all, Browne actually had military duties to perform in the field, for he had been appointed colonel of the "First Battalion Cavalry, Local Defence, Virginia," popularly known as "Browne's Reconnaissance Corps" and as "Browne's Cavalry Battalion." This rank for aides-de-camp had been authorized by the Confederate Congress in an act approved April 2, 1862, and the raising of the troops was in pursuance of an act approved on August 21, 1861. The troops were for local defense or special service and were to be called into action only when needed. Browne's Battalion varied in numbers from 250 to 300 and was made up of those in Richmond whose military enthusiasm led them to join or could be induced to do so. There were four boys in it who were only fifteen years old, there were twenty-one who were sixteen years old, and there were some as old as fifty-seven.[31] Many of them were government workers and there were several executives of private businesses, as for instance the Superintendent of the Southern Express Company in Richmond.[32] One company was composed entirely of employees of the Quarter-master Department.[33]

As these troops were especially valuable for reconnaisance purposes, they needed mounts not only for this service but to qualify as cavalry. As government horses were always in short supply for combat service in the field, these local defense troops were forced to provide their own horses, which were listed in the records as "private horses." They were valued anywhere from $500 to $2,500, depending on the age and condition of the horse as well as the year in which the value was set, reflecting the degree of inflation of the Confederate currency.

In assuming his rank as Colonel of Cavalry, Browne called on the Ordnance Department for aid in getting his saddle repaired. He had a "very good McClellan tree" which he wanted covered with new light-colored leather. He gave minute instructions as to how the whole work was to be done. Also, he wanted an English sword and asked the price—he had learned that some had recently been imported. He also needed a pair of spurs. For driving around in Richmond, he wanted some repairs for his carriage and new curtains provided.[34]

Browne's salary was $210 a month in addition to commutation of fuel and quarters. He was allowed five rooms, which for the month of July, 1863, cost $20 each. For the same time he burned one cord of wood (for cooking, no doubt), which cost $32. In 1864 his five rooms had advanced to $30 each per month, and wood was $40 a cord in January and February; in April, with warmer weather he burned only two cords. As Browne provided his own horse, he received commutation for feed, which amounted to 6 pounds of corn a day and 15 pounds of hay. In making inspection trips and "running errands" for Davis to battlefronts some distance from Richmond, when he would need to go by railway, he received 10 cents a mile.[35]

As has been noted, Browne was only one of nine members of the President's Military Family, which varied with time and included among the others George Washington Curtis Lee (General Lee's son), Joseph R. Davis (the President's brother), James Chesnut (husband of the diarist), and William Preston Johnston. And, of course, all had their missions and military duties to perform. It must not be understood that Browne was in sole charge of local defense in Richmond. General John Henry Winder was provost marshal of Richmond and had broad powers in preserving order in the city and apprehending spies; there were military camps not far from the city, as well as commands stationed nearby, depending on the general military situation in Virginia. All these were vigilant against Federal raiders.

One of the greatest scares in Richmond, apart from McClellan's campaign in 1862, was a movement of Federal troops up the Peninsula under General John Adams Dix in late June and early July of 1863—probably intended to restrain Lee from marching into Pennsylvania. To head off the attack, troops were got together from every quarter, and G. W. Curtis Lee was advanced to a brigadier-generalship on June 25 and placed in charge of the defense of Richmond. Browne now brought his battalion into active service, organizing reconnaissance squads and scouring the neighborhood for horses which were left as being too jaded or too small for active service in the field. He soon had two "Mounted Reconnaissance Corps" in the field and two more were in the process of organization. These were a part of General Custis Lee's much larger force which had been got together in the city, and when the Federal outriders appeared a few clashes took place, resulting in some casualties on both sides. For the next few weeks Browne's troops were busily picketing all roads leading into Richmond, ill-mounted and ill-drilled as they were, "but full of fight," according to Browne.[36]

In the spring of 1864, there took place the ill-fated expedition of Colonel Ulric Dahlgren with about a hundred cavalrymen as part of General Judson Kilpatrick's force threatening Richmond. Kilpatrick's troops were hotly pursued by the Confederates and prevented from attacking Richmond, but Dahlgren's cavalrymen reached the outskirts of the city where they ran into the stiff fire of the local defense troops and were all killed or captured. Dahlgren was among the killed, and on his body were found papers involving him in a plan to free the prisoners in Libby Prison, to assassinate Davis and his cabinet, and to burn Richmond. The dispute never ceased to rage over whether these papers were genuine. It is not known that Browne was involved in this fight, for Davis was more frequently using him on more important missions out of Richmond than in commanding a battalion of home defense troops. The next month he was to leave Richmond permanently, except for a brief trip or two back to report to the President.

⚜ IX ⚜

Commandant of Conscription in Georgia

WAR ENTHUSIASM which swept the Confederacy during the first few months of its existence began to simmer down before a year was out, and the wisest heads decided to adopt a conscription system, which declared that every able-bodied white man from one end of the country to the other was automatically now in the army. Three acts of Congress set up the system: that of April 16, 1862, included those between the ages of eighteen and thirty-five; that of September 27, 1862, increased the age limit to forty-five; and that of February 17, 1864, embraced all from seventeen to fifty, the age limits inclusive in all three acts. Amending legislation to the first two acts provided for occupational exemptions, and an act of May 1, 1863, allowed governors of states to exempt all their officials whom they considered necessary for carrying on governmental operations. The act of February, 1864, abolished occupational exemptions with few exceptions and instituted a system of details whereby the President might fill occupational needs at his discretion.

In the light of the opposition that grew up against the whole system of forcing men to fight and the consequent lowering of morale and support for the Confederate government, conscription seems to have been a mistake. A basic principle of the secession movement which led to the organization of the Confederacy was states' rights, and it is not too much to assume that if the states had been put to the stern test of providing the troops themselves they would have done so. They could hardly have failed more miserably than the Confederate conscription system.

As has been noted, Georgia was the least co-operative of all the states in supporting the conscription laws, and, also, it has been noted that Davis appointed Browne in late 1862 to go to Georgia to inspect the whole performance there and to mollify Governor Brown, who was bitterly opposed to the system. Colonel Browne was much concerned over the working of conscription not only in Georgia but else-

where. He believed, as did others, that great injury was being done
to the execution of the conscription laws "by the indiscreet appeals
for volunteers to escape the disgrace of conscription and thus aid in
making the law odious." He said in a letter to Howell Cobb in 1863,
"The law has almost failed in Ga., owing in a great measure to the
utter imbecility of those appointed to administer it." And he charged
that "bad designing men in Crawfordsville, in Hancock Co., and
elsewhere are doing all they can to bring Joe Brown into open rebellion." As Vice President Stephens' home was in Crawfordsville
the reference here was unmistakably to him, as Cobb would naturally
infer.[1]

Colonel Browne was the logical man to keep an eye on Governor
Brown and Georgia, and no one knew this better than President
Davis. So, in early 1864 (January 25), Davis ordered Browne to
"proceed without unnecessary delay to such points in the State of
Georgia as may be necessary to carry out the instructions which you
have received. Having performed this duty you will return to Richmond and report in person." [2] No copy of Browne's instructions has
been found, but it is not difficult to imagine what they were. He
was to find out the sentiment of the people toward the war and the
Confederacy as well as the hold that Brown had upon them. Also,
he was to see what supplies could be got from Georgia and how well
the people were observing the tax-in-kind, which required them to
turn over one-tenth of their agricultural products, with a few exceptions, to the Confederate agents.

Colonel Browne set out immediately but was slow in getting there,
as he noted in a letter to Davis from Atlanta on February 5, "from
failure of the trains to connect, & running off the track." Browne
reached Georgia at Augusta, going from Richmond by way of Petersburg, Weldon (North Carolina), Raleigh, Charlotte, and Columbia.
Once in Georgia, he criss-crossed the state, visiting Augusta, Macon,
Milledgeville, Atlanta, Dalton, Columbus, Athens, and Albany, as
well as the intervening towns, returning to Richmond by the same
route he used in coming. He traveled 3,062 miles at an allowance of
10 cents a mile.[3] When he had been in Georgia but a short time, he
wrote Davis from Atlanta (February 5) that he found the sentiment
of the people greatly improved over what he had previously sensed,
that the people were coming forward with supplies which they were
offering for sale, and that they were bringing in their tax-in-kind
products. But he found the conscription situation bad. The director
was well meaning but not competent to fill the position, and the
officers and agents under him were of a low caliber and gifted only

in antagonizing the people. He reported that the Georgia State Road (the Western and Atlantic), which was of the first importance in taking supplies from this region to Richmond, was performing better than he expected, but that he intended to see the Superintendent to suggest improvements.[4] This was Browne's preliminary report, but it was most likely in line with what he told Davis when he returned to Richmond.

The dark side of the picture was conscription, which was being brightened none by the cantankerous disposition of Governor Brown. No one was more aware of this fact than Davis, and as the need for troops heightened and conditions in Georgia worsened, the President a few months later decided to put Colonel Browne in charge of conscription there. On April 5 he assigned him "temporarily to the duty of superintending and directing the conscript service in the State of Georgia" and to "proceed without unnecessary delay to such point or points in the State as you may deem necessary for the proper performance of this duty."[5]

Browne was already well known in Georgia, where in Athens he had bought property and established a residence when circumstances permitted him to be there. In welcoming him to the state, the editor of the Athens *Southern Banner* said, "The high position of Col. Browne socially and officially, as well as his well known efficiency in the various positions held by him, is a sufficient guarantee of his ability to discharge the delicate and responsible duties connected with the position to which he has been assigned." He added that the position was "doubtless in consequence of the large share of official and public confidence enjoyed by him."[6] But this was not the universal opinion, for the choleric John Beauchamp Jones, the clerk in the War Department and later of diary fame, was to have his explanation of the appointment. It was to get him out of Richmond, where he had offended someone in Davis' family, "domestic or military"; and then too, "The *people* had long been offended by his presence and arrogance."[7]

The Athens editor was in hopes that Browne would become "our neighbor; as it is understood he intends, so soon as his public duties will permit, to live amongst us."[8] But this was not to be until after the war had ended, for Browne chose Macon as his headquarters, and later he moved them to Augusta. After conferring with the Superintendent of the Bureau of Conscription, who was at this time John S. Preston, Browne set out for Georgia. The most direct route would have been by Lynchburg and Knoxville to Atlanta and on to Macon, but the fall of Knoxville after the Battle of Chickamauga in the autumn of 1863 had cut this railway route. So Browne went, as he had to do in his previous trip to Georgia, by Petersburg, Weldon, Raleigh, Charlotte, Columbia, and Augusta. The Confederate dollar had fallen greatly in value by this time—the trip cost him $339. Inflation had not hit the railway fare very severely, for it was $10.00 from Richmond to Petersburg, the same from Petersburg to Weldon, and likewise from Weldon to Raleigh; but from Raleigh to Charlotte it was $19.00; from Charlotte to Columbia, $15.00; from Columbia to Augusta, $10.00; and from Augusta to Macon it was $12.00. The cost of portage from one railway station to another or to hotels ran from $2.00 to $10.00, but generally $5.00. Meals were uniformly $5.00, whether breakfast, dinner, or supper. Hotel rates were terrific. One night in Charlotte cost $25.00 (not including meals); hotel rates in Columbia and Augusta were even higher, $35.00, which probably included two meals. Colonel Browne left Richmond on April 16 and reached Macon on April 22.[9]

A few days after reaching Macon, he sent in to the Quartermaster Department a requisition for furnishings needed for his office: "You will purchase for the use of my own office a wash stand or table, pitcher, basin, soap & towels. Also a bucket & glass or gourd for drinking water. I also require some blotting paper, steel pens, red tape, and red sealing wax." Three days later he received a letter press, a pitcher, a basin, a tin dipper, a gourd, four towels, two balls of twine, and three sheets of blotting paper. In asking this requisition to be honored he wrote that "these were absolutely necessary for the proper discharge of my duties." Later he asked for, and no doubt received, three tables, an armchair, a writing desk, two water buckets, four corn brooms, a wash stand, a dozen office chairs for conferences, and ten pencil erasers.[10] With all of these furnishings, his office could hardly be called plush.

As in Richmond, Colonel Browne was entitled to quarters and fuel, to five rooms, and whatever amount of wood was needed. For the month of November, when he was now making his headquarters in Augusta, his rooms cost $20.00 apiece, and the four cords of wood he burned came to $400, which even in depreciated Confederate currency seemed high at $100 a cord. In his work of inspecting camps of instruction, Browne traveled extensively over the state, by railway wherever possible and by buggy or horseback otherwise. He fed his horse daily 9 pounds of threshed oats and 14 pounds in the sheaf. The hire for a horse and buggy for three days cost him $100.[11]

Colonel Browne went to Athens whenever possible, for from April to September he was having his house built there, and naturally he wanted to supervise the work as far as he was able. During this time, and later, when his wife Lizzie was not in Augusta, she was living in the home of General Thomas R. R. Cobb's widow; and, of course, she and Colonel Browne were much entertained in the home of General Howell Cobb, who was now in command of troops in Georgia.[12] In June both Colonel Browne and Lizzie were not well (as usual) and the Colonel was especially troubled with cramp colic. Mrs. Howell Cobb asked them to come to Athens from their Augusta headquarters and spend a few days in her home.[13] And the next month Mrs. Cobb was especially anxious to have Colonel Browne up for a birthday party, for the Colonel and her son Howell had the same birthday, July 7. Mrs. Cobb got quite a group together and there was much refreshment of mind and body. Colonel Browne appeared in a white linen suit, which seemed appropriate to him for hot July, but later describing the affair to her husband (who was not there) Mrs. Cobb remarked that the other gentlemen were dressed differently. To add to her mildly upset disposition, she noted that the Colonel before leaving Athens for Augusta did not call on her but merely sent his love verbally. She now made a comment on him, which was certainly only a passing whim, probably never to be felt again. She called him a gossip and added, "To commit anything to Colonel B. is to blow it to the four corners of the globe. He is as leaky and unreliable as a sifter. There is one thing certain, he has played himself out with me and my sons. [How completely Mrs. Cobb misjudged herself and her sons here.] Mrs. Clayton is right [her comment on the Colonel has been previously noted]—he is a [word illegible]—neither more nor less, and his wife is as much a 'reflector' as he is." [14]

When rumors were out the next month (August) that Yankee raiders were approaching Athens, Mrs. Cobb held her ground bravely but felt constrained to write Colonel Browne in Augusta that "Mrs. Browne, Mrs. T R R Cobb and daughters retreated upon the first report of the approach of the Yankees—and are safely housed at Dr. Sims in Lexington, Geo. [a town a few miles to the eastward]." [15]

When Colonel Browne came to Georgia to enforce conscription, he entered an atmosphere badly poisoned against the Confederacy, made so by such outstanding leaders as Governor Brown, General Robert Toombs, and Vice President Alexander H. Stephens. And, of course, this poison was spread by the press, the *Augusta Chronicle & Sentinel* being one of the chief purveyors. Browne found in conversations with many people a rising disapproval of Stephens' course of opposition to Davis and Confederate policy in general. The most bitter enemies of the Confederacy got the state's official advertising; and Browne noted, "This is not encouraging & we need help in this State against the noisy handful of traitors & demagogues who have control of the press." [16]

One of Browne's first problems was to come to some terms with Governor Brown. That was basic to any success in accomplishing his mission. Of course, his ultimate task was to raise troops in Georgia to be sent wherever they were most needed. To do this he needed to reorganize as far as possible the personnel of the Georgia conscription establishment. Also, it was important to bring in deserters and skulkers.

Several points had to be settled with Governor Brown. Most of them hinged around the Governor's orders exempting men as needed in the state's governmental operations, including militia officers, and thus removing them from the operation of the Confederate conscription laws. At first it seemed that the Governor was to assume a gentle and peaceable attitude. Colonel Browne had scarcely got settled in Macon when he received on May 4 a letter from the Governor on a minor matter but written in a friendly spirit. In an emotional plea he asked Browne to exempt from conscription a man and his son from Cherokee County (the Governor's home). There were five or six children in the family, the mother was dead, and now the husband and a son about to become seventeen would be taken away unless Browne exempted them. The Governor closed by saying, "I appeal to you to relieve him and save his little orphans from destitution if not starvation." [17] As conscription regulations provided no exemptions for family problems of this sort, it is not known what action Browne took.

As civil officials whom Governor Brown had declared were needed in governmental service were exempted in pursuance of Confederate law, a clever way of avoiding conscription was to secure election or appointment to such a position. The question soon arose as to whether a person already in the Confederate army could get out by this method. On May 10 Colonel Browne wrote a very clever and strategically worded letter to the Governor, intended "to catch him on the hip" relative to this question, in which the Colonel assumed that the Governor had already settled his policy in favor of the Confederate army, but the Colonel wanted a statement from the Governor to that effect. After stating that in many counties soldiers in the Confederate army were using that device "under the erroneous impression that you will protect them in their claims, I have the honor, very respectfully, to request you to authorize me to inform the officers under my command that you will not countenance claims for exemption from military service on the ground of election to State offices subsequent to enrollment in the C. S. Army." And then the Colonel ingratiatingly added, "It [is] my earnest desire to avoid, by myself and my officers, any real or apparent conflict with the officials of the State, and am therefore very desirous that Your Excellency should make such a declaration as would remove the difficulty to which I have referred and which is of constant occurrence." [18] It should be noted that at this very time General Cobb was in a bitter argument with the Governor over this matter of the exemption of civil and military officers of the state.

A week or two later (May 21) the Governor wrote in good temper a lengthy letter agreeing with Colonel Browne's point but informing him that this was the interpretation of the Governor alone and that some citizens disagreed with it, and that if the courts decided against the Governor he would not interfere with their decision. The Governor also drew the attention of the Colonel to the fact that the Confederate Congress itself had allowed exemption for any Confederate soldier who might be elected to a state legislature, to a judgeship, or to several other positions specified, and he assumed that, of course, the Colonel would respect that law. Governor Brown ended by saying, "Appreciating your personal courtesy and reciprocating your desire to avoid all misunderstandings, I am, with great respect, your obedient servant." [19]

Colonel Browne in assuming his duties as Commandant of Conscription in Georgia ordered his officers and agents to make "a thorough military registration of all white males resident or found within their respective districts who are between the ages of seventeen and fifty years." One of the purposes of this registration was to find out how many men the Governor had exempted by their appointment to civil or military positions. Finding it impossible to secure the desired information by this method, Colonel Browne resorted to the records of the Adjutant and Inspector General of the State, and from those records he obtained this information: There were 5,478 civil officers exempted, which included 1,350 each of justices of the peace and of constables, 660 justices of inferior courts, and lesser numbers of twenty-one other categories of civil officials. There were 2,751 military officers exempted, including 1,098 second lieutenants, 549 each of first lieutenants and of captains, and lesser numbers in fifteen other categories of officers. The Colonel stated that it was his impression "from all the information I can gather that most of the State officers, civil and militia, the latter especially, are composed of able-bodied men between the ages of eighteen and forty-five years." [20]

Assuming that there was some justification in the Governor's civil appointees, many Georgians wanted to know, and so did Colonel Browne, what the military officers had to do to merit their exemption from conscription. The Confederate conscription laws embraced all white males between seventeen and fifty, and, therefore, those left for the Governor's military officers to command were boys under seventeen and old men over fifty. As one Georgian expressed his indignation in a letter to President Davis, "The idea of keeping up such a militia organization is simply absurd," and he looked to him "to stop this outrageous wrong." Davis sent this letter to Colonel Preston, Superintendent of the Bureau of Conscription, who sent it to Colonel Browne, who endorsed it and said that there could be no doubt "of the truth of the statement of the within letter or of the justice of the writer's appreciation of the facts." [21]

On the same day (April 5) that President Davis appointed Colonel Browne to take charge of conscription in Georgia, General Cobb was ordered to Macon to begin organizing the State Reserves. This force was authorized by the third Conscription Act, of February 17, 1864, which directed all white males "between the ages of seventeen and eighteen and forty-five and fifty years" to enroll themselves for service in the field for the duration of the war. They should constitute a reserve and "not be required to perform service out of the State in which they reside."

In setting about collecting and organizing his Reserve Force, Cobb immediately ran into cantankerous Governor Brown over the matter of the Governor's exempting all civil and military officers whom he considered necessary for running the state government. Hoping to make a friendly approach to the Governor, Cobb addressed him on April 21, and after stating the self-evident fact that Georgia was then harder pressed by the enemy than ever before and that there was an urgent necessity to gather together all men able to serve their country, he shrewdly added, "It is only necessary to state the proposition to receive your responsive approval." [22] Cobb then asked the Governor to release as being actually unnecessary for governmental service those thousands of state officials and military officers whom he had exempted. Instead of giving his approval, Brown responded with a highly emotional and intense argument that he was the judge of whom he needed, and that the Confederate government had no constitutional power to override state's rights. He argued further that the state legislature by a recent resolution had exempted these officers and that he as governor could not violate state law. Furthermore, the Confederate conscription officers ought all to be sent to the army, and Cobb should forget about the Governor's own exempted state officers. Governor Brown said that the outcry against his exempted state officers came from "the almost countless swarms of Confederate officers, agents, and detailed men, who, as the favorites of power, have obtained safe and comfortable positions in the rear, while their less-favored comrades, who seldom get furloughs or details, are required to meet the enemy in front. This class of protected men—vastly more numerous than all the protected State officers—all in the pay of the Government, who can be found in every city, town, backwoods village, railroad car, and hotel in the State, or almost anywhere else but in front of the Army," should be sent to the front.[23] The Governor said that he was not moved by all of General Cobb's arguments; and after a month of intemperate letters that passed between them, which degenerated into personalities, Cobb endorsed Brown's letter of May 31: "This communication and the author are alike unworthy of further notice." [24]

General Cobb in his tussle with Governor Brown over the conscription officers was arguing the case for Colonel Browne, whose business it was to carry out conscription. Browne and Cobb worked closely together in Georgia, and the General was duly appreciative of the Colonel's efforts, remarking in early June that he gave "not only cordial but efficient aid" in raising the Reserve Troops.[25] Both argued much with the Governor over the detailed men whom he sent into industries and agricultural work; and the Governor was equally excited over the many men who were detailed by the Colonel to engage in his conscription work. Governor Brown insisted in August that Colonel Browne had not sent a single man into the Reserves to repel the Yankees who under Sherman were deep in the invasion of Georgia.[26] The Governor wanted a certain category of the Colonel's agents sent to the front, to which Browne replied, "The members of the advisory boards in the several counties are indispensably necessary to the execution of the law. They are enrolled men in the Confederate Army. They are in actual service, and as such cannot be required to serve in the State Militia." The Governor's Adjutant-General Henry C. Wayne informed Colonel Browne that the Governor had finally agreed to respect the detailed men in Brown's conscription service if he would certify them to the Governor; but Wayne, echoing the Governor, insisted that Colonel Browne would not raise as many men for the service as those being kept out for that work.[27]

In fact, General Cobb wanted some supporting troops whom Colonel Browne had in his conscription service. These were the companies which had been designated one each for the ten Congressional districts. They were mostly cavalry and as Cobb said, "men liable to serve in the reserve," and they were "doing little or nothing, as their one business . . . [was] to arrest deserters and skulkers, but could be made very efficient as a part of the reserve." Cobb said that he could detail from his reserves men who could perform the work well enough.[28] Though the records are silent, undoubtedly Browne turned over to Cobb these troops, for the two worked in perfect harmony.

Secretary of War James A. Seddon wrote Browne early in July that in the matter of details, and in all other disputes with the Georgia Governor, he should proceed strictly according to Confederate law and his instructions and ignore the Governor, and that when the controversy should come to an impasse, to appeal over the head of the Governor to the Georgia people. Secretary Seddon said that it was his "conviction that the spirit and temper of the Governor, especially in the late correspondence with General Cobb, preclude all hope in a change in his policy and render further attempts at conciliation, harmony, and co-operation useless." He added, "I am weary of vain attempts to obtain his good will or assistance in the work of conscription, and am, moreover, inclined to believe that a course of firmness and decided action in dealing with him will be both wiser and more effective." [29] Governor Brown had been feuding not only with Colonel Browne and General Cobb, but also with Secretary Seddon and President Davis.

Near the end of the month (July 29) President Davis had increasingly felt the absence of his right-hand man Browne, especially since Custis Lee was in the field and other members of his Military Family were not at hand. He wrote Browne, "Cannot General Cobb relieve you from further duty in Georgia?" He noted "your absence is felt even more than usual." [30] Browne referred the request to Cobb, who replied, "His presence is most important now in view of efforts of Governor to force a conflict with Administration. Colonel Browne has conducted controversy with great prudence, and baffled every attempt to entrap him. Unless you need his services urgently I respectfully request he be continued in Georgia."[31] A month later Davis was still wanting Browne back in Richmond, and Browne answered that he thought to relieve him from the controversy with the state authorities "would much damage public service," but ever faithful to the Chief, he telegraphed him, "Order and I obey. If you leave me here temporarily I will hasten the matter." [32] Davis left him in Georgia.

Governor Brown was not the only one to oppose conscription; General Braxton Bragg was adept at disparaging the operations of the Conscription Bureau. In fact, before he had been relieved of service in the field and sent to Richmond as military adviser to President Davis, he had set up his own service under Gideon J. Pillow for service in his Department of the West, who held on until January, 1864. He sent a note to Davis the following September 7 decrying the service in Georgia as indicated in the reports to the War Department. "Though quite defective and especially wanting in details by which errors could be corrected, they develop a startling state of our affairs in our conscript service." He said that results in Alabama and Mississippi were no better. He then offered this solution: "Stern, rigid administration can correct the evil; nothing else will. A complete renovation of the Bureau and its ramifications will be indispensable." [33]

This attack on the Bureau produced an immediate reply from Superintendent Preston. He immediately vindicated Colonel Browne "from the aspersions of General Bragg." "The violent denunciation of the service in charge of Colonel Browne is avowed to be made on defective reports, wanting in those attributes which are necessary for the correction of errors." These were likely not reports from Browne's agents but "perhaps the reports of ignorant and prejudiced persons sent rather as detectives than as military inspectors." After showing how Bragg's conscription service under Pillow had employed over 1,000 officers and 6,000 men, he said that it had "not sent one man to the Army of Northern Virginia," about which lack of service to that army Bragg was now complaining. Now, following out Bragg's remedy, Preston asked for "instant relief as superintendent" and he furthermore resigned the major-generalship, which Davis had conferred upon him in the preceding June.[34] Davis prevailed upon Preston to withdraw his resignation and continue as superintendent.

The third Conscription Act, of February 17, 1864, with supplementary orders and circulars, made important changes in the administration of the conscription service and divided authority with the military commanders. Preston said that in pursuance thereof "this Bureau set to work to collect, conscribe, and organize for military service the scattered and unwilling remnants of a war wasted population." [35] So, when Browne took over the conscription service in Georgia in the following April, he had a dismal outlook in addition to having to deal with the hostile Governor, Joseph E. Brown.

The Colonel inherited an organization in Georgia which could hardly have been worse, as he judged it. And although he was empowered to relieve such officers as he deemed "incompetent or unnecessary to the service," [36] such action was so entwined in red tape that he made no effort to do so or to attempt a more extensive housecleaning. In explaining to Superintendent Preston why some reports that were being sent to him were so incomplete and inaccurate, Colonel Browne said "there are not twenty who profess one qualification for the office." But to displace them and put others in "would be simply to put incompetent men who know nothing whatever in the place of incompetent men who have learned something small tho' it be." The "light duty men," the sick and wounded who had been relieved from active service and who were made enrolling officers and sub-enrolling officers, belonged "to the lower and poorer order of society," and they were "ignorant and stupid" even when they were "not lazy and inattentive to their duties." The best of these "light duty men" when let out of active military service always chose positions in the quartermaster, commissary, or tax collection service, and Browne received the refuse, "men who can even by courtesy be said to read & write." So long as the system "of appointing disabled stupid and illiterate men to perform duty requiring activity, intelligence, and education persists, the result will be failure."

And what was more, Browne said, "I have alluded only to the incompetency of enrolling officers. I have not mentioned the frauds and corruptions which mark their track everywhere carefully covered and yet observable and keenly felt." He ended this commentary on his conscription force by observing, "It is vain to pass laws unless the proper agents be allowed to execute them." [37] According to the report Colonel Browne sent in for August, he had on his rolls 1,043 men. It must be kept in mind that Browne in these comments was writing about his "light duty men" and was not including all of his force, for in his August report he listed one colonel, seventeen majors, thirty-two captains, twenty first lieutenants, and thirty-six second lieutenants —and about all of these he could hardly have made his strictures.[38]

Colonel Browne had some pertinent explanations favorable to his men. Reporting in August, he said that it had been five or six months since they had received "a dollar of their pay." They had been receiving credit at the stores, for they were generally remote from government commissaries, but now merchants were unable to extend credit to them further. Many of them were compelled by the duties of their offices to serve far away from their homes and in counties where there were no railroads. In many counties no horses or mules for hire could be found at any price, and $30 or $40 a day was the "common price for a horse and conveyance of any sort." Browne said that constant inspection was necessary for the service, "and I have hitherto, by myself and by inspecting officer, maintained a close scrutiny of the acts of subordinates"; but when an allowance of $10 a day "and transportation in kind" are not provided, "this inspection must be abandoned in the counties not served by railroads." [39]

Despite all his trials and tribulations, Browne did make some progress in his search for additional soldiers, "the scattered and unwilling remnants of a war wasted population," although he could never satisfy the needs of the commanders in the field who begged for more troops to bolster their forces. Colonel Browne had scarcely got settled in his conscription work before Major-General Lafayette McLaws, at Savannah, was calling on him for six companies, even if he had to supply them from forces he was using to round up conscripts and deserters. [40]

As Sherman cut deeper and deeper into the state in his invasion down through the mountains of north Georgia, Browne used every device to raise troops. On October 17 he issued his ringing "Circular No. 18," in which he called on all enrolling officers to redouble their efforts to bring in the many men between seventeen and fifty who had never been in the service and the many who were deserters. "Let constant efforts be directed to the arrest of these men," he urged. "Let every hole and corner; let every swamp and forrest [*sic*] in your respective counties in which these wretched men now find a precarious shelter, be reached and penetrated by yourselves and assistants, until every deserter has been arrested, and your vigilance and energy have proved that escape from capture is no longer possible. . . . The battle scarred veterans, who, for four years have stemmed the tide of invasion and held at bay the savage and powerful foe which still pollutes our soil, must be strengthened and animated by the presence of fresh men by their side." [41]

A few days later (October 20), General Cobb, whose forces stood directly to gain from any men Colonel Browne might raise, issued a circular calling on the enrolling officers to speed their work; he sought to raise morale by saying: "A few weeks of faithful service by every man in Georgia able and liable to do it, would drive the last enemy from our soil and rid the State forever of their hateful presence. Georgians! the destiny of your State is in your hands. Now is the time to strike the blow; and if the enemy is not driven from your soil, it will be your fault, not theirs." [42] Browne wrote Cobb the next day, "Every man able to take a musket *shall* go to the field." [43]

On September 2 Sherman captured Atlanta; on November 15 he put the torch to the city; and the next day he set out toward the southeast to a destination the Confederates could only guess at. About this time in a "Circular to Inspectors of Conscription," undated, Browne called for all who could bear arms to come forward. These

Inspectors of Conscription had been appointed by General Cobb on Browne's recommendation, in pursuance of military regulations which required them to see that the enrolling officers do their duty, not be absent and wasteful of public money and property, and not engage in fraud, favoritism, and bribery. Browne said in this circular, "Were the whole arms-bearing population in the ranks where they belong, and whither every consideration of duty and every manly feeling loudly call them, the soil of our country would not be defiled by the tread of a single Yankee soldier in arms, and peace would be a certainty." If the enrolling officers would bestir themselves sufficiently, "thousands of young and healthy men who have hitherto held aloof from the path of patriotism and tried to satisfy their consciences by the delusion that by a detail on a Rail Road, in a mill, on a farm, or in a counting house they are serving their country, will be added to our armies. And thousands who have deserted, or who have expired or forged furloughs and certificates of detail, who are now scattered over the State, would be arrested and sent back to the army."[44] One of the Georgia newspaper editors declared that this circular's "clear and vigorous statements, its earnest appeals, its true-hearted and patriotic sentiments" were inspired by a "fervent and elevated spirit."[45]

A few days previously (November 10) Colonel Browne wrote President Davis how he was sending forward able-bodied men who had been detailed for work that was far less important than carrying a musket. He said that he had tried the experiment on the Express Company in revoking their detailed "indispensables" and that within the past thirty days he had "sent forward *one half* of their ablebodied men and purpose taking another quarter" and they did their business just as before, "perhaps with more trouble, but they do it." If a quartermaster or commissary "threatens that he will be unable to clothe or feed the army if his able-bodied clerks, watchmen, and messengers, be sent to the front, let him be told that his want of capacity to encounter difficulties render him unfit for his position, that he will be dropped, and sent to the field with a musket, and I venture to say the army will get half the 'indispensables' and the clothing and subsistence dept. not suffer in the least." Browne said that he was now "getting large numbers of men" and that he had "detected scandalous corruption and fraud, but hope to clean the stable yet. The work is neither easy nor pleasant, but it is useful, has been intrusted to me by you, and it shall be done faithfully to the best of my ability."[46]

Naturally, as Sherman's forces burned their way deeper into Georgia, great excitement prevailed. Davis, in Richmond, ordered Colonel Browne to get in touch with the commanders of troops in the southeastern part of the state and urge them to make "every effort" to impede the Yankees "by destroying bridges, felling trees, planting sub-terra shells and otherwise, to obstruct the advance of the enemy."[47] Browne did not countenance rumors that Sherman was marching on Augusta, but he informed Davis that he could put in the trenches there about "2,000 locals and convalescents."[48] He wrote the President that he would keep him informed of Sherman's movements as far as he could learn them.[49] On November 23 Colonel Browne wrote Davis of Sherman's progress through central Georgia and of a threat to Augusta by Judson Kilpatrick's cavalry. He added that General Bragg had ordered him to take command of the local brigade.[50]

It was soon evident that Sherman was headed for Savannah, and by this time all available troops in Georgia were ordered to join General William J. Hardee and move to the support of that city. Included was Browne's brigade, which he hastily got together, made up of a motley group of mechanics, clerks, and convalescents, or, as he later described them, "Hastily organized, gathered up in a hurry, without officers, the lame, the halt and the blind."[51] Some were operatives brought down from Athens, where they had been at work in the Athens Armory and the Princeton Factory nearby. In all there were about 700. They reached Savannah on November 30 and were placed on General A. R. Wright's sector of the defense line on the left and were directly under the command of General Hugh W. Mercer.[52] On December 9 Browne sent President Davis a telegram informing him that General Hardee was confident that he could hold Savannah if he could secure about 3,000 more men.[53]

But there was hardly a chance for Sherman to be denied his prize, especially after he had captured Fort McAllister, at the mouth of the Ogeechee River. Nevertheless, with an army six times the size of the Confederates (60,000 to 10,000) Sherman settled down for a siege, which on the night of December 20 caused Hardee to evacuate his whole army on a pontoon bridge across the Savannah River and retreat into South Carolina. This was one of the most clever and strategic escapes of the whole Civil War, a feat which General Hardee looked back upon with greater satisfaction than on any other part of his military career.[54]

It was only through the lack of military genius in this instance on the part of Sherman that saved Browne and his brigade, as well as Hardee's whole army, from being captured. Colonel Charles C.

Jones, Jr., the historian of the Savannah siege, who was chief of artillery there, made this comment ten years later:

Had he [Sherman] indicated that activity and energy demanded by the situation, the probabilities are that he could have captured the entire Confederate army. That he did not do so, reflects severely upon him as a soldier and a commander. The evacuation of Savannah and the subsequent seizure of many thousand bales of cotton afforded the Federal general an opportunity for a festive interchange of dispatches with the President of the United States, in which his famous "Christmas present" figures largely; but he pillaged a nest from which the eagle had flown, and all the balderdash which has been written and spoken about his vaunted "march to the sea" can never, in the clear light of history, cover up or excuse the lack of dash and the want of ordinary military skill and precaution betrayed by General Sherman, with the formidable force at his command, in permitting the Confederate garrison to retire unmolested by a route so precarious in its character, and by a flank movement which could have been easily frustrated by a simple division.[55]

Browne was proud of the performance of his brigade in their defense of Savannah as well as of their bravery on the retreat. In a letter of January, 1865, addressed to "My dear Johnston," who probably was Richard Malcolm Johnston, an aide of Governor Brown's and active in organizing the state militia, General Browne rather boastfully described his Savannah expedition:

I had to organize as I went along, and you would be surprised and gratified if you had seen how rapidly I got an efficient command. They fought well, worked well (built all the defences along a front of three miles) marched thirty miles on the retreat with only three halts and only ten stragglers who came up in three hours after we reached Hardeeville and I had not one man reported for punishment. [Browne overestimated the distance from Savannah to Hardeeville, unless he marched his troops in a very circuitous route.] We had a very tight place for twelve days and nights. Under fire of sharpshooters and shells all the time. The enemy being only about two hundred yards distant along the whole line. If I could have dared to weaken my attenuated line, I would have tried to drive the rascals off [typical English talk]; but all I could do was to hold my own and I did it.[56]

On the retreat up the South Carolina coast, when only a few miles out of Charleston at Adams Run, on January 3, 1865, Browne could no longer refrain from addressing President Davis. "My dear Mr. President," he wrote, "Aware of the kind interest you take in all that relates to me I take the liberty of sending you the enclosed copy of my report of the operations of my brigade near Savannah. [Not found.] I trust you will not think my doing so a display of egotism but believe it is due to my anxious desire to prove to you that I did my best and am to some extent worthy of the favor you have shown me and of which I am so justly proud." [57]

It was now Brigadier-General William Montague Browne (no longer Colonel) who was writing, and the favor he referred to was his nomination by the President to this higher rank. Davis made the nomination on December 13, while Browne was in the line of battle before Savannah. The rank was temporary and was to take effect as of November 11, more than a month earlier. [58]

General Browne with his brigade was back in Augusta before the end of January. Still commanding his brigade, which was part of a considerable concentration of troops in and about Augusta awaiting Sherman if he should come that way, General Browne in early February was ordered by Major-General Daniel H. Hill to leave part of his men to burn Rae's Bridge and bring the rest to Spirit Creek, outside of Augusta. [59]

When Browne had led his brigade to the defense of Savannah, he left Major John F. Andrews as acting Commandant of Conscription, [60] but under the supervision of Major-General Cobb. On his return Browne resumed his old position as Commandant. In active command of troops and also in charge of conscription, Browne was sorely beset, especially when Cobb was urging him to get more energetic action out of his enrolling officers. Answering a communication from Cobb on January 28, 1865, Browne reminded him of his protestations to the Bureau of Conscription, in Richmond, of "the incompetency of the great majority of the enrolling officers and of their failure to discharge their duty." And he reminded Cobb of the great difficulty of executing the conscription laws in Georgia and of his awareness that the "Executive of this State and his officials and partisans, aided by a few prominent and influential public men in the State, have persistently labored to oppose the execution of these laws and to create public opinion not only hostile to their execution but commendatory of their evasion." By way of further personal defense, he explained, "I think, general, you will do me the justice to acknowledge that so far as my personal exertions could secure the faithful execution of the law they have not been spared. I have exposed the evils while I was powerless of myself to remedy them." One reason why this was so was the absence of a military court in the state to try those whom Browne had had arrested. [61]

To add to the turmoil was the "terrible condition" of affairs in

Augusta and elsewhere; "Toombs et id omne genus reviling the
Prest. hourly on every street corner." It was General Browne's
opinion that the people of Augusta were "not only ready but willing
to embrace the Yankees."⁶²

Browne had another worry. He had been nominated to a brigadier-
generalship, as previously noted, on December 13, together with a
great many others who were nominated to ranks from lieutenant-
general down to first lieutenant. Confirming during the next month
practically all of these nominations, the Senate was slow in reaching
Browne.

Browne probably never received any other honor that he prized
as highly as his promotion to a brigadier-generalship. He could not
understand why the Senate was so slow in taking up his confirmation, and he did not hesitate to call on some of his friends for help.
In his letter to "My dear Johnston," he asked him to write "me fully
and *confidentially of course* whence comes the opposition. Let me
know particularly where the *Ga.* Senators stand. I confess, my friend,
I am anxious. To be defeated would be such a triumph to the many
enemies I have made by doing my duty, that I should be sorely morti-
fied. I know that you will do all you can." He continued, "Write me
fully and you may rely your letter will be strictly private. I have not
written on the subject to anyone but you. I *know* your friendship
and good heart and rely firmly on both being used to influence the
proper parties. I cannot see why I should be opposed. I have tried
hard as you know to do my whole duty. I have not been unsuccessful
either. I must however bear my fate even though it be adverse. To
be left hanging when Congress adjourns is hardly less dreadful than
rejection. Save me from both."⁶³

It may be that War Clerk Jones partly answered Browne's question on the origin of the opposition to him, as prejudiced and mistaken as the Clerk was when he called Browne "an Englishman and
a Northern reporter," neither of which he had been for some years.
Jones passed this further comment on Browne's nomination and on
his military ability: "This does not help the cause. Mr. B. knows no
more about war than a cat; while many a scarred colonel, native-
born, and participants in a hundred fights, sue in vain for promotion."⁶⁴

Finally on February 18, 1865, Senator Louis T. Wigfall of Texas
reported Browne's nomination out from the Military Affairs Committee, without a recommendation recorded in the minutes. After
debating the question, the Senate by the surprising vote of 18 to 2
rejected the nomination. Senator William A. Graham of North

Carolina, for some reason, was interested in having the yeas and nays recorded. One-fifth, the required number of the Senators present being found agreeable, the vote was recorded by name. The only two Senators who voted for confirmation were Gustavus A. Henry of Tennessee and Robert M. T. Hunter of Virginia.[65] One of the Georgia Senators, Benjamin H. Hill, was absent, and the other, Herschel V. Johnson, voted against Browne.

Any hostility to Browne personally doubtless played a lesser part in his rejection than other considerations. It was a slap at President Davis whom many Senators heartily disliked and who had made Browne one of his favorites, and also with some little pique at Davis for standing by this former Englishman whose native country was now at a low ebb in Confederate friendship. But there might have been a much higher ground for the rejection. Browne had been appointed under an act of Congress, passed May 31, 1864, which specifically provided that all appointees under this act should "hold their said rank and their said command, for such time as the temporary exigency may require, at the expiration of which time they shall resume their previous permanant rank and command."[66]

By the time the Senate took up Browne's nomination, the exigency which put him in command of troops for the defense of Savannah clearly had passed, and by the terms of the law on which his appointment had been based he would have to revert to a colonelcy; but presumably he would have had the right still to be addressed as "General" had his nomination been confirmed. Did his nomination without confirmation give him that right? Mrs. Browne thought so and always called him "General," and so did almost everybody else, except his close friend of pre-war days, Barlow, who after the war was to resume that friendship. He would always say "My dear Browne."

But the highest and most powerful authority in all the land judged him to have held the rank of general, for the only two of the fourteen exceptions to general pardon listed in President Andrew Johnson's Amnesty Proclamation of May 29, 1865, which were made to apply to Browne, were the first and the third, and the third only, if he had held a rank in the Confederate Army above colonel. The first applied because he had held a civil office in the Confederacy, Assistant Secretary of State. Unquestionably apart from the trouble it caused Browne in securing amnesty, the title of "General" pleased him, though there is no evidence that he ever argued the point after the Confederate Senate turned him down, and no instance has been found where he ever signed himself as "General" after the Senate's action.

❧ X ❧

Athenian Browne

BEFORE THE end of March, 1865, Browne was back in Athens, which he considered his home and where, off and on, he lived for the rest of his life. He would now have plenty of time to reflect on the reasons why the great Southern dream of national independence failed, why self-determination was denied to the South though all enlightened nations, including the United States, advocated it for other parts of the world, even for Browne's native Ireland. But as Kati Thompson said, the Confederacy was "a bold struggle and grand failure."

Browne had done his part; he had sacrificed everything but honor and principle. He had given up wealth, position, security, and friends in Washington and the North; and what money he had when the Confederacy was organized in Montgomery he had invested in Confederate bonds. As he later said, he had invested his "little all in Confederate bonds, of the 15 Mil. loan, paying for them at par *in gold*."[1] How much he had he did not mention; but it has been variously stated that he had $8,000 in gold and that he had $20,000 without specifying how much was in gold.[2] On January 1, 1865, he received $1,200.28 interest on Confederate Treasury Notes, in money whose value had dwindled to almost nothing.[3]

Browne did not sit down and weep at a Confederate "wailing wall" for the "Lost Cause," and he did not publically enter into any vendettas as did some of the ex-Confederate generals. But all during the war he noted weaknesses and did not fail to point them out privately.

The sound and fury that brought on and accompanied the secession movement never welded itself into a unity nor sublimated itself into support of the central government—all for one, one for all. The name Confederacy never held the charm for many, though in later times it was to call forth nostalgic sentiments which would have prevailed mightily if they had come earlier. Browne saw all this. Before the Confederacy was scarcely more than six months old, he observed that patriotism was "not a common plant." "There are a great many fungus imitations of it;" he observed, "but of the real article there is scarcely enough to keep alive for one day the 'sacred fire of liberty.' " He then alluded to the besetting sin of the army officers, their lack of *esprit de corps,* their bickerings with one another and with President Davis, their struggles to get ahead in army promotions. With the dissentions following the Confederate victory at First Manassas in mind, Browne wrote, "From all I can see and hear there is most abundant discord and dissatisfaction among the generals in the army of the Potomac." It was being rumored that Beauregard had resigned, and Congressman Wigfall "says that a man like B-g-d [who] has 'steamboats, studhorses and children named after him is a hard man to beat before the people.' " And Browne observed also that Toombs was fanning the flames against Davis, all to make a big man out of Alex. Stephens.[4]

As a further example of these army dissentions, which, of course, Browne could not cite, was some observations which his good friend Howell Cobb wrote to his wife in March, 1862, in which he said that Major General Braxton Bragg was "a contemptible puppy and I hope I shall not be called upon to serve under him." He said further that he would "feel very strongly inclined to resign as I should have no respect for him and no confidence in him."[5]

As the war wore on, morale began to sink to the point where some people were advocating making peace and getting back into the Union; Browne called these croakers "timid fools, and disloyal Yankee reconstructionists tories."[6]

But what Browne could not understand was the incompetency and timidity of the Confederate Congress, and especially so in its interminable delay in passing a general tax measure to ward off galloping inflation and financial chaos. The Confederacy had been in existence for more than two years, and yet Congress was shying away from taxing the people, fearful that it would make the Confederate government unpopular. Finally in early 1863 Congress was debating a tax bill, and Browne hoped that they would speedily pass it. "If something be not done," he said, "we shall soon have to pay $27,000 for a barrel of flour." Congress, he said, was "discussing the organization of a Supreme Court and neglecting everything requiring attention."[7] In March, 1863, he wrote Cobb, now in Georgia, "The tax bill hangs fire. 'The assembled wisdom' is employed discussing the constitutionality of taxation, and other interesting questions, and Treasury notes are now worth 15 cents on the dollar as compared with gold."[8] He observed to Cobb, "You and I agree as to your estimate of Congress. That they will stay and will howl and will misrepresent the people. They are afraid to pass a good tax bill and nothing else can save us from ruin."⁹ Finally on April 24, 1863, Congress passed the tax bill—too much, too late!

When Browne went to Washington in 1859, he probably ceased to consider himself a citizen of New York; if still then, he soon would not be, for he fell in with the Southerners there and especially with Cobb, and since citizenship in Washington meant little or nothing, he would soon be considering a Southern home, especially if secession came. And where could it more logically be than in Georgia, and Athens, at that, the home of the Cobbs.

The prominent part Browne was playing in the Confederate government at its very birth, at that time led a Georgian by the name of Gaulden to bitterly attack him as untruthful and untrustworthy. Gaulden had been a delegate to the National Democratic Convention in Charleston in 1860 and had refused to secede with the other Georgians. A slave-trader and an advocate for reopening the African slave trade, Gaulden was unworthy of serious notice, but Browne was much upset by this attack, fearing that it would injure his reputation with those with whom he was planning to make his home. (After the war, Gaulden turned Radical and was referred to by Browne as "the roaring lion of liberty [Liberty County]."¹⁰

Browne now called on his friend Cobb to defend him in the public prints, for "as Georgia is my State and the place where I mean to live and die, I want to stand well with the people."¹¹ Cobb wrote a generous defense of Browne, which was published in the Athens *Southern Banner* and probably copied in other Georgia newspapers. Cobb recalled Browne's yeoman service in behalf of the South from the time he edited the Washington *Constitution,* "the ablest press of the Southern school"; how he had denounced as "disgraceful and dishonorable" Holt's attempt to sneak troops into Fort Sumter; how he gave up his newspaper at great loss and "could neither be driven from his course by northern abuse nor purchased with government patronage." Identified with us in spirit and feeling," Cobb continued, "he determined to cast his lot with us and share whatever fate might befall us." If Browne was not trustworthy, why did the great Toombs, whose good judgment no one could doubt, have him as his Secretary of State, Cobb wanted to know.¹²

Browne, now in Richmond, received from Mrs. Cobb, still in Athens, a copy of the *Southern Banner* containing her husband's defense of this prospective Georgian. Overjoyed, he thanked Mrs. Cobb for sending the paper, which contained "so generous and flat-

tering defence of me against the unjust attack of unprovoked enemies
. . . [and] when my truth and loyalty are questioned by unworthy
men, it is doubly precious and consoling." He wanted her to thank
her husband "and beg him for me to do everything he can to set me
right with the people of Georgia with whom I have determined to
associate myself for the rest of my life."[13]

It was not in sentiment and name only that Browne was to become an Athenian. Determined to be a more substantial Athenian
and to live there when peace should make it possible, he bought on
March 4, 1862, for $986.25 ten acres of land on the south limits of
the town, on the road to Watkinsville.[14] To make complete payment
for it, he borrowed on the same day from Thomas R. R. Cobb
$728.50.[15] This was only the beginning of Browne's landholdings in
and about Athens. The next year he bought from Alexander M.
Scudder, an Athenian schoolmaster from Connecticut, 39 acres in
and on the edge of town, and a half-interest in a town lot of one-
and-a-half acres.[16] The next year he bought a half-acre lot from
William N. White, a Connecticut-born New Yorker who had moved
to Athens and become a well-known agricultural editor;[17] and later
the same year he bought a one-and-a-half acre city lot with a two-
story house on it, for which he paid $10,000, in Confederate money
of course, and, therefore, not a very high price.[18]

Although Browne did not consider himself a financial wizard, he
had the feeling that what little money he might have to invest (after
having given his all to the Confederacy at its birth) might well go
into something more substantial than Confederate bonds. Hence, he
had been buying land in and around Athens, and in 1863 he was
thinking about buying a small plantation in Oglethorpe County,
adjoining Clarke County, in which Athens was located. At this
time his original investment in Confederate bonds (the $15,000,000
Loan) had appreciated to 190, and he had been advised to convert
them into the $100,000,000 8% Loan. Here he had doubts, for he
feared that these bonds might soon depreciate; and "as everything
I have to leave my wife in case of my death is invested in them [the
$15,000,000 Loan], it strikes me I ought to put their value either in
whole or in part in some more safe security."[19] Here he was asking
Cobb what he thought about it.

Thoroughly pleased with the prospect of living in Athens, and feeling that "in beauty of situation and arrangement"[20] it was "not surpassed by any I have seen anywhere," in 1864 he employed Ross
Crane, a Yankee architect and builder who had become a citizen of

Athens, to build him a house on his property on the Watkinsville road. The house, plastered inside, had two stories, two large chimneys, and four fireplaces—and the inevitable Southern piazza. There was also a servants' house. Not paying for it all at the time, Browne was slow in making settlement after the war, but finally in 1869, acknowledging service in court, he settled a much larger debt measured in Confederate money for $200 in good United States coin.[21]

Growing up around the University of Georgia, founded in 1801 but chartered in 1785, Athens was the most cultured little town in Georgia, delighting to call itself the "Classic City." Soon after the end of the war, not counting students, Athens boasted a population of 4,000, about 1,700 of whom were Negroes.

Back in Athens a few weeks before Lee surrendered at Appomattox, Browne was a man without a country, defeated in all but spirit (and sometimes in that). As proof of his lowly estate he was arrested on May 8 by Brevet Brigadier-General William J. Palmer, who with his Fifteenth Pennsylvania Cavalry in search of Jeff Davis had swept into town four days previously. Palmer paroled Browne the same day,[22] but this did not restore him to citizenship. On August 12 he was administered the oath of allegiance by Major Matthias S. Euen, who with his 156th New York Regiment Volunteers was now in military occupation of Athens. On his allegiance document he was identified as of fair complexion, having dark hair, blue eyes, being six feet tall and forty-four years old; and since he had to give some occupation, he declared himself a farmer.[23] But not until Browne should be pardoned would he be restored to full citizenship. Before Palmer's cutthroats passed on, they held up and robbed Athenians of watches and jewelry and plundered their homes of whatever suited their fancy. Browne's home did not escape their sticky fingers.[24]

Browne lost no time in moving for a pardon. On the very day he took the oath of allegiance (August 12) he made application for a pardon, which was recommended and approved by Major Euen, who noted that he had personally known Browne since June 20, when he first arrived in Athens, and that "in my opinion he will make a good and loyal citizen of the United States."[25] Euen then forwarded the application to the commander of the military district, Major-General Steedman, in Augusta. On August 19, Steedman sent it on to Provisional Governor James Johnson in Milledgeville for an "investigation and report as to the merits . . . and for his recommendation as to final action." Governor Johnson, taking plenty of time for the investigation or more probably for looks' sake letting the application lie on his desk, reported on November 22: "This applicant is represented as being worthy. As such I recommend him for pardon." The application was then on its way to Washington.

In the meantime, following the procedure for requesting amnesty and pardon, Browne on the day he took the oath of allegiance wrote a letter to President Johnson: "I, William M. Browne, citizen of the State of Ga. take leave most respectfully to ask to be included in the amnesty offered in your Excellency's Proclamation of May 29th. 1865." He then proceeded, without any apologies or expressions of regret for what he had done, to make a straightforward factual statement of his career in the Confederacy. He said that he had in his possession no property belonging to the late Confederacy and that no prosecutions or suits had been entered against him. He had on that day, he said, subscribed to the oath of allegiance, "and it is my purpose to keep religiously and in good faith the obligations which I have thus assumed." [26]

Anxious to speed up the course of his pardon application and feeling that there must be a hitch somewhere in Washington, Browne on September 15 wrote Barlow, with whom he had renewed his old friendship, asking him to interest himself and to do what he could in getting the pardon. "Until I get it," Browne wrote, "I can do nothing to earn a livelihood and having lost everything the need to go to work to subsist is very urgent as you would suppose were you to see me. I can form no plans for the future while I continue a paroled prisoner. The little land I own is unproductive to me by my being unable to cultivate it, and I cannot sell as I cannot give a title even could I find anyone with money to buy. My moveables with some inconsiderable exceptions were appropriated soon after the surrender by a raiding party of federal cavalry, and my Confederate money— all I had—has not been able to replace my hopes." Could Barlow influence some Democratic journal up his way to pay "for interesting letters from Ga.?" If he could, Browne added, "it would be a very great relief of one to whom specie is an old tradition and greenbacks a forbidden luxury." [27]

Again, on November 16, Browne wrote Barlow of the inexplicable delay in the progress of getting his pardon and asked him to intercede with the President. "Having no friends in Washington to interest themselves about it, I venture to trouble you. While 'unpardoned' all avenues to earn a livelihood are virtually closed, therefore it is of the most urgent moment." [28] Barlow replied that he was doing all he could, but that President Johnson was going slow. [29] Browne must have known that Barlow would have no easy approach to the

President or influence with him, for though Johnson was shaking off his earlier Radicalism, he still would not relish Barlow's extreme Democracy.

Using every avenue of approach to the President, Browne sent his wife Lizzie on an errand to Washington to deliver to his old New York newspaper friend, Henry J. Raymond, now a member of Congress, a note asking his aid. He wrote on November 29: "This will be delivered to you by Mrs. Browne who goes to Washington tomorrow to endeavor to procure my pardon from the President. Relying confidently on our former friendship, I appeal to you most earnestly to aid her by your influence and do all you can to relieve me from my present trouble which, I can assure you, can hardly be more distressing." [30] Whatever else Raymond did to help, at least he saw that this letter reached those concerned with recommending to the President the granting of special pardons.

The records of Browne's pardon are confusing as to the date when it was granted and issued. Written in different hands, several dates are recorded. "Pardoned Oct. 28," which manifestly is wrong, is written at one place; at another, "Let this Pardon issue Robt Johnson *Priv Sec,*" without date; and, then, "Filed Dec. 12, '65. Pardoned same day, by order of the President." And, then, on another sheet of the group of papers is written in ink: "Resp'f'y forwarded—" and under this in pencil in another hand, "July 5—66." In the rising tussle between the President and the Congressional Radicals, the House passed a resolution requesting of Johnson a list of names of all persons "engaged in the late rebellion" whom he had pardoned. In addition to three previous reports, the President made his final report on December 4, 1867. The confusion in the record of Browne's pardon is reflected in this report, in that his name is recorded twice: first as "Petty civil officer," pardoned December 12, 1865, and second, "Rebel assistant secretary of state and brigadier general," pardoned July 5, 1866.[31]

Figuratively, and even by his own admission, Browne would have starved to death had he been unable to secure remunerative employment before either of the dates given for his pardon. He might well be considered as having been among the six hundred or so leaders in the Confederacy, civil and military, who survived the war. Among the positions they continued in from pre-war days or entered anew after the war were educators, farmers and planters, journalists, lawyers, merchants, ministers, officeholders, and so on.[32] Browne was to try his hand at the first four.

Home from the wars, apart from some farming he hoped to do, he

centered his attention on the law. In Athens there had been going for
some years a law school, loosely attached to the University, known as
the Lumpkin Law School. Browne enrolled in it in the early fall of
1865 and assiduously applied himself to the subject for about six
months, when he was graduated with a diploma, which apparently
entitled him to the school's Bachelor of Law degree. On February 5,
1866, he and Henry Jackson (who would become an important leader
of the Atlanta Bar) appeared in the Superior Court and took the oath
to support the constitutions of the United States and Georgia, and
on producing their diplomas without any further ado, they were admitted to the practice of law in all the courts of the state except the
state Supreme Court.[33]

Browne immediately formed a partnership with John C. Rutherford, a son of the well-known Williams Rutherford of the University
faculty, and under the firm name of Browne and Rutherford established offices in the *Southern Banner* building. According to custom
they placed their "card" in the newspapers, and to lend confidence
and respectability, Browne gave as references a galaxy of names:
Chief Justice Joseph Henry Lumpkin of the Georgia Supreme Court;
Howell Cobb, who was now practicing law in Macon; Henry R.
Jackson, Georgia lawyer, judge, Confederate brigadier general, and
foreign diplomat; Henry L. Benning, Georgia lawyer, judge, and
Confederate major general; Samuel L. M. Barlow, outstanding New
York lawyer and Browne's close friend; and other lawyers of prominence.[34] Anticipating his actual admission to the bar, Browne wrote
Mrs. Jefferson Davis on January 24, 1866: "I have been admitted
to the bar, but even were there not five hundred other Attorneys at
Law—thick as leaves in Vallombrosa, there is no business and no
money. The sight of a five dollar greenback in this [place?] would
draw more crowded houses than Jenny Lind, and a twenty dollar gold
piece would require the dispatch of a large force of *national* troops." [35]

Law was not Browne's forte, and even if there had been money in
it, he would probably not have stayed with it longer than to find a
newspaper opening. In fact, while he was waiting for clients, the smell
of printer's ink from the press of the *Southern Banner,* operating in
the same building, led him to accept the editorship of that paper. But
there was not much more money in this position than in his law practice, as he wrote Mrs. Jefferson Davis. In informing her of his position on this newspaper, he said that it had about five hundred readers,
"but the profits are about equal to the interest of Mr. Memminger's
bonds [some of which Browne doubtless still had unless the Yankee
raiders who had plundered his house carried them off as souvenirs

of their victorious Athens campaign]. I have some idea of driving a dray. I would were it not for the confident belief that were I to do so, people would immediately cease to need that species of transportation."[36]

Because of "feeble health and the demands of other business" Browne gave up his editorship on May 9, 1866, which he had held for the past six months. In his valedictory he wrote, "I have endeavored to vindicate justice, to maintain truth, defend the rights of our suffering people, sustain and encourage their manly patience, and, whenever I saw a prospect however dim of their emerging from their present condition to a position of liberty and equal rights, I have hailed it with joy and tried to impart the hope to others." [37] The editor of the other Athens newspaper, the *Southern Watchman*, wished Browne a speedy restoration to good health "and an early return to a profession in which he has ever displayed ability of the highest order, and which has won him a National reputation as a Journalist."[38] For a short time in 1868, in the absence of the *Banner* editor, Browne assumed "political control" of the paper.[39]

Browne's friends and acquaintances were always eager to help him in whatever way possible, but since most of them were in as strained circumstances as he was, they could do little more than offer suggestions and information of possible openings. And so it was that about the time that he first became editor of the *Banner,* a friend of his in Atlanta suggested that the *Era* paper owners there were interested in employing him, and also that C. R. Hanleiter, another newspaper man of Atlanta, might well be approached. But nothing came of these hints,[40] and Browne, therefore, went with the *Southern Banner.*

Being now permanent residents of Athens, the Brownes would play their part in the social and cultural life in the little University town, as far as their worldly goods permitted. Their background in this respect in New York, Washington, Montgomery, and Richmond entitled them to the highest rungs on this ladder. The Cobbs and their kindred by blood and marriage would be their special circle; this would include the Colonel David Crenshaw Barrows, but there were other important families such as the Williams Rutherfords, the Augustus Longstreet Hulls, the Andrew A. Lipscombs, the Patrick Hues Mells, the Henry Clay Whites, the Charles Morrises, and others of the University community; and, of course, in the town proper there were other notable families.[41] Mrs. Howell Cobb, greatly beloved by the Brownes, would move to Macon in early 1866 to be with her husband, but she would maintain her home in Athens and would be there frequently, and permanently in later life. Browne in writing to Mrs. Jefferson Davis at this time said, "We feel their loss very much indeed. She was about the only companion my wife had with whom she could talk freely."[42]

The Brownes' home was what we would call suburban; despite their poverty, they had servants and needed them, in view of the fact that both were in delicate health. Their servants were a problem, for they were Negroes who could hardly be trusted with the household when both of the Brownes wanted to be absent; apparently the Negroes were carried away by their heady freedom. Late in 1867 Mrs. Browne wrote Mrs. Cobb, in Macon, "The negroes here are beginning to show signs of riot and violence. Last week they formed an armed mob to attack the college boys and were only dispersed by the soldiers [Federal occupying troops]."[43] The widow of Thomas R. R. Cobb remarked that the Brownes "have had many troubles with their servants and I feel truly sorry" for them.[44] Of course, the Brownes had been used to Irish servants in Washington.

But it must not be assumed that the Brownes never found Negro servants to their liking. Although General Browne never found dependable Negro workmen for his lands and would lash out sharply against Negro politicians, he showed a generous attitude toward his domestic servants and was beloved and respected by them. In fact, the son of one of his servants was named for him and was always called Willie. Browne provided medicine for his servants when they were sick. In 1870 the Brownes had a family of servants named Ray, Seneca, Leanna, and Ben.[45] But at one time, Mrs. Browne tried to get white house servants.[46]

For a few months after the war the Brownes had no servants, as indicated in a letter Mrs. Jefferson Davis wrote to her husband, then in prison in Fortress Monroe: "I have a very affectionate letter from Browne. It took a gentleman born to write it—says his wife is doing her own work—and is in better health than she has been."[47]

Mrs. Browne's health was always a worrisome burden for herself as well as for her General, and illness was never lifted far from her until the end. Browne wrote Mrs. Davis September 18, 1865, that "Lizzie's health is better than it has been for years, mine is indifferent."[48] Now and then her General could not accept invitations out because she was not well enough to be left alone; but, as will appear later, when she was better, Browne spent many weeks away from Athens as occasion dictated. In 1868 he wrote Barlow that Lizzie was "still feeble and ailing constantly. She bears her privations and sufferings nobly and never adds complaint from her to my other sources of distress."[49] And the next year Lizzie dropped a note to Mrs. Cobb, who was now back in Athens, in which she said, "I have been greatly unwell since I last saw you and have been confined to the house and partly to my room, else I should certainly have been to see you. . . ."[50]

When her husband was away, Mrs. Browne missed him much. As she told Mrs. Cobb in 1867, he had returned to Atlanta, "leaving me very lonesome as you may suppose, as few people come to see me now."[51] But Lizzie was never to sit and mope; she was as active as her health would permit—a defense against loneliness and, what was just as important, a way to add to the family income. She early became interested in growing strawberries both as gifts to her friends and for sale. In 1869 she reported that she had been working in her strawberries all day and was "very tired."[52] She had taken up some fine ones and would like to present them to Mrs. Cobb for a new bed she might want to make. She could report that she had ripe strawberries even in December, which she was able to produce by keeping them covered with pine straw. She said that she expected "to make a great deal" from her strawberries.[53]

Mrs. Browne occupied herself also in other gainful activities. She raised chickens and turkeys, and with, of course, the help of her servants, she fixed up her yard periodically, planting hedges and pruning her roses. In the fall of 1867 she reported raking leaves, cutting down small pine trees, and sowing grass—and whitewashing her dining room. She was getting her house in order "for the short days and long evenings. And as she told Mrs. Cobb, "Everything looks very cozy but how long we may be allowed to enjoy this comfort is not very clear."[54] Her chronic bad health was now worsened by a cold which she had caught at the town theater where she attended a performance by the Crisps.[55]

The Brownes had their carriage and horses for getting about in town and for short trips; when her General needed them for some more extended trips in his business, Lizzie was house-bound.

She was permanently mind-bound when it came to forgiving the Yankees; she remained unreconstructed. She reminded the more open-minded Mrs. Cobb, "I fear you give the Yankees credit for good feeling which they do not deserve."[56] Doubtless she had in mind the fact that they were the cause of the poverty that beset the Brownes; but, in the light of the house they lived in, which must have been in keeping with the better houses in Athens, and of the fact that they had servants most of the time, their poverty seems to have been genteel.

Yet Lizzie's womanly instincts required that she have a new bonnet now and then and less often a new dress. She always admired Mrs.

Cobb's bonnets, which she got in Macon while living there, and in the early summer of 1867 she wrote Mrs. Cobb to have her milliner send her one, as she was unable to find one to her liking in Athens. Later that year Mrs. Browne welled up enough courage to buy a new dress, and as in the case of the new bonnet she asked Mrs. Cobb to approach her dress and bonnet maker, a Mrs. Wyche, with minute instructions as to measurements and other details, and ask her to make one for Mrs. Browne. "The price is the only obstacle," Mrs. Browne wrote, "but Genl. Browne says I must have it as I have got nothing else." She reminded Mrs. Cobb, "Do persuade Mrs. Wyche to be as reasonable as possible. I doubt the propriety of my getting a new dress at all, and fear I am doing wrong at this time in going to any expense." [57] Musing over it later, she said, "I ought not to have incurred any expense not absolutely necessary." [58]

General Browne wrestled with his health as unsuccessfully as he did with his poverty. About this time Lizzie wrote Mrs. Cobb that her General "suffered intensely last night," that he was grateful for Mrs. Cobb's "consideration and kindness," and that he promised that "the bottle marked old Madeira shall be visited exactly as you prescribe." [59]

The Cobbs were always mindful of Browne's birthday (July 7) and accompanied their well wishes with some little present. This was true not only of Mrs. Howell Cobb, but also of her son Howell, who had studied law with Browne and who was now living in Milledgeville, the former home of his wife, Mary McKinley Cobb. In a note to his mother on May 16, 1866, Howell, Jr., said: "Mary begs to be kindly remembered to Genl. Browne and assures him that there are none of her friends that she would go farther to see than himself & Mrs. Browne, but the thought of the hours at Gordon [a railway junction] disheartens her." [60] It was not long until July 7, when both Browne and Howell, Jr., who had the same birthday, would be exchanging presents and good wishes. Howell's gift to Browne was a picture of himself.[61]

Mrs. Howell Cobb ("Mary Ann" to her close friends, but Browne never took such liberties) was a brilliant, sensible, practical woman; apart from her interest in her husband and her children, her greatest interest was literature, at least to the extent of liking poetry and good fiction. As Browne himself was an avid reader and was, probably, as great a bibliophile as there was in Georgia, if not the greatest, he kept Mrs. Cobb up to date on some of the best books which were coming out and now and then sent her copies. At an unspecified date he sent her "the latest and, I think, the best novel that has been published." What the novel was is not known.[62] As soon as another book was available, Browne wrote Mrs. Cobb's daughter Mary Ann ("Mayon," short for Mary Ann): "Allow me to present to you what I think a very interesting book The Life and Letters of Miss Mitford [London, 1870], and please give Sarah ["Mayon's" young sister] for me 'Lost in the Jungle.' " [63] Being a sort of clearing house for information on books and poetry, Browne was asked by Mrs. Cobb to locate if possible a copy of the poem, "Jacob's Ladder," which she thought had appeared in the *Macon Telegraph;* Browne was unable to find it.[64] Brown and Mrs. Cobb exchanged not only books and literary information but also seeds and tomato plants, since their interests in the vegetable world were kindred. On one occasion he wrote Mrs. Cobb: "If you have one or two little plants of Kenelworth ivy that you do not need I would be greatly obliged to you for them. They are the prettiest trailing plants & most easily cultivated that I know." [65]

The Brownes were not always to reside in Athens, but they would always consider Athens their home. In addition to their cultural contributions to the community, in the end they would also contribute their ashes, to be deposited far away from their birthplaces in Ireland and in England.

❧ XI ❧

Defender of the South

BROWNE WAS NOT ONLY an Athenian and a Georgian, he was
also a Southerner, and he made this amply clear throughout the rest of
his life in his defense of what the Confederacy stood for and of the way
of life in the South. And in this defense he would not spare those whom
he considered to be false leaders, either during the war or after. Among
these against whom he would level his lance, the most important was
Joseph E. Brown, whom he would attack early and late. The war
was hardly over when someone writing under the name of "Vindex,"
who could have been Browne himself, composed three long letters
condemning Governor Brown's Confederate career. Browne sent
them to Mrs. Cobb on August 5, 1865, and noted that they had
been "written some months ago by a friend of mine & intended for
publication"; but as no paper to which they had been submitted was
prepared to publish this long document, he was sending them to her,
thinking she would "find them amusing & well written." He added,
"If Joseph is again a candidate they may prove of use." [1]

Browne's opinion of Toombs varied with time and circumstance.
By 1867, Toombs was back from his self-imposed exile in France and
Cuba, and when Browne heard that he was to speak in nearby Lexington in a law case, he went over to hear him. On mentioning his
name he gave him this accolade—Toombs, "whose voice so long has
been hushed, and whose great intellect we are required to declare as
unworthy of rights which we have accorded to the servant who blacked
his boots on the day he fought and bled at Sharpsburg." [2] Stephens,
Toombs's long-time friend, Browne admired less than he did Toombs,
though at times he would find it possible to praise him. In 1866,
Browne was not much pleased with Stephens's answer when, asked
his opinion of the rising clash between President Johnson and the
Radicals, he replied that if the Radicals did not prevail, then Johnson would. This was reminiscent of his so-called clever answer to the

question of when the war would stop. His reply was: it would last until it ended.

Writing to Barlow, Browne said that Richard Taylor was the "greatest soldier in our army, not excepting any but Lee, & I have doubts if he was not greater even than that great man." Browne recalled that when he himself had been promoted to brigadier general, he wanted to be assigned to Taylor's command, but against his will he was sent to Savannah.[3] He had a high regard for General G. W. Custis Lee: "It was our good fortune to serve with General Custis Lee during the war [on Davis' military staff], and it is our pride to number him among our most valued friends."[4] Also, he had high praise for Albert Sidney Johnston, though he had no liking for Joseph E. Johnston. He said, "Albert Sidney Johnston was a rare combination of great qualities, a great soldier, a great statesman, a great diplomat, a great administrator. There were few of our generals who really understood what the Confederate war was about. He did not fight because he was a Kentuckian, a Virginian, a Texan; but because he was a Southern man who believed that constitutional liberty, the foundation of which is the separate sovereignty of the States, was assailed."[5]

Looking further at Confederate military leaders after the war, in 1866 Browne said, "Our ex-Confederate Generals are engaged in various branches of industry, working hard with their heads and hands, and both to earn a subsistence. Some succeed and some do not, but where all are poor together the degrees of poverty are not always discerned. All live in hope that a good time is coming, and that with God's blessing, the aid of President Johnson, and with a good crop this year, they will be able to live like a NABOB."[6]

The Confederate leader who constantly received Browne's affection and praise was Jefferson Davis, and, of course, his wife Varina too. Knowing that Davis was in prison, Browne began in May, 1865, writing to Mrs. Davis to console her and help her in any way he could. After writing her three letters and receiving no answers, in September he found out that she was in Augusta. He then wrote her that he would come to see her, but "locomotion is impossible. My poverty and not my will keep me from going at once to see you." He added, "If I can serve or aid you in any way tell me how and it shall be done with devotion sincerity & alacrity." Letting her know that his condition was even worse than hers, he said, "My house and a few acres of poor land are all I have left. You know how, contrary to the advice of wise friends, I gave all I had to the govt. I never tried to get it back, but lost all when all was lost. The consequences of this and of the disabilities to which I am subjected, depriving me of the power of earning a livelihood, make our condition one of privation and to some extent hopelessness." [7]

Early the next year (1866), learning that Mrs. Davis might visit Athens, he wrote her on January 24: "It will delight us beyond measure to see you and to talk of the past, present & future." Her letter of January 21, he wrote, "by a strange spasm of postal activity . . . reached here today, and gave Lizzie and myself much pleasure not unmixed with sadness rendered more intense by our inability to relieve you of any portion of the burden you have to bear. If our power were even remotely equal to our will, how quickly would your sorrow be turned into joy. But alas, the truer, the more zealous the friendship for the fallen, the more helpless and unavailing." [8]

Browne was not writing to his wartime chief, who was now imprisoned in Fortress Monroe, because either his letters would not reach Davis or it would be impolitic to write him anything more than banalities. But he was not forgetful of this national disgrace in holding Davis in chains or even in prison at all. When the National Union Convention ("Arm-in-Arm Convention") was held in Philadelphia in August, 1866, which was designed to promote Johnson and his liberal policy toward the South, Browne was undecided how wise it might be for Georgia to send delegates, fearing that some over-zealous Northern delegates might call them traitors, for not one of them could take the test oath (of not having helped the Confederacy). And when the Convention had come and gone, he was not enthusiastic about its work for, he wrote, "If the North wants to shout and hurrah and fraternize, let the gates of Fortress Monroe be opened, let our venerable Davis come forth, and then we will give a shout of joy which will tell all the earth that peace is restored." He questioned the Convention's failure to say anything for Davis.[9] On Christmas Day, 1866, Browne wrote that Davis was gradually sinking—"He is emaciated almost to a skeleton, walks totteringly." [10] He was always ready to come to the defense of Davis whenever he was attacked, and when Edward A. Pollard, the well-known Richmond newspaper editor who attacked Davis unceasingly, wrote a pamphlet in 1868 in further pursuit of Davis, Browne wrote a Northern friend: "I hear that that unmitigated scamp Pollard in a paper called the Political Pamphlet has made a slanderous attack on my beloved chief Jefferson Davis." He was wondering whether his friend could get a copy for him.[11]

As a champion of the South, Browne naturally could not remain passive to the transpiring scene in Washington, where the Radical

Republicans were quarreling with President Johnson over policies for reconstructing the South; but, of course, he could do nothing about it beyond expressing his opinions. To Cobb in early 1866 he divulged his extreme pessimism, saying that "gloomy ill-conditioned and ill-natured thoughts" on the political outlook had occupied him for some time. "Politics to us now," he said, "are as completely useless for all practical purposes (I mean the discussion of them) as diamond shoe-buckles would have been to Robinson Crusoe on the desert island. To talk without any power to act; to assert rights when we have none except what Thad Stevens would allow us; to invoke the Constitution when no one respects that instrument except those of us who have recently sworn to support it and Lincoln's Proclamation,—is degrading to a man who has self respect and is useless to his fellows." [12]

He here had in mind particularly the Civil Rights Bill, and if Johnson should veto it "I shall have hopes," for it would prove "that he is resolved not to allow the spirit or the substance of State sovereignty to be invaded if he can help it." The bill, he said, did not contain "a provision in reference to the legal equality of the nigger and the white man in everything relating to life, liberty and property that our legislature has not already passed. But Congress has no right to pass any such law." [13] Johnson's veto of the Civil Rights Bill greatly endeared him to Browne, who declared that he would "have no other politics now than opposition to the Radicals and cordial, grateful support of President JOHNSON and those in power who sustain and approve his policy," which was nothing more than compliance with the Constitution. He would await the fall Congressional election (1866) and until the verdict was pronounced "we may expect renewed injustice, repeated insults and continued exclusion from the councils of the nation. We have only to bear and forbear, and to pray that ANDREW JOHNSON whose firmness, justice and fidelity to his duty have protected us thus far against the fury of the radicals, may be spared to continue his good work, and receive the applause of a united people." [14] From his conservative convictions and detestation of the Radicals Browne was never to depart—he remained to the end unreconstructed.[15]

On February 20, 1866, in a letter to W. Stuart, an old New York friend, Browne advocated a combination of Southern and Northern conservatives into a new party to save the country from Radical reconstruction, which was being promoted by Thaddeus Stevens and Charles Sumner. "The more I think of it," he said, "the more certain I am that great political good would result if leading conservative republicans like Mr. [Thurlow] Weed & Mr. [Henry J.] Raymond would make some overtures toward an alliance with leading conservatives in the South. The field is wide open. All old political parties in the Confederate States have disappeared. Here and there like the blackened chimneys of our burned and ruined towns and dwellings, a man may be found who believes in the reorganization of the democratic party or 'The resurrection of the Old Whig party,' but they only represent a view with not enough even of debris to form the humblest shelter."

The attempt to disfranchise "practically all the late rebels" to cut down Southern influence "only tends to alienate, anger, and humiliate the Southern people, without the remotest chances of obtaining a party of the smallest proportions or of any influence to act with the North." If Republicans such as William H. Seward, Weed, and Raymond would come out boldly against the Radicals, leave suffrage to the states, and insist on Presidential pardons for all, they "would rally to themselves as by magic a powerful party" in the South.

But these conservatives in Congress "must not 'run with the hare & hold with the hounds' as at present." For instance, that was just what Raymond was doing, making a speech one day "which brightens the heart & raises the hopes of the South" and the next day "he is found voting for the enlargement & perpetuation of the Freedmen's Bureau, placing the liberty of the citizen at the mercy of the tribe of obscure, corrupt, ignorant & utterly worthless agents of the most iniquitous system ever devised for the purpose of spreading discontent & *not* doing what it is avowedly designed to effect, while it also deprives the citizen of the writ of habeas corpus & trial by jury, if the agents aforesaid, wish to deny him either or both of these great bulwarks of freedom."

Continuing, Brown said:

I tell you and I know what I say to be true (no man can have better or more trustworthy sources of information) that the Southern people are heartily loyal, anxious to bury the past, wipe out old scores, reknit the closest relations of good friendship and good neighborhood, and work together for the common good, advancement & glory, if they are not driven off by taunts, insults, threats, & punitive legislation. . . . Is reconstruction possible if you exclude from association all these men by placing them under a perpetual ban, and declaring them infamous? If on the contrary conciliation, kindness, a willingness to forgive and forget are manifested by the conquering side, depend on it thousands of brave men of intellect & power & honor and truth will meet the kindly advance more than half way, and they who extend the hand of fellowship first will assuredly receive the reciprocal fruits & the corresponding devotion of heart. . . .

In political calculations, it is not wise to treat the South as a vassal that can be ordered & kicked into obedience, or to suppose that a party can be made to spring up like mushrooms by the power of Congressional enactments which drive ninetynine hundredths of the people into the outer darkness & isolation of the pariahs. . . . I am vain and stupid enough to believe that if I could see & talk with Mr. S. Mr. Weed & Mr. Raymond for a couple of hours, I could persuade them to adopt my views, at least to examine them by personal observations.[16]

In his opposition to the Radical reconstruction program, Browne went even beyond the Cobbs. Howell, who was busily practicing law in Macon, had less time to think about the pestilences of the times, but he and Browne kept in close touch, and now and then Cobb offered him advice on courses of action.[17] In answering a mild rebuke by Cobb for not being more prompt in answering his letters, Browne replied that it was because he had nothing to say and emphatically explained, "You know my silence was not from lack of friendship. Of the whole human race of my own age, I believe you are the only man whom I can confidentially call a friend and who cares one straw whether I am prosperous or the reverse. With this firm conviction, made firmer by daily experience, it is impossible that I should fail in anything that constitutes friendship—the genuine article—the pure metal, not the greenback." [18]

On a trip to New York, largely for pleasure and relaxation from confining work, Cobb dropped dead in a hotel there on October 9, 1868. The shock to Browne was as genuine and as great as to any member of Cobb's family. Judge Jeremiah Black had given Cobb a dinner the evening before his death, and in deploring his death Black wrote Browne that Cobb "spoke frequently of you and showed the deepest anxiety for your success." [19]

At a meeting of the citizens of Athens called to memorialize Cobb, Browne moved that a Committee of Seven be appointed to draft resolutions, and, of course, it was logical that Browne be made the chairman. Before presenting the resolutions, Browne eulogized Cobb in chaste and appropriate words. "Howell Cobb was the dearest and best friend I had on earth," he said. "Never during the course of a not-uneventful life, have I been required to discharge a duty which caused me profounder sorrow or severer pain. . . . He was one of the greatest and best men I have ever known. He was the most generous, tolerant, unselfish man I have ever known. . . . The place which knew him once so well will know him no more, and all that is left to you and to me is to drop a tear upon his grave and treasure his memory in our hearts so long as we live."[20] And appropriately Browne was selected to convey to the Cobb family the condolences of the community. Also, he was one of the pallbearers, with crepe on his hat and a long white sash across his shoulder, taking the coffin into the University Chapel where the obsequies were held and then to the Oconee Hill Cemetery to a plot, near which Browne himself later would rest.[21] Browne declared that this cemetery was "in beauty of situation and arrangement, . . . not surpassed by any I have seen anywhere." [22]

It was in this cemetery that the Athens Ladies' Memorial Association began decorating the graves of Confederate soldiers the first year after the war. This was on May 4, 1866, and the Athenians instinctively turned to General William Montague Browne to make the address. And here he had a grand opportunity to pour forth his praise of Confederate soldiers and his undying support of the principles which the Confederacy stood for. For three days the ladies had been preparing for the occasion. The procession formed at the University Chapel, headed by little girls carrying baskets of flowers, followed by young ladies with wreaths of evergreens, by matrons bearing crowns and anchors, and then by the citizens of the town—all going to the topmost hill of the cemetery where there had been erected a broken column on which the names of the soldier dead were written. After a prayer by Chancellor Lipscomb of the University, General Browne made the address, purposely short "in a few simple yet touching and eloquent words." He paid a special eulogy to Thomas R. R. Cobb, fallen at the Battle of Fredericksburg. "Far more impressive than any words which I can employ—," he said, "than any words which the most gifted orator can utter—is the voice which proceeds from the graves which you are met to adorn. . . . It tells us of noble effort, of gallant endeavor, of dauntless courage, of purest patriotism, of unsurpassed self-sacrifice. It tells us of duty performed. . . .

"If it be permitted to departed spirits to observe the acts and the thoughts of those whom they have left behind, and to feel emotions akin to those of this world, there can be to them no more acceptable tribute than that which you have laid upon their graves." [23]

As reported in the Athens newspaper, which he had only then ceased to edit: "At first his voice became tremulous with emotions as he beheld gathered around him, the heart stricken wife and weeping daughters of the noble dead. The tremor of his voice showed that he too, in common with the others, felt deeply the loss of those in honor of whom he spoke. The whole address was replete with the tenderest pathos and the deepest feeling and constituted of itself a most beautiful and touching tribute to the gallant dead." [24]

Browne later remarked that the placing of flowers on the graves of Confederate soldiers had given great offense "to the extra-loyal. . . . To place wreaths of flowers on the graves of Sidney Johnston or Leonidas Polk or Thomas R. R. Cobb is flat rebellion." [25]

Year after year the Athens ladies decorated the graves of Confederate soldiers in Oconee Hill Cemetery, and again, in 1874, they called on General Browne to make the address—"an address, which for beauty of thought, eloquence of expression, and appropriateness of conception, could not be excelled, and which not only bespoke a sentiment of soul, commensurate with the poetry of mind, but found a responsive chord in every heart." [26]

The procession to the cemetery was arranged in this order: members of the Ladies' Memorial Association, the Mayor and Council, children of the Sunday Schools of the several denominations, students of the Lucy Cobb Institute (named for a daughter of Thomas R. R. Cobb), students of Madam Sosnowski's Select School, members of various fraternal orders, the local fire companies, the faculty and students of the University, and the commonality of citizens, on foot and in carriages. After a prayer and a song, Colonel B. C. Yancey introduced Browne. Browne began by referring to the same occasion eight years previously when he made the address; it was a time when "there was added to the poignancy of recent bereavement, the humiliating scene of defeat—the belief that our sacrifices had been profitless, and that the precious blood of our fallen heroes had been shed in vain," and when he saw the "venerable mother, bound with sorrow and with age, . . . the crushed and broken hearted widow, . . . [and] the weeping daughter, . . . my heart overflowed and my voice almost refused to give utterance to the words which I desired to speak."

"Now, my friends, time has mellowed grief; the wounds which then were fresh and quivered at the slight touch are now partially healed, and the thought of our soldier dead has become a hallowed memory which affection tells us it is our duty to keep green forever." The flowers which were being scattered over the graves were "not merely the symbols of your tears"; they were "the repetition of the great truth which embodies the protest of the entire Southern people that all just government derives its authority from the consent of the governed."

However, these occasions, he said, were not for perpetuating sectional hostility or to recall past wrongs suffered, for the South shielded the sword in good faith. "But this submission did not carry with it the admission that we were wrong, that our cause was not just or that we are sorry for our participation in the conflict." And now he made a thrust at the Southern turncoats (Joe Brown, Longstreet, and others, without mentioning them by name): "Eternal infamy be the lot of the Confederate soldier who for present profit or future reward would stultify himself and attempt to dishonor his comrades, as to make any such admission." The feeling of hostility to past enemies was dying away and the Northern people were beginning "to recognize the valor and fortitude of the Confederate soldier, and the day is fast approaching when they will proudly acclaim as their fellow citizen and count among the most illustrious Americans JEFFERSON DAVIS, the peerless patriot, and ROBERT E. LEE, the greatest soldier of the age."

He did not like the term "Lost Cause"; it was a mistaken expression. Might never made right: "Does truth crushed to earth cease to be truth? Oh! no, my friends, our cause is not lost." In time to come the United States would be compelled in order to save itself "to invoke the very principles for which we fought in war and which we still hold in peace." Browne would never think of trying to renew the struggle on the battlefield, yet he hoped that the time would never come when the "memories of this day will be less fondly cherished . . . , when the sight of our furled battle flag or of a tattered gray jacket, will lose its power to awaken our pride and quicken our admiration. . . . For myself, humble though the part I was able to take in the struggle, and feeble though the services I was permitted to render, when it shall please God to take me hence, I ask for no other epitaph to be inscribed upon the stone which will cover my last sleep than that I 'wore the gray.' "[27]

Not far from where Browne stood when he made this memorial address, a few years previously he had taken part in the burial of a lady who would have shouldered a musket with alacrity had she been a man; and though the records do not say so, her grave also might have been decorated with flowers on this memorial day. She was Elizabeth Church Robb, wife of James Robb of New York and a daughter of the late Alonzo Church, President of the University. She had lived in Chicago during the war, and, overcome by the prison horrors in Camp Douglas, where seven thousand and more Confederate prisoners were held, she spent much time and money in nursing and otherwise caring for them—in doing which she lost her health. She died in New York on January 6, 1868; her remains were brought back to Athens and buried in the Oconee Hill Cemetery. Browne was one of those in charge of making all arrangements, and in writing about it he said that Mrs. Robb was "born here, & is so endeared to us Confederates for her munificent kindness to our poor prisoners of war." [28]

Browne's strong Southernism did not mean any less regard for his friends in the North of former days. He was not one to harbor a grudge or a hostile feeling against anyone; nor was he one ever to forget a friend, whether Yankee or not. One of the bad features of the war, which he felt keenly, was that it cut him off from his Northern friends. And chief of all of them was, of course, Samuel L. M. Barlow. Their correspondence ceased in 1861, but as soon as the war was over, Browne began trying to establish contact with him, difficult because of the almost nonexistent mail service. In June, 1865, he wrote Barlow: "Unless four years separation have changed you very materially you will be glad to hear from me as I shall be to hear that you, your wife and children are all well and happy. . . . I have worked hard for the independence of C. S. A. and thereto have devoted mind, body & estate. My mind is sound, my body survives, too much the worse for wear, and my estate, all I had [is gone]." Then in a spirit of levity, referring to Confederate notes and bonds,, he said that he had left a few thousand scraps of paper, "paralellograms," 2 by 4 inches, "telling me that two years after the *ratification* of a treaty of peace between the C. S. A. & the U. S. A. [the former] will pay the bearer ('that is me') several thousand dollars." Being in this low estate, he continued, "I can do nothing at present. I rarely stir beyond my house, but whenever I can I try to stimulate harmony & get everybody who can to go to work. . . . If famine and its attendant horrors can be averted until fall we will have done well. Where food is to come from I do not see. . . . No one has a dime." He said that he had a few pieces of bacon and corn bread, and "when they are out, God knows where I shall find food." Many people lost more "in amount" than he did, he said, but he lost all. "Give me your advice and if you can encouragement for the future." He closed by wanting to be remembered to his New York friends.[29]

To make sure that this letter would reach Barlow, Browne sent it by express; but he anxiously awaited a reply he never received. Writing again on August 27, Browne told Barlow that he thought that his June letter had not reached him, for "judging by my own feelings for you I cannot think that you have renounced the friendship which existed between us or that the fact we were on opposite sides during the recent struggle would cause you to refuse to shake hands now especially as you are among the conquerors & I among the conquered." [30]

Barlow had received Browne's June letter and had answered it, but his reply never reached Browne. Barlow did receive Browne's August letter and he answered it the next day (September 6), saying

that it was "a revelation from the dead in the shape of a letter from
W. M. B. which gratified me beyond measure." He was sorry his
previous letter had not reached Browne and to have him think "I had
forgotten my old friends at the South. . . . Write me as to your plans,
what you expect to do, and what I can do to help you, if anything." [31]
Browne immediately wrote Barlow that he was rejoiced to know that
their old friendship still held.

Barlow's offer of help availed Browne little, for there was little that
a New Yorker could do to help a Georgian establish himself in the
South. As the years 1866 and 1867 wore on, Browne began to think
of what opportunities there might be beyond the South; but he was
never carried away by those Southerners who were emigrating to
Mexico and Brazil. Yet, rather facetiously he said that the glowing
accounts he had heard of opportunities in Honduras had about set
him to packing his bag to go there. It was reported that in Honduras
cotton grew perennially and all that planters had to do was to pick
it, that corn grew 100 bushels to the acre and required no cultivation, and that coffee could be gathered like blackberries. But on a little
reflection, he had come to the conclusion that if all this were
so, Yankees from New England would already have grabbed Honduras.[32] More seriously, in 1868 he wrote Barlow, "I did think of
going to California, & have bitterly regreted not having accepted
Butterworth's generous offer." But he was engaged in some farming
at the time which he could not let loose "and the entire failures of
my labors had added to my regret." It is not known what Butterworth's offer was, but he was then in San Francisco and was able to
accumulate an ample fortune there. Barlow had informed Butterworth, who had gone to California at the end of the war, of Browne's
distress. Barlow wrote to Browne, giving him a message from Butterworth: "that whenever everything else fails he will give you honest
meat and bread in Cala. [California]." And the next May (1866)
Butterworth did more than invite Browne to California; he asked
Barlow to mail him a check for $200.[33]

For a period during 1867 Browne was slow in his correspondence
with Barlow, and when Barlow chided him for it, he wrote: "I confess I began to fear that the poor rebel general, hid away in a secluded
corner of this conquered territory" had been forgotten by his New
York friends; but "I did not write because I had nothing to tell you
but the cruel and wicked oppression and degradation of the whole
people with whom I have cast my lot. I knew *you* would alleviate
their condition if you could, but as I knew you could not, I felt it was
unfriendly perhaps to trouble you needlessly with a detail which could

only wound your honest heart, & that it was unmanly to complain
when complaint is unavailing." He asked Barlow to "remember me to
all who are friendly enough to care to know of my existence. In old
times I would send remembrance to several, but I have learned during three years of severe adversity not to obtrude myself on those to
whom I am not welcome." [34]

A few months later, in the same refrain, he wrote Barlow, "If
I do not write to my friends as often as they are kind enough to desire to hear, it is not from any forgetfulness or want of interest. I
remember my friends of better days with very pleasant feelings. But
as I have nothing to say that is not gloomy and discouraging, I refrain from obtruding the griefs of those by whom I am surrounded
on those whose happier fate has placed in a more prosperous and
freer country." [35]

With another friend of happier days Browne hoped to re-establish
good relations in 1867. This friend was Frederick Law Olmsted. On
February 19 Browne addressed him:

My dear Olmsted: It is upwards of six years since you and I have
had any news of each other. Our last letters referred to the great conflict
then about to commence, and in that which you wrote me, altho' I
thought you were grievously mistaken at the time, you predicted events
with marvelous minuteness and accuracy which has frequently astonished
me, when presented forcibly to my mind by the hard teachings of dire
adversity.

"The fact that during all this time we were on opposite sides of a
terrible war, has never diminished or suspended the sincere, cordial
friendship which I have felt for you for many years, & it is in the confident belief that you have not withdrawn from me the good union & the
kind feeling which I so much prized, that I now write you & seek to
renew our intercourse. At all events the fortunes of war have been so
decidedly and overwhelmingly in your favor and against me, that even
did you at any time think of me harshly (which I do not believe) you
can afford to banish such thoughts now, forgiving and forgetting.

Browne could not forego detailing his low estate, which cleverly
served as a preface to a little request he was about to make:

Few even of those who have suffered most have been so completely
crushed by defeat as I have been. Having invested every dollar of the
modest competency which I possessed in Confederate securities, and being
in the field when the blow came and thus unable to save anything, when
I surrendered my command & returned to my house at this place [Athens],
I found myself penniless with nothing of value but my horses. My house
plundered, my furniture destroyed, and my wife's clothes torn to shreds
by a cavalry raid, and my health so broken by exposure, fatigue and

anxiety that for months it was thought that there was no hope for my recovery. I have made various attempts to work. I have been willing to do almost anything to earn a livelihood; but my being a rebel cuts me off from all employment at the North, and the impoverished condition of all classes in this country renders it impossible to obtain anything to do here of which I am capable. Between $8 and $10 a week writing for a newspaper, have been all that I have been able to earn, & you may judge what this is when you remember the prices of the barest necessities of life. I could bear this, however, with a murmur, & strive on with hope, but for the terrible affliction which has befallen me in the sickness of my wife, which is now pronounced hopeless altho' it may continue for months. To witness her intense suffering, and be powerless to procure her the alleviating remedies which were recommended, but the requisite nourishment, has, I confess more than once almost unmanned me. Such has been my fate, Olmsted, and such my sufferings.

And now came the real purpose of this letter, beyond that of re-establishing a genuine friendship with Olmsted, which had flourished before the war: Did he know of anyone whom he "could induce to lend me $300?" He would pay it back the first of January, 1868. He needed the money to buy mules and farming implements for a plantation which he controlled, which would produce a cotton crop that would make him independent. "It is impossible to borrow a cent here," he wrote, and even when money could be borrowed, 4 and 5 per cent a month was demanded. "On my house and place valued before the war at $8000 I could not raise money enough to buy a bushel of meal. I have tried it." (Browne was projecting the value of his Athens property, which he did not own before the war, back to that period. The cotton plantation which he mentioned will be discussed later on in this narrative.) Before closing his letter, Browne could not refrain from asking about a mutual friend: "Where is our friend Kapp? I wrote him since peace but not getting any reply, thought perhaps he had returned to Germany. Should he be in N. Y. remember me to him warmly." [36]

It is not known what Olmsted said in his answer, but from Browne's reply of March 7, it is evident that Olmsted inferred that Browne wanted the loan from Olmsted, which he was unable to make, or from some Northern relief agency, and much more that Olmsted did not have the forgiving spirit which Barlow displayed in his correspondence with Browne. In this letter, after expressing sincere pain at the news that Olmsted and his family were not in good health, Browne wrote:

I fear you construed my letter to you as an application to the Relief

Commission. No. I only asked my friend F. L. Olmsted to help me in getting a small loan, which I could and would have repaid with interest, which would have secured me and my family from distress, and which to some extent would have enabled me to relieve the distress of others. I confess I was not prepared for the account you give of the temper and disposition of your people. It has shocked and pained me more than anything I have heard during the last two terrible years. Knowing as I do that all this passion and hate are based on false information and feeling the powerlessness of this people to stem such a torrent of misrepresentation, I abandon all hope of peace and rest.

You, yourself, benevolent, kindhearted, and intelligent as I know you to be, evidently believe firmly that we murder, maim, and whip the negroes, persecute Northern men and unionists, and are insincere in our professions of allegiance to the government and laws of the U. S.

You evidently believe that the "bayonet" is the only instrument by which conciliation can be secured, and though your goodness of heart causes you to regret the indisposition of the people who have to give to those who have not & save them from famine, your judgment does not. condemn as unnatural or as unjustifiable the sentence which closes the avenue of relief. In yr. disappointment you do not seek the cause in any error or delusion of those to whom you have applied and who have refused yr. petition, but you throw all the blame upon those famine wasted hands which are extended to you for bread.

Now, my friend, however hardly you may judge my "rebellion," I know you give me credit for sincerity and truth, and feel assured that I would not for any consideration on earth put my hand or tongue to a falsehood. And I tell you with all earnestness of solemn conviction derived from positive knowledge, that so far as Georgia is concerned, the negroes are not ill treated, Northern men insulted or unionists persecuted; that I do not know of a single case, nor have I heard of one where any outrage of the kind has been committed, and that the people of every class and shade of opinion have obeyed and do obey and will obey the law, asking for nothing but peace and goodwill. The prominent position I held in the civil and military service of these States made me acquainted with the people, (leaders and led). I have their confidence and know their disposition, and I will swear that they are *not guilty* of what is brought to their charge. If they were, I should be the first to condemn them. There may be intemperate individuals, there may be isolated cases of outrage and crime, just as there are and must be in every community; but it is as cruelly unjust to say that the individual malefactors are representative men, as it would be to say that Ketchum who robbed his father's safe is a representative man of the bankers & brokers of New York.

You are cruelly deceived, Olmsted. The excited and angry public opinion which you describe is caused by the same deception. Why are not the outrages against negroes and union men published with names and dates?

Why do the informers always write anonymously or request the suppression of their names? Why are not the governors and magistrates asked for information? Is it not fair to hear both sides? Must denunciation be true, and exculpation be false?

The insulting letters you describe as receiving are not and cannot be from representative men. They are from lunatics or *forgers,*—men who adopt demoniac mode of poisoning public opinion and preventing peace. Publish their names. Let us at home know who they are who rob the starving widow and orphan of the bread you are willing to give them.

If your health will permit, come South, see for yourself. I will go with you in Georgia, and I promise you on my sacred honor to give you an opportunity to see every thing you desire without the least effort at concealment. But in God's name do not allow slander and misrepresentation to silence humanity.

I write feelingly because your letter has produced a profound impression and I know that you will believe in my truth however you may distrust my judgment. Since the surrender I have done all I could to produce peace, secure submission to authority and obliterate the traces of war. I have "accepted the situation" honestly and unequivocally, and so far as my humble ability goes I mean to persist in welldoing. I own to you that I have but little hope, and think the prospect as gloomy and disheartening, as despair can picture it.[37]

No record has been found to indicate that Olmsted continued the correspondence, but Browne, never willing to give up a former friend, seemed to harbor no ill will. His friendly feeling toward Olmsted did cool somewhat, as indicated in a short letter he wrote Olmsted about two years later. Instead of addressing him as "my dear Olmsted," it was now "My dear Sir," and instead of "Very truly yr. friend," it was "Yours very truly." This letter consisted of three sentences. Browne said that while in New York the previous summer, he noticed in Central Park "a grass clipping machine." He wanted to know "what they are called, who makes them or what they cost." He wanted to have one, and so did some of his neighbors.[38]

When the war ended and Browne had established connections with Barlow, who was as rich in money as Browne was poor in everything but honor, integrity, ideas, and the ability to express them in writing and in oratory, he sought to interest Barlow in the grand opportunities for investments in the conquered South. Many Yankees were buying up cotton lands, and Southerners were glad to welcome them and their money— though later the carpetbaggers, who were interested in the offices and the opportunity to ride into them on the backs of the Negroes, were not so welcome.

On December 4, 1865, he wrote Barlow of a grandiose speculative scheme, though he did not so term it, which was far less nebulous than the South Sea Bubble, but which the practical Barlow did not take to. This was a capitalistic venture into raising cotton. Browne wrote that he and "three experienced cotton planters of this state of high standing and character" proposed to associate themselves with Northern capitalists to buy cotton lands for raising cotton and auxiliary crops such as corn. He said that Barlow could easily assemble the capital, his own, August Belmont's, and others'. There was a fortune to be made. "You know me well enough to be assured that I believe what I say and I believe this because I know it," Browne wrote. "No time is to be lost. Lands will be sold or rented between now and Christmas, negroes hired, &c. Therefore, if anything be done, it must be done quickly. If you come you can satisfy yourself *in two days*."

These were the details: The capitalists would buy the land, stock, implements, provisions for the workmen, and pay their wages. The planters would superintend all the operations and in return receive one-third interest in the plantations and in the profits. Browne estimated that $250,000 would be needed the first year: 10,000 acres would cost $125,000; stocks, implements, provisions, would come to $100,000; and wages for workmen would total $25,000. Of the 10,000 acres, 5,000 acres would be in cleared land. Of these 5,000 acres, 3,000 would be put in the money crop of cotton and 2,000 acres in feed and food. The cotton lands would produce 1,500 bales (500 pounds each), which at 30 cents a pound would amount to $225,000; but if the season was good, 2,000 bales would be realized and cotton might well go up to 40 cents a pound. As for expenses, 250 hands at $10.00 a month would be $30,000; 170 mules would cost $40,000; corn and fodder, if not raised, $25,000; meat, syrup, salt, and so on, $20,000; implements, wagons, and so on, $10,000. The total expenses for the first year would, thus, be $125,000. The clear profit would, then, be $100,000.[39] In fact, it would be more than that, for in Browne's apparent excitement over the press of time, he counted mules, implements, and wages in expenses when he had already counted them in the capital investments. Therefore, the profits, would have been much more than $100,000 and in subsequent years even more, for the full capital investment would not be repeated.

But, as already stated, the proposition looked too good for Barlow's practical sense. He wrote Browne, "I do not believe I can help you in the cotton scheme. I tried for two months to carry out a similar scheme for Genl. [Richard] Taylor & afterwards for Genl. [William R.?] Peck, but without success." But always wanting to be helpful to Browne, he said, "I have however sent your plan to Providence, where parties are inclined to make investments of this character and if I can do anything you may rest assured that I will." And then, like the man who was asked to have a drink and who replied that there were two reasons why he could not: first he had quit drinking, and secondly he had just had two drinks, Barlow said: "My own funds, not very large, were exhausted months ago in similar projects in Georgia & North Carolina so that I cannot just now do anything."[40] In the spring of 1866 Barlow was in North Carolina and Georgia looking after his investments, but he came nowhere close to Athens, he informed Browne.[41] At about this time, Browne wrote for publication in a newspaper that British capitalists were beginning to invest in cotton lands and that Northern capitalists were not faring well in these ventures because they were loosing their Negro workmen by charging them exorbitant prices in their plantation stores.[42]

Browne believed that there was money to be made in land investments, not only by raising cotton but by speculating. In 1869 there was a tract of 30 acres to be sold at an administration sale in which he became interested. It lay on the outskirts of Athens and not far from the Princeton Factory, a mile or two to the south. If divided into lots, he believed it would easily bring from $3,000 to $3,500. According to his estimate, it would bring about $600 at the sale, and certainly not more than $1,000. He thought it would be a good investment for Barlow, and he was especially anxious for him to buy it because it joined "the 70 acres on which my house is built and I am very anxious it should fall into hands that will not sell it to negroes who will surround me with nigger cabins, thieves, w---s and vagabonds."

If Barlow should not be interested, then Browne would like to borrow the money from him to make the purchase himself. He would repay Barlow at a fixed time with interest at 12 per cent; in the fall when his crops were gathered, he would have the money. He would secure the loan by a mortgage on his house and land, which were valued for taxation at $5,750,[43] and he would repay the money on the day he promised.[44] The sale took place on April 6 and Browne bid $550 on faith that he could get the money from someone, hoping that it would be Barlow. So anxious did he seem that now he promised to repay Barlow on November 15 "to the hour."[45] Previously he had named November 20 as the due date.

Browne was not only anxious to make a little money in land speculation, but in acquiring land he was just as anxious to prevent unwelcomed and unworthy persons from becoming his neighbors, as he had mentioned to Barlow. Hence, when Mrs. William N. White had for sale some land adjoining Browne's, he said he was anxious that "the land should not fall into other hands if I can help it."[46]

But as for the neighbors he already had, he always wanted to keep on good terms with them, even though he found it difficult in the case of one of them, a man by the name of B. J. Parr, whose lands bordered Browne's on two sides. The trouble with Parr broke out in 1869. Some four or five years previously they had agreed to keep in repair the fences on their lines, Browne to keep up the fence on one side and Parr on the other. Now, in rebuilding the fence on his side, Browne lacked some material and he got permission from Parr to cut what poles he needed from an old field belonging to Parr. Browne's laborers cut about two hundred pine saplings, and after it was done Parr objected and threatened to sue him. "I offered to pay for the poles," Browne said, "to buy the land they were cut on, to return them, to pay whatever the estimated damage might be, or anything else to rid myself of all obligations to Parr. He never replied to my letter."[47] It is not known what the outcome was.

Browne was never able to induce Barlow to make any investments in Georgia, but Barlow did give Browne encouragement in the form of good counsel, honest friendship, and money. And Browne responded by doing anything he could for the pleasure and comfort of Barlow and his wife and children. Browne's Georgia provided things which all of Barlow's money in New York could scarcely buy. The Georgia peach was on its way to becoming well known, and he found out that the Barlows had an insatiable taste for them. In the fall of 1868 Browne sent twenty-four "cans of preserved peaches," and as "Mrs. Browne superintended the preserving . . . I know that part was well done." Probably in explanation of why he did not send more, Browne said, "The negroes stole all my peaches, and I was unable to buy any under eight and ten dollars a bushel."[48]

A little later in the year Browne sent Barlow a half-bushel of "first class dried peaches," and informed him that he had hired a "wild turkey killer" to provide turkeys for the Barlows during the winter; furthermore, if he could secure from some deer hunter some "*fat* venison," he would send it. In making these gifts, Browne wrote Barlow, "You must allow a poor rebel the gratification in a very weak way his appreciation of the vast number of kindnesses you have done him."[49] Year after year Browne was to keep up his gifts of peaches, preserved and dried, and in the peach-ripening season, some fresh ones. And, of course, the Barlows were quite appreciative of Browne's gifts; and though Browne infrequently made trips to the North, Barlow entertained him when he visited New York. In 1871, he expressed his regrets that Browne would be unable to visit him on his Long Island estate at Glen Cove.[50]

❧ XII ☙

Reporter Browne

ATTORNEY BROWNE HAD QUICKLY seen that there was no money for him in practicing the profession of law in Athens; likewise, Editor Browne had soon discovered that there was little, if any, more money in editing an Athens newspaper. In fact, there was little money in Athens for doing anything. But he had no intention of deserting his adopted country to return to the country of his birth, or even to leave his beloved South for the prosperous North or for the Golden Far West, unless hunger should drive him to it. Yet he and his Lizzie must eat to live; and, if possible, they would remain in Athens.

As he still had a facile pen, a fertile mind, and a quick grasp of what was going on around him, why should he not use those gifts to obtain even a pittance from the more prosperous parts of the nation? So he set about looking for a job to report to newspapers the conditions and happenings in the South.

In canvassing the possibilities, he happily hit upon the *Louisville Daily Courier,* and apparently the *Courier* was happy to be hit upon by Browne, for its policy fitted in exactly with Browne's Southernism and philosophy of government. This paper was edited and owned by Walter Newman Haldeman, a Kentuckian of the "Old School," who had founded the newspaper more than a dozen years before the Civil War. Being strongly for states' rights, Haldeman had bitterly condemned the Lincoln government in 1861. He escaped with his paper before it could be suppressed, and thereafter he edited it within the Confederate lines as they were forced southward. At the end of the war, he returned and re-established the *Courier* in December, 1865. It now became one of the leading newspapers in the South and Southwest.

It is probable that Browne and Haldeman, two highly competent newspaper editors, met during the war, and it seems only natural that when Browne was looking for a reportial job none appeared more promising than with the *Courier.* The man and the paper met.

Haldeman announced on May 16, 1866, the appointment of Browne, though not by name: "Our Georgia Correspondent.—We publish this morning the first of a series of letters we have arranged to receive regularly every week hereafter, from the Empire State of the South. They are from one of the finest intellects in the nation, who, whom the reader will readily perceive, wields a ready, graceful and trenchant pen. We can promise the readers of the COURIER much entertainment and instruction in the admirable letters of 'Nabob'."[1] Thereafter for the next two years there appeared, frequently in a prominent place generally on the first page of the *Courier,* the "Letter from Nabob," followed by the byline, "From Our Own Correspondent."

Soon the Georgia readers of the *Courier* were intrigued by the nom de plume "Nabob" and the identity of the reporter in their midst who was writing such interesting dispatches. The editor of the *Augusta Daily Constitutionalist* remarked: " 'Nabob'—Considerable curiosity is manifested in our community to identify *'Nabob,'* the clever and accomplished Augusta correspondent of the Louisville *Courier.* We do not know of any nabobs in Georgia, unless the witty correspondent be one of the returned gold men from Montana." He then referred to a dispatch in the *New York Times* stating that the police of that city had arrested a party of five men who had $108,000 in gold and silver in their possession, and who said that they had been mining in Montana since 1859 and were then returning to Georgia. The editor then exclaimed, "Whew! Just think of Georgia men returning in that style? Bless you, my children, bless you."[2]

Nabob replied:

I was gratified to find by a paragraph in the local columns of the Constitutionalist, of Saturday, that "considerable curiosity is manifested here to identify Nabob." I would make many sacrifices to gratify the good people of their delightful city; but were I to reveal myself I fear that it would be discovered how little I merit the flattering terms in which the Constitutionalist has referred to me, and prefer, therefore, to preserve an ungracious *incognito* to a declaration of my identity, which might bring disappointment to those who "want to know," and the loss to myself of the modicum of favor now so generously accorded to Nabob.

It is, however, due to myself to state that my *nom de plume* was not suggested by my acquisitions in Montana. To have been in that auriferous territory since 1859 is a confession which few citizens of Georgia would be willing to make, even though the same were paid for by the possession of $108,000 in gold and silver coin. There are other possessions besides gold which may justify me in signing myself as I do; and may I not count among them good will and friendship of many of the good people of Augusta.[3]

Neither Browne nor the *Courier* were ever to reveal that Nabob was, indeed, William Montague Browne.[4] If Browne had written under his own name he would have been greatly limited in what he could say about prominent people.

Indeed, Browne deserved the curiosity that was aroused by the unusual brilliance and cleverness of his dispatches to the *Courier*. He deserved as much being termed a columnist in the twentieth-century meaning attached to the word as anyone of his time. It was not all opinion and prejudices as the twentieth century columnists make it; instead, it was news cleverly festooned with opinion and slants which got across what Browne wanted. With a light literary touch he characterized almost every important person whom he took occasion to mention, either to praise or to pierce with stinging barbs. His deep knowledge of the literary and historical past was revealed in frequent references to and comparisons with figures from Greece and Rome, as well as allusions to such historians as Macaulay and Gibbons, to economists such as Ricardo and John Stuart Mills. There were also frequent references to his travels, as, for example, something about the olive groves of France and Italy. But in all this, he did not write above the heads of the ordinary reader or to show off his learning.

He traveled widely over Georgia to interview people, to see what was going on, and to get the feel of the various sections of the state; he always included in the dateline of his dispatches the town from which he wrote. Most of his dispatches came from Atlanta and Augusta, but more than a dozen other towns were represented. Naturally there would be such additional news centers as Macon and Savannah, but to get back to the grass roots he visited such places as Dahlonega, Stephens, Millen, Waynesboro, Darien, Union Point, and, of course, he had to write a dispatch from Athens, his home.

His first letter was written from Atlanta, May 10, 1866. He said that the topics on all tongues were: how are the crops, how are the freedmen doing, what will the Radicals in Washington do next? Replying, he said that crops were good, that the Radicals were up to no good for the South; and that the freedmen were doing better than expected, but, "whenever a religious festival, a good chance for a fishing frolic, or a funeral occurs, they assert freedom by a total absence from plows and hoes."[5] As he traveled around, he said he saw great poverty in the country where a few years previously there had been wealth and contentment.[6] He went by train when possible, but to out-of-the-way places he used whatever methods were at hand. To get to Dahlonega, in the gold region, he used "a buggy of primeval architecture, a horse advanced in life, and of sedate habits, and harness of very peculiar construction, needing reconstruction much more than the State of Georgia."[7]

On a trip to Savannah and southward, Nabob spent a night at the Millen hotel, apparently one of the structures Sherman did not burn as he passed through. Nabob spent a most miserable night there, and the food was terrible. Those wartime travelers who had had to spend a night in Weldon, North Carolina, waiting for train connections, or at the Trout House in Atlanta, could gain some idea of what Nabob suffered in Millen.[8] On reaching Savannah, where he had done his only actual military combat service during the war in the defense of the city against Sherman, he found it prosperous and elegant: "Here are all the bustle and noise of a really commercial city, and together with that hurly-burly all the elegance and refinement and comfort of the most luxurious ease." The cellars of the "fine old residences," he said, "in which reside those men of elegant leisure, who used to own, and drink, and give others to drink, the finest madeira and sherry to be found anywhere on our continent," were now empty, despoiled by Sherman and his hordes. He noted that a number of Confederate generals resided in the city, including Henry R. Jackson, Alexander R. Lawton, and Hugh W. Mercer.[9] But many familiar faces that Nabob had known in time past were gone, and whimsically he added, "there was one old family which enjoyed a great reputation here, and was one eminently popular, of which not a member is left, as I am informed. It was called old Madeira. As it was the most numerous slave owner in the city, and all its slaves were white, the Federal army captured the whole family and put them to death. They are deeply and deservedly lamented."[10]

Passing on down the coast, Nabob came first to Darien and then to Brunswick. Both were port cities and had good harbors. He was greatly impressed with the possibilities of these two cities and of this whole coastal region, in agriculture, lumbering, and in shipbuilding. Always conscious of the whipping-boy status of the South, he said that if they were situated in Pennsylvania or New York or elsewhere in the North, aided by special favors of the federal government, they would have a combined population of 200,000. The natural resources of this region were unlimited and awaited only capital to develop them.[11] Nabob probably knew that he was overenthusiastic in this assessment, but he was anxious to turn the people away from the enervating cotton economy into the industrial age, thus antedating Ben Hill and Henry Grady in their preachments.

Anxious to make his dispatches appealing to his Kentucky readers, Nabob brought that state into his narrative frequently and especially when he could advocate directing trade to it. He said that Georgia planters bought their ropes and three million yards of bagging for their cotton bales from the Yankees. Why could not Kentucky provide these things? "Hitherto all this is procured from [Henry Ward Beecher's] Plymouth Church choristers of the Chittenden stripe, who swear by Thad. Stevens, pray with Brownlow, curse with Beast Butler, drink with Jack Hamilton, and subscribe for the New York Tribune and Tilton's 'Independent'. . . . Sitting in velvet arm chairs they coin millions from the sweat and toil of thousands of Southern men, and then rack their brains to invent some new process by which they can more effectually plunder, persecute and punish the very men who have enriched them." He called on Kentucky to produce this bagging and rope and to set up cotton factories to spin Southern cotton and to make the many things which Southerners must buy, so that no one would ever have to deal with the Yankees again.[12] Already Nabob was seeing sold on the Augusta market the Louisville-made Brinly plows, which he considered the best of all for Southern soil.[13] The *Courier* was much pleased by Nabob's campaign to direct trade to Kentucky, especially to Louisville, and agreed with it in an editorial, calling Nabob "our very able and intelligent Georgia correspondent."[14]

Kentucky, which had come out of the war in a better condition than the other Southern states and which was not included in the punishments inflicted by the Reconstruction program, was able to send aid to the impoverished Georgians for a year or two after the close of the war. Nabob gladly included his thanks in his letter which appeared in the *Courier* on August 1, 1867: "The noble munificence of your people in feeding the hungry, clothing the naked, and succoring the afflicted of ours, is gratefully appreciated in every home in the State. 'God bless the people of Kentucky,' is a portion of the daily prayers of all classes."[15] In wishing the people of Kentucky a merry Christmas, he could by contrast say of the people of Georgia, a land of woe, "No holly and ivy can gladden the desolate hearts, and no simulated mirth can deaden the gnawing sensation of hopeless misery which seems to dwell under every roof tree." And for the freedmen, Christmas was no longer the merry time it was in plantation days. The Negroes were now wandering around with only memories of their former masters' kindnesses.[16]

Though threatened but never under the heel of the Radical Reconstructionists, Kentucky was of all the Southern states "the last stronghold of constitutional liberty."[17] In Kentucky alone of all the Southern States," Nabob wrote, "is freedom regulated by law, cherished and maintained." He was hearing that many Georgians were thinking of migrating there.[18] When, in 1867, the state of Georgia was merged into Military District Number III and subjected to the mercies of its overlord John Pope, Nabob could tell his Kentucky readers, "All this forms a sad picture, and one which the free people of Kentucky will regard with horror. Where are our sufferings to end? and how much more are we required to bear? are questions which men ask each other in the agony of despair."[19]

In trying to steer the South out of Yankee colonialism, Nabob tried not only to include Kentucky in a new trade zone but he would also add the Northwest, of which Kentucky might well be considered the southern extremity. The combination of the South and the Northwest was an old dream of Southerners from the days of John C. Calhoun, which, had it been completed, might have saved the country from civil war. Nabob was now for reviving the plan. A trade and economic alliance between the two was logical and mutually helpful. Both were being exploited by the "saintly Puritans" and were being "ground to the earth by tariffs and every species of tact which Yankee ingenuity, sharpened by Yankee greed, can invent." He was frank to say, "We have done with revolutions which depend on Generals, Colonels, battalions, bayonets, big guns and quartermasters for their success. We have tried that, at an outlay of many thousands of millions of dollars and at a sacrifice of human life which can only be counted by the sobs and tears of our people." What was the solution? "The Northwest is rich and prosperous. The South is poor but productive."[20] One of the hurdles to be leaped was the iniquitous freight rates, which were already putting the thumbscrews on trade between the two sections.[21] Equitable rates must be established; but Nabob was never to live long enough to see that happen.

Always with Nabob was his ill health, which never seemed to mend for long. When, in the latter part of 1866, there was a skip of a letter or two, he explained, "Severe illness for the past ten days has been the cause of my silence since the 20th of November."[22] At other times he had to cut short trips which he had intended to make in search of news, as when he expected to go to South Georgia to give an account of the lumber industry "to be written under a venerable live oak on the banks of the Altamaha."[23] In an attempt to gain some strength, in the fall of 1867 he decided to spend a few days at the

Madison Springs, a famous ante bellum watering place, about twenty miles from Athens. He described its former glories and its deserted condition after the war; but it was still attended by a few guests and by people from the neighboring countryside on week-ends to hold their "twistification" dances. Nabob had been sent there by his doctors "to drink iron water and get strong." "During my brief stay," he explained, "I worked indefatigably to attain my object. I drank the water until the needle of a surveyor's compass would have been diverted from its true direction by my approach, and I became so strong that I could digest a chincapin, which are [sic] a staple article of food among the natives of this country." On leaving, he was presented a gallon of them, which he did not eat, and for that reason he was "still able to subscribe myself your, respectfully, NABOB."[24]

Perhaps the debilitating hot weather which he experienced in Macon and which he described in his letter of July 24, 1866, had something to do with his health. In an effort to ward off the heat, he said that the natives were fluttering and swaying back and forth palm leaf fans, and "every man, woman and child has got one or wants to get one, for the heat is intense, and real comfort only to be attained by Sidney Smith's recipe: 'Take off your skin and go about in your bones.'"[25]

For some time in 1868 Haldeman had been planning important innovations in the Louisville newspaper world. The other two dailies in the city besides his *Courier* were the *Democrat* and George D. Prentice's *Journal*. Haldeman gained control of these papers and consolidated them in November under the title of the *Louisville Courier-Journal*. In the meantime, on June 1 he had engaged Simon Boliver Buckner, the great Kentucky Confederate general, to take charge of the editorial page, a position which he held for only five months. Nabob was a casualty of this reorganization. His last letter appeared on May 16. Browne had seen it coming; May 12 he had written his friend Howell Cobb that the *Courier* had begun to take his letters fortnightly instead of weekly "and even for that pays very slowly."[26]

Earlier in the year, Browne had been trying to get some of his New York friends to interest the Brooks brothers, Erastus and James, of the *New York Express,* to hire him as their Southern correspondent, but nothing came of this. Browne wrote Barlow: "I wanted to make known the truth about the people and make a little money but like everything else I have tried since 1865, I have failed."[27] After the *Courier* ceased taking his letters, Browne wrote William Cassidy, editor of the Albany (N. Y.) *Atlas and Argus,* an intensely Democratic paper, hoping to interest him in taking weekly letters from the

South during the approaching presidential campaign. Even with the aid of Barlow, to whom he wrote "I need the employment sorely," Browne failed again.[28]

Never to give up, Browne wrote his old friend William Bradford Reed in September, 1868, that the *Philadelphia Age,* the principal Democratic newspaper in Pennsylvania, should publish more about what was going on in the South, and that if he would bring it to the attention of the editor, Browne thought that he could make arrangements to get a correspondent, if the paper could afford to pay "a moderate price, say $10 a letter. If it could, I could make the arrangement."[29] This was Browne's evasive way of securing the position for himself. Failure was again recorded.

But at this very time success came his way. Interest in the presidential campaign then going on induced the New York *World* to hire Browne as its Georgia correspondent. He chose to appear under the nom de plume "Auster," the Latin word meaning "south wind" or "south country." Browne as a newspaper correspondent never used his own name, no doubt to give him the freedom to say what he pleased without any embarrassment to any friend. His letters to the *World* continued through January, 1869, and they were all written with the dateline of Atlanta and Augusta. His letters were more political than they had been in the *Courier,* for he judged that there would be less interest in New York in local happenings in Georgia. It was probably Barlow who got him the position with the *World,* for Browne wrote him that he hoped the position would be permanent. "The 'pay' will be a great help," he said, "although it will not be much."[30] It was $10 a letter.

Browne could be as extreme as he pleased with his political philosophy, for the *World* was a Democratic paper (and, of course, Browne could have got a position on no other kind). Paying his respects to the Southern correspondents of Radical Northern newspapers, Browne recommended that when the Prayer Book should be revised there be added to the other plagues and calamities from which the people should be spared: "and from the correspondents of Northern Radical papers, 'Good Lord deliver us!' The plagues of Egypt were a tolerable infliction as compared with the swarm of letter-writers who are daily slandering and abusing the unfortunate people of the Southern States, and who are daily lying for hire to keep alive the animosities of the war, and thus furnish a bogus justification for the bogus laws of a bogus Congress." Their effusions were "no more like the truth than fusel-oil, tannin, and hydrant water are like *esprit de cognac,* or terra alba and ground beans are like extra family flour." As an example of their reporting, he cited the case of a fracas between some Negroes and white boys in Athens, in which one of the boys who was shot in the leg was unarmed, and as the old Irish expression had it in similar happenings, "he had nothing in his hand but his fist."[31]

As Browne's assignment with the *World* was of short duration, he was soon looking for other means to keep the wolf away from his door. Apparently he gave up trying to secure employment with Northern newspapers, and now he began looking for something from the less prosperous Southern fraternity. In May, 1869, the Augusta *Press* announced Browne's connection with "the political department of that journal" and praised him as "a trained and accomplished publicist and a ripe scholar." "Among the boldest and most earnest defenders of the rights of the South," it continued, "there was none bolder or more earnest than General Browne; and in the hour of her peril and distress, she had no more faithful and unselfish adherent than he proved himself to be."[32]

The *Press* was not one of Augusta's old and well-established newspapers, and it therefore had little to give Browne. After being with it for two months, he became the editor of the Macon *Daily Journal and Messenger,* which was now owned by the well-known book publisher, J. W. Burke and Company. As correspondent of the various aforementioned newspapers, Browne did not move his residence and his Lizzie from Athens—he merely traveled around for news from his home base; but now his editorship required him to stay in Macon. However, he still maintained his home in Athens for some time. Macon had a reputation for being in the summer unusually hot for Georgia towns, being down in a depression. Browne was soon being bothered by the heat and by mosquitoes, too, and he developed "a severe face ache which Dr. Hall calls 'malarial neuralgia.' " He began taking "immense quantities of quinine."[33] Browne made quite a success as editor of Burke's paper, which was to stand him in good stead at a later time. He was given credit for having started the "State News Column," which became a standard format with many newspapers.[34]

◀ XIII ▶

Commentator Browne

AS REPORTER FOR the *Louisville Daily Courier* and for the New York *World*, and in his correspondence with Barlow, Browne, with his keen mind and fixed philosophies of constitutional government and public policies, could not help but report, criticize, praise, and condemn men and measures of the passing scene. Hence, in this respect, he approached closely the role of a twentieth-century columnist, a Walter Lippmann, a Drew Pearson, but much more closely a David Lawrence or a William F. Buckley, Jr.

Unreconstructed and always to remain so, Browne disliked those Yankees who also were unreconstructed in their ways, and he could scarcely write about any one of them without characterizing him with some disparaging characteristic, as for instance one to whom he referred, too obscure to be mentioned by name, as a "sleek-faced, maple sugar eating Yankee from the other side of the White Mountains." [1]

But there were many who were notorious, and there was none against whom Browne liked to pour out his most choice expletives than Benjamin Franklin Butler of Massachusetts. "To call him a highway robber would be to compliment him," Browne wrote, "to elevate him from the degradation of the sneak thief, and slander the memory of Claude Duval and Dick Turpin." Browne said that he first saw Butler at the Democratic National Convention in Charleston in 1860.[2] When William D. Kelley ("Pig Iron Kelley"), long-time Congressman from Pennsylvania, visited the South after the war and passed through Georgia, Browne in noting him quoted an Irish couplet, which he thought quite appropriate,

> The d——l go with him and a bottle of moss,
> If he never comes back, he's no great loss.[3]

Browne was harsher in referring to Henry Wilson, a Senator from Massachusetts who visited Georgia in 1867. Wilson was "an unctious looking individual, heavy in the jowls, a sort of cross between Peck-

sniff and Uriah Heep—that is, Pecksniff without the shirt collar and
with his hair slick, and Heep without the blear eyes."[4] In characterizing George W. Julian, a Radical Congressman from Indiana, Browne
said that had he lived in the days of the Spanish Inquisition, his
"peculiar genius would have invented something which would have
thrown the rack and the thumb-screw into the shade."[5] As for John
Pope, the erstwhile commander of Military District Number III,
which embraced the State of Georgia, Browne took delight in playing on the name of the Pope of the Vatican. The Pope who was
tyrannizing the Georgians did not "wear a triple crown or carry the
keys of St. Peter." Instead, his brow was "adorned by a simple blue
cloth forage cap, and the symbols of his office are rather of the 'long
sword, saddle, bridle, whack-rowdy-dow' order."[6]

Of course, Sherman, who, had he been more resourceful in seizing
Savannah, might have captured Browne and his brigade, received no
praise. Browne was glad to report that he had attended the Presby-
terian Church in Athens and had heard a Reverend Mr. Murchison, a
Methodist minister from Columbia, South Carolina, tell of the terrible night in which Sherman had ordered the firing of the city. One
of Sherman's officers told Murchison that if the city was to be burned,
a blue rocket would be sent up, and a white one if the city was to be
spared. A blue rocket went up, and immediately soldiers with torches
swept the streets, and soon 84 of the 124 blocks of the city were
aflame.[7]

Browne could not help but dislike the Yankee "schoolmarms" who
came South to teach the freedmen social equality and other impracticable notions, which were sure to bring on a clash of the races, "the
consequences of which are horrible to contemplate." They "visit the
negro cabins on a footing of perfect equality, breakfast, dine, and sup
with the negroes."[8]

Browne kept track of what Congress was doing and made comments appropriate to his philosophy of government policies. An un-
speakable iniquity was the cotton tax, which was to take millions of
dollars from an impoverished South while farm products of a prosperous North remained untaxed. The Freedmen's Bureau, with many
broken-down preachers, politicians, and office-seekers, was stirring
up bad feeling between the races by dealing out partial decisions in
its courts.[9] The Civil Rights Bill of 1866, naturally, met the hostility
of Southerners. Calling it the "Civil Wrong Bill" of the "Central
Directory," Browne said that it did not "receive flattering notice at
the hands of the people of Georgia, and if their practical operation
depends on their receiving the popular ratification, I fear the gentle

Sumner and the impetuously philanthropic Thad. will have devoted their genius and energies to an unprofitable purpose."[10]

Of course, the proposed Fourteenth Amendment, which was submitted to the states in 1866, was anathema to Georgia as well as to the rest of the South. Browne said that to have accepted it would have "degraded the State and misrepresented the people" and dishonored and disfranchised those who had fought to uphold the honor of the state.[11]

The Congressional plan of Reconstruction, which was embodied in the three acts of March 2, 23, and July 19, 1867, was a bitter pill for Browne to contemplate, let alone to swallow. Referring to the Act of March 2, before knowing what was to follow in the next two acts, Browne said: "The whole bill is infamous. It commences with a falsehood and ends with a crime. Its every line is an outrage on the liberty it pretends to protect, and the climax of audacity is reached when it requires us voluntarily to accept it as the legitimate and proper exercise of constitutional power."[12] Reaching back into the history of Georgia when Governor George M. Troup had defied the Federal Government in the dispute over the removal of the Indians from the state, Browne exclaimed, "Oh! how the bones of Governor Troup must rattle in his grave if he is permitted to know how 'a Republican Government' is guaranteed in 1867 to the State he loved so well."[13]

The oath which was included in the second Reconstruction Act (March 23), which all voters were required to take and which excluded the old leaders of the South, prompted Browne to remark sarcastically that Southerners would not sear their consciences by stretching the facts to take the oath, for "we are a simple agricultural people, only just emerged from the barbarism of slavery, and not sufficiently instructed by the school marms to appreciate the beauties of false swearing."[14]

Lies, lies, lies—"Lies, infamous, disgusting lies," Browne said, "are the foundation on which public opinion is formed and which gives sanction to the lawless usurpations of the Radicals."[15] Looking at other components of Congressional Reconstruction, Browne mused: "If Job had been obliged to submit to the Freedmen's Bureau and Treasury agents, and then been required to perjure himself, in order to be allowed to earn his living, do you think he could have stood it?"[16] But after all, Browne's opinion of how effective workers the freedmen were varied with the times. In 1867, answering charges (constantly being peddled in the North) that atrocities had been leveled against them, Browne said that freedmen seemed to be doing very well after two years of freedom. "If the white men murder and lacerate negroes every morning, their victims do not seem to be aware of it, or have any dread of their persecutors."[17]

Under the Congressional plan of Reconstruction, the South was divided into military districts and over each a general of the Federal army was appointed to preside, with powers to supplant any state civil government if he should deem it desirable. This was the first step toward organizing a convention that would make a constitution agreeable to Congress. After this, new state governments should be set up; if each legislature ratified the Fourteenth Amendment, then the state might have representatives in Congress. Under rules requiring that an oath be taken by all prospective voters, an oath to which Browne had so strenuously objected, an election would be held to determine whether there should be a convention and to elect delegates to that convention if it should be agreed to. Browne predicted that the white people would vote the convention down, but, because he overemphasized the number of those who were disfranchised as rebels and the difficulty of getting by the Radical registers, Browne was mistaken; for 95,214 whites and 93,457 Negroes were registered, but the whites generally stayed away from the polls, and the convention carried by 102,283 to 4,127. As Browne beheld Negroes voting for the first time in their lives, he commented, "For the last five days every shade and hue of niggerdom has been voting early and often." Out of the 169 delegates elected, 37 were Negroes. And again Browne commented, "The delegates, with few exceptions, are 'to fortune and to fame unknown.' Outside of their villages no human being ever heard of them."[18]

To strengthen the organization of their party, the Conservatives, as the Democrats chose to call themselves at this time, held in Macon a convention on December 5 and 6, 1867 (a few days before the Constitutional Convention would meet in Atlanta). Browne was a delegate from Athens. The unterrified Benjamin H. Hill was chosen chairman. The convention resolved that it accepted the "legitimate results of the late war" but opposed the Reconstruction Acts and declared that the Constitutional Convention had been elected by "votes illegally authorized, forcibly procured, fraudulently received, and falsely counted."[19]

In furtherance of the program of the Macon Convention to resist Radical domination, the citizens of Athens held a meeting in the Town Hall on January 8, 1868. Browne was put on the committee to prepare resolutions, and with his facile pen he called on all citizens to give up partisan politics and work for the preservation of their liberties: "We ask them not to join a political party as party men, to secure the spoils of office. We are engaged in no such unworthy undertaking. The liberties of the country are at stake, and all that freedmen hold dear, and all that freedom means, is now in jeopardy, and we shall be unworthy our once proud State—unworthy representatives of American freedom—unworthy the race to which we belong—were we to cowardly yield our birthright without one effort to preserve it."

After the adoption of the resolutions, Browne was loudly called on to speak. He responded by attacking the Constitutional Convention and declaring that any constitution such a body should make could not be accepted by the white people of Georgia "without degradation." A Committee of Twenty Five, including Browne, was appointed to work in conjunction with the Central Executive Committee, which had been appointed by the Macon Convention.[20]

It was now Browne's pleasure for the next few months to attend the Constitutional Convention (December 9, 1867-March 11, 1868) in Atlanta and to write for the *Louisville Daily Courier,* and in his private correspondence, stinging denunciations of the personnel of the convention and of its activities. Mrs. Browne wrote Mrs. Howell Cobb, in Macon: "Genl. B. is going to see the monkey show and 'take notes.' "[21] Browne referred to it as the "Great Combination Show," likening it to a collection of animals impersonating prominent members of the convention. Mrs. Browne remarked that her husband's "description of the Menagerie at Atlanta is sickening. What will become of us if these people are not stopped in their course?"[22] Varying his epithets, Browne called the group the "Great Reconstruction Constitutional Free Nigger and Mean White Convention"[23] and declared that such "a collection of ignorance, knavery, malice and degeneration was never seen before."[24]

In characterizing individual Negro delegates, he said he was somewhat at a disadvantage in assessing their antecedents since he did not have "access to the plantation books" of their former owners;[25] but he added, "You can easily recognize a delegate when you see a wooly head tied up in a number of plaits like the mane of a race horse."[26] There was Henry M. Turner, whom Browne called "Demosthenes Turner." He was "a heavy, slate colored, pock-marked mulatto, of a dingy kind, with a round bullet head, clad in a long, clerical-looking black coat, a slouch hat, looped up at one side, carries a big black stick, walks wide, and looks greasy"; but Browne awarded him this compliment: He "avoids giving offense."[27] However, Browne could not offer as much to Aaron Alpeoria Bradley, a South Carolina Negro, whom Browne dubbed "Sing Sing Bradley" because of his penitentiary record in New York. Before the Convention had completed its work, Bradley was expelled unanimously for his use of obscene language and constant interruptions. Browne said that those who had heard "the obscene language and insolence of the negro dog, thought that a thousand lashes, well and honestly administered, would have been the appropriate punishment."[28] Browne called G. W. Ashburn, a North Carolina white delegate, "a night-blooming cereus."[29]

General John Pope, one of whose duties as commander of Military District Number III was to get a new constitution made for Georgia, was, of course, not a member of the Convention, but he was frequently asked to occupy a seat. As has already appeared, Browne described him as having only slightly less power than the Pope in Rome; and as for Irish-born Judge A. O. Lochrane, who had praised General Pope and was working in with the Radicals for the plums he was later to get, Browne remarked, "All that he is he owes to the South and Southern men, and when he undertook to laud his new masters he need not have rejoiced in the downfall of his benefactors."[30]

President Johnson, somewhat displeased with Pope, replaced him with General George G. Meade, who soon displeased the Georgians much more by dismissing Governor Charles J. Jenkins and appointing General Thomas H. Ruger in his place. Browne joined by many other Georgians began asking, "Who the—is Ruger?" Browne answered by saying that Ruger "helped to burn Atlanta with Sherman, took part in the great march to the sea, and after the war, was detailed to grind, oppress, bully and torture the people" of North Carolina, and "knows as much of the duties of Governor as he does of infinity of space."[31] Ruger took charge of his new satrapy on January 13, 1868, while the Convention was laboring to make a new constitution.

Among the numerous subjects that came under discussion at the convention, one of the most important was the relief of people who owed money; for days in and days out time was being devoted to this subject. Browne noticed on December 19, 1867, that the Convention "did nothing to-day but discuss repudiation as the essential to salvation."[32] Borrowing a thought from Lord Macaulay's writings, Browne drew a picture of a native of New Zealand visiting this "Great Speckled Reconstruction Convention" to see how democracy worked in the United States—and what a spectacle of rule under Radical Reconstruction met his eye![33]

Joseph E. Brown, whom General Browne had disliked since the war and whom he derisively dubbed "Our Jo," was not a member of the Convention, but now and then he was invited to occupy a seat; and he was not without influence and axes to grind. Always looking to the main chance, he was now working in with the Radicals. Besides making a constitution, the Convention moved the capital from Milledgeville to Atlanta, where it was holding its meetings. Joe Brown was in favor of the move because it would increase the value of property he owned in Atlanta. General Browne said that he "worked and talked and button-holed and hunnifuggled continually and persistently to effect this removal." "Never," the General said, "was so much whisky and so many bad cigars consumed by a population of the same size in the same space of time."[34]

After the adoption of the constitution there would come next the election of officials for the new state government, which the Radicals expected to fill from top to bottom with their own selections. And, of course, there were new Representatives and Senators to be sent to Washington, to take the seats which were denied to the Conservative Democrats in the first elections after the war. General Browne said that all the Yankees in Atlanta were "training for Congress" or for high state jobs. "Never since the world was made," said the General, "in any age or country, was such a scene presented as the scramble for office" when the Convention adjourned.[35] One of the chief powers in the Convention had been George W. Ashburn, who was expecting the new legislature to elect him a United States Senator; but before the election he was killed in Columbus, Georgia, under circumstances unbecoming an aspiring high official—his death blamed by the Radicals on the Ku Klux Klan, but General Browne said, "The belief is that he offended some Yankee soldiers, and that they and some negroes killed him."[36]

The other outstanding hopeful candidate for the Senate was General Browne's favorite whipping boy, Joe Brown, whom the General accused of "damnable treachery" and of "unrivalled meanness and falsehood." These charges were proved, the General argued, by the fact that Joe Brown, in campaigning throughout his North Georgia mountain counties for the adoption of the new constitution, told the people that the Convention's giving the Negroes the right to vote did not confer on them the right to hold office; and later, when the new legislature had been elected containing a good sprinkling of Negroes and Brown was asking their votes, he explained that he had to tell the North Georgians that, in order to get them to vote for the new constitution, which now gave the Negroes all their rights. The General asked whether Robert Toombs had not been justified "in his memorable allusion to Jo Brown? 'Ignoble villain! He has fa-

tigued public indignation by his infamy. He is buoyant only from corruption. He rises only as he rots.' "[37]

The election, which took place in April, 1868, was an all-inclusive
one. The voting was not only for the adoption of the constitution, which
authorized the election, but also for the legislature, the governor, and
the Representatives to the House in Washington, as if the constitution
were already in effect. Rufus B. Bullock, an erstwhite New Yorker,
was put up by the Radicals for governor; and General John B. Gordon, last at Appomattox, was allowed by General Meade to be
nominated by the Democrats after Meade had turned down two previous selections.

Writing for his Kentucky readers and appropriately using the language of the race track, Browne characterized the opening of the campaign in this fashion: "The saddling bell was sounded. The horses are
stripped and the jockeys are up, taking their preliminary canter in
front of the stand. The betting men are busy laying their bottom dollar, and though I am accustomed to 'this kind of thing,' never have
I been at a race which seemed to excite greater interest than that
which is just to come off. The entries for the first and most important
prize, the Governor's slate are as follows." Browne then produced
Gordon, the perfect thoroughbred, festooned with garlands of flowery
compliments. "His competitor," Browne continued, "is a big, flabby,
long-haired, beefy looking animal, raised in some one of the river
counties in New York, of what stock nobody knows, lately imported
into Georgia *to draw an express wagon,* of heavy lumbering action
docile only to negroes, bites and kicks at white people, and ridden by
an awkward light weight, utterly unscrupulous, named Scalawag, one
of his owners." Gordon was ridden by "White-man."[38]

Browne never referred to Bullock without using the initials
"C. O. D.," a play of words on his express business when he first
came to Georgia, or "his bovine excellency," a play of words on his
name, or "express Bullock." Walter L. Clift, a candidate for the
Congress from Chatham County and a carpetbagger of less than a
year's standing in Georgia, Browne called "the 'little he-school-marm'
from Skowhegan [Maine]."[39] And Ben Conley, who succeeded in
getting elected to the legislature, Browne later termed "the ex-shoe-
maker, who now presides over the Senate of Georgia, by the grace of
Radicalism."[40]

The Radicals, of course, expected to ride into power on the backs
of the Negroes, bringing in a few for the aid given. One of the ditties
of the campaign, entitled "The Song of the Radicals," ran this way:

I'm glad the niggers free,

I'm glad the niggers free.
The niggers free,
And votes for me,
I'm glad the niggers free.[41]

Browne said that the "loyal leagues will compel the negroes with very few exceptions to vote for the radicals. Poor devils they ought to be forgiven for they know not what they do."[42] As he looked on the "gallant Gordon" and then on the "bovine Bullock," he had the deep feeling that Providence would "never afflict Georgia to the degree of allowing her gallant son to be defeated by a Radical carpet-bag Yankee."[43] But he was really whistling in the dark, and he knew it.

The election was to continue over a period of four days and thus prolong the agony of Browne and the Democrats and give the managers of the election machinery every opportunity to engage in corrupt practices. On April 22, 1868, in the midst of the voting, he wrote Barlow, in New York, "We are in the throes of an election on the result of which depends everything that can make life desirable to a decent man. We have all the odds against us." Those in charge of the election were "without a single exception rampant radicals. . . . Our people have no spirit, no energy, and no money to prosecute a successful canvass." Writing from Athens, he continued, "In this little town a negro blacksmith and a cornfield negro from the country are the favored candidates for the legislature and I have great fears that they will be elected. Neither is above the ordinary run of field-hands but both as vindictive as rattlesnakes. The town swarms with negroes. To get to the polls you have to take your place in a long line of bustling elbowing negroes, & bear the bustling and elbowing for hours before you reach the registers, who regard you as an enemy & put you to every delay, inconvenience and humiliation they possibly can."[44]

In his dispatch to the *Louisville Daily Courier,* Browne gave a vivid description of Negroes going through the act of voting. "It is impossible," he wrote, "for the imagination to conceive such a scene as the election. It must have been seen to be appreciated." The ignorant black masses chanted as they approached the ballot boxes, " 'I'se gwine to wote."[45]

When the voting and shouting were over, Browne wrote Barlow: "Bullock is our Governor. This town [Athens] containing the seat of learning is represented by a negro blacksmith and a cornfield *nigger,* neither of whom can distinguish B from a bull's foot. Aaron Bradley a negro felon is a senator from Savannah. A negro now in jail for stealing [Henry M. Turner] represents Macon. [Foster] Blod-

gett whom two grand juries (one of his own selection) have indicted
for perjury is to be one of our U. S. Senators and Jo Brown will be
the other."[46] (Browne was here guessing, and he was wrong in both
instances.)

In this evaluation of the outcome of the election, Browne was more
pessimistic than usual, for although losing the governorship, the
Democrats and their kindred Conservative Republicans carried by a
majority of four the lower house of the legislature. And among those
elected to this branch was John A. Cobb, Browne's friend since the
war, from a county having a majority of Negroes.[47]

In the division of the spoils of the election, the Negroes won three
places in the Senate and twenty-nine in the House; but they were not
allowed to hold them, for it had been widely understood that the right
to vote did not include the right to hold office. Soon all were expelled
and their places given to white candidates. Browne represented the
Negroes as cursing, " 'de de——d carpet baggers, scalawags, and
white folks who want to deprive de nigger of his rights.' "[48] He put
the spotlight more particularly on Turner, quoting him as asking,
" 'Am I a Man?' " and Browne replied: "a question which has not
yet been answered, and on which his own doubts were somewhat
justifiable."[49]

Soon other dissensions in addition to those between the Negroes
and the whites in the legislature arose in the Radical camps, much to
the glee of Browne, who reported in the New York *World* that "the
rogues have fallen out, and the scalawags, carpet-baggers, and niggers
—the unholy political trinity of modern times—are no longer a happy
family. The scalawags for the most part are 'down on' the carpet-
baggers, and the carpet-baggers are 'down on' the scalawags, and the
niggers, convinced of the utter perfidy of both, have come to the very
sensible conclusion that they 'haint no use' for either." As for Governor Bullock, "He is so elated by his extraordinary rise from the express wagon to the Executive chair that he fancies himself omni-
present,"[50] but his "bovine excellency" still had to have his secretary
correct some of his Yankee language, such as "hadent orter."

Browne emphasized that the Negroes were not content with the
political crumbs they were getting from the Radical table and that
they might attempt serious trouble. "A few negroes and white radicals
are very turbulent," he said, "and would be violent if they dare, but
they have no Toussaint l'Ouverture to lead them, and their white allies
have not the love of carnage and bloodshed which Homer attributes
to Ajax."[51] This situation might portend something good for the
Democrats, Browne thought: "There are encouraging reports of

democratic conversions among the negroes but I do not attach much importance to them. Political steadfastness among our African 'citizens' can only be secured in one way and I fear that in our impoverished condition that way cannot be much followed."[52]

The year 1868 saw not only the election of a new state government in Georgia under Radical blessings, it also saw the election of a new president of the United States, and the South was now considered to be so Radicalized that it would help to put a Radical candidate in the president's chair. For a time it looked as though President Johnson might not be allowed to serve out his term, as the Radicals had impeached him in the House and were now holding a trial in the Senate to remove him. Browne was somewhat concerned over the probability of his removal, for if that happened, Benjamin F. Wade, a most vindictive Radical who was president of the Senate, would succeed to the presidency. Browne asked Barlow, "Do you think our friends here who are unpardoned are in any danger if Wade is made president? Let me hear from you on this."[53]

It soon became evident that General Ulysses S. Grant would become the candidate of the Radicals, who now controlled the Republican party. Who would become the Democratic candidate was not so certain. For a time Browne had the feeling that he should keep out of national politics, for he had lost faith in Northern Democrats as a source of any protection or sympathy for the South. "Why does not the Democratic Party at the North do something to encourage us," he asked Barlow, "and identify itself in sympathy at least with the Conservatives at the South?"[54] Browne was now wallowing in the pessimism that siezed him now and then. Barlow suggested to him some plan of procedure for the South, the nature of which is not known. Browne replied that he would see what he could do, but he feared it would be very little, for most Southern leaders were disfranchised: "I will do what I can. Broken down in health and fortune as well as in spirit I cannot do as much as I once could 'in the brave days of old.' "[55]

Writing again, he poured forth more pessimism. "I can see no hope for this country [the South]," he said. "It has gone down, down, down ever since the surrender. . . . And with negro legislatures, juries, and executive officers, we must sink into a deeper abyss than any we have yet sounded. . . . The law is really silent for the protection of the white man. No one who has money enough to emigrate will remain here, and in the not distant future I see that most dreadful of all calamities, a war of races." "If I could sell my land or raise enough money to pay my railroad fare," he said,

"I would not stay here a week." He pronounced both parties no good, "with their swindling platforms and claptrap confessions of faith . . . [which are] worthless to us." But the South would support the nominee of the National Democratic Convention, which was to meet in New York, whoever he might be. As for the Republicans, "Grant is not one whit less radical than Wade, and he [has] far less sense & capacity."[56]

Browne agreed with Barlow that the South should stand back and play no part in nominating the candidate and writing the platform and thus keep as far as possible out of the campaign the "bloody shirt" and "rebel atrocities" battle cries which the Radicals were sure to play up.[57] Browne told Howell Cobb that Georgia could "stand any candidate that may be chosen at New York."[58]

Browne was being asked to be one of the delegates to the New York Convention, but health and finances, he said, prevented his going. George H. Pendleton of Ohio, Thomas A. Hendricks of Indiana, and Winfield S. Hancock of Pennsylvania were the main contenders in the voting for eighteen ballots, with Hancock and Hendricks becoming the leaders on the twenty-first, when suddenly Horatoio Seymour, the chairman of the Convention, whose name had not been voted on previously, was nominated unanimously.

Browne now took on new life and became actively engaged in the campaign. A meeting of the citizens of Athens was held in late June with Browne in the chair. It organized a Democratic club with a constitution and by-laws and with Browne one of the vice presidents. The meeting could not adjourn without a speech from Browne, who spoke "in his usual effective and happy style."[59] A few weeks later he attended as a delegate from Athens the State Democratic Convention in Atlanta and was appointed to the Business Committee for his Congressional District (the Sixth).[60]

Determined that Georgia should cast her electoral votes for Seymour, Browne in August made a trip to New York to see Barlow, Samuel J. Tilden, erstwhile Confederate General Dick Taylor, and other New York friends and leaders, in the hopes of securing a campaign fund of at least $15,000.[61] Apart from the cordial reception given him by his close friends, he found in others a somewhat condescending and patronizing attitude, as if to say that they would not let the past interfere with private relations, but "let the South row her own boat. If she wins, so much the better, if not it does not matter as Seymour can be elected without Southern votes." [62]

Browne was able to raise only $500, and he reported, "I regret to say [I] utterly failed in my mission, and impressed with the belief that

Georgia must take care of herself." [63] Though disappointed, he was
not discouraged. He wrote Barlow, "We are jogging along here. We
shall carry Georgia without a doubt." To sample Democratic prospects
in the Middle West, Browne returned by way of Ohio, Indiana, Kentucky, and Tennessee. In Tennessee he found "conditions of things
. . . really appalling. I expect every day to hear of a war between
the radicals & negroes and the mass of the white citizens." He was
told in Nashville that thousands of Negroes were drilling every day
"and that at any moment a spark may fire the magazine and envelope
the whole State in ruin & blood."[64] In a dispatch to the New York
World, Browne repeated his prediction: "The people of Georgia
are determined to carry their own State, if she is the only State in
the Union which casts her vote for the Democratic candidates." [65]

Browne did not neglect to comment on the campaign the Radicals
were waging in Georgia. In describing a mass meeting which they
held in Atlanta, he said,

White scalawags were invariably the orators. They "talked powerful,"
and the poor darkies looked on in blank amazement, utterly unconscious
of one word that was said. The only regret was that so many able-bodied
cotton-pickers were drawn away from their proper field of usefulness to
listen to the ungrammatical bosh of a set of unprincipled vagabonds, who
are trying to use the poor negro for their own benefit. The love of the
carpet-bagger for the freedman is aptly expressed in the following verse:

> "I know not, I ask not,
> How much you can tote;
> I know that I love you,
> Because you can vote." [66]

Browne was not troubled by any inconsistency in his feeling of outrage at the act of Negroes voting, if they voted the Democratic ticket.
As the campaign neared its end he predicted that "thousands of negroes, tired of Radical promises and disgusted with Radical acts,
will vote the Democratic ticket. Georgia's nine votes may be counted
on for Seymour and Blair as certainly as if they had been already
cast." He said that he had traveled over North Georgia counties, and
they were sure to go Democratic.[67]

But Browne could not forget that the mass of the Negroes were in
the Radical camp, and he did not miss an opportunity to use his
most choice derogatory phrases in commenting on this combination.
He described for the readers of the New York *World* a meeting of
the ebony blacks and scalawag whites in Macon to nominate a candidate for Congress:

I have seen the stock brokers at "high change," I have seen a number of Neopolitan ass-drivers trying to make their way through one of the narrowest streets in Pompeii. I have seen an Irish fair after some adventuresome individual has tread on the tail of some pugnatious individual's coat, and I have seen the House of Representatives in Washington during a nights sojourn, but were all these—stock brokers, ass-drivers, Irishmen and Congressmen—rolled into one, they would be an ordinary assembly compared with the fifty or sixty negroes and three or four white men whom I saw assembled in a dilapidated school-house to select a representative in the Congress of the United States! . . . When I got to the door of the room, I found everybody, white and black, yelling, screaming and stamping like howling dervishes in the last stage of religious fervor, the chairman pulverising his table with his hammer in the belief that he was thereby preserving order.[68]

If the Macon meeting nominated anyone, Browne apparently was unable to find out who he was; but he was well informed on the Radical hopefuls throughout most of Georgia. There was blackman *"Senator* Aaron Alpeoria Bradley, of Sing Sing Penitentiary," who hoped to be the Radical nominee in the Savannah District; and up the river in Augusta, Charles Henry Prince, "from Maine or Vermont [Maine being correct]," was the Radical candidate. Browne was uncertain whether Prince was from Maine or Vermont, but he did know this: "He is truly loil all over, is partial to negro society, and from what I can learn, is quite a *beau* among the wenches of Augusta, with whom he trips it on the light fantastic toe after they get away from the cooking stove, the wash tub and the sweeping brush." [69] In fact, Browne thought it would be good strategy for Georgia to send her "most odiferous" Negroes to Congress: "Indeed, I think it would be preferable to send Africans to Washington, unless it be cruel to force good hoe or plow hands to associate with Beast Butler, [James M.] Ashley and Joe Holt." [70]

One of the most effective weapons to win support in the North and, it was hoped, to win votes in the South was the battle cry of "rebel atrocities and outrages." Whether planned for campaign purposes or not, a riot took place at Camilla in September, in which a half-dozen Negroes or more were killed. In proper sarcastic language Browne told his New York readers about it: "The Georgia branch of the 'Outrage Factory,'" . . . has just turned out a most admirable 'outrage' with rebel attachment, negro escapement, and a lie condenser of remarkable capacity. . . . For a long time it has been clear to the impartial observers that the Radicals in Georgia were in special need of an outrage of goodly proportions, in which large numbers of gentle, unoffending and intelligent negroes, exercising their Constitutional rights in the most peacable manner, were to be killed and wounded by rebels, traitors, copperheads, and democrats, acting under the immediate orders of Seymour and Blair, and the Democratic party." [71]

In early October, Browne gave a further description of Radical campaign activities: "The Radicals have a lie manufactory established here [Atlanta] in connection with and auxiliary to the outrage factory which turned out its first piece of work at Camilla on the 19th ultimo. They are using documents by the millions for circulating among the negroes to be read to them by the schoolmarms and bureau agents, in which the art of lying is carried to a degree of perfection which cannot be excelled by the most ingenious Butlerite of the 'Spoon district' of Massachusetts." [72]

In the presidential election, Georgia cast her votes for Seymour and Blair, a performance which as greatly pleased General Browne as it disappointed "Jo" Brown. "Jo" had hoped to get a seat in Grant's cabinet, but with Georgia going Democratic there was now no chance. However, "Jo" was strengthening himself with the Radicals for future favors by letting it be known that he no longer believed that the right to vote did not qualify a person for holding office. This change gave General Browne a chance to get in a devastating blow against "Jo": "He accounts for this little diversity of opinion by saying that 'them was my senti*ments* (great emphasis on *ments*) with lights then before me.' This is no exaggeration of the perfidy of this infamous man. It is literally true." [73]

Not only "Jo" but also the whole Radical establishment was disappointed at the Radical defeat in Georgia. It delighted General Browne to be able to say, "The small circle of notorious characters which constitutes the Radicals of Georgia are beside themselves with anger and mortification because the State has given a majority of probably 30,000 [actually 45,688] for Seymour and Blair. What intensify their rage and chagrin is that thousands of African citizens voted the Democratic ticket openly, defiantly and exultingly." [74] And as for "bovine Bullock," "he pulls his long red mustache, winks one eye with an urbanity and dignity all his own, and alluding to the Democratic party of Georgia, declares confidentially to the select company by which he is surrounded, 'Them fellahs is a bad egg, sure.' " [75]

It must not be inferred that Browne because of his deep interest in politics, state and national, was an office-seeker; apart from the four years of the Confederacy, he never held at any time in America a political office of any kind. Yet his interest in politics continued to the very day of his death, not in just practical politics but in how it conformed to his theories of good government and of the application of constitutional limitations on the national authority. As election followed election, Browne was never without his comments. His political conversations with his acquaintances and in letters to his friends, especially to Samuel Latham Mitchill Barlow, continued all his life, but after 1869 he was never again a newspaper correspondent pouring forth his comments on men and measures, as he had been doing in the *Louisville Daily Courier* and the New York *World*.

In the presidential campaign of 1872 he remained comparatively silent. He did not like the way the Democrats ran off in the "New Departure" to accept Horace Greeley and his Liberal Republicans. "We believe in Democratic principles pure and simple," he said, "and think that the people of the South, if they are wise, will have nothing to do with 'national conventions.' " [76] Not always agreeing with Alexander H. Stephens, in this instance he could write him: "Heartily, most heartily do I concur with your noble defense of constitutional liberty & your scathing exposure of the new departurists. I mean to follow your lead with all my might, feeble tho' it be. I detest expediency. It is only another name for lying." [77]

There were early signs that 1876 would be a Democratic year; and Browne began picking up interest again in national politics. He was attracted by an "Open Letter to General Garfield," [78] a devastating attack on Garfield and the Republican party, written by Jeremiah S. Black, whom Browne had known well when he was Attorney General and later Secretary of State in Buchanan's cabinet. In a letter to Black, Browne said that he was speaking not only for himself but also for "the people of the South" in thanking him for his "recent scathing exposure of Yankee intolerance, cruelty, lawlessness, hypocrisy, and dishonesty." It was "one of the ablest defenses of the Constitution I have read during the last fifteen years."

In re-introducing himself, he began his letter, "You have not forgotten altogether, I hope, William M. Browne, who was Editor of the Constitution, in those better days of the Republic, when the Constitution of the United States was in fact, as in name, the supreme law of the land, and when public officials who would not steal were the rule and not, as now, the exception." He hoped "you will think of me with the same kindness you always manifested toward me in the good old days." He had often thought of Black and had desired to see him again, but he rarely went North "and our ways are so wide apart, I have not had the pleasure of seeing you, since we parted in the White House in December 1860." Browne said that he would like to hear from Black should he find the time and the inclination to write. He then mentioned his present situation, "now alone in the world," having lost his wife three years previously. He had "entirely abandoned editorial & political life" and was at that time a professor in the University of Georgia, "where I teach our young men Constitution as the fathers framed it," not as the Radicals were then interpreting it.[79]

It is not known that a correspondence followed between these two "old-timers" of the Buchanan administration, but they were certainly kindred spirits in their interpretation of the United States Constitution. As usual, Browne exchanged views with Barlow, with whom he had scarcely ever disagreed except on secession and the Confederacy. Barlow was always glad to hear from Browne and, writing on April 25, 1876, he said:

. . . still more at this time when the views of our Southern friends & allies are so important to us. As a matter of mere policy, I assume that the South will have no candidate, in the sense of presenting and pressing anyone for the nomination until the wishes of the Northern Democracy, and especially of their friends from the States which we can control are first plainly announced, and that they will unite in making the nomination. Tilden or Bayard can carry N. Y. & Conn. Possibly Thurman might do the same. Hendricks can carry neither in my judgment and I look upon his nomination as nearly impossible, his election entirely so. I think Tilden has today the best hope of a nomination, but until the forces of all candidates are arrayed, no one can predict the action of the Convention. I am of course for Tilden. He will be earnestly presented by N. Y. He is an able, honest man with some elements of strength not possessed by any other person. But in the conflict he may be put aside by the friends of Hendricks or some other Western man and then it seems to me Bayard must be nominated. Personally I prefer him to any other candidate and I believe we can win with him.[80]

Browne liked Bayard best, but he was willing to take Tilden just as heartily, and he believed that Tilden would run just as well in the South. In fact, he felt that any Democrat could be elected.[81] Barlow had the same belief, but he suggested this qualification: "No one can tell how much force there may be in the old cry of *Rebel* nor in the [power?] of the bloody shirt. I hope our people have learned something in ten years." [82]

Tilden was nominated and almost everyone thought that he had been elected until the Republican conspirators decided that they might be able to count in their candidate, Rutherford B. Hayes. And thus developed the famous disputed election of 1876.

Though Georgia and all the rest of the South had cast their electoral votes for Tilden, South Carolina, Florida, and Louisiana (where the Radicals were still in control) were counted for Hayes, and he was declared elected by one vote. This outcome left Browne disconsolate. The democratic processes of government had failed, and he looked upon the future of the country with deep foreboding. He wrote Barlow: "Fifteen years of unconstitutional government, of 'military necessity,' of expediency and all for saving the Union, (God save the mark!) have so accustomed the people to the lawlessness of lawgivers, that they will even accept as truth the decision of a Louisana Returning Board." Continuing, he said, "No, my good friend, the Government is gone, the Constitution is as dead as the hieroglyphics on Cleopatra's Needle, and you and I and those who thought and acted as we did in better days, must submit unconditionally to Grant, Morton, Logan, Kellogg, and Chamberlain. O tempora, O mores!"[83]

Browne seemed to get some consolation in pouring out his soul in letters to Barlow as he was losing faith in the salvation of his country from dishonesty and military dictatorship, expecting Grant to bridge the gap before Hayes might take over. "Men" he said, "do not commit forgery, purgery, murder, arson, and robbery, not to talk of such petty offences as treason or such a menial crime as violating the Constitution without a settled purpose." He was writing this letter on December 18, before Congress had adopted a method of settling the election. In black despair, he told Barlow: "What little of life is left me is not worth much to anyone; but God knows I would yield it up today if by so doing I would avert the terrible calamity that I believe threatens this country in the immediate future."[84]

When Hayes had been seated and the worst of Browne's fears had faded, Barlow wrote him on August 10, 1877, in a hopeful spirit. "Hayes seems inclined to do justice to the South," he said, "& so glad am I at this, that I sometime forget the fraud & swindle of his election. The fact is that while I earnestly supported the Candidacy of Tilden, I did so simply because no other person was available, and I fear that I did not in the end shed half as many tears on his account as I might have dropped for a more [worthy?] and less self seeking a man."[85]

Browne stood steadfastly for the " 'lost' cause," and the principles of government that it represented; and he believed the "cause" was not "lost" if the people would stand back of it. In his Confederate Memorial Address in 1874 he had referred to the "demoralization of our people as the saddest and most hopeless sign of the times, . . . [their] barter of honor and principle for a dirty office excused, and the worship of expediency openly recommended." As for himself, "I aim to lift the flag, revive the faith and stay the progress of demoralization." And he told Jefferson Davis in a letter, when he mentioned him as a supporter of that point of view lusty cheers from a thousand voices greeted the mention of his name. On reporting to Davis on the condition of some of the Georgia leaders of a more heroic age, he said that Alex Stephens was dying, that Ben Hill wanted to go to Congress, and "Toombs is drunk all the time. Every second man in the state is a candidate for office. The people are as poor as they can be and escape destitution."[86]

Four years later (September 10, 1878), in bringing Davis up to date on Georgians, Browne said that he sensed their gradual acceptance of the supremacy of the national government to the negation of states' rights and sovereignty. It was disquieting to see people he had trusted and respected " 'accepting the situation' and eating the leek with apparent gusto." He was "astonished to see how wide & complete the demoralization has become. The total abandonment of the Constitution and the acceptance of the supremacy of the *nation* & the *national* government are regarded as 'the fruits of the war.' " Browne was, of course, not advocating another secession and war, but he was forever opposed to meekly abandoning a manly attitude toward the principles the South had fought for. Again giving a rundown on the Georgia leaders, Browne wrote Davis, "Toombs is still going about swaggering, blustering, boasting,—amusing the gaping multitude and disgusting all sober people. Stephens is hobbling all over his district making furious speeches, with all the dramatic effect of wheel chair, crutches, being 'toted' by a negro boy & defending his record, and no opposition, a unanimous nomination. . . . Joe Brown is sneaking about trying to defeat Gordon for the Senate, a vain effort." But General Browne had to put in this little reservation on Gordon: that although "he has been unnecessarily and disquietingly vociferous for one nation, one government &c he is the best we have & he will be reelected. . . . [Alfred H.] Colquitt [governor of Georgia], true, honest, manly, ever ready to defend the right," held his own in the hearts of the people. "Without any intellectual superiority of a marked kind, he is really great. I like him especially because he has been & is undeviatingly devoted to you." James Jackson, a judge on the Georgia Supreme Court, was "universally esteemed & respected—deservedly so." All of these men Davis had known, but there was "a host of small fry of whom you know nothing, making a great stir in their respective little puddles, in their eagerness for office from the Senate down to the county court bailiff. There is not one of them who does not apparently believe he could instruct you, Calhoun or Clay."[87]

Browne vacillated considerably in his evaluation of Stephens, from ante bellum days, through the war, and on down. Undoubtedly Stephens never had much love or respect for Davis, not only covertly but also openly making cutting remarks about him. Referring to something which Stephens had recently said about Davis, Browne in 1881 wrote Davis about it and threw out the question, "When were you scared of Mr. S. or any one else?"[88] But when Stephens died two years later, Browne exerted special efforts to attend his funeral in Atlanta, now forgetful of all but the good in him and remarking, he "has been so long and earnest a friend of mine, I feel bound to show his memory every respect in my power."[89]

In national politics, Browne came around somewhat to the belief of Barlow, that Hayes was making a better president than his theft of the office had ever suggested to anyone in the South. But his interest in presidential elections had subsided by 1880, and even the gubernatorial campaign of that year in Georgia repelled him. This was so because of the bitter factional struggles within the Democratic party, which were evident in its nominating convention this year, when five uncompromising candidates sought the nomination and the convention had to adjourn without making a selection. The convention merely recommended Browne's friend Colquitt, who had in the election the unsuccessful opposition of Thomas M. Norwood, another Democrat. The Republicans put up no candidate. Browne expressed his general disgust in this wise: "There is a line in the National Anthem of England which I sing in spirit, if not in voice every evening after I read the newspapers giving the news of the present disgusting canvass in Georgia. It is, 'Confound their politics, frustrate their knavish tricks.'" [90]

Browne could not make a living in politics when he never ran for any office nor was there much to be made in writing dispatches for the *Louisville Daily Courier* or the New York *World*. He had first tried the legal profession without success and then newspaper editing and reporting without much more success; but at the same time he had in mind other things to try, and in the course of his varied activities, they must come next.

⚜ XIV ⚜

Farmer

IN AUGUST, 1865, when Browne took the oath of allegiance to the United States after having been a Confederate citizen and soldier for four and a half years, he gave his occupation as "farmer." Tilling the soil being one of the oldest occupations of civilized man, Browne felt that farming would be the easiest to fall back into; as the owner of about fifty acres on the outskirts of Athens he had something to begin with.

True enough, his land was not much in quality. It was "poor grey surface, and red clay foundation," and some of it was "old second-growth pine field," which he did not clear until the next year.[1] And the workmen, who were the Negroes recently freed from slavery, could not be depended upon. "No system of compensation, no amount of pecuniary interest [whether wages, part of the crop with house and patches for gardens free, or other forms of tenancy]," Browne said, "has been sufficient to overcome the natural idle and slothful, improvident nature of the animal."[2] And after he had seen the Negroes on the coast below Savannah, he declared: "It is as much a libel on mankind to call him a human, as it would be to assign a gorilla to be the *genus homo*."[3]

As the war ended too late in the spring for Browne to put in a crop of cotton, there was little more that he could do than plant a garden and begin to prepare his land for the following year. In the late fall of 1865 and early spring of 1866 he applied 3,530 pounds of phosphate, which cost him $88.25;[4] and he did what might probably be called the very first thing a farmer should do: he provided a cow for his wife to milk. This Browne did even before the war ended. He borrowed from his good friend Colonel David Crenshaw Barrow, a large plantation-owner in Oglethorpe County a few miles away, a cow and calf. When about a year later when he was ready to return them, he explained that he would have done so earlier, but to do so in the midst of the winter, when there was no grass, "would have been too Yankee for my ideas." The next time Barrow should send any of his men up to Athens, Browne hoped that they might take the stock back with them. He would have sent them back, he explained, "but I have no freedmen on whom I can rely." [5]

When the winter of 1865-1866 broke into welcomed spring, Browne's spirits picked up. In March he wrote Howell Cobb, now practicing law in Macon: "I have quit politics, given up writing letters, and taken to planting Irish potatoes, ploughing, pounding bone dust, and other pursuits of an especially rural and loyal nature." [6] Browne was stretching a point for effect when he said that he was "ploughing," unless he meant that he himself was doing it, for he wrote Cobb about the same time: "I may want to have my field ploughed (and I do by the way and cannot get a freedman to do it) but I will not stand your asserting the right to do it (I wish you would in my case, and I would pocket the invasion of personal rights)." [7]

Offering advice to the public in general, but not accepting it himself, Browne said, "The despotism of King Cotton is, I hope, 'played out,' and with it the old planting system." [8] But he himself could not refrain from planting cotton, for the price in Augusta in the fall of 1865 was 42 cents for good middling. At that price, if he could raise a big crop, he would be on the road to affluence. In a gleeful spirit of anticipation he wrote Howell Cobb that he would be surprised "when you see the bales upon bales of the staple ready for market." But there was one great problem—getting seeds to plant. He explained further: "I can not get seed here for love or money particularly not for love. There are reasons why I do not experiment with the latter."[9] He was hoping to get enough seed from John A. Cobb, Howell's son, whom Browne had got detailed during the war to manage some of the Cobb plantations.

At about this same time, still facetiously building castles, not exactly on thin air but on cotton bales, he wrote Cobb further: "The prospect of my cotton crop (if Johnny [John A. Cobb] sends me the seed he promised, in time) would almost [assure?] Browne & Rutherford [his law firm] in building a [cotton] factory, but with a prudence for which they are famed, intensified by their singular apprehension that free niggers do not work as well as chattels—that moral elevation, social equality & political superiority do not increase the African's capacity to weed a row,—they will abandon the factory scheme.

"If the frost spare us we shall have a good garden & plenty of fruit, and with corn at $1.90 per busl., meat 25c, beef 15c, peas $1.25 [per bushel] and Willie Arnold hanging fire with that fee [reference to a law case], I am interested in the forbearence of frost.

"I whistle loudly to keep up my courage & try to affect fortitude";
and, probably not very seriously this early in his farming activities, he
added that if he could sell his land, "I ought to migrate to some
place where it is easier for a poor rebel to earn an honest livelihood." [10]

Writing in July, 1866, to Howell Cobb, Jr., who was now living
in Milledgeville, about sixty-five miles to the south, Browne asked,
"How are *craps* down your way?" He reported that his cotton was
not doing very well. "My cows are nearly dry," he said, "my mare has
the distemper. The chickens all have the pip or some other fatal complaint, & my turkeys have asserted their independence & taken to the
woods. . . . Seriously we want rain badly." [11] The drought was killing
the corn in much of Georgia during the early summer, and then later
incessant rains were ruining the cotton crop.[12] As a result, Browne's
first year of farming, ending with gathering his crops in the fall of
1866, was almost a failure. And what cotton he was able to pick
brought on the Augusta market in December only 32 cents—a drop
of 10 cents a pound from the previous year.

Undoubtedly, Colonel Barrow had a great deal of influence in
turning Browne to farming and even in arousing in him daydreams
of becoming a great planter, just as Barrow himself was. Browne
referred to the Colonel as "a very particular friend" [13] and as "one
of the largest planters of the State." [14] And on another occasion he
enlarged his compliment by introducing him as "a large planter, a
practical business man, a good presiding officer, and a gentleman
of considerable culture and intelligence." [15] In 1863, Browne had
asked Barrow if he knew of any Oglethorpe County property for sale
"valued at about $20,000" which he would recommend for him to
buy.[16] Later in the war, Browne saw that three overseers were detailed
to Barrow's Oglethorpe plantation, and when Browne came to Georgia in 1864 to manage conscription, he made Barrow a member of
the Advisory Board of Clarke County.[17]

Now, even with a bad taste in his mouth made by his first year
of farming, and in the face of his belief that King Cotton was being
dethroned (and should be) and that big plantations were fast fading
into history, Browne decided to act on Colonel Barrow's recommendation that he buy an Oglethorpe plantation adjoining the Barrow one.
On November 8, 1866, Browne bought from Ferdinand Phinizy, a
large landholder and businessman, a tract of 810 acres of land
on the waters of Big Creek. The price was $3,600, or a little less than
$4.50 an acre. With money "as scarce as Radical honesty," [18] as
Browne put it, and interest from 2 per cent to 3 per cent a month, he
was able to complete the transaction by giving Phinizy two promis-

sory notes of $1,200 each, one falling due after two years and the other running three.[19] Browne counted on keeping on the place a freedman and his wife who were there and bringing in other freedmen as he could.[20]

Clara Elizabeth, one of Colonel Barrow's attractive daughters, who was known to her friends as Bessie, took great pleasure in telling how Browne was carried away with his new plantation. "You would be amused if you could hear him talk of Oglethorpe," she wrote. "One would really suppose he expects to accomplish wonders on these old fields of broom corn [sedge?]." [21]

Having no corn left from the little he gathered during his first year of farming, now with a big plantation and stock and Negroes to feed, he found it necessary to be constantly buying corn from Colonel Barrow during the first half of 1867;[22] and to add to his worries, a carload of corn which he bought from Louisville, Kentucky, was damaged by a freshet it ran into in Tennessee—and the railroad company refused to pay damages, claiming that it was an act of Providence.[23]

His labor supply was uncertain, as, indeed, it was with all planters during the summer of 1867, when elections were on the minds of the Negroes, now that they were to vote on delegates to the Constitutional Convention. They became "uppity," and without giving notice they would go to town to "tend to their business," as they put it. Also a disturbing factor was the Freedmen Bureau agents, "who before their appointment did not possess a dime or a whole coat to their back, now drive buggies and fast horses, drink brandy, smoke cigars and dress sumptuously." [24] Browne made it almost a habit to predict: "The day of large cotton plantations has come to an end. Bankruptcy and free negro labor have killed king cotton. The war caused his throne to totter but it did not fall till now." [25]

But by the middle of April, Browne was half through planting cotton—no doubt, working in the fields with the Negroes much of the time. Cotton did well this year, and as the bolls burst open in the fall, Browne's fields looked as white as snow. His wife Lizzie wrote Mrs. Howell Cobb, in Macon, that the General had been down on the plantation much of the fall "trying to coax the freedmen to pick his cotton." She reported him "in despair about the terrible fall in the price. I have never seen him so depressed." "Had the price of last year continued," she wrote, "all our trouble would have been over; but now they are more grievous and complicated than ever." As for her home in Athens, she was about to engage an Irishman and his wife, who "says she can cook, wash, and iron." [26]

Well might Browne have seen the hope of a bright financial future fade, for the price of cotton in Augusta had dropped to 14 cents. A drop from 42 cents to 14 cents in a period of two years was enough to take the heart out of the whole South, which was trying to recover from the desolation of the war. But instead of being aided by the National Government, the South was burdened with the iniquitous cotton tax. No wonder Browne could report that the South was prostrate, its trade dried up, and everything at a standstill or sinking. "There is no bustle to be seen, no hum to be heard," he wrote. "The anvil and hammer are mute. The scaffolding round splendid blocks of buildings, in progress of erection, are still standing but deserted by the artizans, standing evidence of hopes disappointed and of fortunes broken." And all of this because of the fall of the price of cotton to less than half within two years, of the production of a small crop which was planted and capitalized at high prices—and because of the barbaric meanness of the Radicals in Washington. Plantation lands were selling at a dollar an acre. "Never since the close of the war have the prospects been so dark as now," he wrote. "Never were all hopes of help so crushed and every avenue of escape so cut off as now." [27]

Browne's pessimism is evident in a letter to Barlow. "At one time this year," he said, "I hoped that I should make money enough to give me a start. Everything proceeded well. But the negro laziness, and the fall in the price of cotton made me come out a loser." He had tried to sell his house and land, but "no one has a dollar so that no one can buy anything. Land is really valueless. I worked harder than any negro I employed and made less, because they got their food and clothes for themselves and families, and I got nothing. You can have no conception of the condition of this country." [28]

Preparing for his next year's crop, Browne hoped to avert some of the pitfalls of the previous year. He was eschewing cotton to a great extent and would plant wheat. In this way he would need fewer freedmen to pay and feed, and the price of wheat, unlike cotton, would not fluctuate of itself or be manipulated. But even this change of plans did not buoy him much. His wife wrote in January, 1868, to her constant friend, Mrs. Howell Cobb, that he was "greatly depressed and out of spirits at his year's labor lost and still unable to pay his debts. He tried to sell this place but could not get an offer of any sort. He has been quite unwell for some days." [29]

To add to his little income, he set his workmen to cutting some cross-ties from the timber on his plantation for the Georgia Railroad Company, but they cheated him out of two-thirds of them—just as Cobb had predicted they would.[30] When his wheat had sprouted up and had attained some height and his fruit was taking on full growth, Browne was beset with calamities worse than Job of old; he wrote Howell Cobb on May 12, 1868: "We had almost a hurricane and drenching rain last night which blew down half of my fine wheat and greatly damaged my fruit." And this was not the end of his woes: "My black mare is dying, and all around I have nothing to cheer or encourage me, absolutely nothing. . . . In short things are as blue as indigo." [31] In the fall he reported to Barlow that cotton was "tumbling and the hopes of a few weeks ago like most of the hopes of this doomed people, are turning to dust." [32] And although he had little cotton this year to lose money on, yet he could feel the plight of the people in general almost as keenly as he did his own. But even so, the price of cotton in the fall of 1868 was much better than in 1867; it was now selling in Augusta at 22 cents a pound. If the hurricane left any wheat for him to sell that fall, he got the very good price of $2.50 a bushel.

Browne was not a harbinger of doom in everything he wrote; whenever he thought he could brag about Georgia prospects without perjuring his soul, he did so—although he would never have qualified for the chairmanship of a chamber of commerce. In a dispatch to the New York *World* in December, 1868, he wrote of a movement to bring emigrants from Europe to Georgia and predicted that before long Savannah would become another Castle Garden. "People are going to work everywhere," he wrote, "and if we are left alone, and allowed to attend to our own business, it will not be long before we can produce hog and hominy for ourselves and our neighbors in abundance." [33] At this very time he was appointed a delegate to the Cotton Planters' and Manufacturers' Convention which was to meet in Macon;[34] the next year he was made a delegate to the Memphis Commercial Convention;[35] and in subsequent years he attended agricultural conventions in Columbus, Georgia, and in other cities.[36]

In fact, if Browne had stuck more to his philosophy of less cotton and more grain, as a farmer and planter he might have fared better and enjoyed a brighter frame of mind. Soon after the war he became one of a group of "gentlemen planters" in Athens who made wheat raising a sort of hobby or game in which the winner was the one who could raise the most wheat on an acre of land. As Athens' corporate bounds were a little large and not yet completely occupied, it embraced a considerable area of farming land, and the contest was limited to land within the city.

The group went under the name of the Wheat Club of Athens, but later when its activities were to be extended beyond the limits of

the city to embrace the raising of other crops, its name was changed
to the Athens Agricultural Club. At this time (in 1869), Browne
was appointed chairman of the Committee on Superintending, Gathering, and Threshing of Wheat for Prize. The meetings were generally
held in the Town Hall; and the person who was adjudged of having
raised the most wheat on an acre of land was awarded a silver pitcher.
To add to the club's usefulness, contestants were required to tell how
they prepared their acre, how they prepared the seed and what kind,
and how they sowed it. Also, they were expected to inform the group
what kind of fertilizer they used, and how much.

In 1867, the Wheat Club raised 1,000 bushels of wheat inside the
limits of Athens. Browne raised 27 bushels on one and a half acres
of worn-out land. The next year he won the notice of John H. Christy,
editor of the *Southern Watchman,* who went out to Browne's "beautiful place up-town" to see his patch of oats. Christy said that it beat
anything he had ever seen anywhere; it looked more like stalks of
corn than oats. Browne told him that he had gotten the seed in
Pennsylvania.

In this same year (1868), Browne reported to the Club in detail
how he had managed his acre. He had had wheat on it in the previous year, and after cutting it he plowed it across the old furrows
and broadcast peas on it. After ploughing them under in September,
he sprinkled about a half-bushel of lime (all he could get) over the
land. After the pea vines had rotted, he ploughed into the soil to a
depth of 6 inches 100 bushels of decomposed cotton seed. When he
sowed the wheat, he used 250 pounds of Peruvian guano and a like
amount of Reids Superphosphate. All of this material (lime, peas,
cotton seed, and fertilizer) cost him $43.75. With wheat selling at
$2.50 a bushel, he made $97.50 on this one acre.[37]

Browne maintained, contrary to the opinion often expressed that
wheat would not thrive this far south, that in fact it was a proper
crop for middle and northern Georgia.[38] Now, for several years he
was to be in a position to argue about agricultural practices and to
pass along much information on the best methods of running farms,
planting gardens, setting out and caring for orchards, selecting and
arranging ornamental plants, and even how to run the household—he
was to become the editor of a farm journal.

❧ XV ❧

Farm Editor

IT IS not known whether Browne's experience as a farmer or his success as editor of the Macon *Daily Journal and Messenger* suggested to the publishers that they start a farm journal and make Browne the editor; nor is it certain that Browne himself did not suggest starting the journal. The J. W. Burke and Company, publishers of the newspaper, had begun as printers and booksellers in 1862 and had in 1868 bought the *Journal and Messenger*. The next year, Browne was made the editor. In November of 1869 they sold the paper and brought out their farm journal. They entitled it *The Southern Farm and Home, A Magazine of Agriculture, Manufactures and Domestic Economy*.

It was of the ordinary book size (6½ inches by 10, smaller than most farm journals), was to issue monthly, and was destined to run about 500 pages per year, counting the advertisements. After publishing the magazine for two years, the Burke company sold it to Browne for an unannounced price. Regardless of what he might have been able to pay, he divulged to the United States census in 1870 that his real estate was valued at $10,000 and his personal effects, at $5,000.[1] In announcing his sole proprietorship, he said that "in consequence of a very large addition to the subscription list, and other business arrangements of an advantageous character," he would move his publication to Memphis and would have it printed in the plant of Boyle and Chapman.[2] The distinguished format with neat clear type and good paper, which characterized the magazine when in Macon, was continued in its new home, and the price per annum remained the same, at $2.00. The first number issued in Memphis was for December, 1871.

There were a few eyebrows raised in Georgia when this new farm journal made its appearance, for it was asserted that Georgia already had more such journals than any other Southern state. There was one especially which was probably more concerned than any other[3]—

189

The Southern Cultivator, published in Athens. Its editors, William
and W. L. Jones, having been fellow townsmen of Browne's, in taking note of the new publication, said, "The editor makes his bow in
a graceful salutatory, and if he succeeds in conducting an agricultural
paper as well as he has done various political journals, will make the
Southern Farm & Home a valuable addition to Southern agricultural
literature." [4]

A chorus of compliments greeted Browne. His first number, November, 1869, was praised by the Athens *Southern Watchman* as being
edited "with great ability"; [5] and soon it was receiving enthusiastic
welcomes from New York to Texas. A New York editor declared it
to be "a model of neatness and beauty, and filled with the choicest
and most valuable information"; and from Kentucky came this:
"among the finest publications of its character in the United States."
A South Carolina editor reckoned it to be "one of the best family
magazines that is published anywhere," and a Selma, Alabama, newspaper said Browne was "one of the clearest thinkers and ablest writers
in the Southern country." This sentiment was echoed by a Louisiana
publication, and a Texan declared that no "farmer should be without" the *Southern Farm and Home.* Back in Macon, where Browne
should have been best known, he was judged by an editor there to
be "not only an accomplished gentleman and finished scholar, but a
thorough, practical agriculturalist, who writes of what he knows and
has proved by his own experience." [6]

And even the poet Francis Orray Ticknor noticed Browne, Burke,
and the *Southern Farm and Home* in one of his poems, called forth
by some of Browne's previous political editorials as much as by his
new venture in agricultural editorship:

> But oh! disloyal Burke!
> And oh! that "wight" at WORK!
> And oh! rebellious Browne!
> Beware the Doodle's frown!
> Where *do* you 'spect to go
> When — you sarve po' DARKIE so?
> When you hit his photo-phiz
> Tangential to his "biz"—
> That "nigger-way" of his,
> Exactly as it is!
> He is swarming "Home," perplext!
> Please HIVE him in your next!
> And never more disfigure
> Your sun-shine with "cold" nigger.
> While a radiant maiden's arm,
> Illumes your HOME AND FARM. [7]

With these encomiums of man and journal, it might well be expected that the *Farm and Home* would become a strong and healthy publication. By the time it was two years old it had "upwards of six thousand subscribers," [8] and six months later, it could boast of having subscribers in every Southern state and many Northern ones.[9] When Browne became both editor and owner of the journal and moved it to Memphis, he made a special effort to increase its circulation. He quoted an Arkansas subscriber as writing: "How any intelligent farmer is willing to plod along without subscribing for your or some periodical of the kind I cannot see." [10] And he made a special appeal to his old Georgia friends not to forget to keep up their subscriptions, although the publication had now left the state. "To our friends in dear old Georgia," he said, "whose kind patronage and generous support encouraged and cheered us during the two years we published the FARM AND HOME in Macon, we would offer our warmest thanks, and ask them for a continuance of their favor by a renewal of their subscriptions. If the FARM AND HOME published at Macon deserved their support and commendation, we can assure them that the FARM AND HOME printed at Memphis shall be equally meritorious." [11]

Deeply sectional in almost every respect, Browne was pleased to quote from a letter written by a person of similar feelings, who chided his fellow Southerners for their lack of pride in their own literature in preference to Yankee stuff and in high humor told Browne how he had made a mistake: "Had you called it the Cape Cod Agriculturalist, or the Plymouth Rock Cultivator, and published it somewhere in the White Mountains, your circulation in the South would have been immense by this time, and you would be sufficiently rich to build a marble palace, and drive a 2:20 horse." [12]

Browne had something more substantial to offer in his campaign for new subscribers than quoting compliments and good wishes. He published a table of premiums to be won by persons who should secure between three and two hundred subscribers, the prize varying, of course, with the number of subscribers turned in. Prizes that would appeal to the ladies were "a Work-Box, Photograph Album, Chromos for your Parlors, a Washing Machine, a Sewing Machine or a fine Organ." Gentlemen would be interested in "a valuable Library, a Gold Pen, a finely finished Revolver, a beautiful Picture, a reliable Time-keeper, or a Fire Extinguisher." And for the boys and girls there was "an excellent Pocket Knife, some pretty Books, an elegant Watch, a beautifully finished Work-box or a Gold Pen." For anyone sending in three subscribers there was the choice of a novel by Bulwer, Scott, Dickens, Thackeray, or Charles James Lever, the Anglo-Irish writer.

For two hundred subscribers, a library worth $125 might be selected from various authors.[13]

As a bit of information for both old and new subscribers, Browne warned them about the bad mail service which was being handed out to Southerners by the Radical Reconstructionists in Washington. "With route agents and postal officials from Africa, who do not 'know B from bull's foot,' the wonder is that we receive our mail as regularly as we do," he said.[14]

Of course, the greatest source of profit came from the advertisers, who paid from $5,000 to $7,000 a year for between twenty and twenty-five pages of advertisements; but even with the cost of producing the journal, an income of $12,000 a year would flow from 6,000 subscribers and would leave some profit.[15]

The advertisements were varied and designed to appeal to a farm population, although there were some advertisements that were not intrinsically associated with farming. First on the list were fertilizers: Peruvian and Orchilla guanos, superphosphate, dissolved bone, raw bones, bone ash, Dickson's Compound, and so on—Baltimore, Richmond, Charleston, Augusta, and Macon being the chief sources of supply. Farm implements and equipment had prominent places in the advertisements: cotton and hay presses, cotton gins, grain drills, Brinly plows (a specialty with Browne) and cultivators, water wheels, wagons, steam engines, cider mills, water pumps, saddles and harnesses —Louisville, Kentucky, being an important source for farm implements. Livestock scarcely ever commanded full-page advertisements, but readers of the *Farm and Home* were alerted to where they could buy cattle, sheep, goats, pigs, and poultry, too. Suppliers in Massachusetts, Pennsylvania, Ohio, Kentucky, and Tennessee were ready to serve. The Mason-Dixon Line was completely obliterated when it came to securing nursery supplies, for advertisements frequently appeared representing Massachusetts, New York, New Jersey, Pennsylvania, Onio, Illinois, Wisconsin, and Missouri, as well as Louisiana and Browne's own Athens, Georgia. Medical remedies for both man and beast found their places in Browne's advertising pages. Few patent medicines were included, though Simmons' Liver Regulator ("A sure and effectual cure for all diseases") commanded a full page.

For the home were sewing machines, cooking stoves, washing machines, lamps, and glass fruit jars, as well as groceries, clothes, and boots and shoes. There were watches and diamonds for ladies and gentlemen, toys for the children (a steam engine that ran), musical instruments, sheet music, and stereoscopes for the parlor, wines and liquors, guns and pistols for the hunters and marksmen, and monuments and tombstones. Gamblers could participate in a New York lottery, though Browne disapproved of lotteries, and only one lottery advertisement appeared in the *Farm and Home*. Summer vacationists might go to the Chalybeate Springs, in Meriwether County, Georgia. The Civil War had receded sufficiently into the past to lead a New Yorker to advertise for Confederate postage stamps. Railroad schedules were a constant insertion, and after the *Farm and Home* moved to Memphis, steamboat sailings were included.

Hotels such as the Galt House in Louisville, Kentucky, the Peabody in Memphis, and the Lanier House in Macon found it desirable to announce themselves. And though later it was not ethical for lawyers to advertise, now firms in Georgia and Mississippi let themselves be known, and a New York lawyer announced that getting divorces was his specialty. Various newspapers and other publications took a page or less—*Atlanta Constitution, Atlanta Sun, Macon Daily Telegraph & Messenger, Memphis Appeal, Columbus* (Mississippi) *Democrat, Burke's Weekly for Boys and Girls* (Macon), *Independent Farmer* (Philadelphia), *New Monthly Magazine* (Nashville), *Floral Guide* (Rochester, New York), *Western Methodist* (Memphis), and *Southern Musical Journal* (Savannah). *The South,* published in Yankeeland (New York), let it be known that it was all for the progress and development of the South. The reprinters of such English periodicals as the *Edinburgh Review, Blackwood's Edinburgh Magazine,* and *Westminster Review* made their announcements.

Book publishers and booksellers (especially J. W. Burke and Company of Macon) announced their offerings; and a few schools inserted information about themselves. The University of Georgia announced the beginning of the lectures under the "Terrell Professorship of Agriculture," and Richard Malcolm Johnston informed the public of his Pen Lucy, School for Boys, in Maryland.

One of the ways by which Confederate leaders returning from the war hoped to make a living was by organizing insurance companies. Browne became interested in one, as will be seen later, and he early began running their advertisements in the *Home and Farm*. Among those which found a place in this magazine were: Bluff City Insurance Company of Memphis, Carolina Life Insurance Company of Memphis, Cotton States Life Insurance Company of Macon, Georgia Life Insurance Company of Columbus, Mississippi Valley Insurance Company of Memphis, Peoples Insurance Company of Memphis, Phoenix Insurance Company of Memphis, Planters Insurance Company of Memphis, and Southern Life Insurance Company of Atlanta and Memphis.

These insurance companies were not humbugs, though most of them failed and led to the same results as humbugs. Browne frequently warned his readers against humbugs and tried to prevent them from finding space in his advertisement section. Yet, it seems that several did slip in, to ensnare the unwary, as one in which agents were solicited to sell a "wonderful invention" whose nature was not described, and another which offered for sale a corn sheller with an illustration that made it look like a humbug. But a more cunning Yankee on Long Island, New York, slipped in his advertisement offering seed corn at $5.00 a bushel yielding "upwards of one hundred bushels per acre." An unsuspecting Georgian ordered a bushel, which cost him a total of $10.35 before he got it in hand. He planted an acre, using the best of land, fertilizers, and care, and in the fall gathered about "twelve bushels of inferior corn." In detailing his experience to Browne, he said, "All who wish to plant Sanford corn can do so, and I am satisfied, feel swindled as I judge all do who deal in such yankee notions. This, Mr. Editor, is a part of what I know about farming." [16]

Advertisements were the money-making section of the *Farm and Home,* and before Browne became the owner of the publication it was not his primary business or interest to have anything to do with that part. The remainder of the magazine was very definitely his to produce. To enliven the magazine, Browne used a frontispiece for every issue and through its pages he used illustrations appropriate to farm life; every department was surmounted by an attractive woodcut. In his frontispieces he could not resist paying his respects to Confederate generals and other leaders—Jefferson Davis, Wade Hampton, John B. Gordon, Alfred H. Colquitt, Ben C. Yancey (an agriculturalist), the Steamboat *Cleburne* (for Pat, killed in the war). Others were Charles Dickens (one of Browne's favorite authors) and the Grand Duke Alexis of Russia (on the occasion of his visit to America). Also to Tallulah Falls, in North Georgia, whose grandeur he loved, he gave a place. But, of course, many of the frontispieces were related to the main purpose of the magazine: Cotswold and Merino sheep, shorthorn bulls, Jersey cows, goats, swine, a "Steam Plow in Operation," various fair grounds, horses, and so on.

In making his salutation, Browne said that his purpose was to aid "so far as our means and opportunities will permit in the great work of reform and improvement of our industrial system." As for the other agricultural magazines, "We propose to aid and not obstruct or injure them. The field is wide enough for us all." [17] His editorial opinions were not for sale: "No Puffs, paid special notices, or other expressions of what purports to be our opinion, for which we are paid, shall appear in these columns. We intend to preserve perfect independence of opinion as to men and things, and if we are fortunate enough to benefit anybody by anything we write for the information of our readers, we desire no further reward than the satisfaction the knowledge of the fact will afford us." [18] The nearest Browne came to offering a little puff to an advertiser was in recommending Hunt's Fan & Fly Driver on the basis of his own experience with one, adding that he had no interest in its manufacture but was authorized to sell county and state rights; he also referred to Richard Malcolm Johnston's Pen Lucy School, near Baltimore, "where boys are not simply taught from books, but where their morals, manners, and health receive constant attention—where they will become gentlemen as well as scholars." [19]

Having been for many years engaged in political editorializing and reporting, Browne must have exerted much self discipline in resisting the temptation to let a little politics get into his agricultural magazine. He announced that although he had been urged as a " 'Democrat' of the old school" to publish his views on politics, he could not do so "because we think that an agricultural paper to be useful ought to confine itself exclusively to the things which pertain to agriculture." [20] Yet he departed slightly from the rule of carrying editorials on other subjects, but in three special cases they related to the deaths of eminent men. When Horace Greeley died, he felt impelled to call him "the greatest of American journalists," recount his many fine qualities (though Browne had crossed swords with him in his Washington days), and to say that when "he was most wrong he believed he was most right." Referring to the election of 1872, Browne said that one of the anomalies of Greeley's life was that the race he labored most for voted against him, "and those whom he had persistently maligned and deeply injured, were his most earnest supporters." But Browne preferred to remember only his truthful, generous nature, his eminence as a journalist, and the example he has left of the power of self-help.[21] The other instances were his long appreciative editorials on Lord Lytton (Edward Bulwer-Lytton), and Napoleon III.[22]

Browne could probably be charged with straying from agricultural and industrial subjects in his intense defense of the South and in some of his philosophizing and moralizing with especial reference to the pestilences of the times. He found it easy in his New Year's greetings to go off on these angles. His greeting for 1870 was a masterpiece, long and learned—probably a little above the appreciation of some of his readers: "Thanks to the ordinance of threescore and ten, we cannot live to the age of Methuselah, but if we could, woe to the sense of time! Twenty years bring the new years closer together; forty years narrow the span magically; and fifty—so we learn from disinterested witnesses [he being one approaching that age]—fifty years mystify the traditional twelve months until yesterday, to-day, and to-morrow intermingle in a manner very perplexing." Then a good deal of moralizing. "Heaven knows, the world is wicked enough; iniquity never had such gigantic resources at command; treachery was never so insidious and crime never so barefaced; trade is bloody warfare between man and man, and the gold-gladiators strip in the arena for each other's lives; private faith and private honor, the final break-water against the surges of evil, are fast giving way; while neither public law nor public opinion has a tithe of the force that once made it omnipotent." He predicted a great future for the South: "we do insist that the South is destined to be the final victor in this fiery conflict of the forces of civilization; that the collateral changes going on in other parts of the world are necessitated to accrue in a pre-eminent degree to her welfare; and that the delay and postponement of inauguration into her rightful place of intellectual and industrial power will only serve to bring larger accesses to her eventual greatness. . . . A welcome, therefore, to the New Year 1870. A suffering race shall not be cheated out of its heritage of joy. A misunderstood and maligned race must not enter a verdict against its own capacity to outlive any accumulation of misfortunes, nor array itself against its own splendid possibilities of culture, wealth and happiness."[23]

The next year, in saluting the New Year and wishing his readers prosperity and happiness, Browne cried out against the evils that permeated the air and that were fostered by degeneracy in high places. "The ruling passion seems to be to do something 'big,' and to do it in less time than anything was ever done before," he said. "A thing that is big of its kind commands general respect and admiration until something bigger has been produced with more startling rapidity. Even the worst of crimes, command approval and excite emotion. The complete overthrow of a system of government based on the antiquated notion of the consent of the governed, and the substitution in its place of a system of corruption, fraud, violence, contempt for law and open violation of every right human and divine, is 'a big thing in harmony with the age,' and which it is disloyal to disapprove."

Although Browne tried to be optimistic in all things, he could never get over the hurdle of a pessimistic outlook when he thought of the course the national government was taking. "If we consult 'the signs of the times' we find the portents far from encouraging. tion was never so daring, venality so barefaced, infidelity was never so tion was never so daring, benality so barefaced, infidelity was never so bold—dishonesty, betrayal of trust, abuse of power, abandonment of principle, immorality of every kind, were never so frequent in all the grades of society, from the highest to the lowest, as they are now." But in the face of all this, the South would never give up: "Though adversity has pressed most heavily upon us, and sorrow and death have visited our dwellings, and pinching poverty was sat by our hearths, our manhood which has never crushed, our intelligence which was never clouded, and our honor which was never sullied, have combined to sustain, strength and encourage us."[24]

It is easy enough to see from Browne's past career how he was led to these moralizings and philosophizings, but when it comes to such a prosaic performance as telling people who had never done anything but farm how to farm, wonderment might arise. But it should be remembered that he spent two or three years at the grass roots and learned from experience what and what not to do in trying to dig a living out of the soil. Also, few if any people in Georgia were as voracious readers of almost anything in print as was Browne. He had his agricultural dictionaries, his encyclopedias, his farm exchanges, his scientific publications (including the annual United States *Report of the Commissioner of Agriculture*), and his engaging personality which made it easy for him to make friends of farmers and find out what they knew. And he called on them to write letters to the *Farm and Home* telling about their experiences. If anyone should object that he could not write well, Browne answered: "To all such, we say, we do not want fine rhetoric or fine writing. We want the aid of your sound common sense and intelligent observation of what is passing around you. We will promise to do the 'writing for the press,' if you will furnish us with the facts." [25] Browne attributed much of the success of his publication to his farm correspondents "who have added to the stock of information by giving the result of their experience and observation, and thus afford light and instruction concerning matters of deep interest and great practical value." [26] In fact, some issues of *Farm and Home* were more than half-filled with these letters. A frequent correspondent was "John Plowhandles."

Browne began every issue of his magazine with "Farm Work for the Month," in which he gave practical information on what to plant, how to cultivate, and how to harvest; but he emphasized that the "gathering of the crop" was "still the principle business of all farmers." [27] Browne had the problem of varying this section to add freshness for his old subscribers, but fundamentally the advice had to be much the same from year to year for any given month. But, of course, new subscribers were constantly coming in, and they must be told; and he suggested that it would not hurt old subscribers to be reminded of what they had read the previous year. Browne gave a summing up of how to complete the year's work in his number for December, 1872, which he did not repeat, except incidentally here and there: "The cotton should be all picked, ginned, and prepared for market; the corn should be all gathered, peas should be all saved, potatoes should be put away safely; the small grain crops should be all in the ground; the wood for fuel should all be cut and piled away for winter use; all the out-buildings and fences should be over-hauled and repaired; the tools and implements of husbandry should be cleaned, oiled and put away in good order; an inventory should be made of the farm property, crops, stock, tools, etc., and an account taken of expenses and income, so as to know, approximately at least, on which side the balance lies; and last but not least, all our debts should be paid, not forgetting the printer, who during the past twelve months has regularly sent you your paper, paying all the expenses, trusting to your honor to pay him when you made your crop." [28]

Browne often took occasion to argue the importance of agriculture and of applying science to farming. "It is unnecessary, at this day to illustrate the importance of the science of Agriculture," he wrote. "It is admitted to be the first and most valuable of all secular pursuits, because it is not only the foundation of the material and physical progress of our country, but it is also closely connected with our moral and social progress—with the maintenance of our independence and of our virtue." A new day was dawning in the farm world. Farmers were abandoning their old errors, which "have given way before the light of science and enlightened effort, and the people generally, are now eager to receive information, to acquire new ideas, atone for their errors, adopt improvements, and elevate the calling of the agriculturalist to its true position as the chief of all the pursuits of human industry." And although farmers were going forward in this new day, still much remained to be done: "The unseemly 'red hills,' the gaping gullies, the 'old fields' which meet our eyes wherever we turn, point out the evil which has been wrought and which it is our duty to repair. The consequences of the war,—the loss of our accumulated wealth, and the radical change of our social system—compel us to make the most of all that is left us—our land—and forbid our migrating to 'new ground' after we have exhausted the old." [29]

As was the custom with farm magazines, Browne divided his *Farm and Home* into various departments, where appropriate discussions could be carried on either by himself or by contributors. There were the "Stable Economy" (sometimes listed "The Stock Yard") department, the "Scientific Department" (using ordinary terms, which farmers could understand), "The Poultry Yard," the "Apiary" (or "Bee-Keeping") department, the "Horticultural Department" (embracing flower, fruit, and vegetable gardens), the "Poetry" department (occasionally), the "Juvenile Department" (for the first few numbers, including illustrated rebuses, enigmas, charades, riddles, and logotrips), and sometimes the "Mechanical Department." There was an "End Novel," which ran serially at the end of every number, sometimes being an original work, such as Mary Faith Floyd's (Mrs. W. G. McAdoo of Milledgeville) "The Nereid." It later appeared in book form. Also of interest was a reprinted work, "The Cruise of the Olustee," by Captain George W. Gift. Very infrequently a joke would fill up a short space.[30]

Three other departments deserve special attention: the "Insurance Department," the "Household Department," and the "Literary Department" (sub-titled "Editor's Book Table"). The chief contributor for some time to the "Household Department" was Mrs. William N. White, the widow of a former editor of the *Southern Cultivator*. (Of White, who died in 1867, Browne wrote, "He was eminently a practical man, and proved himself to be a public benefactor by his labors as an agricultural writer." [31]) Another occasional contributor to this department, under the special heading of "Domestic Receipts," was "Mrs. E. J. B.," who very logically could have been Mrs. Browne (Eliza Jane Browne), a lady amply able to fill this column. Among the recipes she offered were: how to boil potatoes, to make English muffins, French rolls or fresh yeast, how to boil a turkey, to ice a cake, to make orange and quince marmalade, orange chips, raspberry vinegar, vegetable soup, tomato catsup, raspberry jam, rice cake, ginger bread, plum pudding, mincemeat, oyster soup, and how to preserve whole strawberries and plums. Also she told how to make a perfume for a lady's desk: "The Queen of England uses a perfume for the writing paper composed as follows: Powdered starch, one half ounce; attar of roses, ten drops. Put this in a bag, and keep in the desk among the papers and envelopes." [32] There was a series of letters which appeared under this department written by "Mrs. Dustbrush" to her niece "Mrs. Melinda Newbroom," offering homely practical advice to a young married lady just getting started. There is good reason to believe that Mrs. Browne was also the author of these letters.[33]

Browne carried on a special department which he called "Answers to Correspondents," in which he gave specific answers to their questions. He could handle many of their questions out of his own experience; for others he could find the answers in exchanges or agricultural encyclopedias; and for those questions which he could find or devise no answers he said so, quoting a humorous saying, " 'this is one of those things which no fellow can find out.' " [34] Or in answering the inquiry as to which lightning rod was the best, "We regret our inability to advise him," but adds, "Good lightning rods, well put up, are good things. But there are a great many patent humbugs called by that name." [35] And, again, in discussing the advisability of setting up windmills in Georgia, he said he knew their value in Europe and certain parts of the United States, "but we prefer to admit our ignorance rather than mislead our friends." [36]

But not many of Browne's answers to questions were an admission of lack of knowledge. He was most of the time very positive. As for pulling fodder: "This is a very dear crop. It seems to me probable, though not distinctly tested in my own case, that the *loss* of corn by reason of pulling fodder is actually greater than the value of the fodder when gathered." He agreed with many "that the fodder *robs the corn of more than its own value*—of course this hard labor is *worse than wasted.*" [37] Answering which was a safe lottery, Browne said, "We do not know of any 'safe' lottery scheme. Many of the advertised lotteries are deliberate swindles, and those that are honestly managed are mere gambling concerns, with which we advise all Georgia boys and all other boys to have nothing to do." [38] Answering a correspondent about a cotton-picking machine, he said, "All the cotton-picking machines that have been hitherto invented are failures, though they may not be humbugs. The African's hands are the only reliable picking machine which we can recommend"; [39] and he had a similar answer to a patent milking machine, "We do not believe any patent milking machine is worth a three cent postage stamp. We do not know where the humbug is made or what it costs, and recommend our valued correspondent to trust to Dinah or Sambo's hand as the best milking machine to be found." [40] Would it be better to pen up turkeys or let them roost in trees? Browne said it was better to let them have their way, since they generally roosted high where they were "more secure against the evening calls of fifteenth amendments." [41] He said that as hollow horn in cattle was "generally caused by *hollow belly,* we recommend that that be cured first, by good and regular feeding, and the hollow horn will soon disappear." [42] His sure cure for a jumping cow was that if she was "a practical jumper . . . to shut her up, fatten her, and then trade her to a butcher." [43]

Apart from answering specific questions which were sent to him,

Browne sprinkled throughout his magazine information and advice. He recommended that "all corn cribs be supplied with good locks. It is astonishing how they make a pile of corn 'hold out.' " [44] Despite his advice to rely on the Negro's hand for milking cows and picking cotton, he preferred otherwise the machine "to the gentleman from Africa. The machine never votes or wants to go to the Legislature, never 'knocks off' to go hunting or to town, always obeys the direction of the employer, (we almost wrote *master*), never rides our mules at night, makes no inroads, lawful or otherwise, upon the smoke-house and corn-crib, never burns fence rails, and only demands a little grease and shelter to be useful for many years." [45] He prayed for the day when fence laws would be passed to relieve farmers from having to build and "keep up miles on miles of rail fences" as protection against the inroads of "neighbors' cows, mules, hogs, etc." He believed that hedges of osage oranges and Macartney roses would turn the animals; but if the "hideous worm fences" were persisted in, they should be kept in good repair, for, he said, "Nearly all the 'jumping' cows and oxen we have ever known have been taught this miserable vice by bad tumble-down fences." [46]

He warned the farmers against the common practice of giving liens on their crops. They should be avoided as the plague. "They lead to inevitable ruin," he said. "It is better to give the money-lender a deed to your property now, than to be compelled to do so by the sheriff a few years hence, after much suffering, humiliation and anxiety, and the loss of precious time which might be spent in some useful pursuit." [47]

He believed in fairs and attended many, but he wanted them to remain agricultural and industrial and not horse-racing gatherings. "Horse racing at a fair," he said, "is a great mistake, to say the least. The racing is just enough to spoil the fair and the fair is just enough to spoil the race. All reliable experience goes to show that wherever agricultural fairs are most successful horse racing is excluded." [48]

He advised farmers to build fish ponds and to construct substantial barns and homes. Time and again he also advised farmers to plow deep and turn up the subsoil, for it would amount to doubling their acreage since an equal area lay under the top soil. Abandoning for the moment his decrying things Northern, he said that Yankee farmers plowed deep and made thereby about twice as much per acre. Entitling this advice "Plowing vs. Scratching," he said, "We reiterate the recommendation to *break deep* and not scratch the surface. One acre well plowed is worth three scratched over." [49]

He had much to say about fertilizers, and as his magazine carried many fertilizer advertisements, he could not well have advised against their use; yet he believed that farmers could avoid high fertilizer prices by saving their barnyard and stable manures; by banding together they could buy the ingredients of commercial products and make their own. He explained that he had on a small farm of his near Athens, "naturally poor, thin, red land . . . robbed by bad farming," built it up through the use of commercial fertilizers to where on 24½ acres he had harvested an average of 1,118 pounds of seed cotton per acre.[50] On a trip through several Southern states in 1873 "we observed during our journey, both by the senses of sight and smell, the unusual large quantities of the commercial fertilizers [which] are to be employed this year. Every depot along our route was crowded with sacks and barrels of the odiferous compounds." [51]

Echoing what had been preached by agricultural leaders for generations, Browne strongly argued for the diversification of crops. To diversify meant to stop making cotton the principal crop. Browne was not opposed to raising some cotton, for he himself had hoped immediately after the war to make a new start in life by raising cotton. But, as he said in introducing his *Farm and Home* to his fellow-citizens, "We must cease to give all our care and attention to cotton, to the neglect of every other consideration, counting on our cotton crop to furnish us enough of money to buy everything we need, and thus annually transferring to other communities so large a share of what ought to be retained in the State in the form of productive capital." [52] But knowing full well that the most he could expect would be to reduce the amount raised, he gave sound advice on the management of what would inevitably be produced. After having raised it, farmers too often were careless in picking it. Browne advised them to begin picking it as soon as the first bolls had opened, and to continue several pickings until it was all harvested. "It not infrequently happens," he said, "that crops which have been planted and cultivated with vigilant energy and timely care, are gathered in a careless and slovenly manner." [53] Instead of throwing the seed away, as was often done, the farmer should save it as one of the most valuable products of a plantation, to be pressed into oil and cake or to be properly rotted for fertilizer. Oil cake was one of the most valuable feed for milk cows.[54] When the cotton had been ginned, enough should be immediately sold to pay debts to merchants and take care of other obligations, but the remainder should be held for higher prices, which inevitably would come in the spring after most farmers had unwisely disposed of their supply and the speculators had gained control.

Browne was constantly disturbed by farmers' buying their hay and corn from the North instead of raising these crops. A farmer who bought Northern hay at $2.50 the hundredweight would always be poor, and if he lived long enough he would "find the sheriff winding up his business." Georgia farmers had "no money to spare for Yankee hay, and if they had the wealth of Croesus, it would be a crying shame for a Georgia farmer, with his fine soil and genial climate, to send to the barren hills of New England for hay to feed his stock." He hoped that Northern hay would go up to twenty cents a pound, for farmers would then "go to work to utilize the blessings which surround us on all sides." [55] He estimated that the amount Georgia farmers would send out of the state for hay and corn in 1870 "would not be very far from twenty millions of dollars." [56] On a recent trip to other states, in 1873, he observed large quantities of Northern hay and Western corn addressed to Southern planters. How could farmers expect to make money in such a fashion, he asked.[57]

For Southern hay and forage crops, Browne recommended planting lucerne grass (alfalfa) ("the best and most profitable forage crop we know"), millet, Hungarian grass, corn broadcast or drilled; and the lowly crabgrass, which volunteered itself in every fence corner or other place undisturbed, should be harvested, for it made excellent hay. Oats was an excellent forage crop as well as for grain, and instead of buying Northern hay, "for mercy's sake, do all you can to enable you to stop this discreditable and ruinous exercise at as early a day as possible, by providing *a large oats crop.*" [58]

In his diversification program, Browne strongly recommended planting field peas, which when ground with corn made excellent feed for work animals and milk cows—and "field peas, too, well boiled with a piece of sweet middling, with a red pepper or two and a pinch of salt, are not hard to take." [59] He could not understand why farmers did not plant more turnips, which made excellent feed and food. He said that in England there was no more important crop than turnips, so much so that it had been said that "England could bear better the failure of the Bank of England than the loss of the turnip crop for two successive years." [60] Also he called on farmers to plant more sweet potatoes, Irish potatoes, rye, barley, and especially wheat. He argued frequently that wheat be made a principal grain crop, insisting that it grew well outside of the coastal plain country. "Take an average of five or six years, and we are satisfied that wheat, acre for acre, will be found to pay better than cotton." [61]

Although not placing his main emphasis on livestock, Browne did not forget to advocate fine strains of cattle and sheep, and especially did he recommend raising more hogs to escape buying meat from

Porkopolis (Cincinnati)—"we are unmistakeably of the opinion that jowl and turnip-greens well cooked, with nice corn-bread and a glass of sweet-milk, is a dinner fit for the noblest work of God—an honest man." [62] He was favorable to dairy farming, but he warned that it was an enterprise "demanding care, regularity, cleanliness, and unremitting attention," and if entrusted to Negroes, the result would be certain failure. "The man who wants to 'live at home at ease,' dress in purple and fine linen, drive fast horses, spend his summers at Saratoga, and confine his labor to drawing drafts on his factor, cannot make a dairy farm or any other farm pay." [63]

"Manufactures" was included in the subhead of Browne's *Southern Farm and Home,* but he gave much less attention to that subject than to the farm, as might well be supposed; but, nevertheless, when he wrote about manufactories for the South, he displayed deep conviction and interest. How the South could neglect this source of prosperity and leave it to the North he could not understand, thus differing none from other Southern leaders for generations gone by. In a news item in 1872 telling of the recent investment in Fall River, Massachusetts, of $16,000,000 in twenty new cotton mills, Browne found an excellent text: "The Yankees of one town invest sixteen millions of dollars in twenty new mills, to be fed by cotton transported thousands of miles, with heavy freights, and reap large profits, and we do not hear of a single new mill being built, or a single dollar invested at the South, although we have the raw material at our doors, water power enough in any one county, of any State, to drive all the cotton mills of Massachusetts, and better and cheaper labor than the North can obtain." How could and why must these things be?[64] He did not, however, fail to pay tribute to Enoch Steadman, a Georgia factory-master, who had long advocated mills for the South and who had done something about it.[65] Browne's formula for prosperity for the South was: "When we make all that we want, and raise all that we consume, and not till then, can we be either rich or independent, because not till then can we be free from debt." [66]

Browne reprinted from his exchanges now and then any pertinent article representing his way of thinking, but he always gave credit to its source. Sometimes his exchanges were not as careful in giving his publication credit for articles reprinted from it. He was quite clever in calling their attention to this lapse. He said that some of his exchanges had paid him "the flattering compliment of copying articles and communications *verbatim*" but had "inadvertantly omitted to give us the usual credit." As he was "always ready to bear all the responsibility for what appears in our columns, we do not desire any of our friends to share or assume it, and therefore request that the credit be given, whether it be in our favor or the reverse." [67]

Browne was not simply a desk editor; he was too active, gregarious, and too much an extrovert for that. He was soon out of Macon and down to Americus to visit his friend John A. Cobb and to go over Cobb's plantations in that vicinity. In thanking Cobb for his hospitalities, he said, "I had long wished to see your plantations, and was very much gratified by the sight. They are not only the finest estate I have seen in America—beyond all comparison—but they are the best managed and in best order." [68] Mrs. Browne's birthday came while they were visiting, and to properly celebrate it, the Cobbs butchered a 35-pound turtle which had been presented to them and they served turtle in various forms, including turtle soup.[69].

Browne made it a point to travel widely over the state to attend agricultural conventions and to promote the organization of agricultural clubs. He published in the *Farm and Home* a model constitution for an agricultural club [70] and was active in the Bibb County Agricultural Society, whose headquarters were in Macon. He was on a committee that secured space in the new county courthouse for the Society's club room and museum, the latter designed to preserve and put on display different kinds of wood, minerals, soils, geological specimens, seeds, plants, and other objects of interest to agriculturalists. In the club room members might meet, discuss matters of mutual interest, and read agricultural journals, which Browne doubtless deposited there, having received them on his exchange list.[71]

He attended not only the annual conventions of the Georgia State Agricultural Society (submitting a constitution for it at the meeting in Atlanta in 1870), but also various county conventions and fairs, frequently making addresses on such occasions.[72] When, in 1870, it appeared that the secretaryship of the State Society might become vacant, he began a quiet campaign to secure election to it. He wrote his close friend Colonel D. C. Barrow that he would accept the position if offered, as he understood that David W. Lewis, the secretary, had resigned, but "I would not under any circumstances run against Col. Lewis, but if as I understand his resignation is definite and irrevocable I should like to be elected." Assuming so, he wanted Colonel Barrow's support, as "I do not want to be beaten if I can help it." [73] It turned out that Lewis did not go through with his resignation. Browne stood high in the councils of the Society, and the next year it did him and his magazine a signal honor in awarding it a medal for "the best printed agricultural magazine." [74]

As a fluent writer Browne had few equals. It is not known whether his oratory might be called "Websterian," but he had a reputation for speaking, ample to secure all the invitations he cared to accept. In 1870 he was invited by Charles H. Smith, the famous humorist going under the name of "Bill Arp," to "deliver a short and pointed address" at the Rome Fair that fall. Browne accepted and made an address not short but certainly pointed. Here he took advantage of an opportunity to popularize some of the preachments that he had been carrying on in his magazine and to emphasize others. Although using in the beginning many of the oratorical flourishes complimentary to his surroundings and yielding "to none in zealous devotion to the South," glorying not only in its past but in its great future which lay ahead, he soon passed on to things more substantial. As this was an agricultural fair (no horse racing), he felt compelled to pay tribute to country life and agriculture, which made it possible: "We say that it feeds and clothes the whole world, and without it commerce would perish, and mechanical industry would cease to exist. Men of all professions and callings, the statesman, the soldier, the jurist, the orator and the man of letters, look forward to the time when, released from the cares and dangers, the toils and conflicts of their several vocations, they may find rest and solace in a country life, in the simple pursuits of agriculture. This is all true, yet of all the known professions and pursuits of man, agriculture is the only one in which it is supposed that we can engage without any previous knowledge or preliminary education."

Here he was leading up to a strong support for the campaign then in the making to establish agricultural colleges, with experimental farms, to teach agricultural subjects, but also to teach the English language, arithmetic, geometry, land measurements, chemistry, mineralogy, geology, and knowledge "of every process and kind of farm labor." He maintained that no Southern state had ever appropriated a dollar to establish such a school. "If it be right and wise and proper to extend state aid to build railroads through the Okofenokee and Tobesofkee swamps," he said, "connecting these salubrious spots with the Everglades of Florida, surely it cannot be considered wrong, unwise and improper to give State aid to build and support an agricultural college."

Education provided by the colleges then in existence offered little or no training that would fit its graduates for agricultural pursuits: "They may all have university diplomas in their pockets; they may be able to descant glibly on the beauties of the Greek stage, and calculate to an hour the coming of the next comet, but when they come to plant their Irish potato patch, they are obliged to follow the teach-

ings of some old negro, that 'the dark of the moon' in February is
the best time for the operation."[75] Two years later (1872) the state
established the Georgia State College of Agriculture and the Mechanic
Arts, with its land grant fund which Congress had made possible by
granting public lands to the states in 1862, and which Georgia had
received after the war and had sold. Browne was later to have a connection with this school and to make it flower in part into what he
advocated in this Rome speech.

Immediately preceding Browne's purchase of the *Farm and Home*
and his removal of it to Memphis, he was on the point of making a
move in his business connections which would have taken him to
Baltimore. In fact, he had gone to Baltimore to attend the Maryland
Agricultural Fair when certain propositions were made to him. He did
not like the fair, for there was not much to it but horse-racing—little
to see and no competition in the exhibits.[76] The proposition was that
he become political editor of the Baltimore *Gazette.* The news got out
that he had accepted, which led the *Banner of the South and Plantation Journal,* published in Augusta, to regret that this "most excellent gentleman" was to leave the position, which he had "so long
and ably filled," to go to Baltimore to enter the "more boisterous
field of politics" as one of the editors of the *Gazette.*[77] His supposed
going called forth this encomium from the *Plantation,* published in
Atlanta: "An intelligent farmer, an admirable politician, and, for
more than a year past the accomplished Editor of Burke's *Farm and
Home.* Possessed of high social qualifications, of an admirably
balanced temperament, of a cultivated taste, and of a mind stored with
information, his society was sought."[78]

Instead of going through with the Baltimore proposition and moving there, he bought the Macon magazine and moved to Memphis,
as already noted. Although continuing to edit with increased skill
the *Farm and Home,* which he now owned, his routine differed somewhat. Being more centrally located in the Mississippi Valley, he
traveled more widely, making trips into Arkansas, to Sewanee to visit
the new university and renew contacts with old friends (as General
Josiah Gorgas), and to Vicksburg, where he "met there some old
and valued friends, and made many agreeable acquaintances."[79] In
the spring of 1873 he went "through a large portion of Tennessee,
Alabama, northern Georgia, North and South Carolina, Virginia,
Maryland, and Kentucky."[80]

Although Browne found time to make these trips, his comings and
goings were restricted not only by his editorial duties on his magazine but also by a connection he had established with an insurance

company in Memphis more than a year before he moved to that city. This was his position as "State Agent, Macon, Ga." for the Carolina Life Insurance Company, whose president was his close friend Jefferson Davis.[81] In promoting the company, Browne said, "We know of no safer or more perfectly reliable company in the United States. The fact that JEFFERSON DAVIS—a name deservedly dear to every Southern heart—is its president, is enough to commend it to the confidence and support of the public."[82] Charles F. McCay, formerly a professor in the University of Georgia, was Actuary, and soon Browne was promoted to General Agent.[83]

Undoubtedly it must have been Davis who diverted Browne from Baltimore to Memphis, for in the new arrangements Browne was now made Secretary of the company, with offices for his magazine in the same building with the insurance company. Most of the directors were in Memphis, but a branch of the company was set up in Baltimore, with Wade Hampton as president. Policies of $1,000 to $10,000 were written on the lives of males from sixteen to sixty years of age, but from sixty to sixty-five policies could not go beyond $5,000. Policies on the lives of women were at a higher rate and did not go beyond $5,000.[84]

The frontispiece to the second number of the *Farm and Home* after its removal to Memphis was an "admirable likeness" of Davis; this gave Browne occasion for a panegyric on his hero: "To every lover of constitutional liberty; to every admirer of pure patriotism, lofty intellect, cultivated intelligence, spotless integrity and dauntless courage; to every one capable of appreciating true nobility of character and the highest impulses of human action, JEFFERSON DAVIS must ever be the object of reverence and admiration. Although he no longer directs their government, or commands their armies—in the words of Mississippi's gallant orator, Col. L. Q. C. Lamar—'he still lives in the hearts of his countrymen, the President of an invisible Republic as enduring as Time, as indestructible as the stars.' *Semper honos, nomenque tuum laudesque manebunt.*"[85]

Now being actively associated with the insurance company, Browne added to the *Farm and Home* an "Insurance Department" and began to preach the value of insurance[86] and to warn the public against spurious companies and their dishonest representations: "While there is no class of men entitled to higher honors as benefactors of mankind than faithful, honest, and truthful insurance agents, there is none more deserving of reprobation than those who endeavor to obtain business by false representations and fraudulent devices—

by the promise of gigantic dividends and immense accumulation of profits."[87]

But alas! the Carolina Insurance Company fell victim to bad management, if not dishonesty and corruption within,[88] before the end of 1873, and Davis lost his all (the $15,000 which he put into it),[89] and Browne was forced to bring his *Farm and Home* to an end.[90] Browne moved back to Athens and warned Davis against staying longer in Memphis, a place now of unholy memories for both. "It is by far the worst climate I ever knew," he wrote Davis on July 16, 1874. "I do wish you were all away from that fearful place."[91]

Browne had good reason to dislike Memphis, not only for what nature had done to the place, but also for what man had not done. Yellow fever (which Browne called "The Cholera") hit Memphis in 1873 and took a fearful toll. Commenting on it, he said, "It was a fearful disease, whatever its proper name, has carried off a number of our citizens, and has brought desolation into many hitherto happy homes." The city did nothing to head off its spread: "The condition of the streets and alleys . . . was disgraceful to any people having any claim to decency. The highways absolutely reeked with every species of filth and stench, and not an organized effort was made in any direction that we could hear of to abate these nuisances. . . . Considering the amount of taxes levied on and wrung from the citizens of Memphis by the municipal government, there is less value received than in any other place on earth, not even excepting New York. . . . Ours is, it is true, the worst lighted, worst paved, and by all odds the filthiest city in America; but we have the biggest taxes."[92]

❧ XVI ❧

Literary Critic

ALTHOUGH BROWNE did not include "Literature" in the title of his *Southern Farm and Home: A Magazine of Agriculture, Manufactures and Domestic Economy,* he made his reviewing of books and periodicals an especially important feature. Probably no Southern farm journal or any other like journal in the United States carried as lively and wide criticisms of books. He used the title "Literary Department" with the sub-title "Editor's Book Table."

His fluency as a writer; his critical judgment, seasoned with a remarkable knowledge of world literature and history, not to mention his deep Southern sectional feeling; his lack of neutrality on any subject, but especially on religion, science, politics, and American constitutional law; and his varied experiences in Europe and America—all made him an unusual figure in the world of literary criticism. True it was that his audience was not large (never more than 10,000) and that the literary world never looked to a farm magazine to learn about the new books of the day; but the readers of the *Farm and Home* who were interested in such matters were treated monthly to his outpourings; and his reviews gave almost as much an insight into himself as they did to the works he was reviewing.

Although not neglecting agricultural works which came his way, his reviews were in no sense slanted to that field. Rather, he ran to fiction (American and foreign), history, science, travel, and to whatever the principal publishers of the times sent him. Hardly an issue of his magazine came out without reviews of books published by Harper and Brothers, D. Appleton and Company, J. B. Lippincott and Company, Lee and Shepard, and by lesser publishing houses. His newspaper career in New York and Washington before the Civil War had made him well known to publishers, and he became a close personal friend of the Appletons. In March, 1871, he noted that he had recently received in Macon a visit from his "old-time and valued friend, W. H. Appleton, Esq." of the Appleton company.[1]

In the light of the number of books Browne reviewed each month and in addition to the time he had to expend in producing the whole magazine, it must be concluded that he was an exceptionally speedy reader, especially of fiction. He read many of the English novelists of his time and generally gave them a high rating. He held Lord Lytton (Bulwer-Lytton) to be the "greatest novelist, the most versatile writer" England had known "since the days of Oliver Goldsmith."[2] George Eliot's novels had a charm which was "possessed by none other," a comment he had made in reviewing her *Middlemarch, A Study of Provincial Life*. "She can stir the profoundest emotions of her readers," he said "while at the same time she can satisfy the most critical taste."[3] "No novelist of our times approaches Wilkie Collins as a writer of sensational stories," Browne said, in referring to *Poor Miss Finch*. He believed Collins' *The Woman in White* was "incomparably the best."[4] In reviewing Anthony Trollope's *The Golden Lion of Granpere*, Browne said, "Everything that Trollope writes is readable. He cannot write an absolutely stupid book."[5] But he came near changing his mind in his review of *The Eustace Diamonds*, where he said: "It is impossible for Trollope to make a complete failure, but he certainly has not achieved a success. There never lived, we believe, so thoroughly mean and disgusting a character as the heroine, Lady Eustace, so consummate a fool as Lord Fawn, or so stupid a coxcomb as Mr. Greystock."[6]

Browne placed Charles Reade high up on the list of living English writers of fiction. In reviewing Reade's *Put Yourself in his Place,* he said: "There may be more of elegant romance and rhetorical beauty in the writings of Lord Lytton; more ingenuity and elaborate workmanship in the plots of Wilkie Collins; more gloomy power and austere sentiment in the works of George Eliot, and more magnificence of description and of the splendor of high life among 'lords and dukes and noble princes,' in the writings of Disraeli; but, notwithstanding his often insufferable vanity and self-love, his frequent extravagance, and the undue importance he gives to matters of no importance, it must, we think, be conceded that Charles Reade's works are the most powerful, most interesting, and the *best* novels of the day."[7] But when later Browne read Reade's *A Terrible Temptation,* he changed his mind: "A roue, a courtezan, a malignant scoundrel, an immodest chambermaid, a conceited puppy, and a weak, foolish woman are the *dramatis personae*. The incidents of the conduct natural to such characters are detailed with a daring obscenity, surpassing the 'Police Gazette,' and the most unclean intrigues of the scoundrel and the chambermaid are dwelt upon by the author with a lingering fondness which ought to exclude his works forever from the houses of all decent people."[8]

Browne found it refreshing to read the novel *Sarchedon, a Legend of the Great Queen,* by George John Whyte-Melville, the Scottish novelist, wherein "the gorgeous magnificence of Babylon and the wondrous power of the Assyrian Empire" were described. "It is a relief, too," he said, "to read a novel the scene of which is not laid in Mayfair or Belgravia, and the characters of which are not the Earl of Fitzdoodle, the Dowager Countess of Ballyragget, Sir Charles Leatherhead, the Polish Exile, Count Pullhisnoseki, &c., &c."[9]

Victorian correctness was ingrained in Browne's make-up so completely that he could not endure off-color language; but in reviewing a book he had to see it through however revolting it might become. *Folle Farine* was a novel written by Ouida, the pen name of Marie Louise de la Ramée, the daughter of a French teacher and an English mother. Browne called it "another of those coarsely sensuous, cruelly cynical, but powerful and eloquently written novels, for which Ouida has won unenviable but wide-spread fame. . . . On the whole, a more disgusting, wicked, or scandalously immoral book is not to be found in the English language, except it be some other of Ouida's books. What makes these books ineffably odious, is the knowledge that Ouida is a woman."[10] *Queen Hortense, an Historical Novel,* written by Luise Muhlbach (pen name for Klara Mundt, a German novelist) Browne thought was "entertaining and eminently readable," as were all of her novels.[11]

Browne did not find many Southerners or others writing of Southern life except such as Harriet Beecher Stowe in her *Uncle Tom's Cabin* and George W. Nichols in his *The Story of the Great March,* "which were stories certainly in the sense that that substantive is politely used as a substitute for another little monosyllable."[12] But there were some Southerners, mostly women, who did very well, as for instance Christian Reid (pen name for Frances C. Fisher, a daughter of a Confederate soldier killed in the war), whose *Valerie Aylmer* had an "animated and vigorous" style, a plot "full of interest and well sustained," and characters "well drawn."[13] And there was Augusta Jane Evans (later Wilson added), who wrote various books, some better than others. Browne found her *Vashti: or, Until Death do us Part* a rather immature book with characters using language above their station in life and stating facts that they could scarcely have known. It was not "wholly unnatural" though it was "often ridiculously fantastic." In fact it was "neither good, bad nor indifferent." Miss Evans had a great store of facts which she drew upon, often without any connection with the characters in her story, "producing effects quite as preposterous as if she were to write a description of Mount Vesuvius in eruption, and illustrate it with a picture of the Dismal Swamp."[14]

Although John Esten Cooke, Virginia novelist, was highly esteemed generally in his day, yet Browne found his *Hammer and Rapier* not quite to his liking for not giving other states than Virginia credit for what they did in the Civil War. For instance, Cooke in describing the Battle of Fredericksburg did not make "even passing mention of General Thomas R. R. Cobb," who played an important part in the engagement and lost his life there. Cooke should remember that "the monument which has been reared in every Southern heart to the memory of Virginia heroes, cannot be embellished or enlarged by destroying or defacing those monuments which have been erected in honor of the heroes of other States, whose memory is, and ever will be, cherished and revered even though they have not been permitted to occupy a niche in Mr. Cooke's pantheon."[15]

Antoinette Louisa Brown Blackwell was not likely to win Browne's approval either in her own self or for her book *The Island Neighbors, A Novel of American Life;* though as between the two Browne felt that the novel was not as bad as the woman. He commented: "Nobody reading this book would suppose for a moment, that the author is the well-known lecturer and bloomer spouter about 'Woman's Rights.' She presents herself certainly in a more acceptable character as a novelist than she has ever done as an advocate of the unsexing of her sex."[16]

When Browne disliked a book he was able to say so in the most positive terms, as he so well showed in commenting on Lady Blake's *The Lady of Lyndon*: "We have rarely seen a book so entirely void of purpose as this. It has no plot, no incident, no characters worthy of the name, no sensation, no moral, no anything, but one hundred and eighty-nine double column-pages of vapid twaddle, which no human being could ever be induced to read through unless he was weatherbound on a plantation, with nothing to read but this book, or the Patent Office Report."[17] But another lady wrote a novel which Browne thought well of. It was Mrs. J. H. Riddell's *A Life's Assize,* which he said was the "most remarkable novel we have read in many years. The story is unlike that of any novel in existence, and is told with a power, masculine vigor of style, amazing analysis and portraiture of character, and minute acquaintance with things of which women generally are wholly ignorant, that one's admiration of the book is equalled by surprise that a lady is the author." [18] Swinging from likes to dislikes, he had this to say about *Red as the Rose was She,* with no author given: "We tried in vain to discover any connection between the title of the book and any of the characters, but we suppose that in the progressive age in which we live, we ought not to expect that the title should have any relation to the book."[19]

On things Irish, Browne considered himself an authority by having been born an Irishman, and, therefore, James De Mille's "sensational novel" *An Open Question* was not true to the Irish by its "rendering of the Irish pronunciation and of the language of educated Irishmen and women . . . extravagantly exaggerated."[20]

Browne was a conservative in most human relations and a fundamentalist in religion. He was entirely out of harmony with the scientific findings of the day, especially as they came into conflict with the Bible. Of course, then, he found himself in disagreement with Darwin and Huxley and many of the lesser ones who dabbled in scientific writings and investigations; but he was pleased with John Tyndall, the Irishborn British physicist, who popularized science and whose writings did not offend Browne's religious views. Browne rated him the highest living authority on matters relating to natural philosophy: "He makes the most abstruse scientific questions intelligible and attractive to the unscientific reader."[21]

As for Charles Darwin, in reviewing his *A Naturalist's Voyage Round the World,* Browne said that it was "a delightful book," and although the germ of his theory of the origin of man might be said to appear in this book, it was "so small and indistinct" and was "so hid away by the mass of entertaining and instructive matter which the book contains, that it requires a microscopic search to find it."[22] But Browne was not as favorable to Darwin in reviewing his *The Descent of Man.* "But though we do not believe a word of Mr. Darwin's theory, and condemn it utterly as irreligious, and grotesquely false from beginning to end, his book contains much to interest and amuse the reader, and presents many facts in natural history which are not generally known."[23]

In reviewing Thomas H. Huxley's *Lay Sermons, Addresses and Reviews,* Browne admitted that Huxley handled his subjects "with wonderful ability, and that there are few English writers whose style is more admirable, or whose mode of expressing his thoughts in language is more terse, and forcible." He was a "great thinker," yet his book was "bad and dangerous" when he substituted natural phenomena for the works of Providence. Browne could not accept Huxley's theories and the "truth of the Bible" at the same time." "We cannot imagine profounder human misery," Browne said, "than that of him who convinced by Huxley, abandons the consolation and hopes afforded by the Christian religion, to embark with the Professor in search of that 'natural' knowledge, which, as he observes, furnishes 'justification not by faith, but by verification.' " [24]

Then, there was Sir John Lubbock, writer of popular science books, whose *Prehistoric Times* met Browne's strong disapproval. "If Sir John Lubbock's evolutionary doctrine is correct," said Browne, "Moses was necessarily an ignorant imposter, and the Bible is a tissue of fables. . . . To be what is called in the jargon of the day, a 'scientist,' or a man of science, it is essential in the very outset to be an infidel." [25] Browne was even more severe on the Duke of Somerset, a distinguished statesman, who in his leisure hours wrote a slim book entitled *Christian Theology and Modern Skepticism,* in which his "deliberate purpose" was "to unsettle all belief in revealed religion, in the divine origin of the Bible, in the divine nature of Jesus Christ, in the truth of Christianity, and to defend the wide-spread skepticism of the times by showing how science, literature and modern civilization have exposed what he terms the fallacies of the religious belief which was founded at Bethlehem and established at Calvary more than eighteen hundred years ago." [26] There was more scientific guessing in H. Charlton Bastian's *The Beginning of Life.* If "his hypotheses are correct," Browne said, "the Bible must be a fable." [27]

It was more than Browne's composure could stand to have the French writer of popular science, Louis Figuier, to say in his book *The To-Morrow of Death* that the soul had its last resting place in the sun after it had passed through a purifying process. "It is hardly possible to suppose that the author of this strange production is not a lunatick," Browne thought, "if he seriously believes what he wrote. It is the most wonderful confusion of facts and imagination, of science and conjecture that has ever been perpetrated, even by a Frenchman." [28] Samuel Watson, an American, who wrote various books on spiritualism, one of which he called *The Clock Struck One, and Christian Spiritualism,* offended Browne in a different way. Browne had great respect for Watson personally but he could not believe in ghost stories; and when Watson and others "ask us to credit ghost stories and treat them as divine revelations we must refuse, because our reason, as well as our faith, tell us that the stories are hallucinations as gross as that of the man who, though perfectly sane on all other subjects, believed that he was the prophet Ezekiel." [29]

Browne was glad to meet up with and review books which, he believed, refuted scientific infidel writings. He was pleased to recommend *The Desert of the Exodus,* by E. H. Palmer, the English Orientalist, who followed the route of the Israelites in their forty years of wanderings through the Sinai Peninsula. He said that "in these days when book-makers are so fond of producing sensations by attempting to prove 'the absurdities of the Bible' and the fallacies of religion, it is refreshing to find one who entertains the old fogey belief that the Bible history is true, and who devotes himself to the work of demonstrating the truth." [30] Also, he thought highly of Robert Withers Memminger's *What is Religion?* "We have read this book with close attention from beginning to end," Browne said, "and unhesitatingly pronounce it to be by far the ablest, most conclusive and convincing vindication of the religion of the Bible against the attacks of modern infidels that we have seen published." [31] Another book by Memminger, *Present Issues, or Facts Observable in the Consciousness of the Age,* met Browne's equal approval: "Its perusal would be of inestimable benefit to those who are allowing their minds to be influenced by the newfangled and heretical theories of the so-called modern scientists."[32]

Browne found special pleasure in the appearance of *Physiology of the Soul and Instinct, as Distinguished from Materialism,* by Martyn Paine, a writer of books on medicine, physiology, and kindred subjects. It was a refutation of Huxley and proof for those "who do not believe at all in Professor Huxley's worship of the Unknown and Unknowable, . . . [and] who do not believe in Mr. Darwin's theory that man is lineally descended from an 'anthropomorphous ape.' " He said that Paine had "utterly annihilated the entire school of materialists." [33] He applauded the work of St. George Jackson Mivart, an English biologist and critic of Darwin and Huxley, who opposed their theory of natural selection and who sought to reconcile science and Christianity. Browne said that Mivart failed to use one of the best weapons at hand—"the most powerful of all weapons in the vindication of truth—the Word of the Living God." He added: "Scientific writers of the present day seem to think that it is impossible to be scientific without being infidel, and that the least semblance of faith in religion, is wholly inconsistent with progress." [34]

Browne's interest in religion did not stem primarily from his attacks on books by scientists who either ignored the Bible or attacked its interpretation of natural phenomena. He was religious by nature, and any deviation from religion's proper presentation met with his disapproval. In reviewing *Song Life for Sunday Schools* by Philip Phillips, a gospel singer and music author and editor in Cincinnati, Browne said the songs were "really gems of piety, . . . but we cannot see how the woodcuts can illustrate anything but the rudeness of their engraving." They were "ugly and foolish." [35] In reviewing T. de Witt Tal-

mage's *Sermons,* Browne admitted that Talmadge was an orator of
uncommon power but he thought that the divine delved too much into
the scandals of the times, including Jim Fisk's amours and financial
swindles. Such subjects had no place in sermons.[36]

Browne was equally outraged by muckraking authors who dug up
or invented scandals for the sensations they might produce. He found
an especially shining target in *Medora Leigh, A History of an Autobiog-
raphy,* edited by Charles Mackay, for it gave him incidentally an opportunity to attack Harriet Beecher Stowe for raising the Lord Byron slander and to record a word of praise for Byron. "We were in hopes," said
Browne, "that we had done with that mass of garbage, filth, and
abomination of which 'The Byron Controversy' is composed. A more
disgusting compound was never thrust under the noses of people who
affect at least to be moral, refined and decently behaved. From the
time that Mrs. Harriet Beecher Stowe's odious book [*Lady Byron Vindicated*] appeared until the publication of that which is now before
us, we almost wished that we lived in an age and country where publications of such a class were seized by a censor of public morals and
given to the hangman to be burned. They are a disgrace to literature, to civilization and humanity, as obscene and degrading as the
Memoirs of the Marquis de Sade, which, even in Paris, at a time
when morality was not the chief characteristic of French society, was
suppressed by judicial order.

"We all know that Lord Byron was a vicious man, but we do not
know and will not believe that he was the monster that Mrs. Stowe
would represent him." Browne wanted to remember him for his
poems, "which will live as classics, so long as the English language
is spoken," and he did not want his "admiration of the genius of the
poet disturbed by a *post mortem* exposure of the alleged vices of the
man, particularly when the exposure can answer no purpose but to
gratify the greed of literary body-snatchers, and pander to the prurient
tastes of demoralized scandal-loving readers. Now that Spring is coming and we can open our windows and doors, let this ordure be swept
away and buried, and let us enjoy the fragrance of the violets." [37]

Browne was equally at home in reviewing solid historical works,
whether he agreed with them or not, especially English and American,
though Continental as well. In noticing Garibaldi's *The Rule of the
Monk,* Browne thought that "Garibaldi's anxiety to complete the 're-
generation of Italy' by the destruction of the Papacy, makes him a
prejudiced witness, and betrays him into the utterance of slanderous
statements too extravagant for belief." [38]

It took courage to disagree even slightly with John Stuart Mills, whose *Principles of Political Economy* Browne reviewed and admired, but for Mills himself, he had made a perfect failure as a member of Parliament, and though "his ridiculous advocacy of woman's rights and other equally absurd theories, it must be admitted that no writer has ever excelled him in the knowledge of the science of political economy." [39] *The Life and Times of Henry Lord Brougham, Written by Himself,* which was appearing in several volumes, so pleased Browne that he could hardly await the coming of the next one.[40] When William Edward Hartpole Lecky wrote his *Leaders of Public Opinion in Ireland,* even though Lecky was an Irish historian and essayist, Browne could not agree with him as to the causes of Irish discontent and with his saying that the Irish people were prosperous and educated.[41]

It was easy "to raise the Irish" in Browne when someone said unkind things about Jefferson Davis or called Southerners rebels or misstated facts about the late war. When John William Draper, scientist and author (English-born, coming to the United States when twenty) wrote his *History of the American Civil War* (in several volumes), he showed a prejudice and immaturity in his subject that greatly offended Browne. Browne said that a Southern reader would "find himself and his comrades and his fellow countrymen generally, often spoken of as rebels, traitors, murderers, etc., through all the thousands of pages of which the work consists. While the writer affects to be impartial, and desires to be philosophical, he frequently accepts and reissues as truth, all the slanders and exploded falsehoods uttered during the heat of the conflict by the army correspondents of the sensation newspapers of the North, including the stupid fiction of the capture of President Davis in 'female attire,' with the accessories of the 'high top boots,' and the 'tin pail.' " Browne said Draper had attempted an impossible task: "No man on either side, even though he be far the superior of Dr. Draper in all the qualities which constitute an historian, can possibly write now or for many years to come, an impartial history of the War between the Northern and Southern States." [42]

In reviewing *Haydn's Dictionary of Dates,* edited and revised for American readers by Benjamin Vincent, Browne gave high praise to the original edition, but the revisionist had badly strayed from the truth "when he chronicles the battles of Chancellorsville, the Wilderness and Spotsylvania as 'indecisive,' a judgment on which we are satisfied General Hooker and Grant cannot be found to agree with him." [43] Even such a dedicated Confederate-Southerner as Emily V. Mason, who had been a matron of Confederate hospitals in Virginia and had known the great war chief Lee in his home, did not meet

Browne's wholehearted approval in her *Popular Life of General Robert Edward Lee,* in dealing with his military career.[44] But no one could equal Browne in praise of Howell Cobb, and when *A Memorial Volume of the Hon. Howell Cobb of Georgia,* edited by Samuel Boykin, appeared, Browne called it "a touching and eloquent heartoffering to a great and good man by those who knew him best, and is indeed a 'memorial' which surpasses in beauty and enduring value any monument in brass or marble which could have been reared over his grave." [45]

When Alexander H. Stephens' *A Compendium of the History of the United States* appeared, Browne said that it was the only history "wherein the principles of the Constitution and Government perspicuously and truthfully [were] explained . . . without admixture of sectional prejudice or partisan misrepresentation." [46] Commenting on it again, he said that it was the "best work of its kind now extant. It should be a text-book in every school, and should find a place in every library, because it is the only work of its kind published in America which does not mutilate and distort the history of our country." He could not deny himself the pleasure of mentioning that it was published by E. J. Hale and Son, "who are Southern men, long connected with the Southern press, and were the victims of Sherman's houseburners on that notorious commander's 'Great March to the Sea.' " [47]

Although Browne could not claim Buchanan as a Southerner nor as an associate in the late war, yet "Old Buck" had an enduring enchantment over him that was not erased by the treatment he had received at the President's hand on the eve of his secession. Therefore, he could not refrain from chiding W. H. Sparks for writing in his unreliable *Memories of Fifty Years* that Buchanan had had a hand in the "bargain and corruption" accusations circulated against Henry Clay for his support of John Quincy Adams in the election of 1825. Browne said that the charges were false and that he had "heard Buchanan frequently deny the charges made against him with indignant warmth." [48]

In defense of the South and of his interpretation of governmental powers, Browne found a text in praising one dictionary to condemn another. In reviewing Joseph E. Worcester's *A Dictionary of the English Language,* he said that he always used it in preference to Webster's, for Webster had been revised in later editions to make the meaning of words conform to modern Radicalism, citing earlier and later definitions of Congress and state to show how "under the inspiration of reconstruction acts, ku-klux bills, enforcement laws and the like, old Dr. Webster is made to utter . . . stupid falsehoods." Browne cited examples "to show how Yankee progress can amend a dictionary as well as a constitution, even at the expense of moral forgery." [49]

No book on any subject came to Browne's editorial table which he did not feel competent to review (and generally rightly so). Although he had never been in Russia (or certainly not far), he said that William Hepworth Dixon, an English historian and traveler, had made several visits there and had "pleasantly written on the whole, though occasionally abrupt, and not unfrequently oracular and flippant. There is nothing from the Baltic to the Chinese wall on which he is not fully prepared to express an off-hand judgment, from which he evidently thinks an appeal would be absurd." Yet Browne admitted that the book had valuable information on Russia. The book Dixon wrote was entitled *Free Russia.*[50] Another traveler, Charles Nordhoff, a German who was brought to America as a child, wrote among his various works one entitled *California: A Book for Travelers and Settlers,* which greatly interested Browne, for at one time (as has been noted) he had thought of going there. He declared it to be the best guide book he had ever seen.[51] Another travel book that Browne read with great pleasure and amusement, which was "a great deal more than we can say of nine out of ten narratives of American travel," was *Up and Down and Around the World,* by James Brooks, the editor of the *New York Express,* from whom Browne had sought employment a few years previously.[52]

Browne was able to read Latin and Greek, and he was conversant with several modern foreign languages. In reviewing *Waddel's Greek Grammar for Beginners,* whose author (William Henry Waddel) was the professor of Ancient Languages in the University of Georgia, Browne said: "We imagine how we should have felt had such a simple, clear and concise grammar been put into our hands when we commenced the study of Greek, and had nothing to aid us but Valpy's elaborate volume." [53] He was equally pleased with Waddel's *A Latin Grammar for Beginners* and hoped that it would be adopted widely in the schools.[54] Browne said that *A German Reader* by George F. Comfort, a professor of Modern Languages in Syracuse University, was an excellent introduction to the "richest and most powerful of all modern languages." [55]

There was a light side to Browne's mental make-up which led him to enjoy W. T. Thompson's classic *Major Jones Courtship* and to say that "all that appreciate humor, wit, satire and keen perception of the grotesque and laughable, will make haste to buy a copy." [56] But there were limits to humor, Browne thought; and so, in reviewing L. J.

Bigelow's *Bench and Bar,* which he said was filled with witty sayings, jokes, and humor of lawyers and judges, both in America and England, he concluded that enough was enough and too much was a plenty—"There is such a thing as being too funny, and we think that this is the fault of all the collections of wit and humor we have seen." [57]

Browne thought that being a lady or a gentleman and knowing how to conduct oneself in company or out was a natural gift that did not have to be cultivated or directed into senseless artificial rules. Hence he regarded books of etiquette to be "the stalest, flattest, and most unprofitable reading." But since he had before him the *Bazar Book of Decorum,* he was constrained to say that it was the "least objectionable book of its kind of which we have any knowledge. Its object is not merely to instruct its students that clean hands and clean linen are requisite in polite society, that spitting upon a carpet or blowing the nose with the fingers are objectionable indulgences, and that putting one's feet on the table or mantle piece may be a convenient and easy position, but one which politeness forbids." [58]

As has appeared, Browne's book-reviewing was almost completely concerned with intellectual subjects, even though it appeared in a farm magazine; but he did not entirely neglect agricultural, livestock, and other outdoor books that came his way. Charles Barnard, hiding under the name of Mrs. Maria Gilman, wrote a book which he called *My Ten Rod Farm,* telling of the wonderful amounts of farm products raised upon it. Taking the author to be serious, Browne declared that it was "a work worthy of the manufacturer of wooden nutmegs. It is a stupid, palpable fraud, written by somebody who is as ignorant as dishonest, and who takes good care to suppress the name of the locality where the 'Ten Rod Farm' is located." He predicted that before long he would "see a work published somewhere in Yankeedom showing how one square yard of ground can be made to sustain a large family and yield a handsome surplus income." [59] If Browne had known that the same "Mrs. Gilman" was to write a book called *My Handkerchief Garden* and had already written another entitled *Farming by Inches,* he would have sensed that the author was dealing in high humor or was trying to pull the reader's leg.

In reviewing G. Fleming's *Practical Horseshoeing,* Browne agreed completely with the author in decrying the barbarity generally used in that operation. "One half of the injuries done to horses can be directly traced to bad shoeing. For one blacksmith who understands the anatomy of a horse's foot, comprehends the purpose of a shoe and how to put one on, it is no exaggeration to say there are a thousand who are wholly ignorant of these things—who not only leave undone what they ought to have done, but do a number of things they ought not to have done. Especially is this true of the Southern blacksmith, with his frog cutting, burning and paring, and many other barbarous practices." [60] Browne noted that F. O. Morris' *Dogs and their Doings* contained remarkable anecdotes about the wonderful doings of dogs, many of them being "of the Munchausen order, but are interesting, nevertheless." It was a good book for boys.[61]

Browne did not fail to note his magazine exchanges, and often he listed their tables of contents. Now and then he gave more than passing mention to certain of their articles, especially where they aroused his disapproval. Although he received some agricultural journals, most of his exchanges were literary, among which were *Appleton's Journal, Harpers' Magazine, Southern Magazine* (Baltimore), *Littell's Age, Lippincott's Magazine,* and such British journals as *Edinburgh Review, Westminster Review,* and *Blackwood's Magazine.* He mentioned with much approval a newspaper-magazine weekly published in New York and called the *South,* devoted entirely to the interests of the Southern States. "Our people would be largely gainers if they would forswear the Police Gazette," Browne commented, "and other infamous 'picture papers,' published at the North, and buy this really valuable paper." [62]

The periodical that Browne looked upon with the greatest favor was *Appleton's Journal.* The owners were Browne's friends, and he was further drawn to their journal by the respect it showed for the South. In reviewing one of the issues, Browne said, "The entire absence from its columns of the gentle and benevolent allusions to 'rebels,' 'traitors,' 'pirates,' etc., which are to be found in other Northern publications, when reference is made to the South, gives *Appleton's Journal* another great charm for the Southern reader." Browne then suggested that the day had about arrived for "hands across the bloody chasm." "Is it not time, now," he asked, "that the soldiers of both armies have laid aside their weapons and have forgotten the animosities which the war engendered, that those less noble combatants who have never wielded or felt other weapons than the pen and the engraver's *stylus,* should cease from their manufacture of falsehood and misrepresentation, and use their faculties for some better purpose than the promotion of hatred, malice and uncharitableness?" [63]

Lippincott's was not as charitable toward the South, if for no other reason than it published now and then articles by Edward A. Pollard, "that wretched literary outcast, . . . so full of the vilest time serving, gross falsehood, and flagrant misrepresentation, that we wonder how the editor of a respectable periodical would allow such a paper [Pol-

lard's "The Condition of the South"] to deface his columns." [64]
Browne disliked Pollard, the wartime editor of the *Richmond Ex-*
aminer, especially for his attacks on the Davis administration. Noticing again an article by Pollard in *Lippincott's* entitled "The Negro
in the South," Browne said that he showed "mendacity, malignity,
ignorance and impudence raised to the *n*th power." And taking from
this the opportunity to refer to Pollard's life of Davis, Browne said,
"The man who never having seen President Davis except passing in
the street, who never spoke one word to him, and never had any opportunity of knowing anything about him, would have the audacity
to write the 'Life of Jefferson Davis,' is fully capable of writing from
a garret in New York, or from behind a desk in the Custom House, a
vivid description of the present condition and status of the negro in
the South, in relation to labor, society, morals, and politics. He knows
as much of the negro as he does of President Davis. His motive is the
same in both literary efforts—to malign and villify the South, and his
object is also identical—a few dirty greenbacks purchased at the cost
of everything which a decent man values." [65] Browne said *Lippincott's*
was "eminently readable and deservedly ranks high" where its pages
were "not defaced by the malevolent hissing of Pollard." [66]

Seldom noting any article in an agricultural journal beyond listing
it, Browne had to do himself the pleasure of attacking in full force the
editor of the *Rural New Yorker* for his answer to one of his correspondents who asked him, "Shall we go South?" Browne said that the
article equalled "in malice, sectional hate, unscrupulous vindictiveness
anything that we have ever read in the columns of Theodore Tilton's
Independent, either of Forney's 'two papers, both daily,' or any of the
dirty radical sheets which adventurous loyalists have issued in the
Southern States in order 'to get a share of the public printing.' " If
this article had appeared in a political journal, Browne said that he
would not have noticed it, but coming in a farm paper, it showed
how "Northern periodicals, whose interest it would seem to be to
tell the truth and shame the devils by whom they are surrounded, step
out of their appropriate sphere, ignore the avowed objects of their
existence, and in order to gratify their hatred, malice and all charitable-
ness toward the South, publish columns full of slanders with a perfect
knowledge that every statement they contain is a deliberate falsehood."

The advice of the editor of the *Rural New Yorker* had been not
to go, for a Northerner would be ostracized in that barbarous land.
Browne replied that he knew of no place where that was true if the
newcomer came as a respectable person and did not assume a superiority and other insulting manners: "But if you come to preach the doc-

trine of radicalism and social equality—if you come to make us believe and admit that you are our superiors in morals, religion, education, intellect, refinement, manners and politics, we strongly advise you to stay at home and enjoy the society of the editor of the *Rural New Yorker.*" [67]

Browne was always alert to answer any traducer of the South or anyone who denied the glory of the Confederacy. It was, therefore, hard for him to understand why such a respectable English journal as the *British Quarterly Review* admitted to its pages an article entitled "The American Civil War," written by an unnamed American. It was evident, he thought, that it was "the production of a pettifogging advocate hired by his Radical masters to traduce and villify a brave people; and our only wonder is that a British periodical laying claim to respectability would give such a paper a place in its columns." [68]

Always regardful of the people among whom he lived, Browne could hardly have neglected to praise *Burke's Weekly for Boys and Girls,* published in Macon by the firm which published the *Farm and Home* before it moved to Memphis. Of this little magazine Browne said: "We cannot imagine how Southern parents can continue to purchase for their children the frothy, vapid, and often offensive trash of which many of the Northern juvenile books and papers are composed, and neglect to patronize a Southern periodical of high merit, such as that now before us." [69]

And, thus, did Browne, in telling what he thought about the many books on many subjects which he reviewed in his *Farm and Home,* leave no reader in doubt of his deep learning, his facile pen, and the likes and dislikes that helped to make up his character.

❧ XVII ❧

Professor Browne

NOT FOR a year and more after becoming editor of the *Farm and Home* did Browne move his residence to Macon. He much regretted having to leave Athens, and Mrs. Browne was almost disconsolate, for after leaving the Washington of Buchanan days, she never enjoyed living in any place as much as in Athens. In Macon the Brownes did not buy or rent a house, but instead they arranged with the Lanier Hotel to set off an end of one of its corridors with adjoining rooms to which they brought their own furniture.

The situation between Mrs. Browne and Mrs. Howell Cobb was now reversed. When following the war Howell Cobb practiced law in Macon and lived there, Mrs. Browne carried on a correspondence with Mrs. Cobb and kept her informed on happenings in Athens; now it was Mrs. Cobb, who had moved back to Athens after her husband's death, informing Mrs. Browne—and unintentionally adding to her loneliness. In March, 1871, Mrs. Browne wrote Mrs. Cobb that all the people in Macon were very kind, but she missed the friendliness of Athens very much. Still, she felt like a "total stranger," she said, "I have no intimate friends with whom I can talk of old times. Nobody I love as I love you." She said that she had been ill (which was generally her condition), "suffering a great deal from my throat and spine together with some fever, and I have been so nervous as to be almost unable to sit up." She took short walks but returned generally fatigued.[1]

There was at least one pleasant aspect to life in Macon; about fifty miles to the south, in Americus, lived John A. Cobb, Browne's wartime friend, who ran several plantations in the vicinity. As opportunities afforded, there were visits back and forth by these two families.[2]

When in later 1871 Browne became Secretary of the Carolina Life Insurance Company with headquarters in Memphis, Browne bought the *Farm and Home* from the Burke people and moved it and his residence to Memphis. Mrs. Browne was always loyal to her "General" and as a most dutiful wife went to Memphis to live, but with, no doubt, misgivings. However, she found one sentimental attachment there which tied her to the pleasant life she led in ante bellum Washington: the inimitable Kati Thompson (Mrs. Jacob Thompson), burned out of her Oxford, Mississippi, home by the Yankee troops, was now living in Memphis. She wrote Mrs. Howell Cobb, in March, 1872, that she enjoyed Mrs. Browne, "who comes out to see me & stays all night. Her health is not very good. She is boarding at one of the best hotels & takes life easy." [3]

But life was never easy for Mrs. Browne. The climate of Memphis was much more enervating than Macon's, and as a result her health steadily grew worse. In early 1873 General Browne wrote that she was "quite broken. She is but the shadow of her former self, and no treatment, no change of air or scene seems to benefit her. She seems to grow weaker and weaker every day and is so painfully nervous that the falling of a pin seems to startle her." [4] Reporting a little later he said: "For several months she has been growing worse here. The climate seems to disagree with her, she dislikes the place and the people very much, and has no confidence whatever in the physicians, several of whom she has tried and discarded." She was becoming "alarmingly ill & her nervousness becoming greatly aggravated." As a result, in early March he decided to take her to Augusta, Georgia, to a physician whom she had known and in whom she had confidence; but she soon lost faith in him and was suffering from "depression of spirits" and "excitability." Browne could not remain long in Augusta and soon returned to Memphis where his duties "imperatively" required his presence "and I cannot afford to resign." He added, "I am intensely anxious and unhappy and can only pray to God to lighten the burden I have to bear." [5]

Mrs. Browne was soon back in Memphis, and on May 5, 1873, she died.[6] The editor of the *Memphis Daily Appeal* paid this tribute to her: "With feelings of deep sadness we announce the death of the estimable wife of our distinguished townsman General William M. Browne, which occurred in our city on Monday, May 5th. Though the terrible blow was not wholly unexpected, yet it fell with crushing force upon the bereaved and disconsolate husband and a large circle of friends. . . . Mrs. Browne was the youngest daughter of Hon. Denison Beket, Yorkshire, England, and was born April 14, 1830. For many years she had resided in America, and latterly in our city, where she had by her christian graces and fine womanly qualities endeared herself to a large circle of friends who mourn her loss with no ordinary grief. We tender to General Browne our condolence in his great bereavement, and humbly hazard the hope that the father of all mercies will give him strength to bear this deep affliction." [7]

Browne had great love and affection for his wife, which were only increased by her long ill health. He could hardly close a letter, however official, without including his wife's kind remembrances. And often he had occasion to say, "I am in great trouble. My wife is very ill." [8] During her last days Mrs. Browne's thoughts were on Athens and her friends there, as they often were. She wanted her fur cape to be given to Mrs. Howell Cobb, and she left her Episcopal prayer book, which she had used in Washington, to Mary Ann Cobb, a daughter of Mrs. Howell Cobb. [9]

Mrs. Browne was entombed in Memphis, but not permanently, for she had often told General Browne that she wanted to be buried in Athens; and when he asked her why, "she always said 'because I shall be near the Cobbs. I cannot bear the idea of being among perfect strangers.'" In acknowledging the condolences of Mrs. Cobb, Browne said, "Human sympathy is not a cure but it certainly is a balm for grief." [10]

It took Browne a few months to close his affairs in Memphis and make arrangements to transfer his wife's body to Athens. In August, still in Memphis, he said, "I am fearfully lonely and desolate here. Of all the places I ever lived in, this is by far the most disagreeable in every point of view. Situated as I am with my present feelings and tastes, I might just as well be on a desert island." [11]

Browne bought a lot in the beautiful Oconee Hill Cemetery overlooking the river and directly across the driveway from the Howell Cobb lot. [12] He commissioned a rock mason to construct a substantial granite tomb. By early September Browne was back in Athens, for "I must *see* that work done. I must superintend it in person." [13] On September 7, 1873, Jefferson Davis, in Memphis, wrote his wife in Canada: "Browne went to Athens, Ga. with the remains of his Wife & has not returned." [14] Thereafter the anniversary of Mrs. Browne's death was not forgotten, for the General was supplied with flowers by Athens ladies to lay on his wife's tomb. [15]

Brown was never more adrift in his life than now, and never more disconsolate—his wife gone, all his business interests a failure, practically penniless. He was back where he was when the war ended. But he could always depend on his Athens friends for comfort and on that ever-faithful New York friend Barlow for money, and on Butterworth, too. In October, 1873, he managed to make a trip to New York in search of something to do and, of course, saw Barlow; but he returned empty-handed. [16] Always plagued with ill health, he had grown worse by the end of the year, and on December 20 he wrote Barlow: "I have lost the use by paralysis in my left leg and am suffering torture continually from a pain in my spine just below the neck." Having no chance to earn a livelihood, "I am compelled to hope that my struggle may be short." He asked Barlow to "write me when you have leisure. News from an old friend from the outer world" relieved the "desolation" that oppressed him. Reminiscing on the chance he had had earlier to go to California with Butterworth, Browne now regretted not having done so, for he would have found something to do to relieve him "from all further anxiety as to the future supply of bread and meat. Now I feel as if I was in one of those torture chambers said to have been used by the inquisition, the walls of which gradually contract until they crush out life." [17]

Already knowing of Browne's low state, Barlow wrote him on the same day that at "Butterworth's request I send you check herewith for $250—which please acknowledge." And he advised him that "in your present state of health you should not attempt work of any kind, not even weekly letters for the press and until I hear that you are recovered I hope you will not attempt it. When you are well enough let me know and I will do what you want, or if you do not recover your health speedily let me know so that I may serve you in some other manner."[18]

Browne was, of course, hoping to get back into newspaper work, his first love; and Barlow was doing what he could to secure him a position with one of the New York papers. Barlow wrote him in May, 1874: "I am at work with Bennett [of the *New York Herald*] & reasonably hopeful. Failing him I really do not know of anything that you can do here, but something may turn up. For present wants I enclose check for $100."[19]

Browne had no special desire to secure newspaper work in New York City; undoubtedly he would have preferred a position in the South, and probably his choice would have been a sufficiently lucrative position as correspondent for one or more newspapers, which would have made it possible for him to live in Athens. He wrote Jefferson Davis in the summer of 1874 that he had a fruitless trip to Macon;[20] but soon thereafter he was employed as a political editor of the *Macon Morning Star*.[21]

In the meantime he was making his home in Athens, always a welcome guest in the homes of the Cobbs and Barrows. He dined often with the Colonel David Crenshaw Barrows and made the Lamar Cobbs' home his "regular Sunday night resort."[22] He was a great favorite in the home of Howell Cobb, Jr., and he always made it a point to visit in the home of Colonel Barrow at any time, but especially when Mrs. John A. Cobb of Americus, a daughter of the Colonel's, was in Athens staying at her father's. On one occasion she reported to her husband, in Americus, that Browne was in for the evening and that he was "still chatting away & it is now *midnight*." When she came out of the parlor "a few minutes ago, he was in the midst of a journey of his through Poland."[23]

Browne had an incurable social streak which had to be served, and this fact acted as a bracer to his customary bad health. Clara Elizabeth (familiarly called Bessie), an unmarried sister of Mrs. John A. Cobb, was always good company for the General; and so pleasantly did he seem to be attached to her that the rumor was soon going the rounds that they were to be married[24]—even only a year after Mrs. Browne had died; but there was no substance to it, and within a few years Bessie had passed on, carried away by the dread tuberculosis.

Athens was a strategic location for Browne in addition to being the residence of many of his friends; it was the seat of the University of Georgia, which was, indeed, an attraction for a person of Browne's intellectual interests. The University had been closed during the latter part of the war but had reopened early in 1866, and in recruiting its faculty, like other Southern colleges and universities, it was turning to Confederate leaders, military as well as governmental.

First, in the year of its reopening, it offered the professorship of Civil Engineering to Major General George Washington Custis Lee, the eldest son of the great Confederate Commander, but Lee chose instead, like his father, to go to Washington College (later Washington and Lee University). Thereafter the Georgia Trustees elected to the position Major General Martin Luther Smith, a New Yorker long in the United States Army who had married an Athens girl and who from "associations, feelings and interests" went with the Confederacy. Unfortunately, he died soon after his election.

Like most other American universities and colleges, the University of Georgia had no formal history department; but in 1868 it decided to establish one and it named Alexander H. Stephens to head it. For six months Stephens dilly-dallied on acting on the invitation and then reported to the Chancellor that he was compelled "to suspend" his acceptance because of ill health.[25] Browne seems not to have been suggested for the position, but undoubtedly he would have been a willing replacement. At least his attitude was correct in reporting on Stephens, saying that his appointment would "certainly give great *eclat* to the University" but observing that his labor would be "arduous" and that the duties of the position would be "confining and monotonous."[26] Furthermore, to leave his home "Liberty Hall," in Crawfordsville, "and all its comforts, change all his habits, abandon his profession (of law, at which he would make three times as much as at teaching), and enter upon an entirely new way of life, would be a great sacrifice, and although he is anxious to serve the college, he hesitates whether he can do so."[27] Stephens was now in the midst of writing his *Constitutional View of the Late War Between the States,* and to accept the position would interfere with that work.

Although Browne had not liked Stephens' attitude toward the Confederate administration during the war, he had no desire to dissuade "Little Aleck" from accepting the professorship; and later when Stephens was elected a trustee of the University, Browne wrote him urging him to accept: "You can do vast service to the college and to the educational interests of the State."[28]

Browne would have been a valuable choice for the history professorship when the department was created and offered to Stephens; but at the same time there was established a professorship of Modern Languages, to include French, German, and Spanish at a salary of $2,000, and Browne, who knew these languages well, was being strongly promoted for this position. There were other candidates and the election was postponed for six months, during which time the opposition to Browne became strong enough to secure his defeat.[29] At this time Browne was conducting his plantation in Oglethorpe County at a loss and would have greatly preferred dealing with students than trying to get labor out of trifling freedmen.

Now, in 1874, a half-dozen years had passed during which time Browne had edited a newspaper, run a farm journal, helped manage an insurance company, and was again back in Athens. The Department of History had never been filled, and here was a chance for Browne's Georgia friends to do something for him, since Barlow had been unable to secure him an editorship in New York. Browne was doing all he could within proper bounds to promote his chances, using his friends inside Georgia and out. At his request Jefferson Davis was using his influence among his Confederate acquaintances and associates. In July, 1874, less than a month before the Trustees were to meet, Browne wrote Davis: "Fortune has dealt so harshly with me in the past I am, I suppose, inclined to despondency so that I am by no means sanguine of success as to the Professorship." Chancellor Andrew A. Lipscomb was giving up his position for less arduous work, and Browne feared that he might stand for the history professorship, in which case Browne felt that he would be out of the contest. But he thanked Davis for letters he had written and was sure that they would insure his election, if Lipscomb did not stand for the position, adding that he prized Davis' "good opinion above all the rest of the world."[30]

Browne had good reason to feel optimistic. Among the Trustees were Colonel Barrow, his son Pope Barrow, Lamar Cobb, and several other warm friends. A few days before the election, one of Colonel Barrow's daughters wrote, "Pa and Gen. Browne are sitting on the front porch discussing his chances of being elected. He is beginning to feel a little uneasy."[31] Three or four who were especially friendly to Browne had not come for the meeting; there were then twenty-one Trustees in town and Browne thought that he could count on ten. But how would Robert Toombs stand, about whom Browne had written some mean things; and what would Joe Brown's position be, about whom Browne had written meaner things? True enough, Browne had written under pen names, but his identity must have been suspected and what he thought of them was no secret. But fortunately there had been a "bridging over the bloody chasm, created by the black flag war between Toombs and Browne,"[32] and Joe Brown was as adept in forgetting personal feuds as he was in changing his party allegiance in search of the main chance, which he always found. For *mirabile dictu* it was Joe Brown who nominated General Browne for the professorship of history, and although there were other candidates for the position, the minutes of the meeting indicate that no other names were voted on.[33]

Being widely known for his scholarly attainments, Browne was warmly welcomed to his new position. One of the town editors called him "a gentleman of education and learning rarely equalled, and with an experience in the history and government of both this country and Europe." [34] And the *Southern Christian Advocate* said that he was "a worthy Methodist lay-man, and gentleman of polished manners and most liberal culture," and that he brought "to the Chair of History and Political Science, abilities of a very high order." He was a "graduate with its highest honors, of the University of Dublin, and with extensive diplomatic experience."[35]

Apparently Browne was slow in informing his friend Barlow of his good fortune; for Barlow wrote him almost three months after Browne's election: "I want to know how you are—what you are doing and all that—write me fully." He said that because of changes recently made on the *New York Herald*, "I have hopes of doing something for you. Hitherto it seemed impossible."[36] Either Browne had already written Barlow or he wrote immediately on receipt of his letter, telling him of his new position but informing him of his extreme poverty, for Barlow came back at once as handsomely as ever a father responded to the needs of a son. He said he and Butterworth "will put you in shape. Let me know what books and clothes you want, with size of latter, & I will see that they are sent, & draw on me for any ready cash you want, either $50 or $100, whichever is necessary."[37] Browne's New York friends were as thrilled as he was over his securing at last a permanent position.

Not only did Barlow outfit Browne with new clothes and money, but he, probably unnecessarily, provided him with certain American histories for his study, not assuming that Browne could check out of the University Library whatever he needed. As George Bancroft's monumental American history was standard in those days, Barlow scurried around to secure him a set. He also sent him a watch for a Christmas present. It can hardly be thought that Browne put up such a hard luck story as to give the impression that he lacked even a watch; Barlow probably wanted to make him a special present and could think of nothing better than a watch.[38]

Browne was forever grateful for the aid Barlow gave him now, had already given him, and would on occasion continue to give him— never could ingratitude be charged against him, but a suspicion could be aroused that there was a weakness in his character that suggested and welcomed these gifts. But so highly did Barlow regard Browne that it never appeared to him that Browne might be "using" him. And Browne never regarded Barlow's munificence as such, for he was always ready to return favors when he was able. As has already been mentioned, the Georgia peach was a favorite with Barlow, and Browne never wearied in sending him this delectable fruit—even sending him peach trees, hoping that they could withstand the Long Island winters.[39] Barlow often acknowledged Browne's gifts of peaches and suggested more: "Send me some more peaches if you can, those dried whole";[40] "I have to thank you for the peaches, which are excellent."[41] Mrs. Barlow liked the peaches very much.[42] And Browne sent Barlow other presents, especially at Christmas time, not specified in their correspondence.

Barlow's gifts to Browne were not necessarily all in response to Browne's needs, as were clothes and money itself, but generally they were expressions of sentimental considerations, as well as intellectual, and convivial. Barlow sent Browne two copies "of a rare portrait of Jefferson" and suggested that he might want to pass one of them on to the University.[43] And as both were connoisseurs of good wines and fine whiskeys, neither of which might readily be found in Athens, Barlow made presents of them to Browne. In acknowledging a gift, Browne wrote: "Corn whiskey is our native beverage, and my very limited experience enables me to state positively that rather than to drink it I would subit to all the ills that 'flesh is heir to.' "[44]

To the regret of both, they lived too far apart to visit each other as they often had when they lived in New York and in Washington; but Browne occasionally made trips to the North and if he came near New York, Barlow was sure to have him as a guest. In 1876 Browne was hoping to attend the Centennial Exposition in Philadelphia if he could "muster the requisite number of greenbacks," and he informed Barlow that if he made the trip he would try to go on to New York "and shake you by the *hand*."[45] Barlow insisted, "If you come to Phila., you must come on to New York."[46]

The next year Barlow was planning a trip to Georgia during the summer, and he wrote Browne: "If I do I shall try to see you at Athens or somewhere else where you can meet me."[47] He was delayed and informed Browne that he would give him "an early notice"[48] if he did come. It is not known whether the trip was made and whether these two good friends got together in Georgia this year; but the following year (1877), Barlow was again thinking of making a trip to the South and informed Browne that "I mean to hold you to your promise to join me somewhere in Georgia during the spring."[49] Too, it is not known whether this trip was made.

Barlow was always solicitous of Browne's health and often gave him advice. In 1878 he wrote: "I am afraid that you, like myself, have not taken enough out of door exercise & now that you are too stout to admit of much work, with comfort." He inquired of Browne whether he could get good wines in Athens and suggested: "If not I will send you some with much pleasure" and offered the hope: "There is no reason that I can see why your trouble should not pass away with the warm weather."[50] In a pessimistic mood at this time, he wrote Barlow: "There are very few left who feel any interest in me, and I believe you are one of that number."[51] Probably, Browne had in mind his former Northern friends.

❧ XVIII ❧

Service to the University of Georgia

WHEN BROWNE was elected Professor of History and Political Science at the University of Georgia, he became a part of the first American state university to be chartered, though not the first to be established. It was chartered in 1785, but for lack of funds it was not founded until 1801. In the meantime, the University of North Carolina had been chartered in 1789 and was actually set going in 1793.

The University at the time Browne joined it extended its annual activities over one term of ten months, beginning in October and continuing without intermission (except Christmas Day and later one week for Christmas vacation) until August. The students were severely restricted by many rules. There were rules requiring attendance at morning prayers in the Chapel, every Sunday at some church in town, and on Sunday afternoons again at services in the Chapel, conducted by the Chancellor. They were not allowed to leave town without permission; and when a student should accumulate nine unexcused absences he was excluded from the University. During the time of Browne's services the number of students varied from 116 to 229, with an average of about 160.

Coming under the Land Grant Act, the University required military drill of all students unless excused for satisfactory reasons, but drill was limited to one hour three afternoons a week. The uniform consisted of "a frock coat, of standard cadet-gray cloth, single-breasted, military cut, with a single row of Georgia buttons, four in rear, and three smaller on the sleeve cuff, with a scroll of black cord on the sleeves." The pantaloons were of the same material, with a black stripe one inch wide. The vest was of like material, "cut with straight collar, buttoning high, with smaller Georgia buttons." [1]

The University in Athens was organized in three colleges or schools; Franklin College (the academic part), Georgia State College of Agriculture and Mechanic Arts, and the Department of Law. It awarded these degrees: Bachelor of Arts, Bachelor of Science, Bachelor of Philosophy, Bachelor of Agriculture, Bachelor of Chemical Science, Bachelor of Engineering, Bachelor of Law, Bachelor of Civil Engineering, Master of Arts, and Doctor of Medicine (earned at the Medical College, located in Augusta).

Browne had the enviable opportunity of organizing the first history and political science department in the University. He labeled his courses simply as history, but he included political science and especially constitutional history wherever they could logically be added. Students for every degree except Law, Civil Engineering, and, of course, Medicine (in Augusta) were required to take history; but the subject was not taught in any Junior Class. It was required of all Freshmen and Sophomores for these degrees (except only by Freshmen for the Bachelor of Science); and all students working for the Bachelor of Arts were required to take it in their Senior year also. There were separate courses for all Freshmen, all Sophomores, and for Seniors, every one meeting two hours a week. As there were, thus, three courses, Browne had a teaching load of six hours.

Browne stated that the purpose of his courses was to give the student "a knowledge of the facts and leading occurrences connected with the progress of the political and social organizations of the principal nations of the world" and to assist in forming "a correct comprehension of the relations those facts and occurrences bear to each other, and to permanent springs of human action, so that in the pages of history he may find a vital illustration of religion, politics and human progress in their relation to government and the condition of society." [2]

Methods of teaching were the same in all of Browne's courses. He used textbooks "combined with frequent lectures in explanation of the text." His textbooks varied, of course, with the progression of his classes. Freshmen were treated largely to general history and were required to use *Wilson's Outlines of History* as the text. The same work was used for Sophomores with the addition of Alexander H. Stephens' *Compendium of the History of the United States.* Browne gave his Seniors a more extensive fare that included American, English, and French history, and a broader history of civilization, using as texts the appropriate works of David Hume, Henry Hallam, Francois Guizot, the first volume of Stephens' *Constitutional View of the Late War between the States,* and selected parts of the works of John C. Calhoun. Browne listed also more than a dozen special works for additional readings, which included George Bancroft, Macaulay, De

Tocqueville, Henry Wheaton on International Law, and Emerich de Vattel's *Law of Nations.*

Knowing Browne's philosophy of American government, constitutional law, and politics, one should not be surprised at his using works by Stephens and Calhoun and should be no more surprised at the adverse criticism he received in the North for doing so. Even one of Browne's students was reported to have taken his advice "too literally to study Stephens' History slowly & that he has found hunting more agreeable than exploring the depths of constitutional law." [3] But Browne was informed that Stephens himself "spoke in most flattering terms of your lectures on the Constitution" and hoped that Browne would publish his lectures on that subject.[4]

In fact, after a few years of teaching, Browne wrote a long treatise on constitutional law, and, being urged to publish it, he sought to do so, but his work never found a publisher. As the publishing business was largely a Northern undertaking, it is easy to understand why no Northern firm would risk bringing out a work that would be unpopular with those who supported the centralizing influence in government. Browne was especially desirous of supplanting John Norton Pomeroy's *Introduction to the Constitutional Law of the United States, Especially Designed for Students, General and Professional,* which had appeared in 1870. Browne was sorry to know that this work was being used at West Point to indoctrinate the cadets in an erroneous and vicious interpretation of American history and government.

Browne wrote to Barlow in 1878 that because he believed in the limitations set forth in the Constitution, "perhaps I have become fossilized and ought to be put away in some cabinet of political curiosities, labeled 'curious specimens of a Jeffersonian Democrat of the ante bellum period.' " Still, he said that when he read Senator Bayard's speeches, "I think I hold live opinions, but generally I feel very Rip Van Winkleish." [5]

To give Barlow some idea of the content of his course in Constitutional Law and to show him the kind of written examinations he gave his students, Browne sent Barlow a set of questions he used in 1878. "First, demonstrate by historical facts and by the letter of the Constitution, that the U. S. are not a consolidated Nation, but a Confederation of Sovereign States, and that the Govt. of the U. S. under the Constitution, was instituted *by* the States & *for* the States & is one of limited and enumerated powers." Second, how does the United States Constitution make a person a citizen of Georgia, of the United States? Third, what are the meanings of "Supreme Law of the land"

and of "common defence and general welfare"? Fourth, define treason against the United States, piracy, letters of marque and reprisal, ex post facto law, bill of attainder, privilege of the writ of habeas corpus, eminent domain. Fifth, what is the extent of the United States judicial power? Show that "it cannot extend to political compacts." Sixth, "why are appropriations of public money by Congress for an exploration of the Polar Seas, for an observation of the Transit of Venus, or for adorning the capitol, constitutional; and the appropriation for the Centennial Exposition unconstitutional?" Seventh, when and by whom can the writ of habeas corpus be suspended, "and in what cases and under what circumstances does the Constitution warrant federal armed interference in a State?" "Sign pledge in full." [6]

A Senior examination in American history (though more in Political Science than in History, it would seem) involved the following items: constitutional status of the colonies and the causes of the Revolution; "aggressions of the British Government" and colonial reaction and defense; facts showing that the states (colonies) "always acted as separate and distinct political communities, and never as one nation"; defects of the Articles of Confederation; disputes and settlements in the Constitutional Convention of 1787; proof of the federal character of the government; "Vattel's definition of a Federal Republic"; facts showing "that absolute sovereignty was thereby recognized as residing with the people of each State respectively, and not with the people of all the States as one mass." [7]

Having no point of view to promote, Browne's examination in English history were made up of questions involving almost entirely the memorization of historical facts, as: all the Anglo-Saxon and Danish rulers and others down to Henry VIII; the Witanagemot; Domesday Book; feudal system; Macbeth's usurpation; Magna Carta; annexation of Ireland to the British monarchy; causes of the War of the Roses; Wickliffe; powers and composition of Parliament; life of Cardinal Wolsey; and Statute of Mortmain. [8]

Barlow's political philosophy was not far from Browne's, and he probably agreed with the slants Browne gave his teaching. Certainly Browne could expect Stephens' approval and he got it. At the end of his first year, Browne sent him some of the examination papers he received from a class of forty students and remarked that he had "received several nearly perfect papers." He was sending them that "Little Aleck" might see the scope of his examination "and judge of the proficiency of the students." [9] So impressed was Stephens that he provided a "History Medal" to be awarded to the best student in

Browne's department, containing this motto: "He is best fitted for usefulness in the public service, who, is acquainted with the history of his own country." [10]

Entering the teaching profession as probably his final haven, not of rest but, at least, of security, Browne left no opportunity unused to show the importance of the study of history and to make it attractive. He soon employed a local teacher of penmanship to make three large history charts to be hung on the walls of his classroom. They were 6 by 12 feet, beautifully lettered in colors, "giving them the appearance of old illuminated manuscripts." One was a table of the kings and queens of England, with dates, relationships to predecessors, and with the royal houses in different colors. Another was a similar chart for Scotland; and the third was a list of the presidents of the United States with the dates of their terms. [11]

The editor of the *Northeast Georgian,* an Athens newspaper, was much impressed with Browne's work, praising him for his industry and stating that he was ever "anxious to make his branch of instruction one of great usefulness, sparing no pains within his power to render it both attractive and impressive to the student." Browne was proving himself to be "the right man in the right place," and he was making the "study of history an important part of University education." [12]

Almost a hundred students were on an average studying history; but numbers did not indicate popularity, for the student's courses were fixed according to the degree for which he was working. However, proof was ample, both in Browne's day and afterward, that he was probably the most popular teacher on the campus. One of his students many years later remembered him as "one of nature's noblemen," with a big heart, kind and sympathetic. [13]

Browne had been on the campus but a few months when it was reported that he was "one of the most popular Professors in college, and his department is both entertaining and instructive." [14] And at the end of his career, an Atlanta newspaper could say that his "popularity among students was proverbial in Athens." [15] At the end of his first year, so pleased were his Senior students with his teaching that they presented him with a ten-volume set of the English classics, "in appreciation of the ability with which he has filled this most important chair in the University." [16]

Browne was always ready to help students both in class and in their campus activities. There were two literary societies, the Demosthenian and Phi Kappa, founded respectively in 1803 and 1820. They met weekly on Saturday mornings and were vital in campus life. When the

Demosthenian Society held its regular fall debate in 1877, it invited him to preside and to render the decision on the question "Does morality keep pace with the progress of civilization?" In pronouncing his verdict, he said that morality ought to keep pace with the progress of civilization, but he was compelled to say that the negative debaters had put forth the better argument. So pleased was the Society with Browne's performance that it invited him to preside at all their open debates.[17]

The good relations between Browne and the University students did not blind him into a defense of student outbreaks, riots, any violations of proper decorum, or petty crimes. In 1878 there was some performance by some students, the nature of which was not made plain in the records, which met with Browne's deep disapproval. In writing about it, he said: "If this outrage passes unpunished, discipline by this faculty is forever at an end. Insult to the faculty, breach of the peace, blasphemy & profanity, become the form of the students' protest against every effort to control him and the greater the number of delinquents the more certain is total immunity for crime." [18]

It is possible that Browne was referring to certain rumors that had been passed around by some disgruntled students regarding his morality; and there was some talk of not re-electing him. John A. Cobb wrote his wife that he hoped that Browne would be continued, "but things have got to such a pass that some one has got to 'Walk the plank' and the Trustees will have to decide for the best interest of the University and not of the stand point of friendship." [19] Browne had the feeling that some "old Whigs" on the Board of Trustees were trying to oust him, using whatever arguments they could trump up, but they were openly arguing that the financial condition of the University did not warrant continuing the chair of History and Political Science, that those subjects were not essential to a college education. But in writing about it to Barlow, Browne said that Stephens, "who is my friend," was supporting him throughout.[20]

Wholly innocent of the charges made against him, Browne suffered under them for a year, and at the meeting of the Trustees in August, 1879, he decided to bring the movement into the open and to a final decision by handing in his resignation. The Trustees immediately rejected it and asked him to withdraw it.[21] Thus vindicated, Browne wrote the Secretary of the Board of Trustees that "it affords me great pleasure to withdraw my resignation" and "to offer the Board my grateful acknowledgement of the compliment which their resolution conveys." [22]

Browne had always stood well with the faculty, and back in 1866 the Trustees had awarded him an honorary Master of Arts degree.[23] When he joined the faculty in 1874, he was asked to give his first lecture to the whole University, professors and students. In reporting the occasion, the town newspaper said that he gave "expression to the unanimous sense of all who heard him, in saying that he established the absolute necessity of a system of historical training to a complete and thorough University education beyond the remotest doubt," and the reporter exclaimed, "how wonderful is the indifference displayed toward it in our educational systems; above all, how passing strange the apathy hitherto manifested by the University of Georgia toward this grand field of instruction." And how fortunate the University was to have as its history professor William Montague Browne, "a refined and courteous gentleman and a soldier of our 'Lost Cause'!" [24]

Browne was popular with the professors, who recognized his unusual abilities in various fields of learning and his gift at writing and expression. When William L. Mitchell, a prominent Athenian, who for many years had been connected with the University as Secretary and Treasurer and as Professor of Law, died in 1882, the faculty appointed Browne to write his memorial.[25] Browne was also appointed by the Superior Court of Clarke County to address the bar on the "life and character" of Mitchell. The University faculty was in attendance on that occasion.[26]

Since Browne's interest in books and literature and in newspapers and periodicals was well known, the faculty at once requested him to stock the reading room of the Library with current magazines and newspapers;[27] and in 1876 it asked him to take charge of the University Library. At this time the Library consisted of about thirteen thousand volumes, and in addition there was the special Gilmer collection of about a thousand volumes of "select literature," which George R. Gilmer had presented to the University. To enrich further the supply of books available to the students, the two literary societies had their own libraries of about three thousand volumes each.[28] In 1878 the Trustees in commending Browne's services noted that the Library had been "greatly improved in its arrangement and neat appearance" and that "valuable additions" had been made.[29] Browne had added during the year 250 volumes.[30] He continued as Librarian to the end of the college year in 1879;[31] but two years later the faculty requested him "to prepare a list of books and other publications on subjects pertaining to the late war between the Confederate States and the United States, . . . the sense of the faculty being that it [is] eminently proper to place such publications in the Library of the University."[32]

While Browne was in charge of the Library, one of his most famous out-of-town patrons was Charles Colcock Jones, Jr., who, although a lawyer by profession, was a voluminous writer in the field of history and archeology. He borrowed from the Library and in appreciation sent Browne personally his *Siege of Savannah in December, 1864, and the Confederate Operations in Georgia* . . . (published in 1874), an appropriate gift as Browne was in that siege, and so was Jones.[33] Also Jones presented him his *Roster of General Officers, Heads of Departments, Senators, Representatives, Military Organizations, &c., &c., in Confederate Service during the War between the States* (published in 1876), again appropriate as Browne's name appeared in it several times.[34] The University Trustees were anxious to bring Jones to the faculty, and in 1874 when they elected Browne they were angling for Jones, though not in competition with Browne for History. Jones seemed receptive should the offer be made; he wrote Secretary Mitchell of the Board that although he had a very lucrative law practice, his love for Georgia was so great that "my present inclination is, should the Trustees favor me with their choice, to enter at once upon the discharge of the duties of the position, even at the sacrifice of private interests.[35] Three years later the Trustees offered him the chair of Natural Philosophy, but he declined on the ground that he was not an expert in that field.[36]

Browne had a deep love for the University and was thoroughly loyal to it, which he showed after a visit to Vanderbilt University in 1878, which had been founded five years earlier. It is not known whether he made his visit to be "looked over" for a position there, but when he returned he said in an address that with all the finery at Vanderbilt, he greatly preferred Georgia, and he was reported to have asserted that "no one who has a diploma awarded by the University of Georgia need blush when comparing it with those of Vanderbilt. The glorious record made by the former during the hundred years of its existence is worth more than all the grandeur of the latter. This commendation coming from the source it does is a very high compliment. Gen. Browne is not only a well informed but a careful speaker."[37]

Nevertheless, it was difficult for Browne to forget the exciting newspaper career he had in Washington before the unfortunate war. In 1876 he wrote Barlow that the rumor was out that a Democratic paper was to be established there, with a capital of $500,000, and "if so is there any opening for an old democratic editor?"[38] Barlow answered, "I think there is no truth in the report."[39]

The versatility of Browne was well illustrated in the different chairs

he held at the University, one being added to another until the
jokester could say that really he occupied a settee. Combining his
professorship of History and Political Science, which he received in
1874, the Trustees four years later elected him "Professor of Agriculture and Horticulture, Natural History, History, and Political Science,"[40] and the following year he was honored with the position of
"Lecturer on Political Science" in the Department of Law. His law
lectures were only occasional, and no course was listed in the curricu-
lum; but his other new chairs were quite important and required additional course listings.

As incongruous as Browne's professorships might appear, he had
had experience and wide reading in all the subjects included in his
extended title.[41] In listing his new department in the Georgia State
College of Agriculture and Mechanic Arts, which he called the
"School of Agriculture, Horticulture, and Natural History," Browne
stated that its purpose was to fit its students "intellectually and practically to cultivate the soil, develop the agricultural resources of their
country, and meet the coming demand on their capacities, which the
increase of population, and the consequent increased demand for the
products of the earth, imperatively require."

In lectures and textbooks he would go into the classification of
soils, how they could be improved, best methods of tillage, the
advantages of sub-soiling and drainage, and the various kinds and
properties of manures. He would consider plants "botanically, economically and geographically," indicate those best adapted "to the food
of man," and how and where produced. He would include also in
this school discussions of vegetable gardens and orchards; the breed-
ing of domestic animals and their adaptation to farm economy; the
classification of insects, their history and habits, and which ones were
"noxious and should be destroyed, and which beneficial and should be
preserved"; the construction of farm buildings and the uses of farm
machinery; and "landscape gardening, laying out gardens and lawns
and their ornamentation, and the culture and propagation of flowers
and shrubs."

Browne listed for the use of students a large number of textbooks
and books of reference, which would supplement and illustrate his
lectures; but his most practical aid was a great outdoor laboratory, an
experimental farm, where the students would be "taught to apply practically the scientific principles" they had already learned.[42]

This experimental farm was about a mile west of the University
campus and consisted of thirty acres of worn-out land, which was
being brought back into a high state of cultivation by the scientific

principles which Browne would teach his students. The process of reclaiming this land had been started by E. M. Pendleton, who had been Professor of Agriculture in the University from 1872 to 1876.

Having lain idle for two years before Browne's appointment, this land was sorely in need of attention, and his coming was hailed by the editor of the *Southern Banner,* who said that Browne had entered "upon the discharge of the duties of his position with a zeal and earnestness which promises much success." His progress in developing the farm excelled "anything of the kind ever before seen in this part of the country." Not only was he getting the land ready for crops, but he was "so beautifying and improving the grounds as will doubtless make the agricultural farm one of the most attractive spots in and about our city; and all of which must induce the general opinion that he is the right man in the right place."[43]

Browne's first year as Professor of Agriculture (with his extended title) pleased the University authorities as much as his beginnings had been praised by the Athens editor. In preparing their report to the Governor of the State, Alfred H. Colquitt, of July 9, 1879, the Board of Visitors, Chancellor Patrick H. Mell, and Secretary William L. Mitchell visited the farm and gave all activities on it a close inspection. They found the full 30 acres planted in these crops: 9 acres in corn; 10 in cotton; 1 in tobacco, sorghum, and lucerne grass; 1 in sweet potatoes; ½ in forage corn and millet; ½ in Irish potatoes; ½ in various kinds of melons; 1 in vegetables; 2½ in flowers, shrubs, and grasses; 2 in wheat; and 2 in oats. In cultivating these crops Browne was using various "standard compounds" of fertilizers, distributed experimentally. Although the season had been dry, the crops were "green, luxuriant and far above the average of the adjacent country."[44]

When the Trustees met in early August, 1879, Browne asked for an appropriation of $359 for running the farm, which would be offset by almost $400, which he would receive or had already received from the sale of products—in the meantime having used $103.40 of his own funds, which the Trustees repaid. Thus it would appear that the farm, with all the experimental improvements which Browne had made, was practically self-sustaining.[45]

In subsequent years, Browne varied the amount of land given to crops, concentrating in some years on the main crops that would bring in money. The crops he planted to be harvested in 1883 consisted of 25 acres of cotton, 12 of corn, and 10 of oats— the additional area having been rented. The previous year he had planted only 10 acres in cotton but had been able to gather a bale (466 pounds) to the acre. At all times, though, he kept experimentation in the forefront; he tested different brands of commercial fertilizers, applying one brand to five rows of cotton or corn, leaving five rows without fertilizer, and applying a different brand to another five rows, and so on; he experimented with the effect of spacing corn and cotton in the row and the distances between rows; and he tested the effect of nitrogen on cotton and corn and the best sources of it.[46] Browne liked to keep Secretary Mitchell informed on his farm operations; in early May, 1880, he reported to Mitchell: "My crops look very promising. I am now busy planting corn. Cotton all planted."[47]

Often Browne found the supply of help uncertain and good laborers hard to find; as a result, when his health permitted, he himself sometimes worked in the fields. In the fall of 1880 he reported to Secretary Mitchell that he had been "in the field all day and at my desk nearly all night. These last few days I have not been merely an overseer, but a laborer, picking cotton, I find it so hard to hire extra hands. I do very well at it tho' it is rather trying to my back."[48] There was a resident white man on the farm who helped to carry out Browne's instructions as an assistant overseer; for it must be remembered that Browne not only taught his classes in History and Political Science and in the other subjects assigned him, but took his classes in Agriculture out into the fields as occasion required to illustrate what he had told them in class.

When Browne was elected to the University faculty, he lived in his cottage "upwards of a mile" from the campus and was required to walk back and forth every day, "added to the labor of lecturing several hours." This was made necessary as Athens had no public hacks or street cars "& consequently I am like the poetic Irishman,

'When I was rich I rode in chaises
'Now I'm poor, I walk by Jabers.' "[49]

But when Browne had his agricultural duties added, he moved a little farther away to a very substantial three-story building popularly known as Rock College, as it had been constructed from rock found in the vicinity. It was designed to be the residence for the Freshmen and Sophomores of the University and had been completed in 1860. During the late war it was used as a preparatory school for the University and was made up largely of boys who were refugees. At the end of the war it was occupied briefly by Federal troops, after which it became the University High School for a few years and then remained vacant until 1872, when with the organization of the Georgia State College of Agriculture and Mechanic Arts it became headquarters for the experimental farm.

There was an elegance and dignity about it which must have reminded Browne of some English manor house or castle. However, when he took up residence in it, it must have reminded him more of some Irish ruin, for the yard had been allowed to go to waste and the surroundings looked more like an old worn-out field, which, in fact, the 30 acres were. Within a year the Trustees could report that under Browne's care it had "been made to appear as the surroundings of a civilized abode, the result of his labor and taste."[50] Being more specific, the Board of Visitors in their report to Governor Colquitt said that Browne had adorned the grounds adjacent to the building "with graceful beds of lovely flowers, and planted [them] in shrubbery and shade trees." His improvements had "been not only satisfactory but astonishing."[51]

Having lain vacant for a few years, Rock College was as badly in need of an overhaul as had been the grounds outside. Browne soon had the Athens Steam Planing Mills, which seem to have been general contractors too, repairing both the inside as well as the outside. They handed in bills for oil, paint, lime, brick, cement, laths, lumber, "laying two Hearths," "putting in grate," and doing other needed work.[52] Also, Browne had the large assembly hall on the first floor made ready to house "a museum of field and garden implements," which was being stocked with gifts from the manufacturers.[53]

Browne had had much to say about flowers and shrubs in the horticulture department of his *Farm and Home* magazine and was, therefore, well acquainted with landscaping and all that it involved.[54] And now, since he was also Professor of Horticulture, he had occasion to instruct his students to use shrubs and flowers not only to landscape Rock College but also to develop small nurseries. He dealt with Peter Henderson and Company, Seedmen and Florists, of New York, buying a great variety of items: agaves, phyllanthus, various kinds of roses, lautamas, latavia borbuica, dracaena terminala, dion edule, "100 Geranium Genl. Grant," hibiscus, tuberoses, fittonia, echeveria, cobra scandsus, hardy climbing plants, ornamental leaved plants, and many other flowers and plants whose botanical names were unfamiliar to anyone except an expert.[55]

Browne conducted the experimental farm, of course, directly for the instruction of his students, but he also gave it a much wider significance. His findings should be popularized, and as the University was at this time issuing no experimental bulletins, he sent reports to the newspapers, advising farmers on many subjects, for instance, to "cut, save and put under shelter every blade of grass upon your farms"; plant millet and large turnip patches; save all the fodder from cornstalks; sow small grain such as rye, wheat, oats and barley—and lucerne, too.[56] All of this was merely repeating what he had recommended in his farm journal.

By attending the meetings of various farm organizations, especially of the Georgia Agricultural Society, Browne came to be well known among important farm people. He was generally a vice president of the Agricultural Society and frequently spoke at its meetings. When it met in Athens in 1878, he delivered the address of welcome.[57]

As there were some farmers who decried "book farming" and opposed carrying on experiments that could tell them nothing better than what they already knew from their fathers and grandfathers, they naturally belittled Browne's experimental farm. One of his most outspoken and caustic critics was Colonel W. H. Reese of Marshallville, who declared that Browne's experimental farm was "a double-distilled humbug of the first water." [58] Of course, the Agricultural Society did not think so, as it had been seeking to have the legislature to set up several experimental farms over the state; and when it met in February, 1883, in Macon, the issue came before that body. Browne was among the "prominent men present [and delivered] an interesting address embracing 'the report of experiments at the University farm.' " When he had completed his main address he drew from his pocket a copy of the Macon *Telegraph and Messenger,* which contained Reese's attack on him and the movement of the Society to have additional experimental farms set up, and in a "sharp and caustic" retort denounced the article as a reflection on the Society. Browne was "heartily applauded." Reese replied that no one had ever received any practical benefit from Browne's reports and asked anyone in the audience who had, to stand up. Several "instantly arose." Thereupon, a motion was made to support Browne in his experimental farm work, and it was carried with only two dissenting votes.[59]

No one could say that Browne was not learned in history and constitutional law and government; that was attested by his standing in the University faculty and his reputation beyond. Likewise, it could not be denied that he was respected by the agricultural interests in Georgia and over the South generally.

❧ XIX ❧

Citizen Browne

AS A PROFESSOR, Browne was not one to withdraw into himself or into the ivy towers of the University; he considered himself as much a citizen of his town and state as a member of the college faculty. And he could not divorce himself from literary activities beyond those incident to his teaching.

He was always glad to take his part in any movement that centered in or touched Athens. In 1874, when the "great Grange movement" was spreading into Georgia, Browne helped to organize the Co-operative Grange Association, which embraced Clarke and the surrounding counties, and he was elected "Lecturer" for Clarke County.[1] Although he never held a governmental office or sought one, as has already been stated, he was active in local and regional politics and was frequently a delegate to political conventions.[2] In 1883 he attended the Democratic state convention as a delegate from Clarke County and played an important part in securing the nomination of Henry D. McDaniel for the governorship.[3]

In 1875 the Georgia Press Association met in Athens. The University and the citizens of Athens gave a dinner for the members, at which Browne was the principal speaker, responding to the toast "Our common country, 1775 and 1875." His address was reported as eloquent, somewhat whimsical and humorous at times. Naturally he told of the present greatness of the United States, comparing its population and wealth with what they were in 1775. But he could not resist pointing out how wealth and power had corrupted the government, how growing centralization in Washington was endangering the liberties of the people. He could not help but wonder whether the generation of 1875 was "as pure, as honest, as patriotic, as worthy of freedom as the men who for a principle, confronted the most powerful empire in the world." [4]

It should hardly be surprising that Browne was instrumental in organizing the Clarke County Historical Society in 1875. A group, mostly Confederate officers, had founded in New Orleans in 1869 the Southern Historical Society. Four years later it was reorganized and its headquarters moved to Richmond. It was now to be a federation of state historical societies, which in turn should promote local societies; and it was in carrying out this movement that Browne and others acted for Clarke County. Browne was one of the vice presidents and was appointed on a "Special Committee on Historical Collections," whose duty it was to collect facts and documents on the history of the county.[5] This grand federation never took on much life, but the central organization in Richmond did publish for many years its *Southern Historical Society Papers.*

The State College of Agriculture and Mechanic Arts division of the University felt that if it were true to its name, it ought to pay some attention to others than its students and carry some information and inspiration to the Athens mechanics and laborers. Browne began a series of lectures for them, taking as his first subject "The Dignity of Labor and the Value of Economy." He praised the working class and noted their accomplishments in science and literature. His audience was large, and he held its interest with his easy style and manner of speaking.[6]

Browne was probably a Mason; at least he was chosen in 1881 as the principal speaker at the Masonic celebration of the anniversary of St. John the Baptist, a patron saint of the Masons. Instead of having much to say about the Masonic organization, he launched into an amusing speech largely dedicated to the ladies, who made up a part of the audience of three hundred. As the news reporter had it, all were pleased "and we believe it was the unanimous vote that Gen. Browne could not have made a better or more appropriate speech if he had strung it out to an hour's length." [7]

Before coming to America, Browne had been a member of the Church of England, but instead of continuing in that faith as a member of the Episcopal Church in the United States, he joined the Methodist Church, which had originated as an offshoot of the English official church. As a Methodist, he was "an active and useful member" [8] and a fundamentalist in his beliefs of the Bible. In reviewing a book by the Rev. Samuel Watson, entitled *The Clock Struck One, and Christian Spiritualist,* Browne wrote: "As a Methodist who believes that 'the Holy Scriptures contain all things necessary to salvation,' we are sincerely sorry that a Methodist minister has written such a book as that before us, and has attempted to vamp upon our pure and holy religion doctrines which the Bible condemns, and which the same judgment of the Christian world rejects as the result of delusions or impostures." [9]

Browne was much interested in the Sunday School work of the church and was for some time chairman of the Sunday School Committee of the North Georgia Conference.[10] Straitened in financial circumstances though he generally appeared to be, he nonetheless made a substantial contribution to the church, the last $40 being collected from his estate, "being in full balance of subscription for the addition to and improvement on the first Methodist Church Building in Athens, Ga." [11] For the Christmas celebration in 1874, the Athens churches joined in hearing an address by Browne, at the Methodist Church. Describing the First Christmas, he gave an address "chaste, elegant and exceedingly appropriate." His description of Bethlehem and its surroundings greatly charmed his audience.[12]

Browne was a fluent and voluminous writer, a fact which was amply proved in his work on the *New York Journal of Commerce* and especially by his editorials in the Washington *Constitution* and in several Georgia newspapers, his dispatches to the *Louisville Courier* and the New York *World*, and his conduct for four years of the *Southern Farm and Home*. He had never contributed to any of the national literary journals, but the suggestion came to him when Barlow in 1877 sent him a year's subscription to the *North American Review*.[13] Browne asked Barlow whether he thought the *Review* would be interested in an article he had in mind to write on "England's Policy and Power." [14] It is not known what Barlow's reaction was, but apparently Browne gave up the idea and decided to write two articles on a subject more to his heart—an attack on the concentration of power in Washington. Barlow was pleased to learn this, but he warned Browne: "I would make it very short. Long articles are not in vogue—twenty pages are better than forty." [15] Browne wrote Jefferson Davis that he had about completed one of the articles, which he thought he would entitle "Shall the People or the General Government be Sovereign?" Or he might change it to "How did the 13 sovereign & independent states become a consolidated nation?" He said that the subject had been suggested by Pomeroy's *Introduction to the Constitutional Law of the United States,* which was being used as a textbook at West Point and "in a number of Northern Universities." Browne was not oblivious to the supposition "that public sentiment will regard my labor as archaelogical & consign me to the class of explorers of the remains of Nineveh and Babylon." But he felt that the day was "not far distant, if it be not already at hand, when the poor Yankees will be compelled in the effort to save popular liberty from destruction to invoke the principles of the grand struggle for the maintenance of which you were the illustrious leader." [16]

In September, 1878, Browne wrote Barlow that he had completed the article, which ran for twenty pages, and that he had shown it to Alexander H. Stephens and "one or two other friends," who thought it " 'first rate.' " [17] He hoped the *Review* would accept it, for he had avoided sectional bias and had "only endeavored to vindicate the truth of history against the bold misrepresentations of Pomeroy & [Hermann E. von] Holst." [18] He sent it to Barlow, who replied: "I have read enough of your article to be quite sure that it [is] a very able one and have sent it to the Review, signed, as customary." He thought that the editorial board would "see that the work is well done & will print it very soon." [19] Browne hoped that Barlow would do his best to get the article accepted, for he wanted no pay for it but only "the reputation which the paper will give me." [20] The *Review* never accepted this article nor any other by Browne, and it is not difficult to understand why—Browne's point of view on constitutional law and national politics was contrary to that of the *Review,* and even with Barlow's recommendations the editor of that publication could not be made to broaden his pages.

Browne's close association with Jefferson Davis over the years and his literary interests led him to play the part he did in assembling historical material and otherwise aiding Davis in writing his *Rise and Fall of the Confederate Government*. Soon after the war Davis was being urged by his wife to write his book on the Confederacy, but for many reasons there was little he could do for some years, and his interest was not much aroused until the 1870's. Many people besides Browne were to urge him on and assist him, asked and unasked. In 1872 Davis asked Burton N. Harrison, his wartime secretary, to send to Browne in Memphis the papers he had relating to the war period. [21] And after Browne settled down again in Athens as a professor in the University, he was active in aiding Davis, making several trips to Beauvoir, Davis's home in Mississippi. In 1880, explaining how far behind he was in some of his University work, he said that he was just back from Mississippi where he "had some literary work to do for Mr. Davis and all of it left me a close and industrious prisoner." [22] When Davis's son Jeff, Jr., died in 1878, Browne wrote: "How I wish to be with you to throw the arms of my earnest affection and sympathy around you, as you surrounded me with yours in the bitter hours of my sorrow." [23] And in further correspondence with Davis about the contents of the book, writing of the Andersonville prison, he said that the maligners of the good name of the Confederacy would not be convinced: "They will not be persuaded. They lie consistently persistently and all the time, *because they find it pays.*" [24]

To speed up Davis in writing his book, the D. Appleton and Company, who were to publish it, sent down to Beauvoir their long-time reader and editor, William J. Tenney. Tenney called on Browne to send him a narrative of his retreat from Savannah, after its fall to Sherman. Browne was unable to comply fully as he had no official reports and his memory was a little vague as to certain facts which needed to be checked for accuracy.[25] The book was finally published in 1881 in two volumes.

As has been previously noted, Browne and the Appletons were friends of long standing, going back to ante bellum days. It might, therefore, be expected that they would invite him to contribute to their *Annual Cyclopaedia and Register of Important Events;* and they did. His first article appeared in the volume for 1881 and was entitled "International Cotton Exposition." This world's fair was held in October, 1881, in Atlanta, and Browne could write interestingly and factually about it, as he undoubtedly attended it. There were 1,800 exhibits, "embracing apparently every article in the range of American industry from a Corliss engine to a potato-peeler." When the exhibition was over, many of the exhibits were moved to the museum of the College of Agriculture and Mechanic Arts, which Browne had established, though, of course, he did not mention in the article his connection with it. Policy dictated that in a publication of this sort he forego any reference to the sectional feeling that dominated much of his writings. On the contrary, he wrote that some of the important results of the exposition were that "by the interchange of ideas, opinions, and courtesies between intelligent and reflecting men of both sections which it afforded, the men of the North and of the South have learned to esteem each other more, to see the fallacy of the depreciative representations by unscrupulous politicians on both sides, by which they were respectively misled and estranged, and by dissipating the prejudices which made Georgia a *terra incognita* to the citizen of Massachusetts, and Maine a remote foreign country to the citizens of Georgia, to promote social and commercial intercourse between them, and finally exert a good influence in shaping the policy of the Federal government." [26]

Browne contributed extensively to the volume for 1882, for undoubtedly the Appletons were much pleased with his first article. Not until 1881 and 1882 was it the custom to call attention in the preface to outstanding contributors and their articles. Browne was among the contributors so honored. His articles in the 1882 volume were on North Carolina, South Carolina, Georgia, Mississippi, Louisiana, Tennessee, and Texas. All of the articles except the one on Texas were highly encyclopedic, factual, and statistical. There was no sectional bias or expression of opinion.[27]

But on Texas, Browne wrote like a Texan. He waxed eloquent in describing the progress that state had made: "In a vast territory which a few years ago was only accessible to the traveler on horseback, and a serious risk of life from the tomahawk of the Comanche and the lawlessness of the desperado, the whistle of the locomotive, the church-bell calling to divine worship, the voice of the school-teacher, the hum of the machine-shop are now heard in every direction, and millions of acres of fertile lands, as profitless as if they were a desert, are now dotted with the homes of thrifty husbandmen, rewarding with abundant crops the intelligent industry which has subdued them to civilization. Where 'they might take who had the power, and they might keep who can,' was the law of property; where personal rights were defended only by the pistol and the rifle, and where the name of God was never heard but to be blasphemed, law and order now prevail, and the mandate of justice and of preached word are heard and respected." [28] It is not known what rates of pay the Appletons gave their contributors, but after Browne's death in 1883, they paid his estate $130.[29]

It might well be assumed that a person of Browne's literary interests must have accumulated a personal library of considerable proportions. The University faculty in the Browne memorial inscribed in its minutes said: "His fondness for books was illustrated by the selection of the most beautiful and valuable library to be found in any private house in the State." [30] Many of his books he got by purchase and gift, and a great many came to him for review in his *Farm and Home.*

In the settlement of his estate, a catalogue of his books was compiled and printed, but no copy is now known to exist. The library was not disposed of as a unit, but volumes and sets were sold to the highest bidder; and some idea may be got of the nature of its contents from the records of its sales. It consisted of more than 1,500 books, covering a wide variety of subjects; novels made up the largest group, there being more than 400. As Browne taught history, constitutional law, and agriculture, he collected a large number of works on these subjects. He had 104 books on religion and 5 Bibles, as well as 18 works attacking or defending the Bible, including evolutionary works such as those by Darwin and Huxley. He had almost 200 United States government documents, such as the *Congressional Globe* and census reports. He had three dozen bound periodicals, agricultural and otherwise. Various other subjects helped to make up his well-balanced library; literary classics, poems, science, travel, biographies, atlases, dictionaries, wit and humor, four bound volumes of his *Constitution,* and three of its predecessor the *Washington Union,* and many pamphlets.[31]

❧ XX ❧

Death and Settlement of Estate

AFTER BEING elected to the professorship of Agriculture, Browne moved out to Rock College, as previously noted, and there with whatever possessions he had been able to bring south when he left Washington and with those he had accumulated afterward, he must have lived in some regal splendor, for he occupied eleven rooms. The overseer of the experimental farm with his family lived in part of the building and acted somewhat as housekeeper.[1]

Apart from his living room, a bedroom or two, a kitchen, and a dining room, the overseer's quarters and the museum, the rest of his "castle" was given over to his library and his household and kitchen furniture not in use. Scattered through at proper places there were many potted flowers and plants (others being landscaped on the outside), for Browne was an avid horticulturist. On the walls of his library rooms and other appropriate places were paintings and pictures of some of his favorite acquaintances and associates—so many, indeed, that some of them would have had to be stored.

Though not an egotistical person, Browne had a life-size painting of himself, probably a gift from admirers, and of his beloved wife he had six pictures of different sizes. Also he had some smaller ones of himself. Being an active Methodist, he had a picture of Bishop Pierce (whether of Lovick or of George F. it is not known, for either would have been appropriate). There were several of his dearest friend Howell Cobb, one of his wife Mary Ann Lamar Cobb, and pictures of Cobb's children, John A. Cobb and his wife and children, Howell Cobb, Jr., and his wife, and some of his children. Of course, there was one of Jefferson Davis, and several of Browne's other wartime associates were represented in his picture gallery: Thomas R. R. Cobb, Alexander H. Stephens, John B. Gordon, Benjamin H. Hill, and George Washington Custis Lee. Another was one of James Jackson, on the Georgia Supreme Court. Of Browne's University associates he had pictures of Chancellor Andrew A. Lipscomb and of William L.

Mitchell, Secretary of the Board of Trustees. There were, of course, pictures of some of Browne's other friends, acquaintances, and persons whom he admired, even one of Lord Palmerston, strangely, but none of Barlow was listed. He had pictures of a few historic buildings and a Madonna.[2] A few of Browne's collection must have been paintings (in addition to the life-size one of himself), and some were lithographs; but none was of the small "vest-pocket" size, so popular in this period, such as those made by Brady in Washington, Motes in Athens, and most other photographers. Of course, he must have had many of these, too, which were never listed. Also, he had an interesting collection of chromos.

The household furnishings which Browne had at the time of his death, listed in the appraisement of his estate, were voluminous and might well have required the use of much of Rock College for their storage. There were all the furnishings for bedrooms: bedsteads, pillows, sheets, mattresses, blankets, quilts, looking glasses, hair brushes, hand mirrors; for bathrooms: bathtubs, clothes baskets, folding screens, washstand sets, bowls and pitchers, soap stands; furnishings throughout the house: chandeliers, swinging lamps, fly fans, carpets and rugs, leather trunks, valises, cedar chests, small and large ladies' trunks, hand satchels, a child's rocking chair (probably, of sentimental memories), sewing machine, sitting chairs, large armchairs, whatnots, desks and tables, brass andirons, tongs, hearth brooms, vases, flower baskets, and many other items found in a well-furnished house.

The dining room and kitchen furniture and utensils were suggestive of the better days when the Brownes entertained the governmental and military aristocrats in Washington and in Richmond. And departing somewhat from the legal enumerators' expression, "too numerous and tedious to mention," some of this wealth must be, at least, indicated: walnut tables, dining chairs, tablecloths, crum cloths, fruit and flower stands; plates galore of every kind and need, such as tea plates, dinner plates, soup plates, butter plates, sugar dishes, cups and saucers, steak plates, earthenware egg plates, preserve dishes, cake plates, breakfast plates, tumblers, large cut-glass goblets, casters, gravy dishes, cream pitchers, water pitchers and dippers, salt stands; knives and forks, breakfast knives, dinner knives, butter knives, carving knives, pickle knives, silver forks, call bells; table spoons, tea spoons, pickle spoons, silver ladles; silver trays; tin trays, Japanese trays; coffee pots, tea pots, sugar tongs; in the kitchen: cooking stove, lard tubs, demijohns, earthenware, egg boilers, churns, biscuit rollers, pots and pans.

Browne's personal possessions were adequate to all purposes: stationery, letter files, sealing wax, gold pen with pearl handle, ink stand, letter scales, writing desk, easy chair, portfolios, gold spectacles, knives, rings, two watches and chains, gold cuff buttons and clothing, opera glasses, medical supplies, umbrellas, walking canes, and a flute. Reminiscent of wartimes, he had two swords, a pistol, a bowie knife, and a dirk.

Passing to the outside of his Rock College castle, he had a rock-away and a ten-dollar interest in a horse, with harness, saddle, and saddle bags, six hogs, two cows and a calf, eleven chickens, ten ducks, nine guineas, and eight turkeys.[3]

Bad health was Browne's greatest enemy, as has previously been mentioned. He could overcome poverty with the help of Barlow, Butterworth, and his own industry, but he could find no remedy for whatever it was that ailed him; and this fact made him despondent and deeply fatalistic at times. When working on the *New York Journal of Commerce* he was out for a week or more at a time; in Washington he had less trouble; during the war his health gave him trouble; in 1869 he was confined to his home "for some weeks," and his wife wrote Mrs. Cobb: "Genl. B. has been ailing continually. . . . I never saw him so despondent." [4] In 1876 he wrote to Jefferson Davis: "Though able to move about and attend to my duties, I am weak, nervous and miserable. My existence is that of a prisoner on a tread-mill with no hope of release or mitigation of punishment this side of the grave." [5] And this year, as at other times, he disturbed Barlow with reports of his miseries. "I am slowly recovering," he wrote, "from a severe billious fever with congestive chills, which brought me to death's door. Had I crossed the styx, Charon might have landed me in the Elysian fields and would that not have been a good exchange.[!]" [6] A little later he was getting better, he wrote Barlow, who answered: "I am sorry to hear that you have been unwell, but now that you are mending you must not take so gloomy a view but assume you mean to live a hundred years—at least until the next Centennial—of what—the Lord in his mercy only knows." [7]

Browne had a weakness in dwelling on his bad health too much and too often and to too many of his friends. Charles Colcock Jones, Jr., in answering a letter giving such news, said: "I regret to learn that you have been such a sufferer, and trust you have, by this time, shaken hands at final parting with that aristocratic old enemy to comfort and locomotion." [8] Jones was erroneously diagnosing Browne's ailment as the gout, by assuming that since Browne was an aristocrat he could have no other disease than the gout. The next year (1878), Browne wrote Barlow: "Something must be very wrong: My pulse is below 40 and 'mighty unsartin' at that. I feel no pain—nothing but extreme fatigue and langour." He said the doctor called it "nervous prostration."[9] About this time he was too ill for days to meet his classes; but he must have been heartened by one of the greatest compliments that could be paid to a professor, by his students' "regretting very much" missing his lectures.[10] This year and the following one Browne was unable to attend several faculty meetings because of illness; but one of them he missed was for a very opposite reason—he was planting cotton on the experimental farm.[11]

Reporting to Barlow in early 1878: "I am better, stronger, more hopeful, and less disposed to growl,"[12] Browne told him that he expected on his summer vacation to go North to rest near the sea or on the Hudson, but "to do this, I intend to practice an economy which would scare an anchorite."[13] Having tried physicians in Athens, Browne went to Atlanta to consult for three days one of the most eminent doctors in the South, who said that his trouble was disordered circulation produced by nervous prostration. The doctor prescribed complete physical and mental rest, which Browne said was impossible, for he must work for a living.[14]

Never seeming to find a cure for whatever it was that ailed him, to add to his misfortunes he reported to William L. Mitchell, in May, 1880: "I have been laid up, unable to move a step, for nearly ten days with a serious injury to my left foot, which neglected threatened to deprive me permanently of its use." But he was getting better and hoped "to be able to hobble about" soon.[15]

Browne's last illness grew out of his services in the Democratic Convention in early April, 1883, in securing the nomination of Henry D. McDaniel for the governorship. He contracted a cold,[16] which developed into pneumonia. For two weeks, beginning on April 14, Nancy Napier, a colored woman, attended to his care;[17] and beginning a week later Dr. J. E. Pope, a local physician who had had Browne as a patient for some years, visited him every night until Browne's death on the night of April 28.[18]

Browne's desperate illness was of much concern to Athenians and to the newspaper editors over the state. The *Atlanta Constitution,* a morning newspaper, reported on April 28 that Browne was ill of pneumonia and very low,[19] and the next day it carried the news that he had died at 4:00 P.M. the day before.[20] The hour was an error, for Howell Cobb, Jr., telegraphed Jefferson Davis at 6:30 P.M. on April 28: "Gen. Browne very low with pneumonia, thought to be dying."[21]

Funeral ceremonies were carried out in the University chapel on April 30, after which Browne's body, in a metallic casket costing $150, was taken to the Oconee Hill Cemetery and deposited in the granite vault containing the remains of his wife Eliza Jane, on the Browne lot, across the driveway from the Howell Cobb lot. Soon a metal fence was erected around the Browne tomb.[22] Newspapers over the state paid tribute to Browne, his character, his life, and works. The Augusta *Chronicle and Constitutionalist* called him "a man of great ability [who] . . . was in the vigor of matured manhood" and who had twenty more years of usefulness before him.[23] (Having been born on July 7, 1823, Browne lacked a few days more than two months of being sixty years old.) His home-town paper, the *Banner-Watchman,* said: "Finely educated, polished by travel and long and intimate association with cultivated people of two continents he was a charming companion, and elegant writer and altogether an accomplished man."[24]

The editor of the *Atlanta Constitution* said that the "state loses a son whose loyalty was attracted in the days of adversity; one whose heart rejoiced with our triumphs and grieved in our trials. He was a man of graceful accomplishments; varied as a scholar; prudent as an advisor; firm as a friend, and beloved as an intimate. He is one whose memory will long be cherished." [25]

The news dispatch announcing Browne's death, which this newspaper carried, written by someone who must have long been a close acquaintance, gave a factual account of his career and an intimate view of his character. It was "doubtful if he had a peer in Georgia." His information was "wonderfully extensive and accurate," yet "no man was less 'bookish' than he." His intellect "readily assimilated all that it touched." He had "manners of easy grace and dignity" and his "social qualities shone among his fellow men and made him universally beloved. . . . In every station that he filled and in all that he did he 'bore without reproach the grand old name of gentleman. . . . Few men have been more sincerely mourned. He had friends wherever he went." [26]

What Browne's own faculty associates thought of him was well expressed by Williams Rutherford, Professor of Mathematics for more than a quarter of a century, who was appointed by the faculty on May 1 "to draft suitable resolutions" on Browne's death. At the same time, the faculty resolved to wear mourning badges for thirty days and ordered that the chapel, which had been draped for the funeral, remain so for the period of mourning. The memorial noted that he "boldly resigned the high and honorable position of editor of the administration paper under Mr. Buchanan, the democratic president of the United States, to make common cause with the Southern States, in their determination to secede from the Federal Union, in the year 1861." He reached a "high attainment in scholarship [and he] . . .

built a reputation for literary culture rarely surpassed in this country."
"His intercourse with his colleagues was marked by urbanity, the most
cultivated and, at the same time, of the most cordial character. Never
arrogant or conceited, his address was always persuasive and complimentary to the person addressed." Indeed, he was "a pleasant and
agreeable colleague." [27] Chancellor Patrick H. Mell added his meed
of praise in his report to the Board of Trustees: Browne was "an accomplished scholar, a genial and cultured gentleman, and a successful teacher." [28]

Cut short by Browne's death, his work in the College of Agriculture
was taken over to the end of the term by Henry Clay White, Professor
of Chemistry, who in his report to the Board of Trustees said, "I take
this opportunity to express my admiration for & appreciation of the
conscientious labors in scientific agriculture of my lamented colleague.
These labors were performed under many disadvantages—some in-
herent in the man, whose tastes & culture would, perhaps, have led
him to prefer other lines of work: many incident to his position, requiring much of his time and attention to be given to tutorial work
affording but scanty means for the prosecution of truly scientific research. That he labored faithfully and conscientiously none who knew
him will deny: that the results of his labors were valuable to agricul-
turists & creditable to our University, I have had every reason & opportunity to know to be eminently true; that his labors were appreciated
by those in whose special interest they were performed is attested by
the direct, unanimous & enthusiastic expression of opinion to that
effect on the part of the State Agricultural Society at its last meeting
at Macon in February of this year. I am glad to have been permitted,
even for a few weeks, to carry out the work of my esteemed friend
that his usefulness might not terminate abruptly at the grave." [29]

Duly appreciated and praised by his colleagues, Browne was also
memorialized by his students in the Phi Delta Theta fraternity, which
had elected him to honorary membership. In the secretary's chapter
letter to national headquarters, he said: "But in the midst of all our
happiness death has claimed one of our most worthy members. I speak
of General W. M. Browne, who was a professor of history and political science in the university, and was universally beloved by all who
knew him, and more so by the members of his Fraternity who not only
knew him in his every day duties but in his drawing room to be a true,
bold and valiant Phi. The boys of Georgia Alpha will always love to
cherish his name and bear him in their memory to the grave." [30]

Indeed, almost all men of prominence who knew Browne, it seemed,
felt the urge to praise him and to express their sorrow at his death.

Governor McDaniel was much grieved and said: "In his death I lose a friend. I will never forget his sympathy and kindness." [31] And Sylvanus Morris, an Athens lawyer and later dean of the School of Law of the University, in his brochure *Strolls about Athens during the Early Seventies* (n.p., n.d.), said that Browne "knew more people, and was known by more people than anyone the stroller ever saw."[32]

Some discount should always be made of eulogies called forth by death, and by their very nature little, if any, mention should be expected of anything derogatory or, at least, not complimentary to the deceased. But the established facts of Browne's life indicate that there was little that was overdrawn in what was said of him at the time of his death.

A eulogy is never a full characterization of the person eulogized, and this was of course so in the case of Browne; but a full characterization of him should leave little to his discredit. There is little known of the first half of his life, spent before coming to America; but whatever made it up and for whatever reasons the records of it are so meager, there could have been nothing dishonorable in that career. It would certainly seem so, for instead of avoiding Englishmen or other contacts with England, he was often by his position thrown into their company. When the Prince of Wales (Lord Renfrew), who later became King Edward VII, visited the United States in 1860, Browne was prominent in the inner group that entertained him; when William H. Russell came over in 1861 as correspondent of the *Times* of London, he met Browne and wrote about him; Browne sent his English wife on a visit to her Yorkshire home in 1860; and he himself was planning a trip back to England at the time of his death.

One must, therefore, judge Browne by what became known about him after he came to the United States. That he was learned and cultured is evident, for within a short time he had made friends with many of the statesmen (especially of Southerners), and with President Buchanan, Frederick Law Olmsted, and Samuel L. M. Barlow of New York, and many other Northerners, and was accepted socially by them. A few critics thought they saw a studied purpose in the way Browne made his friends and stood by them, that he cultivated especially people who could do him favors—that, in short, there was an element of the toady about him. A full consideration of his life would hardly support this charge.

He was conservative by nature and tenacious of his views of government and politics. It is easy to see why, therefore, that though he had been in the United States less than ten years, he became as ardent a secessionist as could be found anywhere, for Southerners were con-

servative (and the secession movement was ultra-conservative), though
they sometimes referred to it as the "Southern Revolution." His tenac-
ity of position put him above pelf or price. If he had swerved away
from his secession stand and remained in Washington in 1861, as he
had been urged by Barlow and others to do, he could have had both
increased fame and fortune. He gave up and waved aside every Northern prospect; he could take little with him to the South; and in the
war he lost everything except his honor and principles. But he defended
the South and its position to his dying day and never regretted the
course he had taken. Although never abandoning the principles for
which the South stood, in his somber moods of discouragement he
sometimes regretted that he had not taken advantage of opportunities
to move to greener pastures—as to California with Butterworth or
even to a newspaper position in the North, if one could be found.

If Browne had had less stamina, the corrosive effects of his health
would have driven him beyond the despondency which now and then
beset him and would have made him seek a date with Charon to ferry
him across the Styx. But religion was his consolation, for he was a
Methodist fundamentalist and believed the Bible literally.

Despondency was more a misfortune than a weakness with Browne,
for few people who had had the jolts in life he had, could have escaped
being despondent now and then. But he can be charged with weakness
for dwelling on his bad health, especially in his correspondence with
Barlow, and sometimes with Jefferson Davis. He could hardly be
charged with playing on Barlow's sympathy, despite the fact that Barlow sent Browne a check for a hundred dollars sometimes. A more
direct approach by Browne on Barlow's munificence was to refer
occasionally to his own utter poverty. But, Browne never asked directly
for help, though once or twice he asked a loan from Barlow. Certainly in view of the needs of an ailing wife, whom Browne always
adored, he should not be blamed for laying aside pride and accepting
these gifts; but it should also be noted that Browne did his best to
show his gratitude and make slight recompense by sending Barlow
those delicious peaches, which Barlow accepted with paeons of praise
for that delectable Georgia fruit.

Having aristocratic tastes and yet democratic in his dealings with
his fellowman, Browne was a *bon vivant* and a connoisseur of food,
wines, and liquors, and of books and the arts. These were qualities
which endeared him to Barlow to the very end, come secession, war,
disease, and poverty. Proof of these qualities were seen in the library
he collected, in the twenty-one claret and wine glasses, eleven cham-
pagne glasses, wine and brandy decanters, and ordinary glasses for

whiskey he had, and in the fact that he generally had on hand the liquids to fill them, often beholden to Barlow for them. Also, he enjoyed cigars and his pipe. At the time of his death he had several hundred cigars, a box of smoking tobacco, and a "Tobacco stand, Pipes & Cigar Holder," which were sold in the settlement of his estate for $25.00.[33]

Browne was not a seeker after publicity or a prominent place in history. He never saved his public papers or his private correspondence, and by neglecting so to do he made it difficult to reconstruct his life in America and almost impossible to establish a bare outline of his career in Europe.

Immediately on Browne's death, a search for a will was made in order to settle his estate, but none could be found, except for two wills that had been made while his wife was still living and they were inapplicable now. The first Browne made on May 27, 1862, "written in my own hand, and affixed hereunto the seal of my arms." As "Colonel in the Provisional Army of the Confederate States, and Aide-de-Camp of the Staff of the President," he gave to his wife all his property, real and personal, "after paying the expenses of my funeral which I desire to be the simplest and most quiet character." It was witnessed by two of Browne's associates on the President's Military Staff, Colonel William Preston Johnston and Colonel Joseph C. Ives. Browne made his second will on December 11, 1865, which was a repetition of his first except that it was witnessed by John A. Cobb, Pope Barrow, and Edwin D. Newton and that it appointed as executor "my much esteemed friend Howell Cobb, Senior." [34]

Two days after Browne's death, Howell Cobb, Jr., appeared at the office of the Ordinary, Asa M. Jackson, among whose duties it was to probate wills and settle estates, and presented him with the two wills Browne had made. As they were now inapplicable and no subsequent will could be found, Cobb applied "for temporary and permanent letter of administration." On the same day (April 30, 1883), Ordinary Jackson issued to Cobb "Temporary Letters of Administration" and set his bond at $5,000.[35] At the same time he appointed five Athenians to make an inventory and appraisal of Browne's estate.[36]

The appraisers made a listing of Browne's possessions and determined the value to be $5,169.[37] In addition, Browne had a balance of $118.60 in the National Bank of Athens and there was owing to him an unpaid salary from the University of $166.65 and an account of $130 from D. Appleton and Company.[38] As certain parts of Browne's personal property were "of a perishable nature & . . . likely to de-

teriorate in value," Administrator Cobb was given permission to order
their sale, after advertising for ten days. Sheriff John W. Wier held
the sale at public outcry and sold not only the perishable items but
also much of the other property, but there still remained the library,
"pictures, jewelry, trunks, wearing apparel &c &c." [39]

While the liquidation of the estate was slowly going on, there came
an exciting interruption. On December 27, 1883, Jefferson Davis at
his home Beauvoir in Biloxi, Mississippi, received from an unknown
source a will that had been made by Browne in Memphis on June 11,
1873, a little more than a month after his wife's death. Realizing that
now that his wife was dead and that his previous wills were inopera-
tive, Browne made an extensive disposition of his property in this new
will. Desiring that his funeral expenses should not exceed $500 and
should be paid from "my funds on deposit in the Union & Planters
Bank" in Memphis, he wanted a sufficient amount to be used "to purchase a lot in Elmwood Cemetery" and defray expenses in building a
vault "in which my remains and my lamented wife Eliza Jane Browne
shall be laid, there to repose until the resurrection." (His wife's remains at this time were in the private vault of William Donoho.)

Then followed his various bequests. To "my young friend William
Hutton . . . as a very feeble expression of my regard and esteem" he
left $250. (Hutton was Browne's secretary for both the Carolina Insur-
ance Company and for his *Southern Farm and Home*.) He bequeathed
to "Leannah Wray my colored servant" $200 "as a reward for many
years faithful service and for her devoted attention to her deceased
mistress." To John A. Cobb he gave 38 shares of the publishing and
printing house of J. W. Burke and Company of Macon, to be used
in repaying a debt of $500 to the estate of Howell Cobb, Sr., and the
remainder to go to John A. Cobb's children. He gave his library to
Mary Ann Cobb, a daughter of Howell Cobb, Sr., and then the wife
of Alex S. Erwin. To General George Washington Custis Lee and to
General William Preston Johnston (who had witnessed Browne's first
will) he gave each 5 shares of stock in the Union and Planters Bank
of Memphis. To Jefferson Davis he bequeathed 25 shares of the capital stock of the Carolina Life Insurance Company in trust for his children Margaret and Varina Anne ("Winnie"). He gave his watch and
chain (the only one he had at this time) to John D. Adams of Little
Rock, Arkansas, to go at his death to his son Dean Adams. It was his
desire that his "furniture and household effects except certain trunks
containing the wearing apparel of my late wife" to be sold and the
proceeds be used in paying his debts, if any, and the remainder, if any,
be given to his colored servant Leannah Wray for her youngest child,

"whom she named after me." His "silver plate" should go to John A. Cobb, and his "pictures" to Mrs. Mary McKinley Cobb, the wife of Howell Cobb, Jr., "with the request that she give a place of honor and prominence to the two framed portraits of my wife, and that she preserve them carefully." He wanted the trunks containing his wife's clothing to be burned without being opened, and he enjoined his executors to see that "this wish is literally carried out," for he desired "that the things which are sanctified in my eyes by having been used by my wife, may not ever pass into other hands." And finally he gave to John A. Cobb for his children two life insurance policies: one for $5,000 in the Cotton States Life Insurance Company of Macon and the other for $2,500 in the Carolina Life Insurance Company.

To be executors of his will, Browne appointed Jefferson Davis, at this time living in Memphis, and James Jackson of Macon (later Chief Justice of the Georgia Supreme Court) and asked them "as the last favor of friendship not to refuse to act in that capacity." It was witnessed by Samuel Snow, William P. Hutton, and H. H. Booth.[40]

On receiving the will, one of Davis' first acts was to write to Jackson to suggest that in the light of the will the remains of the Brownes should be removed to Memphis. Jackson quite properly objected, for he said that Browne had constructed in the Oconee Hill Cemetery in Athens a vault for his wife costing "some five hundred dollars," and that he had had her remains removed there, and that Browne himself had been entombed beside her, showing "an alteration of intention on his part as to the place of burial. . . . Moreover the deceased left friends in Athens Ga who will care for the place where he is interred and his wife was well known there—and the place of interment will be cared for on account of both. In Memphis they lived but a short time and ten years prior to the General's death." [41]

Jackson also suggested to Davis that since Howell Cobb, Jr., had administered already much of the estate, he should proceed to the end. He said further that all the insurance had lapsed and was now worth nothing, and that exclusive of Browne's library "and an obligation of the Knights of Honor to pay *his heirs at law* two thousand dollars, nothing practical is left in the case—because the debts of our friend more than absorb the remainder, leaving $900 to be paid from the sale of the library, which has not yet been done and will not be done now 'but those debts will be paid' by the legatee." And he felt sure that Cobb would carry out Browne's wishes with regard to burning the trunks that contained his wife's clothing, which Cobb now had in his possession.[42]

Davis agreed with Jackson, and both refused to serve, Davis explaining "because the subsequent acts of the deceased, W. M. Browne, indicate a change of purpose on his part, and in important particulars render the execution of this will impracticable." There was filed in the office of the ordinary on January 28, 1884, the "Renunciation of James Jackson & Jefferson Davis as Exrs of Wm. M. Browne, desd," in which "we do hereby each for himself Renounce said appointment and Refuse to take any part in the probate of said Will, and pray that you will duly file and Record this Renunciation in your Office, and each of us do hereby declare that he has not, in any manner intermeddled with the estate of said deceased." [43]

Since Davis and Jackson refused to serve as executors, it seemed logical that Howell Cobb, Jr., should continue to administer the estate, and so he applied to the Ordinary to be allowed to continue as administrator under the will. In so asking he said that he could qualify, since he was the husband of one of the legatees, Mary McKinley Cobb; and he was, accordingly, appointed administrator.

Although it was assumed that Browne had no heirs at law in the United States, and if any at all, they resided in Great Britain and Ireland and their exact residences and number were unknown, Andrew J. Cobb, attorney for his brother Howell Cobb, Jr., asked that there be a notice inserted in the newspapers requesting any heirs and the legatees to appear at the March, 1884, term of the Ordinary's court. The meeting was held and the hearing was continued; sometime afterward Frederick William Browne of Chicago appeared, claiming to be a nephew of William Montague Browne and demanding the estate. Since he was not one of the legatees, his attorneys at the August term of the Ordinary's court argued that the will should not be admitted to probation, for it was null and void, because Browne "was *mentally* incapable of making a will on account of temporary aberration of mind produced by extreme grief at the recent death of his wife."

In the meantime, in order to establish the authenticity of the will, the Ordinary questioned the three men who had witnessed it. All replied that Browne's signature was genuine. Hutton said, "I saw him sign his name to this paper. . . . He was a man of very clear head—and at the time of the execution of the will, was perfectly sound in mind— and perfectly capable of performing any business intelligently." Booth said, "He was a man of fine sense and in full possession of his intellectual facilities" when he signed the will.

At the next session of the Ordinary's court, Cobb was appointed administrator "with the will attached," and he proceeded to a final settlement of the estate. In the meantime, heirs in England and Ireland had been found and they were convinced by Cobb that the proceeds from the settlement of the estate would not meet its debts; as a result, they and Frederick William Browne dropped their suits.

The estate was long in being settled, the final sale not taking place until December 23, 1885, which was more than two and a half years after Browne's death. And as much of the estate had been disposed of before the will was found, thereafter that document was ignored in the final settlement. Mary Ann Cobb Erwin did not receive the library, for it was sold at public outcry in small lots, bringing a total of $686.27. Since only local people attended its sale, the bidding was not brisk—in fact, it seems that there was little competitive bidding at all. Most of the books sold for less than a dollar each, and some unbound novels brought only one cent each. The highest price paid was $3.50 for a Bible. The item in the will relating to the library was ignored in order by its sale to provide needed funds; other items were of necessity ignored since insurance policies had lapsed and stocks in corporations had become worthless.[44]

In William Montague Browne the elements were mixed. He had a varied career, in every part of which his versatility stood him in good stead. His mind was cultivated and his impulses were noble, but his steadfastness to his principles led him to attack sharply whoever opposed them. He never saw any treason in deserting the government to which he had sworn allegiance and in joining the Confederacy. Suffering the misfortunes of a Job, he did not let his bad health and intermittent poverty embitter him toward his fellow man, whom fundamentally he loved and respected. Despite his varied activities and many accomplishments and the many friendships which he made, his frustrations, failures, misfortunes, poor health, and untimely death add a strong element of pathos to his life.

⚜ *Appendix I* ⚜

BROWNE'S EUROPEAN BACKGROUND

A long and appreciative obituary of Browne appeared in the *Atlanta Constitution,*[1] which was written undoubtedly by some close acquaintance who must have received much of his information from Browne himself. In it are mentioned Browne's birth and ancestry, his education, his travels in Europe, his English diplomatic service, and, of course, the main facts of his career in America.

The main outline of Browne's life before he came to America was "common knowledge" among his fellow townsmen in Athens, Georgia, and his colleagues on the faculty of the University of Georgia—especially his connections with nobility, his education at Rugby and at Trinity College, Dublin, and his extensive travels through Europe. He was reputed to be a relative of the Marquis of Sligo (sometimes stated to be in line to succeed to the title) and of Lord Oranmore.[2]

Sylvanus Morris, a long-time resident of Athens and a member of the faculty of the University of Georgia, who knew Browne well, said: "His family are members of the British gentry, the head of his house is the Marquis of Sligo." [3] A short biography of Browne, which appeared in an Athens newspaper [4] during his lifetime, mentioned his education at Rugby and at Trinity College, Dublin, and stated that he had spent "many years in foreign travel." Brown sent in no corrections to what appeared in the biography.

Augustus Longstreet Hull, an acquaintance of Browne's and for many years Treasurer of the University of Georgia, noted Browne's education at Rugby and at Trinity College, Dublin.[5] Browne himself must have informed the University of Georgia authorities when he became a member of the faculty in 1874 of his educational background, for the faculty in its resolutions on his death stated that the foundation of his education had been laid at Rugby and "completed at the University of Dublin." [6] A student of Browne's in the University remembered in later life that he had heard that Browne had had an adventurous life before coming to America, that he had fought in the Crimean War, and that he was a "son of an English Earl." [7] And Browne himself, in reviewing a book on Eton, remarked that although he was not an Etonian, he was not unfamiliar with life there, which might be considered a mild inference that he had attended some other English boys' school, for instance, Rugby.[8]

In 1870 Browne informed the United States census taker that he was forty-seven years old, which would confirm the year of his birth as 1823.[9] The *Irish Citizen* (N. Y.), in a reference to Browne, with pride called him "a Mayo man." [10] William Howard Russell, famous correspondent of the London *Times,* met Browne and interviewed him in Montgomery, Alabama, in 1861 while the Confederate government was still located there. Russell stated that Browne was "a cadet of an Irish family." [11] The Brownes, indeed, were old Irish families. They had been "the noble families in Mayo and Sligo since the reign of King James the First." [12]

England has been given erroneously by several writers as Browne's birthplace.[13] Also, William Montague Browne has been confused with William Hand Browne in the statement that he was the author of a life of Alexander H. Stephens. In fact, it was William Hand Browne who was co-author with Richard Malcolm Johnston of the *Life of Alexander H. Stephens* (Philadelphia, 1878).[14]

If Browne was a fraud, humbug, or gay deceiver concerning his European background, he did not profit by it in America, where there was still prejudice against Englishmen and especially against titled Englishmen. Albert Gallatin Brown, a United States Senator from Mississippi, bitterly attacked Browne as being a foreigner and in line for a title; and others attempted to discredit him for the same reason. Browne did not try to hide from his English visitors who might have known of any fraud in his life before he came to America, nor otherwise did he try to avoid contacts with England—as for instance his associations with the Prince of Wales and with William H. Russell on their visits to the United States, or his wife's visit to Yorkshire in 1860 and his own contemplated trip to England at the time of his death.

Some foreigners cloaked their identity in their native countries by assuming a new name on coming to America; their reasons were varied: crime, illegitimacy, or mere whim prompted many of them. It is not assumed that Browne did this, but the lack of his identification under the name of William Montague Browne in England and Ireland does not rule out the possibility. If he went under another name on the rolls of Rugby, Trinity College, and of the diplomatic and military service in England, this would explain the absence of the name William Montague Browne. Of course, there is always the possibility that records were incomplete or that researchers were fallible, but due diligence was shown by all who searched for William Montague Browne in English and Irish records.

On October 1, 1853, a passport was issued to William Browne by the British authorities, and on July 17, 1857, a William Browne was naturalized in New York. These two William Brownes could hardly have been the same person, for the William Browne with the passport could not have been naturalized only four years later, since five years' residence was the minimum required for naturalization. But it is possible that the William Browne of the naturalization proceedings could have been William Montague Browne, for it was stated in 1859 by the editor of the *New York Journal of Commerce* that William M. Browne had been in this country eight years, which would have given him a term of residence of six years when the William Browne was naturalized in 1857. But why should the Montague or the initial M. have been omitted in the naturalization proceedings, when at that time he was known as William M. Browne on the staff of the *Journal of Commerce?*

Although no naturalization papers issued to William Montague Browne or to William M. Browne have been found, there can be no question about his naturalization, since he was prepared to offer as evidence his record of naturalization at the Congressional hearing where the matter was being discussed.

These observations are more a futile exercise in puzzlement than of much importance in the life of Browne in America, which is all this book is intended to be—though as a matter of satisfying a curiosity, it would be interesting to know more about the first half of Browne's life before he came to America, and helpful in a full estimate of his character.

A tribute must be paid here to Ezra J. Warner of La Jolla, California, who became interested in Browne in preparing his biography for *Generals in Gray,* a work of great value. After the publication of his book in 1959, Warner centered his interest and attention on Browne's background in Ireland and England. He persistently and most intelligently carried on his researches and employed competent scholars in Dublin, London, and elsewhere to search the records; but no one has been able to find any evidence that a William Montague Browne ever attended Rugby or Trinity College, Dublin, or to establish in the genealogy of D. Geoffrey Browne that he had a son named William Montague, though it was so stated in America.

This is the enigma of William Montague Browne's Irish-English background, the solution of which is open to anyone who cares to wrestle with it in the light of the facts heretofore set forth and of any that might be turned up later.

⊗ *Appendix II* ⊗

THE PICKETT PAPERS

In 1872 John T. Pickett, as agent for the owner, sold to the United States government parts of the Confederate State Department Archives, which have come to be known as the "Pickett Papers."[1] This transaction, which many people believed was engineered by President Grant in the hopes of finding incriminating evidence against the former Confederate leaders, was used by the Republicans in re-electing him. It created quite a stir in the newspaper world and led to various editorials and letters to the press. The *Memphis Daily Appeal* published on July 30 a letter in defense of the Confederacy[2] and elsewhere made some cutting remarks about Pickett's Civil War career, and especially about his mission to Mexico, which turned into a fiasco.[3] Pickett insisted that this letter (or possibly some other letter in the *Appeal*) had been written either by Jefferson Davis or William Montague Browne, Assistant Secretary of State (1861-1862), and it called forth his wrath in a letter which he addressed to "General C. F. Henningsen," on September 15, 1872.[4]

"General" Henningson (he was only a colonel in the Confederate Army) seemed to be a proper person for Pickett to address in the mood of this letter, for he, like Pickett, considered himself neglected and badly wronged in his Confederate service by Davis and his "Flunkey Browne."

Charles Friedrich Henningsen was born in London of German parentage (some say Scandinavian), and before he had reached adulthood he had engaged in warfare in Spain; thereafter he fought in the Russian army, took part in the Hungarian revolt under Louis Kossuth, and fled to America with him. He became a citizen of Georgia and married a niece of Senator John M. Berrien. In 1859 he joined William Walker's filibusters in Nicaragua. When the Civil War broke out he entered the Confederate army.[5] He was the author of several histories and novels.

Pickett's letter follows:

My Dear General: You cannot have forgotten a certain hulking, prize footman sort of fellow by the name of Browne—Wm. M. Browne—otherwise, for reasons unknown to me, called "the Marquis of Sligo," who was employed on the Administration here [Washington] in Buchanan's days, and who spent most of his time toadying the Cabinet and others in authority, and their families. Was he not, as editor &c., in some indirect way responsible for the death of William Walker? Could you give me a few of his antecedents?

This fellow has turned up in Memphis, of course, in his business of flunkeyism; in which capacity he has lately been obliged to father an article in the *Appeal,* which I am now authoritatively informed was instigated and revised, if not penned by his master, Jefferson Davis, and headed "The Pickett Archives." As to J. D., although belittling himself by publishing that which he knew to be false, I shall let him pass, on account of that which he has been or might have been, had he known how to be truly great. But this little incident shows the great mistake the Southern people made in committing their destiny so absolutely into his hands; for here he is, as of yore in Richmond, under the influence of his spies, sneaks, pimps, parasites and informers*—going off half cocked and placing himself in an indefensible attitude toward so obscure individual as myself.

By an inscrutable dispensation of Providence; or rather by the power of toadyism that person was made Assistant Secretary of State of the Confederate States, and I found him in that position at Montgomery when I was summoned thither by telegraph, April 1861, to accept the mission to Mexico. Mr. Toombs referred me to him for instructions, &c.; but he most unaccountably delayed me for some ten or twelve days. At length, pressing him—saying the blockade would cut me off, &c., he requested me to submit a draft of what my instructions should be. I did so in about an hour's time, and in three days he gave me my papers, utterly castrated; ("emasculated" isn't strong enough). I discovered, years afterwards, when getting at the "Pickett Archives," that the Booby had manufactured those instructions, *verbatim,* from *Memoires pour servir* addressed the Department of State by William M. Burwell, a man of brains; but who knew as little of Mexico in such connection, as the cat that Kittens seven times a year knows of the gestation of an elephant; whereas I had lived in that country near ten years. Thus I fixed upon Nincompoop Browne the responsibility for the failure of the objects of my mission in Mexico.

Flunkey Browne says I was "recalled from that mission for having engaged in an encounter with some American in the City of Mexico." Now, we all know that, liars ought to have good memories, and Blather-

*He had honorable gentlemen about him, too; but I fear they had little influence with him. Alas, that the inability of one man to conquer himself should prove to be the source of woes unnumbered to millions yet unborn! Still, regarding him somewhat as a representative man, and deeply sympathizing with his misfortunes I shall let him part in peace. But I am inclined to "go" for Brother Browne.

skite Browne officially knows his statement to be false. I was never recalled, and if he had attended to his duty as such Ass. Secretary and had
me empowered as he should have done, instead of toadying men in
authority, or even answered my dispatches I had not returned as soon as
I did, voluntarily, to enter the military service. It is true that, I gave a
most consummate drubbing to a prominent Yankee in the City of Mexico,
and old as I am would be found quite capable of trying to do it again; or
to "any other man" who would like to test such conclusions. The whole
story, provocation and all—and there's "richness" in it—will appear when
the "Pickett Archives" shall be published.

As to those Archives themselves and my delivery of them in my quality
of attorney there has been, perhaps, quite enough said, both *pro* and *con.*
But I cannot forego the reflection that, it has not escaped my observation
that no one of those who so violently assailed me has said what he would
or would not have done under the same circumstances, nor, indeed, what
I should have done. It must be manifest to all that it was not in my
power any longer to prevent the delivery of the documents. Thus it is
not apparent to me that a moderate and purely professional success should
have justified such harsh comment. Ruined by the war I "accepted my
destiny" and sought to attend to my own business. The Confederate
Gov'nt. owed my friends and myself a colossal sum on liquidated account
—of which I have the most ample official evidence. Yet I have not spent
my time in whining for Southern sympathy and dollars; nor even asking for an Insurance agency. So it may be supposed I care little for the
reviling of the invidious, the prejudiced, the ignorant and the silly. But
I do value the good opinion of men imbued with a sense of justice, and
honor, and truth—among whom I do not rank Mr. Wm. M. Browne;
and this recalls me to my objective point. Please, therefore, let me have
what you know of him.

Pickett then added this postscript:

I have not been able to find anything about Browne in Burke's Peer-
age, or in kindred works; but a little bird whispered me "look in the
'Newgate Calendar'". Now, this must truly have been an inspiration;
for I am not addicted to that style of literature, and pay no attention to
criminal practice. And here we are: "The Marquis of Sligo. Fined and
imprisoned for enticing seamen to desert His Majesty's Navy." It is too
long to transcribe; but it seems The Most Noble Marquis had a yacht
in the Mediterranean, which he manned in part by seamen whom he
had enticed to desert from H. B. M.'s Ship the Warrior; the worst feature
of the business being that, *he pledged his word of honor he had no deserters on board.* Upon his return to England he was indicted, tried at Old
Bailey, found guilty, and sentenced to pay a fine of five thousand pounds,
and to be imprisoned four months in Newgate. This was in 1812. See
"The Newgate Calendar," pp. 526-27. Now, is our Memphian Marquis
a descendant of the aforesaid?

The next day in reply, Henningsen wrote to Pickett the following long, intemperate, and inaccurate letter:

1221 New York Avenue, Washington, Sept. 16th, 1872. Col: John T. Pickett 1422 F. Street. My Dear Sir: You ask me what I know about a certain Wm M. Browne. To any one else I would reply that I know but little about him and thought still less of him. Your reference to his connection, (which was an indirect perhaps unconscious and irresponsible instrumentality), the fate of our friend in common, General William Walker, reminds me that but for that circumstance I should hardly remember the little I do of him.

Meagre as it is I give it you. I first heard of him, and believe met him when he was a subordinate on a second rate New York paper. He was spoken of as a harmless fellow, whose characteristics and foibles, based on aristocratic pretensions had secured for him the nickname of Flunkey Browne, or Jeames Brownee. He boasted of connection with the Marquis of Sligo, and it was said, partly in jest, partly in earnest that he had been a footman in that family; i. e. a domestic official selected on account of a good development of calf, (usually at both extremities) to strut in gaudy small-clothes, gorgeously aiguilletted livery, and powdered hair, to stand behind the ladies' coach, or walk after them carrying the lap-dog, and armed with a five foot long, gold-headed Malacca cane. Hence no doubt his sobriquet "Jeames," from Thackeray's Yellow-Plush Papers. The nickname, however, proved to be an inspiration, as his little career subsequently illustrated. The press-men and the politicians have had their Jenkinses and their toadies; but Brown-ee was the only legitimate Flunkey Jeames of politics or of the press. He was called Brownee, by the way, from his persistence in explaining that he was none of your plain "Browns" (like Gratz,) but a Browne with an "e."

When an Administration organ was started here, in Buchanan's interest, either Butterworth, Superintendent of the Assay Office, or his brother, (I forget which) was largely instrumental in getting it up and claimed to have "the chief say" in the appointment of its editor, whose salary was fixed at $5000 per annum. Whichever it was he told me he had made up his mind to give it to Browne, who was keeping up a creditable appearance on a pittance of $1000, and to whom he wished to give a pleasant surprise, and who would do just as well as any other for a situation wherein only steadiness, docility and reticence — all of which he had — were required.

Butterworth canvassed for endorsement of his recommendation; but the matter was not so easily arranged as expected, and Browne was brought on to help. Though no lawyer he was a very indefatigable solicitor, as you had, subsequently, cause to know in the matter of the Senate printing, wherein you and he were so unfortunate as to be antagonized, ending, if my memory serves, in common defeat—a fact which he has no doubt treasured up.

Amongst other endorsements was one from George N. Sanders, which Browne was about to reject as equivocal if not insulting, to the effect that "no more appropriate selection could be made than that of Mr. Browne, because he neither had independence nor originality enough ever to think, write or act otherwise than as his patrons should direct." Some one, however, who knew Buchanan as well as George Sanders did, said this would be a more effective recommendation with the President than all the other endorsements put together. So it proved. Translated to the editorship Brownee soon ingratiated himself and family at the White House, where he became a sort of Master of Ceremonies and toady-in-ordinary—establishing himself on a light footing with several of the members of the Cabinet.

When General William Walker started on his Ruatan and Honduras expedition there appeared in the "Constitutional Union" (or whatever the name of the Administration organ may have been) an editorial stating (and thereby suggesting) that, the British had a right to treat him as a pirate. On this hint the British Captain Salmon, acted (as he would never otherwise have ventured to do) and handed Walker over to Guardiola, who shot this American representative man, as a prisoner, though afraid to face him in the field. Walker's friends found, however, that Wm. M. Browne was a mere figure head and tool in this matter, too contemptible and irresponsible in all ways to be held accountable for an article which if he did write it, was inspired and revised by James Buchanan, just as his late attack on you was by his present master, Jefferson Davis.

Brownee next turned up at Montgomery, Alabama, whither, his occupation in Washington being gone and his former small berth in New York being occupied, he had followed Howell Cobb and his fortunes. When Robert Toombs was appointed Confederate Secretary of State every one was astounded that Brownee, (who was entirely unknown to the Southern people, and who had never before come South of Washington,) should have been made Assistant Secretary. I asked an explanation from A. H. Stephens, the Vice President. He said it was one of the strange things occurring around us; that Browne was an importation and an importation of Howell Cobb's, who having presided over the Convention which elected Davis, claimed this singular boon in requital. Whilst we were talking, Secretary Toombs came in. He confirmed what the Vice President had said, and then remarked: "Well I suspect there is not much harm done; for I dare say I could carry all the needful papers of the State Department in that hat," (and it was a soft, low-crowned, broad-brimmed one he pointed at—not a stovepipe). He then expressed himself to the effect that, "Brownee would do as well as any other, as usefully subservient enough and a pretty good Flunkey, or Jeames, or Jenkins"— I do not recollect which of the words he used, but it was one of them, and possibly all three; for when Toombs wishes to express himself he neither beats about the bush, nor is sensitively particular as to the word he uses. Now reflect, Pickett, on what might have happened had Toombs continued at the head of the State Department instead of resigning to go into the field, and had circumscribed all the correspondence of the Department within the limits of that hat? Where would have been the ton and a half of Confederate Archives which you delivered for your client, and which it is said was purchased by weight?

It was generally understood that the source of Howell Cobb's romantic interest in Brownee originated from the fact of the latter, when editor of the organ at this place, having manfully vindicated the shortcomings of the former as Secretary of the U. S. Treasury.

Afterwards, Brownee, who, as you know, could never, by virtue of the calf in him, whether below the knee or above the shoulder, write a decent state paper or diplomatic document even by the help of aboundant plagiarism, relapsed into his true vocation as custodian of Jefferson Davis's door. Between the visitors who cursed him for not letting them in and the niggings he got from Jeff. for those he did let in he found this a hard road to travel, but was, at length, rewarded for his faithful services by being made *Aide-de-camp* to the President and Colonel of Cavalry. It was remarked when he donned his uniform (which was peculiarly generous and Yellowplushy) that, J. D. had been a long time putting him into a congenial livery. He chiefly distinguished himself in the defense of Richmond—which never was assaulted, and I was an amused witness of his principal exploit. Scouting at the head of some stay-at-home cavalry on the Mechanicsville road he stumbled on what he conceived to be the van-guard of the whole Federal army, and retired with a celerity which was equally creditable and surprising, considering his weight and the condition of his cattle. This supposed Yankee van-guard proved to be three youths mounted on spavined mules—the two Sizers and Schermerhorn, privates of cavalry, home on furlough to recruit their animals, and two of whom, poor fellows, were afterwards killed in battle. It may have been for this exploit that Brownee was made a "General," perhaps without seeking the promotion, like a General out West, who for many years had borne that title, which had been thrust upon him because he had, on one occasion inscribed himself on an hotel register as "General Agent of Brandreth's Pills."

This is the little I know and the last I heard of Brownee. Did not know he was in this country until so hearing from you. If you will take my unsolicited advice you would let the poor devil alone as entirely beneath your notice. He is back at his proper occupation of toadying Jeff. Davis, and could you wish your worst enemy, could Brownee ever attain the dignity of being an enemy, a more degrading office? As to his master, that were a different affair. You speak of a lingering respect for what he was or ought to have been. I have none, nor much opinion of the judgment of those who, knowing him, have or pretend to have such respect for him. I look upon him as one of the smallest men in History whose name was ever so prominently connected with such stupendous events. I know that, there are some who, when they penetrated the veil of this modern Prophet of Khorassan, or when it was removed to expose not neither a hero or a monster, but a very commonplace, not to say mean personage, denounced him in unmeasured terms, yet who now treat his reputation tenderly, as a representative of the lost Confederate cause. I regard this not only as a morbid sentimentality, but as an injustice to the dead and living Confederates whose cause he so signally mismanaged, and to whom their most bitter opponents cannot deny the meed of heroism, self-sacrifice and sincerity. To spare him is almost to reflect upon the memory of the thousands: —

> "Who died in vain,
> For those who knew not to resign or reign."

It seems to me there is not only an issue of veracity on a matter, not of opinion, but of fact between Jeff. Davis and yourself; but worse: he charges you from his anonymous ambush with forgery and slander in the matter of the Jake Thompson paper. You know best how to act in the premises, but certainly ought not to be restrained by any considerations of false delicacy or magnanimity from dragging him from his retreat if you see fit. Why not publish that exhibit of those sums of Confederate gold which he has received since the war ended, and which by your theory, belongs to the widows and orphans of the South? Also the name of the banker who invested————thousands for————? But all this pales before Jake Thompson's Colossal plunder—which he received for himself individually. I am, very truly Yours &c. Charles Frederick Henningsen.

P. S. Of course this long, rambling epistle is a private communication. Still, as I never write or say anything behind one's back which I am not willing to repeat to his face you may make what use you think proper of the whole or any part of the contents hereof. If I had been called upon to put my impressions in a form fitted for publication I should have felt to be constrained to be quite severe in expressing myself; but as it is I have been as indulgent as the subject would admit of, having lived long enough to subscribe to the sentiment that "charity covereth a multitude of sins." I am afraid you are not so forgiving. Why be so hard on Brownee? Can he help being fat, foolish and a Flunkey? C. F. H.[6]

❧ *Notes* ❧

Numbers in brackets at the top of the following pages indicate the pages in the text to which the notes refer.

CHAPTER I

1. For a further discussion of Browne's European background, see Appendix I.
2. William Howard Russell, *My Diary North and South* (Boston, 1863), 170. There was a passport issued by the British government to a William Browne on October 1, 1853. For a discussion of this point, see Appendix I.
3. *New York Journal of Commerce,* Jan. 19, 1859 (3, 1). The first number in the parentheses refers to the page, subsequent numbers, to the column.
4. Russell, *Diary,* 170.
5. *New York Journal of Commerce,* April 30, 1859 (3, 4). See also *Southern Banner* (Athens, Ga.), May 14, 1869 (2, 2).
6. *New York Journal of Commerce,* Feb. 3, 1859 (3, 1).
7. *Ibid.,* Dec. 30, 1858 (3, 2).
8. *Ibid.,* Jan. 12, 1859 (3, 1).
9. *Ibid.,* Jan. 19, 1859 (3, 1).
10. "The Covode Investigation," No. 648 of *Reports of Committees of the House of Representatives, Made during the First Session of the Thirty-Sixth Congress: 1859-'60,* Serial No. 1071 (5 vols.; Washington, D. C., 1860), 493. See also *Weekly Georgian* (Athens, Ga.), Jan. 4, 1875 (2, 2).
11. "Covode Investigation," 624, 632; *Congressional Globe: Containing the Debates and Proceedings of the First Session of the Thirty-Sixth Congress: also, of the Special Session of the Senate* (Washington, D. C., 1860), Pt. I, 111, 112; *Biographical Directory of the American Congress, 1774-1927* (Washington, D. C., 1928), 1072.
12. Browne, Washington, D. C., July 12, 1859, to Buchanan, in James Buchanan Papers, in Historical Society of Pennsylvania Library, Philadelphia.
13. "Covode Investigation," 16, 176-78, 596-97.
14. *New York Journal of Commerce,* April 30, 1859 (3, 2).
15. There was naturalized on July 17, 1857, in New York City, by the Common Pleas Court of New York County, a William Browne, who could have been William Montague Browne. P. A. Esperdy, District Director, Immigration and Naturalization Service, New York, N. Y., Oct. 5, 1964, to E. M. Coulter.
16. J. B. Jones, *A Rebel War Clerk's Diary at the Confederate States Capital* (A new and enlarged edition edited by Howard Swiggett. 2 vols.; New York, 1935), II, 134.
17. Allan Nevins and Milton Halsey Thomas, eds., *The Diary of George Templeton Strong* (4 vols.; New York, 1952), [III], *The Civil War, 1860-1865,* pp. 89-90.
18. "Covode Investigation," 485, 487; *Atlanta Constitution,* April 29, 1883 (3, 1).
19. *Weekly Banner-Watchman* (Athens, Ga.) May 8, 1883 (1, 6; 3, 5).

20. "Public Printing," No. 249 of *Report of Committees of the House of Representatives, Made during the First Session of the Thirty-Sixth Congress: 1859-'60,* Serial No. 1068 (5 vols.; Washington, D. C., 1860), 96-97.
21. "Public Printing," No. 205 of *Reports of the Committees of the Senate of the United States for the First Session of the Thirty-Sixth Congress,* Serial No. 1040 (2 vols.; Washington, D. C., 1860), 227, 228, 234-35.
22. *Ibid.,* 234.
23. For instance, see Mary Boykin Chesnut, *A Diary from Dixie* (Edition edited by Ben Ames Williams. Boston, 1949), 7.
24. "Public Printing," No. 249, p. 52; *Congressional Globe,* 36 Cong., 1st Sess., Pt. I, 473; *Constitution,* (Washington, D. C.) Jan. 20, 1860 (2, 4).
25. *Congressional Globe,* 36 Cong., 1st Sess., Pt. I, 478. See also Roy Franklin Nichols, *The Disruption of American Democracy* (New York, 1948), 246-49 *et passim.*
26. "Public Printing," No. 205, p. 2; "Covode Investigation," 544.
27. "Public Printing," No. 205, pp. 2-3.
28. *Ibid.,* 3-4.

29. "Covode Investigation," 511; "Public Printing," No. 249, p. 29.
30. "Public Printing," No. 205, pp. 17, 31, 211 (testimony), 333 (testimony); "Covode Investigation," 599-602.
31. *Constitution* (Washington, D. C.), April 13, 1859 (3, 1).
32. Of course, Browne did not write every editorial. Besides those which Bowman wrote, now and then an outsider was invited to write one, as, for instance, Joseph Holt. See Scrapbook in Joseph Holt Papers, Manuscript Division, Library of Congress.
33. *Constitution* (Washington, D. C.), Dec. 14, 1859 (2, 1).
34. *Ibid.,* April 7, 1860 (2, 1).
35. *Ibid.,* June 7, 1860 (2, 1).
36. *Ibid.,* June 11, 1859 (3, 1).
37. *Ibid.,* Oct. 11, 1859 (3, 1).
38. *Ibid.,* Aug. 23, 1860 (3, 1-2).
39. *Ibid.,* Dec. 22, 1860 (3, 1-5).
40. *Ibid.,* Jan. 26, 1860 (2, 2).
41. *Ibid.,* Aug. 6, 1859 (3, 2).
42. *Ibid.,* Aug. 20, 1859 (3, 1).
43. *Ibid.,* Feb. 15, 1860 (2, 3).
44. *Daily National Intelligencer* (Washington, D. C.), July 9, 1860 (3, 1).
45. *Constitution* (Washington, D. C.), July 24, 1860 (2, 1).

CHAPTER II

1. *Constitution* (Washington, D. C.), Feb. 2, 1860 (2, 1).
2. *Ibid.,* Dec. 8, 1859 (2, 1).
3. *Ibid.,* Jan. 26, 1860 (2, 2).
4. *Congressional Globe,* 36 Cong., 1st Sess., Pt. I, 165. Browne in the *Constitution* commented: "This feeble little band of mercenaries, on every division which has been taken for Speaker, voted not for Sherman, nor for Bocock, but for each other; and the steady devotion which Hickman voted for Haskin, and Haskin voted for Hickman, would have been the subject of universal admiration, were it not that both Hickman and Haskin are too well known to admit of the existence of such a feeling for a moment." Dec. 10, 1859 (2, 1). See

also *Congressional Globe,* 36th Cong., 1st Sess., Pt. I, 1, 87, 158.
5. *Constitution* (Washington, D. C.), Dec. 10, 1859 (2, 1). *Congressional Globe,* 36 Cong., 1st Sess., Pt. I, 112. "Black Republican" was a term which was first used to designate a certain wing of the Republican party, but later it was applied widely to the whole party. As explained by the *New York Journal of Commerce,* May 16, 1856 (2, 1), it was applied to those Republicans "who make the *black* man their principal stock in trade," and because they promote sectionalism as "decidedly a black-hearted business."
6. *Constitution* (Washington, D. C.), Dec. 10, 1859 (2, 1). It was quoted

in the *Congressional Globe,* 36th Cong., 1st Sess., Pt. I, 112.

7. *Congressional Globe,* 36 Cong., 1st Sess., Pt. I, 111.
8. *Constitution* (Washington, D. C.), Dec. 13, 1859 (2, 1).
9. *Ibid.,* Dec. 16, 1859 (2, 1).
10. *Ibid.,* (2, 2).
11. *Ibid.,* Dec. 13, 1859 (2, 1).
12. *Ibid.,* Dec. 14, 1859 (2, 1).
13. *Ibid.,* Dec. 13, 1859 (2, 1).
14. "Public Printing," No. 249, p. 97. The editorial appeared in the Washington *Constitution* (Washington, D. C.), Dec. 16, 1859 (2, 2).
15. *Congressional Globe,* 36 Cong., 1st Sess., Pt. I, 434-35.
16. James Byrne Ranck, *Albert Gallatin Brown, Radical Southern Nationalist* (New York, 1937), 177 ff.
17. *Constitution* (Washington, D. C.), Nov. 26, 1859 (2, 1-2).
18. *Congressional Globe,* 36 Cong., 1st Sess., Pt. I, 476.
19. *Ibid.,* 472.
20. *Constitution* (Washington, D. C.), Jan. 20, 1860 (2, 2).
21. *Ibid.,* Jan. 18 (2, 1), Jan. 20 (2, 1), Jan. 21 (2, 2), 1860; *Congressional Globe,* 36 Cong., 1st Sess., Pt. I, 471-81 (esp. 471, 473, 475, 478).
22. *Constitution* (Washington, D. C.), Jan. 21, 1860 (2, 1) (Saturday evening edition).
23. "Public Printing," No. 205, p. 1.
24. *Ibid.,* 8, 44, 46, 194, 198, 226-36 (testimony); "Public Printing," No. 249, p. 23; *Constitution* (Washington, D. C.), Jan. 21, 1860 (2, 1).
25. "Public Printing," No. 249, p. 96.
26. *Ibid.,* 98.
27. *Ibid.,* 101.
28. *Ibid.,* 97-110.
29. *Ibid.,* 104.
30. *Ibid.,* 98.
31. *Ibid.,* 102. Hindman added: "Under the circumstances, it is wrong and unjust thus to assail a man who has no redress on the face of the earth, being here, as it were, bound hand and foot, liable to be committed for contempt if he ventures to defend himself by word or deed, and compelled to listen to denunciation of articles published in a paper, of which he is one of the editors, as infamous, libellous and slanderous." *Ibid.,* 103.
32. "Covode Investigation," 59.
33. [James Buchanan], *Mr. Buchanan's Administration on the Eve of the Revolution* (New York, 1866), 239-40.
34. *Constitution* (Washington, D. C.), March 10, 1860 (2, 1) (Saturday evening edition).
35. *Ibid.,* March 31, 1860 (2, 1).
36. "Covode Investigation," 202.
37. *Ibid.,* 487, 489.
38. *Ibid.,* 176-78.
39. *Constitution* (Washington, D. C.), June 5, 1860 (2, 2).
40. "Covode Investigation," 28.
41. *Ibid.,* 58.
42. June 20, 1860 (2, 2).
43. June 5, 1860 (2, 2).
44. George Ticknor Curtis, *Life of James Buchanan, Fifteenth President of the United States* (2 vols.; New York, 1883), 261.
45. "Public Printing," No. 249, pp. 112-13.
46. To Barlow, New York in S. L. M. Barlow Papers, Henry E. Huntington Library, San Marino, Cal.
47. *Ibid.,* July 3, 1860.
48. *Ibid.,* July 6, 1860.
49. "Public Printing," No. 205, p. 210.
50. *Ibid.,* 210. See also 17.
51. *Constitution* (Washington, D. C.), July 7, 1860 (2, 1) (Saturday evening edition).
52. *Ibid.,* July 6, 1860 (2, 2).
53. *Ibid.,* July 7, 1860 (2, 1).
54. *Ibid.,* Dec. 13, 1860 (3, 2). See also *ibid.,* Dec. 7, 1860 (2, 3).
55. *Ibid.,* Jan. 16, 1861 (2, 3).
56. *New York Journal of Commerce,* Dec. 23, 1858 (1, 1).
57. March 20, 1860 (2, 2).
58. George P. Sanger, ed., *Statutes at Large, Treaties and Proclamations, of the United States of America from December 5, 1859 to March 3, 1863 . . .* (Boston, 1865), XII, 118, 119-20. See also *Constitution* (Washington, D. C.), Dec. 13, 1860 (3, 3).

CHAPTER III

1. *Atlanta Constitution,* April 29, 1883 (3, 1); Henry C. Tuck, *Four Years at the University of Georgia, 1877-1881* (Athens, Ga., 1938), 127; Ella Lonn, *Foreigners in the Confederacy* (Chapel Hill, N. C., 1940), 88.
2. Chesnut, *Diary from Dixie,* 16.
3. "Covode Investigation," 178.
4. William M. Browne, Washington, D. C., May 10, 1860, to Barlow, New York, in Barlow Papers.
5. *Ibid.,* Jan. 14, 1861.
6. *Ibid.,* July 1, 1860.
7. *Ibid.,* Jan. 10, 1861.
8. Kati Thompson (Mrs. Jacob Thompson), Washington, D. C., July 10, 1859, to Mrs. Howell Cobb, Athens, Ga., Howell Cobb Papers, University of Georgia General Library, Athens, Ga. See also Browne, Macon, Ga., April 18, 1871, to "My Dear John," Americus, Ga., John W. Bonner Collection, in possession of John W. Bonner, Athens, Ga. See also *Weekly Banner-Watchman* (Athens, Ga.), May 1, 1883 (3, 6).
9. Browne, Washington, D. C., Aug. 19, 1860, to Barlow, New York, in Barlow Papers. See also *ibid.,* May 18, 1860.
10. Chesnut, *Diary from Dixie,* 18.
11. Allen Johnson and Dumas Malone, eds., *Dictionary of American Biography* (Authors Edition) (New York, 1937), I, 613-15. See also *Harper's Weekly, A Journal of Civilization* (New York), XXXIII, No. 1701 (July 27, 1889), 607.
12. Curtis, *Buchanan,* II, 170-73.
13. Barlow, New York, Aug. 14, 1860, to Browne, Washington, D. C., in Barlow Papers. See also *ibid.,* May 11, Aug. 9, 1860.
14. *Ibid.,* Aug. 16, 1860.
15. Browne, Washington, D. C., Sept. 6, 1860, to Barlow, New York, *ibid.*
16. *Ibid.,* July 20, 1860.
17. *Ibid.,* July 30, 1860.
18. *Ibid.,* Aug. 19, 1860.
19. *Ibid.,* Oct. 19, 1860.
20. *Ibid.,* Dec. 14, 1860.
21. *Ibid.,* Dec. 18, 1860.
22. Russell, *Diary,* 170.
23. P. 28 of "8th Census 1860 [Population], District of Columbia: Georgetown, City of Washington, 1-890, No. 101," Microfilm, National Archives, Washington, D. C.
24. Kati Thompson, Washington, D. C., July 10, 1860, to Mrs. Howell Cobb, Athens, Ga., in Howell Cobb Papers.
25. *Constitution* (Washington, D. C.), Sept. 27, 1859 (3, 1).
26. Browne, Washington, D. C., Nov. 25, 1860, to Barlow, New York, in Barlow Papers.
27. *Ibid.,* Aug. 20, 1860.
28. Joseph Holt Papers, XXIII, 3125.
29. *Constitution* (Washington, D. C.), Dec. 31, 1859 (2, 3). In fact, Buchanan sometimes publicly referred to himself as "an old public functionary." See James D. Richardson, comp., *A Compilation of the Messages and Papers of the Presidents, 1789-1897* (11 vols., Washington, D. C., 1899), V, 553.
30. *Constitution* (Washington, D. C.), Dec. 30, 1859 (2, 1).
31. *Ibid.,* Jan. 26, 1860 (2, 1).
32. *Ibid.,* Feb. 22, 1860 (2, 1).
33. *Ibid.,* July 23, 1859 (3, 2).
34. *Ibid.,* Aug. 3, 1859 (3, 1).
35. *Ibid.,* Aug. 25, 1860 (2, 2). See also *ibid.,* May 18, 1860 (2, 1-2).
36. In Barlow Papers.
37. *Illustrated London News* (London, England), XXXVII (July 21, 1860), (53, 1).
38. *Constitution* (Washington, D. C.), Aug. 10, 1860 (3, 1). Browne said: "Capt. Hall asked me to visit the engine room. I declined on the ground that I did not wish to visit Hell before my time."
39. *Ibid.,* Oct. 3, 1860 (2, 1).
40. *Ibid.,* Oct. 6, 1860 (2, 1-2).
41. Chesnut, *Diary from Dixie,* 271.
42. Browne, Washington, D. C., Oct. 7, 1860, to Barlow, New York, in Barlow Papers.
43. *Constitution* (Washington, D. C.), Oct. 6, 1860 (2, 1) (Saturday evening edition).

CHAPTER IV

1. Browne, Washington, D. C., June 14, 1860, to Frederick Law Olmsted, New York, in Frederick Law Olmsted Papers, Manuscript Division, Library of Congress, Box 4. This and subsequent citations to the Olmsted Papers were most generously supplied to me by Col. H. B. Fant of the National Archives, Washington, D. C.

2. Browne, Charleston, S. C., April 22, 1860, to James Buchanan, Buchanan Papers. See also *Constitution* (Washington, D. C.), April 28, 1860 (2, 2); Browne, Athens, Ga., April 29, 1876, to Barlow, New York, in Barlow Papers.

3. *Constitution* (Washington, D. C.), April 19, 1860 (2, 1).

4. *Ibid.*, Feb. 25, 1860 (2, 1) (Saturday evening edition).

5. *Ibid.*, May 4, 1860 (2, 3).

6. May 9, 1860, Barlow Papers.

7. Browne, Washington, D. C., June 9, 1860, to Buchanan, in James Buchanan Papers.

8. *Constitution* (Washington, D. C.), June 19, 1860 (2, 3).

9. *Ibid.*, June 21, 1860 (3, 6).

10. *Ibid.*, June 22, 1860 (2, 3).

11. *Ibid.*, *June* 18, 1860 (3, 1).

12. *Ibid.*, Oct. 9, 1860 (2, 1).

13. *Ibid.*, Sept. 22, 1860 (2, 2).

14. *Campaign Constitution* (Washington, D. C.), July 19, 1860 (3, 2).

15. *Ibid.*, July 19, 1860 (2, 5).

16. *Constitution* (Washington, D. C.), May 8, 1860 (2, 1).

17. *Ibid.*, Aug. 11, 1860 (2, 1).

18. *Campaign Constitution* (Washington, D. C.), July 19, 1860 (2, 2).

19. *Constitution* (Washington, D. C.), Oct. 24, 1860 (2, 2).

20. *Ibid.*, Sept. 1, 1860 (2, 2) (Saturday evening edition).

21. *Ibid.*, Sept. 11, 1860 (2, 4).

22. *Ibid.*, Nov. 6, 1860 (2, 1).

23. *Ibid.*, Sept. 12, 1860 (2, 2).

24. *Ibid.*, Oct. 31, 1860 (2, 2).

25. *Campaign Constitution* (Washington, D. C.), July 19, 1860 (1, 1).

26. Browne, Washington, D. C., July 20, 1860, to Barlow, New York, in Barlow Papers.

27. *Ibid.*, Aug. 17, 1860.

28. *Constitution* (Washington, D. C.), June 27, 1860 (3, 1).

29. Quoted in Philip Shriver Klein, *President James Buchanan, A Biography* (University Park, Pa., 1962), 351.

30. *Constitution* (Washington, D. C.), July 10, 1860 (3, 1-2).

31. *Ibid.*, July 19, 1860 (2, 1).

32. *Campaign Constitution* (Washington, D. C.), July 19, 1860 (2, 1).

33. *Ibid.*, July 19, 1860 (2, 5).

34. *Constitution* (Washington, D. C.), Jan. 28, 1860 (2, 1).

35. *Ibid.*, Aug. 6 [7], 1860 (2, 1). See also *Campaign Constitution* (Washington, D. C.), July 19, 1860 (2, 3).

36. *Constitution* (Washington, D. C.), Nov. 1, 1860 (2, 1). Browne wrote in his *Campaign Constitution,* July 19, 1860 (2, 3): "Every sane man in this country must know that the predominant feeling in the bosom of every black-republican at the North—the bond which binds together that large and powerful party—is hatred against the inhabitants of the fifteen states of the Union where the institution of slavery exists; and every man who knows anything of Southern sentiment must feel that were the black-republican party, by the force of sectional numerical majority to acquire the ascendancy in the National Government—were ABRAHAM LINCOLN to be elected President —disunion, sooner or later, must be the inevitable result." "That it must come, in such an event," was as certain as anything in the future.

37. *Constitution* (Washington, D. C.), Dec. 29, 1860 (2, 4) (Saturday evening edition).

38. *Ibid.*, Dec. 20, 1860 (2, 2).

39. *Ibid.*, March 9, 1860 (2, 3).

40. *Ibid.*, March 10, 1860 (2, 2).

41. *Campaign Constitution* (Washington, D. C.), July 19, 1860 (2, 1).

42. *Constitution* (Washington, D. C.), May 19, 1860 (3, 2) (Saturday evening edition).

43. *Ibid.,* Aug. 14, 1860 (2, 3).
44. *Ibid.,* Oct. 23, 1860 (2, 1).
45. *Ibid.,* Oct. 31, 1860 (2, 1).
46. *Ibid.,* Nov. 3, 1860 (2, 1).
47. Browne, Washington, D. C., Oct. 19, 1860, to Barlow, New York, in Barlow Papers.
48. Nov. 7, 1860 (2, 1). Continuing, Browne said: "We can understand the effect that will be produced in every Southern mind when he reads the news this morning—that he is now called on to decide for himself, his children, and his children's children" whether he would submit to a rule hostile to him and to his section.
49. Horatio King, *Turning on the Light. A Dispassionate Survey of Presi-*
dent Buchanan's Administration . . . (Philadelphia, 1895), 25.
50. *Constitution* (Washington, D. C.), Nov. 9, 1860 (2, 2).
51. *Ibid.,* Dec. 13, 1860 (3, 1).
52. *Ibid.,* Nov. 22, 1860 (2, 2).
53. *Ibid.,* Nov. 22, 1860 (2, 1).
54. Nov. 23, 1860, in Barlow Papers.
55. *Constitution* (Washington, D. C.), Nov. 24, 1860 (2, 2).
56. *Ibid.,* Nov. 23, 1860 (2, 1).
57. *Ibid.,* Jan. 5, 1861 (2, 1).
58. *Ibid.,* Nov. 29, 1860 (2, 1).
59. *Ibid.,* Nov. 8, 1860 (2, 1).
60. *Ibid.,* Dec. 22, 1860 (2, 2).
61. *Ibid.,* Dec. 12, 1860 (2, 3).
62. *Ibid.,* Jan. 25, 1861 (2, 2).
63. *Ibid.,* Jan. 26, 1861 (2, 1) (Saturday evening edition).

CHAPTER V

1. *Constitution* (Washington, D. C.), Jan. 4, 1861 (2, 2).
2. *Ibid.,* Jan. 22, 1861 (2, 2).
3. *Ibid.,* Jan. 30, 1861 (2, 1).
4. Quoted in Hudson Strode, *Jefferson Davis, American Patriot, 1808-1861* (New York, 1955), 364.
5. *Constitution* (Washington, D. C.), Sept. 3, 1859 (3, 2).
6. *Ibid.,* Dec. 12, 1860 (2, 2).
7. *Ibid.*
8. *Ibid.,* Dec. 18, 1860 (2, 1-2).
9. *Ibid.,* Dec. 21, 1860 (2, 1).
10. Browne, Baltimore, Dec. 14, 1860, to Barlow, New York, in Barlow Papers.
11. Dec. 29, 1860 (1, 4-6).
12. *Ibid.,* Dec. 22, 1860 (2, 1).
13. *Ibid.,* Dec. 25, 1860 (2, 1-2).
14. *Ibid.,* Jan. 10, 1861 (2, 1).
15. *Ibid.,* Jan. 11, 1861 (2, 2).
16. *Ibid.,* Jan. 25, 1861 (2, 2).
17. *Ibid.,* Jan. 1, 1861 (2, 1).
18. In Barlow Papers.
19. Barlow, New York, Nov. 20, 1860, to Browne, Washington, D. C., *ibid.*
20. Browne, Washington, D. C., Nov. 22, 1860, to Barlow, New York, *ibid.*
21. Barlow, New York, Nov. 26, 1860, to Browne, Washington, D. C., *ibid.*
22. Browne, Washington, D. C., Dec. 10, 1860, to Barlow, New York, *ibid.*
23. Browne, Washington, D. C., Dec. 10, 1860, to Olmsted, New York, N. Y., in Olmsted Papers, Box 4.
24. *Constitution* (Washington, D. C.), Dec. 22, 1860 (2, 1).
25. Browne, Washington, D. C., Dec. 26, 1860, to Barlow, New York, in Barlow Papers.
26. *Ibid.,* Jan. 4, 1861.
27. *Constitution* (Washington, D. C.), Jan. 10, 1861 (2, 1).
28. *Ibid.,* Jan. 17, 1861 (2, 1).
29. In Barlow Papers.
30. *Constitution* (Washington, D. C.), Jan. 15, 1861 (2, 2).
31. *Ibid.,* Jan. 15, 1861 (2, 2).
32. *Ibid.,* Jan. 17, 1861 (3, 3).
33. *Ibid.,* Jan. 19, 1861 (2, 2).
34. *Ibid.,* Jan. 30, 1861 (2, 2).
35. *Ibid.,* Dec. 18, 1860 (2, 1).
36. *Ibid.,* Jan. 1, 1861 (2, 1).
37. *Ibid.,* Dec. 21, 1860 (2, 1).
38. *Ibid.,* Sept. 28, 1860 (2, 2).
39. *Ibid.,* Jan. 26, 1861 (2, 2).
40. *Ibid.* (2, 1).

CHAPTER VI

1. Browne, Washington, D. C., no date, to Howell Cobb, Washington,
D. C., Howell Cobb Papers.
2. *Constitution* (Washington, D. C.),

June 23, 1859 (3, 2).

3. *Ibid.,* Dec. 30, 1859 (2, 1).
4. *Ibid.,* Dec. 19, 1860 (2, 2).
5. *Ibid.,* Dec. 13, 1860 (1, 4-6; 2, 1-3).
6. *Ibid.,* Dec. 12, 1860 (2, 1) (Saturday evening edition). See also *ibid.,* Dec. 15, 1860 (2, 3). Browne said further: "The black-republican journals and their allied contemporaries of every stripe, here and elsewhere, seem to have drawn with more than ordinary recklessness on their stack of slander, vituperation, and mendacity, in order to assail the late Secretary of the Treasury, Hon. HOWELL COBB. There is not a day that some of the pack may not be heard yelping at the heels of the ex-Secretary, and the noisiest of them are those who, having got all they can from the democratic party, are now hoping, by their disgusting readiness to bite the hand that fed them, to earn a few crumbs from the party that will soon have some loaves to divide."
7. Browne, Washington, D. C., Dec. 30, 1860, to Barlow, New York, in Barlow Papers.
8. *Ibid.,* Jan. 8, 1861.
9. *Constitution* (Washington, D. C.), Jan. 8, 1861 (2, 3).
10. *Ibid.,* Jan. 12, 1861 (2, 5).
11. *Ibid.,* Jan. 16, 1861 (2, 1). Of a speech that Judah P. Benjamin made in the Senate about this time, Browne wrote that it was "one of the most masterly, eloquent, logical, earnest, and perfectly convincing speeches . . . which have ever been delivered in the halls of Congress." *Ibid.,* Jan. 1, 1861 (2, 3).
12. *Ibid.,* Jan. 30, 1861 (2, 2).
13. *Ibid.,* Dec. 28, 1859 (3, 1).
14. W. O. Bartlett, New York, Feb. 24, 1860, to William M. Browne, Washington, D. C., in James Buchanan Papers.
15. Browne, Washington D. C., Feb. 25, 1860, to Buchanan, *ibid.*
16. *Ibid.,* June 9, 1860. It is not known that Buchanan did it, but it seems evident that he must have done so. See John Bassett Moore, ed., *The*

Works of James Buchanan, Comprising his Speeches, State Papers, and Private Correspondence (12 vols.; Philadelphia, 1908-1911), XII, 289-315.

17. Browne, Washington, D. C., June 9, 1860, to Buchanan, in James Buchanan Papers.
18. Browne, Washington, D. C., Oct. 12, 1860, to Barlow, New York, in Barlow Papers.
19. *Ibid.,* Nov. 25, 1860.
20. *Constitution* (Washington, D. C.), Dec. 5, 1860 (3, 3).
21. *Ibid.,* Dec. 15, 1860 (2, 4).
22. *Ibid.,* Dec. 19, 1860 (2, 1).
23. *Ibid.,* Dec. 21, 1860 (2, 2).
24. *Ibid.,* May 18, 1860 (2, 1).
25. King, *Turning on the Light,* 24.
26. Horatio King Papers, III, 5582-83, in Manuscript Division, Library of Congress.
27. King, *Turning on the Light,* 26.
28. *Ibid.,* 27.
29. John A. Dix, New York, Nov. 27, 1860, to Horatio King, Washington, D. C., in Horatio King Papers, IV, 5692.
30. King, Washington, D. C., Dec. 14, 1860, to Black, *ibid.,* pp. 5708-09.
31. King, *Turning on the Light,* 35.
32. Dec. 20, 1860, to Nahum Capen, Boston, *ibid.,* 36.
33. Buchanan, Washington, D. C., Dec. 25, 1860, to Browne, Washington, D. C., in Moore, ed., *Works of Buchanan,* XI, 75.
34. *Constitution* (Washington, D. C.), Dec. 27, 1860 (2, 1).
35. *Daily National Intelligencer* (Washington, D. C.), Dec. 28, 1860 (3, 2).
36. *Constitution* (Washington, D. C.), Jan. 3, 1861 (2, 3). In a satirical vein, Browne likened those who were speculating on who wrote the *Constitution* editorials to those who had long been trying to establish the identity of Junius: "In a month or two book-buyers may expect the first of a series of quarto volumes, designed to prove that the political articles of the *Constitution* emanate from gentlemen of the highest distinction in the cis-atlantic world." *Ibid.,* Jan. 5, 1861 (2, 1).

37. Clipping in Scrapbook, Joseph Holt Papers.
38. Nevins and Thomas, eds., *Diary of George Templeton Strong,* III, 89-90.
39. King, Washington, D. C., Dec. 30, 1860, to I. Toucey, in King, *Turning on the Light,* 37.
40. *Ibid.,* 38. Years after the war, King assessed Buchanan as having been a friend of the South but one determined to maintain the authority of the United States. That was "what President Buchanan endeavored to the utmost of his power to do, while at the same time he deemed it prudent, in the cause of peace to avoid bloodshed, to pursue a conciliatory policy toward the South." *Ibid.,* 43.
41. Jeremiah S. Black, Washington, D. C., Jan. 10, 1861, to Browne, p. 354, in Records of the Department of State, Domestic Letters 53, Aug. 8, 1860-April 30, 1861, in National Archives, Washington, D. C.
42. Jeremiah S. Black, Washington, D. C., Jan. 12, 1861, to Stanton, pp. 357, 359, *ibid.*
43. Black, Washington, D. C., Jan. 15, 1861, to Department Heads, 361, *ibid.*
44. Browne, Washington, D. C., Jan. 14, 1861, to Barlow, New York, in Barlow Papers.
45. King, Washington, D. C., Jan. 12, 1861, to Nahum Capen, Boston, in King, *Turning on the Light,* 42.
46. Browne, Washington, D. C., Jan.

(no day given), 1861, to Buchanan, in James Buchanan Papers.
47. *Constitution* (Washington, D. C.), Jan. 3, 1861 (2, 2).
48. Chesnut, *Diary from Dixie,* 18.
49. *Constitution* (Washington, D. C.), Jan. 9, 1861 (2, 4).
50. *Ibid.,* Jan. 19, 1861 (2, 1) (Saturday evening edition).
51. To Cobb, Athens, Ga., in Howell Cobb Papers.
52. *Constitution* (Washington, D. C.), Dec. 29, 1860 (2, 3) (Saturday evening edition).
53. In Barlow Papers.
54. *Constitution* (Washington, D. C.), Jan. 26, 1861 (2, 1-2).
55. *Ibid.,* Jan. 12, 1861 (2, 4). See also *ibid.,* Jan. 15, 1861 (2, 4).
56. Browne, Washington, D. C., Jan. 15, 1861, to Howell Cobb, Athens, Ga., in Cobb, Erwin, Lamar Collection, University of Georgia General Library, Athens, Ga.
57. *Ibid.*
58. Jan. 30, 1861 (2, 1).
59. *Ibid.*
60. *Ibid.,* Jan. 31, 1861 (3, 4).
61. *Ibid.,* Jan. 30, 1861 (2, 2).
62. *Ibid.* (2, 1-2).
63. *Ibid.* (2, 2).
64. *Ibid.,* Jan. 31, 1861 (3, 4).
65. *Daily National Intelligencer* (Washington, D. C.), Feb. 1, 1861 (3, 2); *New-York Daily Tribune,* Jan. 31, 1861 (5, 1).
66. *Washington Confederation,* Jan. 30, 1861. This item was discovered and copied for me by Col. H. B. Fant of the National Archives, Washington, D. C.

CHAPTER VII

1. Browne, Washington, D. C., Jan. 28, 1861, to Cobb, Athens, Ga., in Howell Cobb Papers.
2. Feb. 6 1861 (2, 6).
3. Feb. 13, 1861 (1, 1).
4. *Weekly Montgomery* (Ala.) *Confederation,* Feb. 22, 1861 (2, 4).
5. *Southern Banner* (Athens, Ga.), Feb. 27, 1861 (3, 1).
6. *Montgomery Weekly Advertiser,* March 20, 1861 (1, 4). See also *ibid.,* March 20, 1861 (4, 2; 1, 6).

7. *Journal of the Congress of the Confederate States of America, 1861-1865* (7 vols.; Washington, D. C., 1904-1905), I, 87.
8. March 1, 1861, (2, 1).
9. Jones, *Rebel War Clerk's Diary,* I, 43.
10. Writer unknown, Tuskegee, Ala., May 21, 1861, to "My Best Friend [Mrs. Howell Cobb]," in Howell Cobb Papers.
11. Chesnut, *Diary from Dixie,* 7.

12. *Ibid*, 16.

13. Browne, Washington, D. C., March 6, 1861, to Barlow, New York, in Barlow Papers.

14. "Instructions of the Department of State to Hons. Martin J. Crawford, John Forsyth, and A. B. Roman, Commissioners of the Confederate States of America to the United States. Dated February 27th 1861," signed by William M. Browne, in Packet No. 1, Pickett Papers of Confederate States of America Collection, Manuscript Division, Library of Congress; Browne, Montgomery, Ala., March 14, 1861, to Martin J. Crawford and John Forsyth, Washington, D. C., *ibid.;* Browne, Montgomery, Ala., March 28, 1861, to Martin J. Crawford, John Forsyth, and A. B. Roman, *ibid.* See also *War of the Rebellion: A Compilation of the Official Records of the Union and Confederate Armies* (127 books and index. Washington, D. C., 1880-1901), Ser. I, Vol. I, 284; "Diplomatic Correspondence, Commission to Washington," 73-78, in John G. Nicolay Papers, Manuscript Division, Library of Congress.

15. "Confed. State Dept. 140, 141, 142 (Pickett)," Folder 140, in Pickett Papers of Confederate States of America Collection, CV, 26-28; *Journal of Confederate Congress*, II, 53, 84; Rembert W. Patrick, *Jefferson Davis and his Cabinet* (Baton Rouge, 1961), 101-102.

16. *Official Records of the Union and Confederate Navies in the War of the Rebellion* (30 vols. and index; Washington, D. C., 1894-1927), II, 363-64. See also pp. 284,298-303; Browne, Richmond, Va., Oct. 23, 1861, to Judah P. Benjamin, Richmond, Microcopy 437, Roll 13-6869, National Archives, Washington, D. C.

17. *Official Records, Navies,* Ser. II, Vol. III, 248; James D. Richardson, comp., *A Compilation of the Messages and Papers of the Confederacy, Including the Diplomatic Correspondence, 1861-1865* (2 vols.; Nashville, Tenn., 1905), 18-19, 26ff., 76-77, 77-80, 151-52.

18. Russell, *Diary,* 176.

19. *Official Records, Navies,* Ser. II, Vol. III, 289-90.

20. *Ibid.,* 125.

21. Microcopy 437, Roll 9-4168, in National Archives; Browne, Richmond, Va., Aug. 14, 1861, to A. Fullarton, Savannah, Ga., in Keith Read Collection, Emory University General Library, Atlanta, Ga. See also *ibid.,* July 29, 1861.

22. Browne, Richmond, Va., Nov. 1, 1861, to Judah P. Benjamin, Richmond, in Microcopy 437, Roll 14-7243, in National Archives.

23. *Official Records, Navies,* Ser. II, Vol. III, 252.

24. *Ibid.,* 253-55. See also pp. 116-17; Richardson, comp., *Messages and Papers of the Confederacy,* II, 151-52; Frank Lawrence Owsley, *King Cotton Diplomacy. Foreign Relations of the Confederate States of America* (Second edition, revised by Harriet Chappell Owsley; Chicago, 1959), 98-99, 113-16.

25. Juan A. Quintero, Monterey, Mexico, Feb. 9, 1862, to Browne, Richmond, Va., in Microcopy 437, Roll No. 31-169B, in National Archives.

26. Browne, Richmond, Va., Sept. 4, 1861, to Walker, Richmond, Va., *ibid.,* Roll 8-3947.

27. *Montgomery* (Ala.) *Weekly Mail,* March 15, 1861 (3, 2).

28. Chesnut, *Diary from Dixie,* 30.

29. *Ibid.,* 25.

30. April 15, 1861, to Mrs. Howell Cobb, in Howell Cobb Papers.

31. Chesnut, *Diary from Dixie,* 18-19.

32. *Ibid.,* 17.

33. *Ibid.,* 30.

34. Writer unknown, Tuskegee, Ala., May 21, 1821, to "My Best Friend" [Mrs. Howell Cobb], in Howell Cobb Papers.

35. Russell, *Diary,* 177.

36. *Ibid.,* 183.

37. Chesnut, *Diary from Dixie,* 46.

38. *Ibid.,* 18.

39. Browne, Washington, D. C., March 6, 1861, to Barlow, New York, in Barlow Papers.

40. Browne, Montgomery, Ala., March

18, 1861, to Barlow, New York, *ibid.*

41. *Ibid.,* March 22, 1861.

42. *Ibid.,* April 16, 1861.
43. Browne, Richmond, Va., July 16, 1861, to Barlow, New York, *ibid.*

CHAPTER VIII

1. Browne, Montgomery, Ala., May 28, 1861 to Cobb, Athens, Ga., in Howell Cobb Papers.
2. *Journal of Confederate Congress,* II, 206. Browne had long been interested in foreign affairs and would continue to be. In 1863 he wrote that foreign affairs of the Confederacy were "not very encouraging." "Neither England nor France will have anything to do with us. England is afraid of Lincoln," and France was too busy in Europe. "Seward will apologize for the Peterhoff seizure. England will be abundantly satisfied & will go to work seizing our ships to prove her neutrality." Browne, Richmond, Va., May 19, 1863, to Cobb, in Howell Cobb Papers.
3. Charles C. Jones, Jr., *Roster of General Officers, Heads of Departments, Senators, Representatives, Military Organizations, &c., &c., in Confederate Service during the War Between the States* (Richmond, Va., 1876), 5.
4. July 29, 1859 (3, 2).
5. Cobb, Richmond, Va., July 25, 1861, to wife, Athens, Ga., in Thomas R. R. Cobb Papers, University of Georgia General Library, Athens, Ga.
6. *Ibid.,* Camp Cobb, Sept. 10, 1861.
7. *Ibid.,* Camp Marion, Feb. 3, 1862.
8. *Ibid.,* Camp Helen, Nov. 14, 1862.
9. *Ibid.,* Nov. 17, 1862.
10. Browne, Richmond, Va., Oct. 23, 1861, to Howell Cobb, in Howell Cobb Papers.
11. Feb. 8, 1862, in Thomas R. R. Cobb Papers.
12. Chesnut, *Diary from Dixie,* 72.
13. *Ibid.,* 347. See also Hudson Strode, *Jefferson Davis, Confederate President* (New York, 1959), 515.
14. Chesnut, *Diary from Dixie,* 270-71.
15. *Ibid.,* 264.
16. Mrs. Howell Cobb, Athens, Ga., June 8, 1862, to Cobb, Richmond,

Va., in Howell Cobb Papers. See also Appendix II; Howell Cobb, Camp Comfort, June 19, 1862, Howell Cobb Papers.
17. Camp Comfort, June 19, 1862, to wife, Athens, Ga., *ibid.*
18. Cobb, Charlestown, Va., Sept. 17, 1862, to Browne, Richmond, Va., in Microcopy 437, Roll 35-10083, National Archives.
19. Browne, Richmond, Va., Oct. 31, 1862, to Howell Cobb, in Cobb, Erwin, Lamar Collection.
20. Jan. 3, 1863, in Howell Cobb Papers.
21. *Official Records, War,* Ser. IV, Vol. II, 211.
22. Dunbar Rowland, ed., *Jefferson Davis, Constitutionalist. His Letters, Papers and Speeches* (10 vols.; Jackson, Miss., 1923), V, 378-79. See also *Official Records, War,* Ser. IV, Vol. II, 216; William M. Browne, Richmond, Va., Nov. 25, 1962, to Howell Cobb, in Howell Cobb Papers.
23. Jefferson Davis, Richmond, Va., Nov. 29, 1862, to Joseph E. Brown, in Rowland, ed., *Jefferson Davis, Constitutionalist,* V, 379.
24. Browne, Richmond, Va., Dec. 23, 1862, to Davis, in Jefferson Davis Papers, Duke University General Library, Durham, N. C.
25. Browne, Augusta, Ga., Dec. 5, 1862, to Mrs. Howell Cobb, Athens, Ga., in Howell Cobb Papers.
26. Browne, Richmond, Va., Feb. 5, 1863, to "My dear John," *ibid.*
27. "Wm. M. Browne, War Department Letters Received, 420-B, 1863," Microcopy 437, Roll 94-139, National Archives, Washington, D. C.
28. *Ibid.,* Roll 94-102; Roll 95-309; Roll 109-293R. As another example, see William M. Gwin, Jackson, Miss., March 1, 1863, to "Friend [William M.] Browne," a holograph letter inserted opposite p. 20 in

Charles C. Jones, Jr., *Siege and Evacuation of Savannah, Georgia, in December 1864. An Address Delivered before the Confederate Survivors' Association, in Augusta, Georgia, . . . on Memorial Day, April 26th, 1890* (a pamphlet of 30 pages bound into a thick volume by laying in many letters, photographs, clippings, etc., with the binder's title: *Siege and Evacuation of Savannah, Georgia in December 1864 . . . Illustrated.* Augusta, Ga., 1890). This is Jones' unique copy, now in the University of Georgia General Library.

29. Browne, Richmond, Va., March 28, 1864, to James A. Seddon, Richmond, Va., in "Browne, War Department Letters Received," Microcopy 437, Roll 144-169W. See also *ibid.*, Nov. 7, 1863.

30. Chesnut, *Diary from Dixie*, 266.

31. "1st Battalion Cavalry, Local Defence—Va. Formerly Known as 'Browne's Reconnaissance Corps' and 'Browne's Cavalry Battalion.' " Microcopy 324, Roll 15, National Archives.

32. *Ibid.*

33. *Ibid.*

34. Browne, Richmond, Va., Aug. 22, 1862, to Capt. Downer, in Compiled Service Records of Confederate General and Staff Officers and Non Regimental Enlisted Men, Microcopy 331, Roll 37, National Archives. See also letters dated Aug. 23, 1862, and Nov. 13, 1863.

35. Vouchers, *ibid.*

36. Browne, Richmond, Va., July 16, 1863, to Maj. Gen. Elzey, Richmond, *ibid.* See also Browne, Richmond, Va., July 13, 1863, to Cobb, in Howell Cobb Papers.

CHAPTER IX

1. Browne, Richmond, Va., Jan. 21, 1863, to Howell Cobb, in Robert Preston Brooks, ed., "Howell Cobb Papers," in *Georgia Historical Quarterly*, VI (1922), 363. The standard work on conscription is Albert Burton Moore, *Conscription and Conflict in the Confederacy* (New York, 1924).

2. Jefferson Davis, Richmond, Va., Jan. 25, 1864, to Browne, Richmond, Va., Compiled Service Records, Microcopy 331, Roll 37. See also Browne, Richmond, Va., Jan. 26, 1864, to Col. J. S. Preston, in Manuscript Collection, New-York Historical Society Library, New York City.

3. Compiled Service Records, Microcopy 331, Roll 37.

4. Browne, Atlanta, Ga., Feb. 5, 1864, to Jefferson Davis, in Jefferson Davis Papers, Louisiana Historical Association Collection, Manuscript Division, Tulane University Library, New Orleans, La.

5. *Official Records, War*, Ser. IV, Vol. III, 269. See also Rowland, ed., *Jefferson Davis, Constitutionalist,* V, 220; Jones, *Rebel War Clerk's Diary*, II, 193.

6. April 27, 1864. (3, 2).

7. *Rebel War Clerk's Diary*, II, 193.

8. *Southern Banner* (Athens, Ga.), April 27, 1864 (3, 2).

9. Browne, Macon, Ga., Sept. 3, 1864, to Jefferson Davis, Richmond, Compiled Service Records, Microcopy 331, Roll 37.

10. Requisition, April 28, May 1, 1864, *ibid.*

11. Vouchers and receipts, *ibid.*

12. Mrs. M. McH. Cobb (Mrs. Thomas R. R.), n. d., Athens, Ga., to Mrs. Howell Cobb, in Howell Cobb Papers. See also Chesnut, *Diary from Dixie*, 400.

13. Mrs. Howell Cobb, Athens, Ga., June 22, 1864, to Cobb, in Howell Cobb Papers.

14. *Ibid.*, July 11, 1864.

15. Mary Ann Cobb (Mrs. Howell), Athens, Ga., Aug. 4, 1864, to Browne (in possession of E. M. Coulter). For additional activities of Browne in Athens, see John F. Stegeman, *These Men She Gave. Civil War Diary of Athens, Georgia* (Athens, Ga., 1964) 108-109.

16. Browne, Macon, Ga., June 7, 1864, to Jefferson Davis, in Jefferson Davis Papers, Duke.

17. Joseph E. Brown, Milledgeville, Ga., May 4, 1864, to Browne, Macon, Ga., in Georgia Governor's Letter Book, 1861-1865, Department of Archives and History, Atlanta, Ga.

18. *Official Records, War,* Ser. IV, Vol. III, 416. Governor Brown informed Colonel Browne that Georgia law allowed the Governor to detail regularly enlisted men in the State Troops to work in factories and other places to supply materials for Georgia soldiers. Therefore, Colonel Browne should not apply Confederate conscription laws to them. Joseph E. Brown, Atlanta, June 6, 1864, to Browne, in Georgia Governor's Letter Book, 1861-1865.

19. Joseph E. Brown, Milledgeville, Ga., May 21, 1864, to Browne, in *Official Records, War,* Ser. IV, Vol. III, 440-41.

20. Browne, Augusta, Ga., Nov. 25, 1864, to J. S. Preston, Richmond, *ibid.,* 868-70.

21. *Ibid.,* 259-60.

22. *Ibid.,* 347.

23. *Ibid.,* 381.

24. *Ibid.,* 457.

25. *Ibid.,* 475.

26. Joseph E. Brown, Milledgeville, Ga., Aug. 9, 1864, to Browne, in Georgia Governor's Letter Book, 1861-1865, pp. 676-78. Colonel Browne said that he wished to assure Governor Brown "of the earnest desire of myself" and of the Confederate government "to avoid all difficulties and controversies with the state authorities." He wanted to administer Confederate laws "so far as in me lay in a spirit of conciliation." Browne, Augusta, Ga., July 20, 1864, to Brown, in Joseph E. Brown Papers of Felix Hargrett Collection, University of Georgia General Library, Athens, Ga. In a long and intemperate reply, Governor Brown argued against Colonel Browne's position and ended with this threat: "As you are now fully advised of my position upon these points and as I shall maintain it if necessary with all the force at my command which is now nearly ten thousand armed men no further discussion is necessary," and he requested "that you as a subaltern take no steps which will precipitate such a conflict till you have submitted the question to the Confederate Executive and have received his explicit instructions, that he and not you may assume before the country the weighty responsibilities which will attend the act." Joseph E. Brown, Milledgeville, Ga., Aug. 9, 1864, to William M. Browne, *ibid.* Colonel Browne replied that he had never suggested a forced collision with Georgia but had urged the very opposite course. He added, "I would sincerely rejoice if the tone and temper of your Excellency's communications were equally conciliatory with those of mine and equally conducive to that good understanding, which it is so very desirable should subsist between the Confederate and State Governments." He assured the Governor that he would not have to use his ten thousand troops against the authority of the Colonel. Browne, Augusta, Ga., Aug. 20, 1864, to Brown, *ibid.*

27. Georgia Governor's Letter Book, 1861-1865, p. 693. See also Browne, Macon, Ga., May 9, 1864, to J. H. Burton, in Compiled Service Records, Microcopy 331, Roll 37. Browne detailed John A. Cobb to manage five plantations in Sumter and Baldwin counties, but when not needed on the plantations he should serve as aide-de-camp on Howell Cobb's staff. Order signed by Browne, April 30, 1864, in Cobb, Erwin, and Lamar Collection.

28. Howell Cobb, Macon, Aug. 31, 1864 to Browne, in *Official Records, War,* Ser. IV, Vol. III, 613.

29. James E. Seddon, Richmond, Va., July 5, 1864, to Browne, *ibid.* 530.

30. *Ibid.,* Ser. I, Vol. LII, Pt. II, 715.

31. Howell Cobb, Macon, Ga., Aug.

10, 1864, to Jefferson Davis, *ibid.*, 722.

32. Telegram, Jefferson Davis Papers, Duke University General Library.

33. *Official Records, War,* Ser. IV, Vol. III, 624-25.

34. *Ibid.*, 641.

35. *Ibid.*, 786.

36. *Ibid.*, 285.

37. *Ibid.*, 1049-50. See also Browne, Augusta, Ga., Nov. 24, 1864, to Brigadier-General J. S. Preston, Richmond, Va., Jefferson Davis Papers, La.

38. *Official Records, War,* Ser. IV, Vol. III, 871.

39. *Ibid.*, 579.

40. *Ibid.*, Ser. I, Vol. XXXV, Pt. II, 543-44.

41. *Southern Banner* (Athens, Ga.), Nov. 2, 1864 (2, 1).

42. *Ibid.* (3, 3).

43. Browne, Augusta, Ga., Oct. 21, 1864, to Howell Cobb, in Howell Cobb Papers,

44. *Southern Banner* (Athens, Ga.), Nov. 16, 1864 (3, 3).

45. *Ibid.*

46. Browne, Augusta, Ga., Nov. 10, 1864, to Jefferson Davis, in Jefferson Davis Papers, La. See also Browne, Augusta, Ga., Oct. 12, 1864, to Cobb, in Howell Cobb Papers; Browne, Macon, Ga., May 17, 1864, to Henry C. Wayne, Milledgeville, Ga., in Adjutant General File, Letters Received, 1860-1865, Department of Archives and History, Atlanta, Ga. Henry C. Wayne, May 19, 1863, to Browne, *ibid.*

47. Jefferson Davis, Richmond, Va., Nov. 22, 1864, to Browne, Augusta, Ga., in Rowland, ed., *Jefferson Davis, Constitutionalist,* VI, 410. This letter may be found also in *Official Records, War,* Ser. I. Vol. XLIV, 880-81.

48. *Official Records, War,* Ser. I. Vol. XLIV, 672-73.

49. *Ibid.*, 886.

50. *Ibid.*, 900.

51. Browne, Augusta, Ga., Jan. 19 [?], 1865, to "My dear Johnston," in Jefferson Davis Papers, La.

52. Charles C. Jones, Jr., *The Siege of Savannah in December, 1864, and the Confederate Operations in Georgia and the Third Military District in South Carolina during General Sherman's March from Atlanta to the Sea* (2 vols.; Albany, N. Y., 1874), II, 114; *Official Records, War,* Ser. I, Vol. XLII, Pt. II, 1003; *ibid,* Vol. XLIV, 910; Jones, Jr., *Roster of General Officers . . . in Confederate Service,* 30, 31; Joseph T. Derry, *Georgia,* Vol. VI of Clement A. Evans, ed., *Confederate Military History* (Atlanta, 1899) VI, 399.

53. "Mrs. Burton Harrison's Scrap Book, 1859-1909," in Burton Harrison Collection, Manuscript Division, Library of Congress.

54. Nathaniel Chairs Hughes, Jr., *General William J. Hardee, Old Reliable* (Baton Rouge, La., 1965), 270.

55. Jones, Jr., *Siege of Savannah,* II, 115-17.

56. Browne, Augusta, Ga., Jan. 19 [?], 1865, to "My dear Johnston," Jefferson Davis Papers, La.

57. Jones, Jr., *Siege of Savannah,* II, 114. This is a holograph letter laid in opposite p. 114.

58. *Journal of Confederate Congress,* IV, 346, 347.

59. *Official Records, War,* Ser. I, Vol. XLVII, Pt. II, 1093. See also *ibid.*, 105.

60. Andrews, Augusta, Ga., Dec. 1, 1864, to Cobb, in Howell Cobb Papers.

61. *Official Records, War,* Ser. IV, Vol. III, 1048-49. See also *ibid.*, 981; Howell Cobb Letter Book, 1863-1865, pp. 416, 440, 467 (in University of Georgia General Library).

62. Browne, Augusta, Ga. Jan. 19 [?] 1865, to "My dear Johnston," Jefferson Davis Papers, La.

63. *Ibid.*

64. Jones, *Rebel War Clerk's Diary,* II, 427.

65. *Journal of Confederate Congress,* IV, 576-77. See also Patrick, *Jefferson Davis and his Cabinet,* 102; Jones, Jr., *Roster of General Officers . . . in Confederate Service,* 5.

66. *Statutes at Large of the Confed-*

erate States of America, Passed at the First Session of the Second *Congress; 1864* (Richmond, Va., 1864), 255.

CHAPTER X

1. Browne, Richmond, Va., Oct. 22, 1863, to Cobb, in Howell Cobb Papers.
2. Minutes of the Faculty of the University of Georgia, 1881-1889, p. 113, in University of Georgia General Library, Athens, Ga. See also *Atlanta Constitution,* April 29, 1883 (3, 1).
3. Compiled Service Records, Microcopy 331, Roll 37.
4. Browne, Richmond, Va., Nov. 4, 1861, to Cobb, in Howell Cobb Papers.
5. March 29, 1862, *ibid.*
6. Browne, Richmond, Va., April 29, 1863, to Cobb, *ibid.*
7. *Ibid.,* Feb. 12, 1863.
8. *Ibid.,* April 15, 1863.
9. *Ibid.,* March 4, 1863.
10. *Louisville* (Ky.) *Daily Courier,* June 28, 1867 (1, 9); Horace Greeley and John F. Cleveland, *A Political Text-Book for 1860* . . . (New York, 1860), 39-41.
11. Browne, Richmond, Va., June 29, 1861, to Cobb, in Howell Cobb Papers.
12. *Southern Banner* (Athens, Ga.), July 3, 1861 (2, 8).
13. Browne, Richmond, Va., July 8, 1861, to Mrs. Cobb, in Howell Cobb Papers.
14. Deed Record W, p. 287, Office of Clarke County Clerk of Court, Athens, Ga.; Minutes of the Superior Court, Vol. XXIV (1870-1871), 17, Office of Clarke County Clerk of Court; Superior Court Record, Writs, Vol. XXX (1861-1872), 341, Office of Clarke County Clerk of Court.
15. Superior Court Records, Writs, Vol. XXX (1861-1872), 341.
16. Deed Record X, 90-91, Office of Clarke County Clerk of Court.
17. *Ibid.,* 167.
18. *Ibid.,* 208.
19. Browne, Richmond, Va., Oct. 22, 1863, to Cobb, in Howell Cobb Papers.
20. *Louisville Courier,* Sept. 7, 1866 (1, 9).
21. Superior Court Record, Writs, Vol. XXX (1861-1872), 359-60, Office of Clarke County Clerk of Court.
22. Compiled Service Records, Microcopy 331, Roll 37.
23. William Montague Browne Amnesty Papers, Record Group No. 94, National Archives, Washington, D. C.
24. E. Merton Coulter, "Slavery and Freedom in Athens, Georgia, 1860-1866," in *Georgia Historical Quarterly,* XLIX (Sept., 1965), 282.
25. Browne Amnesty Papers.
26. *Ibid.*
27. Browne, Athens, Ga., Sept. 15, 1865, to Barlow, in Barlow Papers.
28. *Ibid.,* Nov. 16, 1865.
29. Barlow, New York, Nov. 22, 1865, to Browne, Athens, *ibid.* Barlow wrote, "I tried to secure action in a number of cases, including your own, pending before the prest. but could not. He is however [word undecipherable] approaching the crisis, and unless all signs fail, we shall soon see the end of Republican rule in Washington, and I think we shall have a general amnesty." *Ibid.*
30. Letters in Browne Amnesty Papers. See also "Pardons by the President," No. 16 of *Executive Documents . . . of the House of Representatives during the Second Session of the Fortieth Congress, 1867-'68* (20 vols.; Washington, D. C., 1868), VII, 104, 105.
31. *Ibid.*
32. William B. Hesseltine, *Confederate Leaders in the New South* (Baton Rouge, La., 1950).
33. Minutes of the Superior Court, Vol. XXII (1864-1868), 30, Office of Clarke County Clerk of Court.
34. *Southern Banner* (Athens, Ga.), April 11, 1866 (1, 1).
35. In Jefferson Davis Letters, Confederate Museum, Richmond, Va.
36. *Ibid.*

37. *Southern Banner,* (Athens, Ga.), May 9, 1866 (2, 6). Only a few issues of this paper for this period have been found.
38. *Southern Watchman* (Athens, Ga.), May 16, 1866 (3, 1).
39. Browne, Athens, Ga., May 12, 1866, to Howell Cobb in Ulrich Bonnell Phillips, ed., *The Correspondence of Robert Toombs, Alexander H. Stephens, and Howell Cobb,* Vol. II of *Annual Report of the American Historical Association for the Year 1911* (Washington, D. C., 1913), 695.
40. John C. Whitner, Atlanta, Ga., Nov. 22, 1865, to Cobb, in Howell Cobb Papers.
41. Augustus Longstreet Hull, *Historical Sketch of the University of Georgia* (Atlanta, 1894), *passim*; Augustus Longstreet Hull *Annals of Athens, 1801-1901* (Athens, Ga., 1906), *passim.*
42. Jan. 24, 1866, in Jefferson Davis Letters in Confederate Museum, Richmond, Va.
43. Dec. 15, 1867, in Howell Cobb Papers.
44. Mrs. Thomas R. R. Cobb, Athens, Ga., Feb. 13, 1866, to Mrs. Howell Cobb, Macon, Ga., *ibid.*
45. MS Census, 1870; Vouchers, 15, 24, in "Vouchers of Howell Cobb, Admr. Genl. Wm. M. Browne, Deceased. Return of 1886," in Records of the Settlement of the William M. Browne Estate, Office of Clarke County Ordinary, Athens, Ga.
46. Browne, Athens Ga., June 3, 1868, to Mrs. Cobb, Macon, Ga., in Howell Cobb Papers.
47. Quoted in letter, Hudson Strode, University, Ala., Oct. 17, 1964, to E. M. Coulter, Athens, Ga. (in possession of E. M. Coulter).

48. In Jefferson Davis Letters.
49. Browne, Athens, Ga., Jan. 26, 1868, to Barlow, New York, in Barlow Papers; Browne, Athens, Ga., Sept. 7, 1866, to Cobb, in Howell Cobb Papers.
50. March 12, 1869, in Howell Cobb Papers.
51. *Ibid.,* Dec. 15, 1867.
52. *Ibid.,* March 25, 1869, May 15, 1869(?).
53. *Ibid.,* Dec. 2, 1867.
54. *Ibid.*
55. *Ibid.,* Dec. 2, 1867. The Crisps were Shakespearian actors, one of whom, Charles Frederick, became a member of the United States Congress and Speaker of the House; his son, Charles Robert, also served in Congress.
56. *Ibid.*
57. *Ibid.* n. d. See also *ibid.,* June 17, 1867.
58. *Ibid.,* Jan. 3, 1868.
59. *Ibid.,* n.d.
60. Howell Cobb, Jr., Milledgeville, Ga., May 16, 1866, to Mrs. Howell Cobb, Sr., *ibid.*
61. Browne, Athens, Ga., July 7, 1865, to Mrs. Howell Cobb, *ibid.*; Browne, Athens, Ga., July 11, 1866, to Howell Cobb, Jr., *ibid.*
62. Browne, Athens, Ga., n. d., to Mrs. Howell Cobb, *ibid.*
63. Browne, Athens, Ga., n. d., to Mary Ann (daughter of Mrs. Howell Cobb), *ibid.* The book was A. G. K. L'Estrange, ed., *The Life of Mary Russell Mitford, Told by herself in Letters to her Friends* (2 vols.; New York, 1870).
64. Browne, Macon, Ga., Aug. 16, 1869, to Mrs. Howell Cobb, Howell Cobb Papers.
65. *Ibid.,* April 14, 1874.

CHAPTER XI

1. In Howell Cobb Papers.
2. *Louisville Courier,* April 23, 1867 (1, 6).
3. Sept. 15, 1865, in Barlow Papers.
4. William M. Browne, ed., *The Southern Farm and Home. A Magazine of Agriculture, Manufactures and Domestic Economy* (4 vols.; Macon, Ga. and Memphis, Tenn., 1869-1874), II (1870-1871), 148.
5. Browne, Athens, Ga., Sept. 10, 1878, to Davis, in Jefferson Davis Letters, Confederate Museum, Richmond.

6. *Louisville Courier,* May 16, 1866 (1, 8-9).
7. Sept. 18, 1865, in Jefferson Davis Letters, Confederate Museum, Richmond.
8. Jan. 24, 1866, to "My dear & valued Friend" (Mrs. Jefferson Davis), *ibid.*
9. *Louisville Courier,* Sept. 3, 1866, (1, 10). See also *ibid.,* July 18 (1, 9), Aug. 10 (1, 9), 1866.
10. *Ibid.,* Jan. 1, 1866 (1, 8).
11. Browne, Athens, Ga., Sept. 7, 1868, to William B. Reed, in Buchanan Papers.
12. Browne, Athens, Ga., March 28, 1866, to Howell Cobb, in Phillips, ed., *Correspondence of Toombs, Stephens, and Cobb,* 678.
13. *Ibid.*
14. *Southern Banner* (Athens, Ga.), May 9, 1866 (2, 6).
15. See Browne, Athens, Ga., June 26, 1882, to Jefferson Davis, in Rowland., ed., *Jefferson Davis, Constitutionalist,* IX, 174.
16. Browne, Athens, Ga., Feb. 20, 1866, to W. Stuart, New York, in Personal Papers—Miscellaneous, Box STER-STY, Folder "Stuart W. Ac. 3240, 1 letter to, from Wm. M—? [Browne]," in Manuscript Division, Library of Congress. This letter was located by Col. H. B. Fant of the National Archives and transcribed through his generosity.
17. Howell Cobb, Macon, Ga., Nov. 24, 1865, to wife, in Howell Cobb Papers.
18. Browne, Athens, Ga., March 28, 1866, to Howell Cobb, in Phillips, ed., *Correspondence of Toombs, Stephens, and Cobb,* 677-79.
19. Jeremiah S. Black, New York, Oct. 12, 1868, to Browne, Athens, Ga., in Howell Cobb Papers.
20. Samuel Boykin, ed., *Memorial Volume of the Hon. Howell Cobb of Georgia* (Philadelphia, 1870), 85-86.
21. *Southern Watchman* (Athens, Ga.), Oct. 21, 1868 (3, 1-2).
22. *Louisville Courier,* Sept. 7, 1866 (1, 9).
23. *Southern Banner* (Athens, Ga.), May 9, 1866 (2, 7). See also

Southern Watchman (Athens, Ga.), May 9, 1866 (3, 1); Hull, *Annals of Athens,* 338.
24. *Southern Banner,* (Athens, Ga.), May 9, 1866 (2, 7).
25. *Louisville Courier,* June 7, 1866 (1, 10).
26. *Northeast Georgian* (Athens, Ga.), April 29, 1874 (3, 5).
27. *Ibid.,* April 29, 1874 (3, 2-7).
28. Browne, Athens, Ga., April 9, 1868, to Barlow, New York, Barlow Papers. See also "Mrs. Elizabeth Church Robb—An Obituary," in *Georgia Historical Quarterly,* XLVIII (Dec., 1964), 471-73. Mrs. Robb was married twice. Her first husband was Col. L. S. Craig of the United States Army (ante bellum), and from this union came descendants who have perpetuated Craig as a family given name.
29. June 17, 1865, in Barlow Papers. Barlow, New York, May 17, 1866, to Browne, said "It is plain that the mail service in Ga. is in [need?] of reconstruction."
30. Aug. 27, 1865, in Barlow Papers.
31. Sept. 6, 1865, *ibid.*
32. *Louisville Courier,* July 4, 1867 (1, 6).
33. Barlow, New York, Nov. 22, 1865; May 17, 1866; Nov. 22, Dec. 11, 1874; Aug. 10, 1877, to Browne, Athens, Ga.; Browne, Athens, Ga., Jan. 26, 1868, to Barlow, New York, in Barlow Papers.
34. Browne, Athens, Ga., Jan. 26, 1868, to Barlow, New York, *ibid.*
35. April 9, 1868, *ibid.*
36. Browne, Athens, Ga., Feb. 19, 1867, to Olmsted, New York, in Frederick Law Olmsted Papers, Manuscript Division, Library of Congress. This and the following two letters were located and transcripts generously supplied by Col. H. B. Fant of the National Archives.
37. *Ibid.,* March 7, 1867.
38. *Ibid.,* Feb. 15, 1869.
39. Browne, Macon, Ga., Dec. 4, 1865, to Barlow, New York, in Barlow Papers.
40. Barlow, New York, Dec. 21, 1865, to Browne, Athens, Ga., *ibid.*
41. *Ibid.,* May 14, 1866.

42. *Louisville Courier,* Aug. 21, 1866 (1, 10).
43. Browne, Athens, Ga., March 12, 1869, to Barlow, New York, Barlow Papers.
44. *Ibid.,* March 22, 1869.
45. *Ibid.,* April 6, 1869. Apparently the sale was not completed, since the deed records of Clarke County do not show a transfer of this land to Browne.
46. Browne, Athens, Ga., March 10, 1869, to Mitchell, Athens, Ga., in William L. Mitchell Collection, in possession of E. M. Coulter, Athens, Ga.
47. *Ibid.,* March 24, 1869.
48. Browne, Athens, Ga., Sept. 29, 1868, to Barlow, New York, in Barlow Papers.
49. *Ibid.,* Oct. 8, 1868. See also *ibid.,* Nov. 18, 1868.
50. *Ibid.,* Macon, July 18, 1871.

CHAPTER XII

1. *Louisville Courier,* May 16, 1866 (1, 8).
2. *Daily Constitutionalist* (Augusta, Ga.), Oct. 20, 1866 (3, 1). See also *ibid.* (2, 2).
3. *Louisville Courier,* Oct. 26, 1866 (1, 9-10).
4. The clue to the identity of "Nabob" is to be found in a letter from Browne to Howell Cobb, written on May 12, 1868, in which he said: "The Courier takes now but fortnightly letters instead of weekly, and even for that pays very slowly." Phillips, ed., *Correspondence of Toombs, Stephens, and Cobb,* 696. Browne made no mention of using the pen name "Nabob"; but an examination of the *Courier* showed that nobody but "Nabob" had been writing letters to it from Georgia. Although Browne did not specify the Louisville newspaper, it seemed evident that he must have been referring to the Kentucky newspaper, rather than to the *Charleston Courier.*
5. *Louisville Courier,* May 16, 1866 (1, 2).
6. *Ibid.,* April 13, 1867 (3, 3).
7. *Ibid.,* Oct. 17, 1867 (3, 6).
8. *Ibid.,* June 25, 1867 (1, 7).
9. *Ibid.,* June 7, 1866 (1, 10).
10. *Ibid.,* June 28, 1867 (1, 9).
11. *Ibid.,* June 18, 1866 (1, 10).
12. *Ibid.,* Oct. 10, 1866 (1, 10).
13. *Ibid.,* Nov. 17, 1866 (1, 8).
14. *Ibid.,* Aug. 21, 1866 (1, 1).
15. *Ibid.,* Aug. 1, 1867 (1, 7).
16. *Ibid.,* Jan. 1, 1867 (1, 8).
17. *Ibid.,* July 23, 1867 (3, 5).
18. *Ibid.,* Sept. 13, 1867 (1, 8).
19. *Ibid.,* Aug. 28, 1867 (3, 5).
20. *Ibid.,* May 24, 1866 (1, 9).
21. *Ibid.,* Aug. 21, 1866 (1, 10). See also *ibid.,* Aug. 2, 1866 (1, 9).
22. *Ibid.,* Dec. 11, 1866 (1, 5).
23. *Ibid.,* June 14, 1866 (1, 10).
24. *Ibid.,* Oct. 9, 1867 (1, 8).
25. *Ibid.,* Oct. 2, 1866 (1, 9).
26. Phillips, ed., *Correspondence of Toombs, Stephens, and Cobb,* 696.
27. Jan. 26, 1868, in Barlow Papers.
28. *Ibid.,* June 24, 1868.
29. Sept. 7, 1868, in James Buchanan Papers.
30. Oct. 8, 1868, in Barlow Papers. See also *ibid.,* Nov. 18, 1868.
31. New York *World,* Jan. 12, 1869 (12, 3-4).
32. Quoted in *Southern Banner* (Athens, Ga.), May 14, 1869 (2, 2).
33. Browne, Athens, Ga., Aug. 16, 1869, to Mrs. Howell Cobb, in Howell Cobb Papers. See also *Southern Watchman* (Athens, Ga.), July 14, 1869 (3, 1).
34. *Weekly Georgian* (Athens, Ga.), Sept. 29, 1875 (2, 2).

CHAPTER XIII

1. *Louisville Courier,* Sept. 20, 1867 (1, 9).
2. *Ibid.,* Nov. 17, 1866 (1, 8).
3. *Ibid.,* June 1, 1867 (3, 7).
4. *Ibid.,* May 21, 1867 (1, 8).
5. *Ibid.,* Jan. 1, 1867 (1, 8).

6. *Ibid.,* April 23, 1867 (1, 6).
7. *Ibid.,* Sept. 7, 1866 (1, 9).
8. *Ibid.,* March 20, 1867 (1, 6).
9. *Ibid.,* May 22, 1866 (1, 9).
10. *Ibid.,* May 16, 1866 (1, 8).
11. *Ibid.,* Nov. 17, 1866 (1, 8).
12. *Ibid.,* March 20, 1867 (1, 6).
13. *Ibid.,* March 28, 1867 (1, 8).
14. *Ibid.,* June 6, 1867 (4, 3).
15. *Ibid.,* April 4, 1867 (3, 5).
16. *Ibid.,* May 24, 1866 (1, 9).
17. *Ibid.,* April 4, 1867 (3, 5).
18. *Ibid.,* Nov. 9, 1867 (4, 6).
19. *Southern Watchman* (Athens, Ga.), Dec. 11, 1867 (3, 1). See also *Louisville Courier,* Aug. 2, 1867 (3, 6); Aug. 26, 1867 (3, 5); New York *World,* Jan. 5, 1869 (3, 4).
20. *Southern Watchman* (Athens, Ga.), Jan. 15, 1868 (2, 4-5).
21. Mrs. Browne, n. p., n. d., to Mrs. Cobb, in Howell Cobb Papers. See also Browne, Atlanta, Dec. 19, 1867, to Cobb, Macon, Ga., *ibid.*
22. Mrs. Browne, Athens, Ga., Dec. 15, 1867, to Mrs. Howell Cobb, Macon, *ibid.* See also *Louisville, Courier,* Dec. 17, 1867 (1, 8); Jan. 2, 1868 (2, 1).
23. *Louisville Courier,* Feb. 27, 1868 (3, 7).
24. Browne, Athens, Ga., Jan. 26, 1868, to Barlow, in Barlow Papers.
25. *Louisville Courier,* Nov. 22, 1867 (1, 8).
26. *Ibid.,* Dec. 7, 1867 (2, 3).
27. *Ibid.,* Dec. 19, 1867 (1, 7).
28. *Ibid.,* Feb. 21, 1868 (2, 3).
29. *Ibid.,* Jan. 24, 1868 (2, 2).
30. *Ibid.,* May 4, 1867 (1, 9).
31. *Ibid.,* Jan. 16, 1868 (2, 3).
32. *Ibid.,* Dec. 22, 1867 (1, 9).
33. *Ibid.,* Jan. 30, 1868 (1, 7).
34. *Ibid.,* March 6, 1868 (3, 7).
35. *Ibid.,* Feb. 27, 1868 (3, 7).
36. *Ibid.,* April 7, 1868 (1, 10).
37. New York *World,* Nov. 14, 1868 (1, 6).
38. *Louisville Courier,* April 23, 1868 (1, 7).
39. New York *World,* Sept. 18, 1868 (2, 1).
40. *Ibid.,* Feb. 1, 1869 (1, 6).
41. *Southern Watchman* (Athens, Ga.), May 13, 1868 (2, 3).
42. Browne, Athens, Ga., April 22, 1868, to Barlow, New York, in Barlow Papers.
43. *Louisville Courier,* April 10, 1868 (1, 7).
44. Letter in Barlow Papers.
45. May 1, 1868 (4, 6).
46. May 15, 1868, in Barlow Papers.
47. *Louisville Courier,* May 16, 1868 (1, 8).
48. New York *World,* Sept. 8, 1868 (2, 1). Georgia's boldness in ejecting the Negro members from the legislature brought about serious repercussions in Washington. Congress, after discussing for a year what should be done about it, passed on December 22, 1869, a law subjecting Georgia to a second reconstruction, setting down a new test oath, guaranteeing the right of Negroes to hold office, and placing the state under military supervision again. Col. I. W. Avery, editor of the *Atlanta Constitution,* asked Browne to give his opinion of what "patriotic members of the Legislature should do" in the approaching session. Browne replied that they should take their seats and do all they could to defend Georgia against those who would ruin the state. He said that the law was "a violation of the plainest provisions of the Constitution and a violent and unscrupulous act of revolution." Avery agreed and added, "Gen. Browne's record makes him a standard Democratic authority." *Atlanta Constitution,* Jan. 5, 1870 (1, 2; 1, 1).
49. *Atlanta Constitution,* Sept. 24, 1868 (1, 6).
50. *Ibid.,* Dec. 24, 1868 (12, 3).
51. Browne, Athens, Ga., September 7, 1868, to William B. Reed, in Buchanan Papers.
52. *Ibid.,* Sept. 7, 1868.
53. Browne, Athens, Ga., April 22, 1868, to Barlow, New York, in Barlow Papers.
54. *Ibid.,* Jan. 26, 1868.
55. *Ibid.,* April 22, 1868.
56. *Ibid.,* April 9, 1868.
57. *Ibid.,* May 15, 1868.
58. Phillips, ed., *Correspondence of Toombs, Stephens, and Cobb,* 695.

59. *Southern Watchman* (Athens, Ga.), July 1, 1868 (3, 2-3).
60. *Ibid.*, July 8 (3, 1), July 29 (3, 3).
61. Browne, New York, Aug. 21, 1868, to Cobb, in Howell Cobb Papers. See also E. B. Hart, New York, Sept. 11, 1868, to Cobb, *ibid.;* Browne, Athens, Ga., Sept. 7, 1868, to William B. Reed, in James Buchanan Papers.
62. Browne, New York, Aug. 22, 1868, to Cobb, in Howell Cobb Papers.
63. Browne, Athens, Ga., Sept. 7, 1868, to William B. Reed, in Buchanan Papers.
64. *Ibid.;* Browne, Athens, Ga., Sept. 29, 1868, to Barlow, New York, in Barlow Papers.
65. New York *World,* Oct. 31, 1868 (11, 1).
66. *Ibid.*
67. *Ibid.,* Oct. 10, 1868 (4, 1).
68. *Ibid.,* Sept. 24, 1868 (1, 6; 2, 1).
69. *Ibid.,* Oct. 3, 1868 (1, 1).
70. *Louisville Courier,* April 7, 1868 (1, 10).
71. New York *World,* Sept. 29, 1868 (1, 6).
72. *Ibid.,* Oct. 10, 1868 (4, 1).
73. *Ibid.,* Nov. 14, 1868 (1, 5).
74. *Ibid.* (1, 5-6).
75. *Ibid.*
76. *Southern Farm and Home,* III (May, 1872), 271.
77. Browne, Macon, Ga., Sept. 4, 1871, to Stephens, in Alexander Hamilton Stephens Papers, Duke University General Library, Durham, N. C.
78. Chauncey F. Black, ed., *Essays and Speeches of Jeremiah S. Black. With a Biographical Sketch* (New York, 1885), 292-311.
79. Browne, Athens, Ga., Sept. 27, 1876, to Black, in Jeremiah S. Black Papers, Manuscript Division, Library of Congress.
80. Barlow, New York, April 25, 1876, to Browne, Athens, Ga., in Barlow Papers.
81. Browne, Athens, Ga., April 21, April 29, 1876, to Barlow, New York, *ibid.*
82. Barlow, New York, May 3, 1876, to Browne, Athens, Ga., *ibid.*
83. Dec. 13, 1876, *ibid.*
84. Dec. 18, 1876, *ibid.*
85. Barlow, New York, Aug. 10, 1877, to Browne, Athens, Ga., *ibid.*
86. Browne, Athens, Ga., July 16, 1874, to Davis, in Jefferson Davis Letters, in Confederate Museum, Richmond.
87. *Ibid.,* Sept. 10, 1878.
88. *Ibid.,* May 2, 1881, in Louisiana Historical Association Collection, Jefferson Davis Papers.
89. Browne, Athens, Ga., March 4, 1883, to Mell, in Patrick Hues Mell Collection, University of Georgia General Library, Athens, Ga.
90. Browne, Sept. 20, 1880, to Mitchell, in William L. Mitchell Collection.

CHAPTER XIV

1. *Southern Watchman* (Athens, Ga.), Sept. 16, 1868 (1, 4).
2. *Louisville Courier,* Oct. 23, 1866 (1, 9).
3. *Ibid.,* June 28, 1867 (1, 9).
4. "Memorandum of Phosphate Sales," Box 1, Folder 32, in Colonel David C. Barrow Papers, University of Georgia General Library, Athens, Ga.
5. Browne, Athens, Ga., Feb. 10, 1866, Box 1, Folder 34, *ibid.*
6. March 20, 1866, in Howell Cobb Papers.
7. Phillips, ed., *Correspondence of Toombs, Stephens, and Cobb,* 678.
8. *Louisville Courier,* June 18, 1866 (1, 5).
9. March 28, 1866, in Howell Cobb Papers.
10. *Ibid.,* March 20, 1866.
11. July 11, 1866, *ibid.*
12. *Louisville Courier,* Oct. 4, 1866 (1, 9).
13. Browne, Richmond, Va., May 16, 1863, to James A. Seddon, Box 1, Folder 23, in Colonel David C. Barrow Papers.
14. *Louisville Courier,* Nov. 17, 1866 (1, 8).
15. New York *World,* Jan. 30, 1869 (11, 4).
16. Browne, Richmond, Va., May 25,

1863, to Barrow, Box 1, Folder 23, in Colonel David C. Barrow Papers.
17. Browne, Macon, Ga., May 24, 1864, leave of absence to Barrow, Box 1, Folder 29, in Colonel David C. Barrow Papers.
18. *Louisville Courier,* Nov. 27, 1866 (1, 8).
19. Deed Record V, 279-81, 360-61, Office of Oglethorpe County Clerk of Court, Lexington, Ga. For land transactions with William N. White, see Deed Record X, 180, 287-88, 311, Office of Clarke County Clerk of Court, Athens, Ga.
20. Browne, Athens, Ga., Oct. 27, 1866, to Barrow, in Colonel David C. Barrow Papers.
21. Fragment of undated letter by Clara Elizabeth Barrow (Bessie) to her sister Lucy (Mrs. John A. Cobb), in Howell Cobb Papers.
22. Browne, New York, Aug. 22, 1868, to Howell Cobb, *ibid.;* Col. D. C. Barrow Diary for 1867, in Colonel David C. Barrow Papers.
23. Browne, "Plantation, Oglethorpe Co.," April 20, 1867, to John A. Cobb, in Howell Cobb Papers. Browne's railroad station was Antioch Depot, on the Georgia Railroad.
24. *Louisville Courier,* Sept. 20, 1867 (1, 9).
25. *Ibid.,* Nov. 15, 1867 (2, 4).

26. Dec. 2, 1867, in Howell Cobb Papers.
27. *Louisville Courier,* Jan. 29, 1868 (1, 8).
28. Jan. 26, 1868, Barlow Papers.
29. Jan. 3, 1868, in Howell Cobb Papers.
30. Browne, Athens, Ga., May 2, 1868, to Howell Cobb, *ibid.*
31. *Ibid.* This letter was published in Phillips, ed., *Correspondence of Toombs, Stephens, amd Cobb,* 695-96.
32. Nov. 18, 1868, in Barlow Papers.
33. New York *World,* Dec. 24, 1868 (12, 4).
34. *Southern Banner* (Athens, Ga), Dec. 4, 1868 (3, 2); *Southern Watchman* (Athens, Ga.), Dec. 9, 1868 (3, 1).
35. *Southern Watchman* (Athens, Ga.), May 5, 1869 (3, 1).
36. *Ibid.,* Jan. 28, 1874 (3, 2).
37. *Ibid.,* July 3, 1867 (3, 1); June 3 (3, 1), June 17 (3, 1), Sept. 16 (1, 3; 1, 4), Sept. 30 (3, 1), 1868; June 2 (3, 4), 1869; *Southern Banner* (Athens, Ga.), June 4, 1869 (3, 4); *Southern Farm and Home,* III (Sept., 1872), 432-33. Tappahannock wheat was the variety used in the contest.
38. *Southern Farm and Home,* I (Oct., 1870), 433.

CHAPTER XV

1. Mortgage Record, Liens, A, 75-76, Office of Oglethorpe County Clerk of Court, Lexington, Ga.
2. *Southern Farm and Home,* III (Dec., 1871) 69, III (Oct. 1872), 471.
3. *Southern Watchman* (Athens, Ga.), Oct. 20, 1869 (3, 2).
4. *Southern Cultivator. A Practical and Scientific Magazine for the Plantation, the Garden and the Family Circle* (William and W. L. Jones, Editors and Proprietors. Athens), XXVIII (Jan., 1860), 29.
5. *Southern Watchman* (Athens, Ga.), Nov. 24, 1869 (3, 1).
6. Quoted in *Southern Farm and*

Home, I (Sept., 1870), 17 (advertisements).
7. *Ibid.,* II (Nov., 1870), 6.
8. *Ibid.,* III (Dec., 1871), 71.
9. *Ibid.,* III (June, 1872), 21. Browne wrote that we "have received unusual encouragement and aid, and that we have had a fuller measure of success than we anticipated." *Ibid.,* II (Nov., 1870), 33.
10. *Ibid.,* IV (Feb., 1873), 152.
11. *Ibid.,* III (Feb., 1872), 150.
12. *Ibid.* (April, 1872), 211.
13. *Ibid.,* IV (Dec., 1872), 2.
14. *Ibid.,* III (April, 1872), 234.
15. *Ibid.,* I (Nov. 1869), 32.
16. *Ibid.,* II (Oct., 1871), 451-52.
17. *Ibid.,* I (Nov., 1869), 1, 2.

18. *Ibid.*, 32; III (Aug., 1872), 39.
19. *Ibid.*, III (June, 1872), 10 (advertisements); (Aug., 1872), 390; (Sept., 1872), 434.
20. *Ibid.*, III (May, 1872), 271.
21. *Ibid.*, IV (Jan., 1873), 111.
22. *Ibid.*, 151.
23. *Ibid.*, I (Jan., 1870), 89, 91.
24. *Ibid.*, II (Jan., 1871), 82. See also p. 81; III (Jan., 1872), 81-82.
25. *Ibid.*, III (Dec., 1871), 71.
26. *Ibid.*
27. *Ibid.* (Nov., 1871), p. 1.
28. *Ibid.*, IV (Dec., 1872), 41.
29. *Ibid.*, I (Nov., 1869), 1.
30. *Ibid.*, IV (Dec., 1872), 76.
31. *Ibid.*, I (Jan., 1870), 115.
32. *Ibid.* III (April, 1872), 268. See also pp. 268, 309, 388, 430.
33. In support of the theory that Mrs. Browne was "Mrs. Dustbrush" and "Mrs. Melinda Newbroom," Editor Browne explained that the absence of these letters was caused by the illness of the author, and said: "She promises to resume her pen for our benefit as soon as her health will permit." After Mrs. Browne's death in May, 1873, there were no more of these letters. *Ibid.*, IV (Dec., 1872), 80. In fact, the last of these letters signed "Mrs. E. J. B." appeared in the Jan., 1873, issue, when Mrs. Browne's serious illness began, resulting in her death in May.
34. *Ibid.*, III (May, 1872), 274.
35. *Ibid.*, II(May, 1871), 264.
36. *Ibid.*, II (Nov., 1871), 21.
37. *Ibid.*, II (Sept., 1871), 411. See also (July, 1871), pp. 321-22.
38. *Ibid.*, III (May, 1872), 275.
39. *Ibid.* (July, 1872), p. 354. See also (Oct., 1872), p. 471.
40. *Ibid.*, II (Sept., 1871), 431.
41. *Ibid.* (June, 1871), p. 309.
42. *Ibid.*, III (Oct., 1872), 472.
43. *Ibid.*
44. *Ibid.*, I (Oct., 1870), 425.
45. *Ibid.*, II (Jan., 1871), 84.
46. *Ibid.*, (Nov., 1870), p. 2.
47. *Ibid.*, III (Dec., 1871), 41.
48. *Ibid.* (Nov., 1871), p. 29.
49. *Ibid.*, IV (Feb., 1873), 121, 125-26.
50. *Ibid.*, II (Feb., 1871), 132.
51. *Ibid.*, IV (April, 1873), 233.
52. *Ibid.*, I(Nov., 1869), 2.
53. *Ibid.*, II (Oct., 1871), 441.
54. *Ibid.* (Sept., 1871), p. 401.
55. *Ibid.* (Oct., 1871), p. 451.
56. *Ibid.*, I (Sept., 1870), 386.
57. *Ibid.*, IV (April, 1873), 233.
58. *Ibid.*, I (Feb., 1870), 121-22.
59. *Ibid.*, II (Oct., 1871), 441.
60. *Ibid.*, I (July, 1870), 312.
61. *Ibid.*, II (Oct., 1871), 442.
62. *Ibid.* (Feb., 1871), p. 122.
63. *Ibid.* (July, 1871), p. 338.
64. *Ibid.*, III (March, 1872), 187.
65. *Ibid.* (May, 1872), p. 257.
66. *Ibid.*, IV (Feb., 1873), 126-27.
67. *Ibid.*, III (May, 1872), 273.
68. Browne, Macon, Ga., April 18, 1871, to "My dear John" (John A. Cobb), Americus, Ga., in John W. Bonner Collection.
69. Mrs. John A. Cobb, Americus, Ga., April 25, 1871, to Mrs. Howell Cobb, in Howell Cobb Papers.
70. *Southern Farm and Home*, II (July, 1871), 2 (advertisements), II (Oct., 1871), 17 (advertisements).
71. *Ibid.*, 467; (March, 1871), 198.
72. *Ibid.*, I (Oct., 1870), 442-43; II (July, 1871), 348; (Aug., 1871), 287; *Southern Watchman* (Athens, Ga.), Aug. 2, 1871 (1, 6).
73. Browne, Athens, Ga., April 8, 1870, to "Dear Colonel" (D. C. Barrow) (in possession of E. M. Coulter).
74. *Southern Farm and Home*, III (Dec., 1871), 69; II (July, 1871), 347.
75. *Ibid.*, II (Dec., 1870), 46-49.
76. *Ibid.*, III (Nov., 1871), 29.
77. *Banner of the South and Plantation Journal* (Augusta, Ga.), I (Sept. 30, 1871), 4.
78. *Ibid.*, III (Nov., 1871), 29.
79. *Ibid.* (Jan., 1872), 109; (July, 1872), 322; (Sept., 1872), 431.
80. *Ibid.*, IV (April, 1873), 233.
81. *Ibid.*, I (Sept., 1870), 10 (advertisements); J. A. Cobb, Sept. 17, 1870, to wife, on letterhead of the insurance company, in Howell Cobb Papers.
82. *Southern Farm and Home*, III (Dec., 1871), 70.

83. *Ibid.*, II (July, 1871), 16 (advertisements).

84. *Ibid.*, III (June, 1872), advertisement on back cover.

85. *Ibid.* (Jan., 1872), 110.

86. *Ibid.* (Dec., 1871), 71.

87. *Ibid.*, 77.

88. Browne, Athens, Ga., July 16, 1874, to Davis, in Jefferson Davis Letters in Confederate Museum, Richmond.

89. Robert W. Winston, *High Stakes and Hair Triggers. The Life of Jefferson Davis* (New York, 1930), 265.

90. The last known issue was for July, 1873. In this number Browne inserted this notice: "To our Subscribers. Serious illness and the advice of our physician that total rest from mental labor is necessary to recover, compel us to omit the issue of our August number, and to ask the indulgence of our subscribers. We hope, God willing, to resume our publication on September 1st, and continue it thenceforward without interruption. Subscribers will of course receive the twelve numbers of the FARM AND HOME for which they have paid, thus losing nothing by the unavoidable interruption of the publication" (p. 351). By early September Browne was back in Athens, and it seems that he never returned to Memphis. It would, thus, appear that his promised September number was never published nor a continuation in subsequent numbers brought out by him. How he disengaged himself from his *Southern Farm and Home* is not known, but it has been stated that it was moved back to Macon for the rest of the year and that it became a weekly in 1875 and continued for an unknown time. See Stephen Conrad Stuntz, *List of the Agricultural Periodicals of the United States and Canada Published during the Century July 1810 to July 1910,* Miscellaneous Publication 398 by the Department of Agriculture. This information was furnished by Oliver M. Shipley, Chief, Division of Reference, United States Department of Agriculture National Agricultural Library, in a letter to E. M. Coulter, Dec. 10, 1965.

91. Browne, Athens, Ga., July 16, 1874, to Davis, Jefferson Davis Letters in Confederate Museum, Richmond.

92. *Southern Farm and Home,* IV (July, 1873), 353. See also Rev. D. A. Quinn, *Heroes and Heroines, or Reminiscences of the Yellow Fever Epidemics that Afflicted the City of Memphis during the Autumn Months of 1873, 1878, and 1879, to which is Added a Graphic Description of Missionary Life in Eastern Arkansas* (Providence, R. I., 1887), 66-123.

CHAPTER XVI

1. *Southern Farm and Home,* II (March, 1871), 197.

2. *Ibid.*, IV (Feb., 1873), 151.

3. *Ibid.* (Nov., 1872), 39.

4. *Ibid.*, III (April, 1872), 231.

5. *Ibid.* (Oct., 1872), 474.

6. *Ibid.*, IV (Dec., 1872), 74.

7. *Ibid.*, I (Aug., 1870), 376.

8. *Ibid.*, II (Oct., 1871), 470-71.

9. *Ibid.*, 471.

10. *Ibid.*, III (Dec., 1871), 74-75.

11. *Ibid.*, I (Aug., 1870), 375.

12. *Ibid.*, II (Dec., 1870), 70.

13. *Ibid.*

14. *Ibid.*, I (Dec., 1869), 79.

15. *Ibid.* (May, 1870), 262.

16. *Ibid.*, III (Dec., 1871), 76.

17. *Ibid.*, IV (Dec., 1872), 74-75.

18. *Ibid.*, II (Aug., 1871), 390.

19. *Ibid.*, I (May, 1870), 262.

20. *Ibid.*, IV (April, 1873), 235.

21. *Ibid.*, II (Aug., 1871), 389-90; IV (April, 1873), 234.

22. *Ibid.*, III (Dec., 1871), 75.

23. *Ibid.*, II (May, 1871), 269.

24. *Ibid.* (Dec., 1870), 70-71.

25. *Ibid.*, III (June, 1872), 311.

26. *Ibid.* (April, 1872), 229-30.

27. *Ibid.*, IV (Nov., 1872), 38-39.

28. *Ibid.*, III (May, 1872), 269.

29. *Ibid.* (Sept., 1872), 434.
30. *Ibid.* (July, 1872), 352.
31. *Ibid.* (May, 1872), 269.
32. *Ibid.,* IV (Jan., 1873), 114.
33. *Ibid.,* III (March, 1872), 192.
34. *Ibid.,* II (June, 1871), 310.
35. *Ibid.,* IV (Nov., 1872), 39.
36. *Ibid.,* III (July, 1872), 353.
37. *Ibid.,* I (March, 1870), 183-84.
38. *Ibid.* (May, 1870), 262.
39. *Ibid.,* III (July, 1872), 352.
40. *Ibid.,* II (Aug., 1871), 389.
41. *Ibid.,* III (April, 1872), 231.
42. *Ibid.,* I (July, 1870), 119.
43. *Ibid.,* I (Jan., 1870), 119.
44. *Ibid.,* III (Aug., 1872), 393.
45. *Ibid.,* I (March, 1870), 180.
46. *Ibid.,* IV (Nov., 1872), 40.
47. *Ibid.,* III (Sept., 1872), 436.
48. *Ibid.,* II (Nov., 1870), 34.

49. *Ibid.,* III (Feb., 1872), 155.
50. *Ibid.,* I (Sept., 1870), 418.
51. *Ibid.,* IV (Nov., 1872), 39.
52. *Ibid.,* III (July, 1872), 353-54.
53. *Ibid.,* I (Dec., 1869), 79.
54. *Ibid.,* III (Dec., 1871), 76.
55. *Ibid.,* II (April, 1871), 234.
56. *Ibid.,* IV (Jan., 1873), 115.
57. *Ibid.,* II (Aug., 1871), 390.
58. *Ibid.,* I (June, 1870), 303.
59. *Ibid.* (April, 1870), 221, 222.
60. *Ibid.,* III (Aug., 1872), 394.
61. *Ibid.,* IV (Jan., 1872), 113-14.
62. *Ibid.,* III (Jan., 1872), 114.
63. *Ibid.,* I (Jan., 1870), 119.
64. *Ibid.,* II (Jan., 1871), 115.
65. *Ibid.,* I(May, 1870), 262-63.
66. *Ibid.,* II (Feb., 1871), 152.
67. *Ibid.,* I (March, 1870), 181-82.
68. *Ibid.,* III (June, 1870), 313.
69. *Ibid.,* I (Feb., 1870), 152.

CHAPTER XVII

1. March 2, 1871, in Howell Cobb Papers.
2. John A. Cobb, Macon, Ga., June 8, 1871, to wife, *ibid.*
3. C. A. Thompson (Kati) (Mrs. Jacob T.), Memphis, March 30 (1872), to Mrs. Howell Cobb, *ibid.*
4. Browne, Memphis, Feb. 24, 1873, to Mrs. Howell Cobb, Jr., *ibid.*
5. Browne, Memphis, March 27, 1873 to Mrs. Howell Cobb, *ibid.*
6. *Memphis Daily Appeal,* May 6, 1873 (1, 6).
7. *Ibid.* (2, 1-2).
8. Browne, Richmond, Va., May 20, 1863, to Cobb, in Howell Cobb Papers.
9. Browne, Memphis, July 21, 1873, to Mrs. Howell Cobb, *ibid.*
10. *Ibid.,* Aug. 8, 1873.
11. *Ibid.*
12. Deed Record AA, 113, Office of Clarke County Clerk of Court, Athens, Ga.
13. Browne, Memphis, Aug. 8, 1873, to Mrs. Howell Cobb in Howell Cobb Papers.
14. Jefferson Davis, Memphis, Sept. 7, 1873, to wife, quoted in letter of Hudson Strode, University, Ala., Oct. 17, 1964, to E. M. Coulter (in possession of E. M. Coulter).

15. Mary McKinley Cobb, *Swallow Flights* (Atlanta, 1929), 156.
16. John A. Cobb, Americus, Ga., Oct. 11, 13, 1873, to wife, in Howell Cobb Papers.
17. In Barlow Papers.
18. Dec. 20, year indistinct, *ibid.*
19. *Ibid.,* May 26, 1874.
20. July 16, 1874, in Jefferson Davis Letters in Confederate Museum, Richmond.
21. *Northeast Georgian* (Athens, Ga.), May 27, 1874 (3, 6) ; *Weekly Sumter Republican* (Americus, Ga.), Oct. 30, 1874 (3, 3).
22. Mrs. John A. Cobb, Athens, Ga., May 24, 1874, to husband, in Howell Cobb Papers.
23. *Ibid.,* May 29, 1874.
24. *Ibid.,* Oct. 19, 1874; June 13, 1878.
25. Minutes of the Board of Trustees, University of Georgia, 1858-1877, Dec. 8, 1868, in University of Georgia General Library, Athens, Ga.
26. New York *World,* Dec. 24, 1868 (12, 4).
27. *Ibid.,* Jan. 5, 1869. See also *ibid.,* Feb. 1, 1869 (1, 6).
28. Browne, Athens, Ga., Aug. 8, 1875, to Stephens, in Alexander H. Stephens Papers.

29. Minutes of the Board of Trustees, University of Georgia, 1858-1877, p. 231; Col. D. C. Barrow, Athens, Ga., Sept. 18, 1868, to "Johnnie" (John A. Cobb), in Howell Cobb Papers.

30. Browne, Athens, Ga., July 16, 1874, to Davis, in Jefferson Davis Letters, in Confederate Museum, Richmond.

31. Mrs. John A. Cobb, Athens, Ga., July 31, 1874, to husband, Americus, Ga., in Howell Cobb Papers.

32. *Northeast Georgian* (Athens, Ga.), Aug. 12, 1874 (2, 2).

33. Minutes of the Board of Trustees, University of Georgia, 1858-1877, p. 516; *Atlanta Constitution,* Aug. 4, 1874 (3, 4), Aug. 8, 1874 (3, 2).

34. *Northeast Georgian* (Athens, Ga.), Oct. 14, 1874 (3, 3).

35. *Ibid.*

36. Barlow, New York, Oct. 29, 1874, to Browne, Athens, Ga., in Barlow Papers.

37. *Ibid.,* Nov. 6, 1874.

38. *Ibid.,* Dec. 11, 1874.

39. Browne, Athens, Ga., Dec. 20, 1873, to Barlow, New York, *ibid.*

40. Barlow, New York, Nov. 22, 1874, to Browne, Athens, Ga., *ibid.*

41. *Ibid.,* Dec. 11, 1874; *ibid.,* Nov. 22, 1874; *ibid.,* Feb. 9, 1878.

42. *Ibid.,* Feb. 9, 1878.

43. *Ibid.,* Oct. 30, 1877.

44. Browne, Athens, Ga., Jan. 10, Feb. 14, 1878, to Barlow, *ibid.*

45. *Ibid.,* July 12, 1876.

46. Barlow, New York, July 17, 1876 to Browne, Athens, Ga., *ibid.*

47. *Ibid.,* Aug. 10, 1877.

48. *Ibid.,* Nov. 11, 1877.

49. *Ibid.,* Feb. 9, 1878.

50. *Ibid.*

51. Browne, Athens, Ga., March 1, 1878, to Barlow, *ibid.* The last of the known correspondence extant between Browne and Barlow ended the following year (1879). Browne died in 1883; Barlow, in 1889.

CHAPTER XVIII

1. *Annual Announcement of the University of Georgia with a Catalogue of the Officers and Students, 1879* (Atlanta, 1879), 40; *Southern Banner* (Athens, Ga.), July 22, 1879 (2, 3).

2. *University of Georgia Catalogue, 1879,* p. 25. In 1878 Browne's office was in the Ivy Building. *Southern Banner* (Athens, Ga.), March 19, 1878 (4, 5).

3. Browne, Athens, Ga., n. d. [1879-1880?], to Mrs. Howell Cobb, in Howell Cobb Papers. See also *University of Georgia Catalogue, 1879,* pp. 15, 17, 25.

4. C. C. Jones, Jr., Sept. 27, 1877, to Browne, in Charles C. Jones, Jr., Letter Book, 1877, Duke University General Library, Durham, N. C.

5. April 30, 1878, in Barlow Papers.

6. *Ibid.,* July 17, 1878. Browne asked, "What do you think of the enclosed examination paper?"

7. *University of Georgia Catalogue, 1877,* pp. 95-96.

8. *Ibid., 1875,* pp. 83-84.

9. July 9, 1875, in Alexander H. Stephens Papers.

10. *Northeast Georgian* (Athens, Ga.), July 28, 1875 (3, 2).

11. *Ibid.,* April 21, 1875 (2, 4).

12. *Ibid.*

13. Tuck, *Four Years at the University of Georgia,* 127.

14. Athens *Northeast Georgian* (Athens, Ga.), Jan. 27, 1875 (2, 4).

15. *Atlanta Constitution,* April 29, 1883 (3, 1). He was "quite fitted . . . his lectures were much appreciated." Hull, *Historical Sketch of the University of Georgia,* 118.

16. *Northeast Georgian* (Athens, Ga.), July 14, 1875 (3, 1).

17. *Weekly Georgian* (Athens, Ga)., Jan. 23, 1877 (5, 1-2); *Banner* (Athens, Ga., weekly), May 31, 1881 (3, 1).

18. Browne, Athens, Ga., July 10, 1878, to Barrow, in Colonel David C. Barrow Papers.

19. Aug. 4, 1878, in Howell Cobb Pa-

pers. See also Tuck, *Four Years at the University of Georgia*, 125-26.

20. Oct. 8, 1878, in Barlow Papers.
21. Minutes of the Board of Trustees, University of Georgia, 1878-1886, p. 142. See also Browne, Athens, Ga., March 7, 1879, to Barlow; Barlow, New York, March 20, 1879, to Browne, in Barlow Papers; Tuck, *Four Years at the University of Georgia*, 39-40.
22. Browne, Athens, Ga., Aug. 4, 1879, to Wm. L. Mitchell, in Trustee Correspondence, University of Georgia, University of Georgia General Library, Athens, Ga.
23. Minutes of the Board of Trustees, University of Georgia, 1858-1877, pp. 158, 160. See also Hull, *Historical Sketch of the University of Georgia*, n. p. (under date 1866).
24. *Northeast Georgian* (Athens, Ga), Oct. 21, 1874 (3, 5).
25. Minutes of the Faculty, University of Georgia, 1881-1889, pp. 82-84.
26. A copy of this address is in the William L. Mitchell Collection.
27. Minutes of the Faculty, University of Georgia, 1873-1881, p. 34.
28. *Ibid.*, 59; *University of Georgia Catalogue, 1879*, p. 46.
29. Minutes of the Board of Trustees, University of Georgia, 1878-1886, p. 72.
30. *Southern Banner* (Athens, Ga.), July 23, 1878 (2, 3).
31. Chancellor Mell's Report to Trustees, Aug. 1, 1879, in Mell Collection.
32. Minutes of the Faculty, University of Georgia, 1873-1881, p. 226.
33. Browne, Athens, Ga., Sept. 19, 1877, to Jones, in Charles C. Jones, Jr., Papers. See also Jones, Augusta, Ga., (month illegible) 1877, to Browne, in Charles C. Jones, Jr., Letter Book, p. 875.
34. Jones, Augusta, Ga., Sept. 22, 1877, to Browne, *ibid*. This copy is in the possession of E. M. Coulter.
35. Jones, New York, April 21, 1874, to Mitchell, in William L. Mitchell Collection.
36. Minutes of the Board of Trustees, University of Georgia, 1858-1877, p. 705. See also Browne, Athens,

Ga., Sept. 19, 1877, to Jones, in Charles C. Jones, Jr. Papers.
37. *Southern Banner* (Athens, Ga.), March 26, 1878 (4, 6).
38. July 12, 1876, in Barlow Papers.
39. July 17, 1876, *ibid.*
40. Minutes of the Board of Trustees, University of Georgia, 1878-1886, session of Aug., 1878. Browne's salary in 1882 was $2,000 annually. *Ibid.*, 361.
41. Nevertheless, Hull said of him as an agriculturalist: "he was a failure. He had no training whatever for the work. He didn't know the difference between nitrogen and ammonia, and he believed that feeding a cow on fodder would dry up her milk." *Historical Sketch of the University of Georgia*, 118. It is difficult to understand how Hull could have made this statement.
42. *University of Georgia Catalogue, 1879*, p. 37. See also Chancellor Mell's Report to Trustees, Aug. 1, 1879, pp. 24-26, in Mell Collection.
43. *Southern Banner* (Athens, Ga.), Dec. 24, 1878 (2, 3).
44. *Ibid.* July 22, 1879 (2, 3).
45. Minutes of the Board of Trustees, University of Georgia, 1878-1886, p. 142.
46. *Banner* (Athens, Ga., weekly), June 28, 1881 (1, 6); Minutes of the Board of Trustees, University of Georgia, 1878-1886, pp. 277-78, 331-34, 421-27.
47. Browne, Athens, Ga., May 2, 1880, to Mitchell, William L. Mitchell Collection.
48. *Ibid.*, Sept. 20, 1880.
49. Browne, Athens, Ga., Feb. 16, 1878, to Barlow, in Barlow Papers.
50. Minutes of the Board of Trustees, University of Georgia, 1878-1886, pp. 140-42.
51. *Southern Banner* (Athens, Ga.), July 22, 1879 (2, 3).
52. Voucher 14, in Records of the Settlement of William M. Browne Estate.
53. *Southern Banner* (Athens, Ga.), July 22, 1879 (2, 3).
54. For instance, *Southern Farm and Home*, IV (Nov., 1872), 24. See

also *ibid.,* III (April, May, 1872), 226, 265.

55. Voucher 40, in Records of the Settlement of the William M. Browne Estate. See also Trustee Correspondence, 1885, University of Georgia Library.

56. *Southern Banner* (Athens, Ga.), Sept. 13, 1881 (2, 2). See also *Savannah Morning News,* Sept. 6, 1881 (4, 5).

57. *Southern Banner* (Athens, Ga.), July 16, 1878 (5, 4); Aug. 20, 1878 (5, 1). See also *Northeast Georgian* (Athens, Ga.), Aug. 18, 1875 (2, 6); *Georgian* (Athens, Ga.), Jan. 4, 1876 (2, 2).

58. *Southern Banner* (Athens, Ga.), Feb. 27, 1883 (2, 1).

59. *Atlanta Constitution,* Feb. 21, 1883 (1, 5).

CHAPTER XIX

1. *Northeast Georgian* (Athens, Ga.), May 6, 1874 (3, 6); Jan. 20, 1875 (3, 1).

2. *Southern Banner* (Athens, Ga.), March 26, 1869 (2, 3-4); *Northeast Georgian* (Athens, Ga.), Sept. 2, 1874 (3, 5); Nov. 25, 1874 (2, 3); John A. Cobb, Americus, Ga., Oct. 5, 6, 1874, to wife, in Howell Cobb Papers.

3. *Atlanta Constitution,* April 11-13, 1883; (*passim*) *Chronicle and Constitutionalist* (Augusta, Ga.), April 29, 1883 (4, 3).

4. *Northeast Georgian* (Athens, Ga.), May 26, 1875 (2, 2).

5. *Ibid.,* Feb. 3, 1875 (3, 1).

6. *Georgian* (Athens, Ga.), March 20, 1877 (5, 1).

7. *Banner* (Athens, Ga., weekly), June 28, 1881 (3, 3).

8. Minutes of the Faculty, University of Georgia, 1881-1889, p. 114.

9. *Southern Farm and Home,* III (Sept., 1872), 434.

10. *Atlanta Constitution,* April 29, 1883 (3, 1). See also *Southern Banner* (Athens, Ga.), April 30, 1878 (4, 5).

11. Journal HH, 539, in Records of the Settlement of the William M. Browne Estate.

12. *Northeast Georgian* (Athens, Ga.), Dec. 30, 1874 (1, 2).

13. Barlow, New York, Nov. 21, Dec. 26, 1877, to Browne, Athens, Ga., in Barlow Papers.

14. Browne, Athens, Ga., May 17, 1878, to Barlow, New York, *ibid.*

15. Barlow, New York, July 22, 1878, to Browne, Athens, Ga., *ibid.*

16. Browne, Athens, Ga., Sept. 10, 1878, to Davis in Jefferson Davis Letters. See also Browne, Athens, Ga., July 17, 1878, to Barlow, in Barlow Papers.

17. Sept. 16, 1878, in Barlow Papers.

18. *Ibid.,* Sept. 25, 1878.

19. Barlow, New York, Sept. 20, 1878, to Browne, Athens, Ga., *ibid.*

20. Browne, Athens, Ga., Oct. 8, 1878, to Barlow, New York, *ibid.*

21. Jefferson Davis, Baltimore, Sept. 27, 1872, to Burton N. Harrison, New York, in "Mrs. Burton Harrison's Scrap Book."

22. Browne, Athens, Ga., Sept. 20, 1880, to Mitchell, William L. Mitchell Collection. See also Browne, Athens, Ga., Sept. 10, 1878, to Davis, in Jefferson Davis Letters. See also Rowland, ed., *Jefferson Davis, Constitutionalist,* IX, 174.

23. Browne, Athens, Ga., Oct. 18, 1878, to Davis, in Jefferson Davis Letters. Five years after Browne's death Davis had occasion to speak affectionately of him. *Weekly Banner-Watchman* (Athens, Ga.), Oct. 25, 1887 (1, 2).

24. Rowland, ed., *Jefferson Davis, Constitutionalist,* IX, 174, 175.

25. Browne, Athens, Ga., Sept. 24, 1880, to Judge W. J. Tenney, Jefferson Davis Papers, La.

26. *Appletons' Annual Cyclopaedia and Register of Important Events of the Year 1881* . . . (New York, 1889), n.s. VI (whole series XXI), 260-71.

27. *Appleton's Annual Cyclopaedia and Register of Important Events of the Year 1882* . . . (New York, 1889), n.s. VII (whole series XXII), 337-

48, 480-86, 560-64, 629-35, 743-49, 786-92.
28. *Ibid.*, 792-98. Quotation on p. 792.
29. Journal HH, p. 538, in Records of the Settlement of the William M. Browne Estate.

30. Minutes of the Faculty, University of Georgia, 1881-1889, p. 114.
31. Sale Bill; Journal FF, pp. 54-61, in Records of the Settlement of the William M. Browne Estate.

CHAPTER XX

1. Journal HH, 539; Vouchers, in Records of the Settlement of the William M. Browne Estate.
2. Journal FF, 54-61, *ibid.*
3. *Ibid.;* Sale Bill, 1883, *ibid.*
4. March 12, 1869, in Howell Cobb Papers. See also Mrs. Browne, Athens, Ga., [June, 1864?] and Nov. 27, 1865, to Mrs. Howell Cobb, *ibid.* See also *Southern Banner* (Athens, Ga.), Feb. 26, 1869 (3, 1).
5. March 24, 1876, Jefferson Davis Papers, La.
6. Browne, Athens, Ga., Dec. 1, 1876, to Barlow, New York, in Barlow Papers.
7. Barlow, New York, Nov. 6, 1876, to Browne, Athens, Ga., *ibid.* "Perhaps I am more despondent as to myself than as to others. Tho' ready and willing for any honest labor, I see little field for anything I can do." Browne, Athens, Ga., Jan. 24, 1866, to "my dear & valued Friend" (Mrs. Jefferson Davis), in Jefferson Davis Letters in Confederate Museum, Richmond.
8. Jones, Jr., Sept. 27, 1877, to Browne, in Charles C. Jones Jr. Letter Book, 1876, 1877.
9. Feb. 8, 1878, in Barlow Papers.
10. *Southern Banner* (Athens, Ga.), 1878, Feb. 19, (4, 5); March 12, 1878 (4, 3).
11. Minutes of the Faculty, University of Georgia, 1873-1881, *passim.* See also *ibid.*, 141-42.
12. Feb. 16, 1878, in Barlow Papers.
13. *Ibid.*
14. *Ibid.*, March 1, 1878.
15. May 2, 1880, in William L. Mitchell Collection.
16. *Atlanta Constitution,* April 29, 1883 (3, 1).
17. Voucher 42, Records of the Settlement of the Browne Estate.

18. Voucher 29; Journal HH, 540, *ibid.* Various writers have been in error in both the day of the month and the year of Browne's death.
19. April 28, 1883 (2, 1).
20. *Ibid.*, April 29 (3, 1).
21. Telegram in Jefferson Davis Letters, in Confederate Museum, Richmond.
22. Voucher 14; Journal HH, 540. Records of the Settlement of the Browne Estate. See also *Atlanta Constitution,* April 29, 1883; (3, 1); *Atlanta Journal,* April 30, 1883 (2, 3).
23. *Chronicle and Constitutionalist* (Augusta, Ga.), April 29, 1883 (4, 3). See also *ibid.*, May 1, 1883 (3, 1-2); *Savannah Morning News,* April 30, 1883 (2, 3).
24. May 1, 1883 (3, 6).
25. April 29, 1883 (6, 1). By 1967, and long before, Browne was as unknown in Athens, in Georgia, and elsewhere as if he had never lived.
26. *Ibid.*, April 29, 1883 (3, 1).
27. Minutes of the Faculty, University of Georgia, 1881-1889, pp. 111, 113-14.
28. Minutes of the Board of Trustees, University of Georgia, 1878-1886, p. 412.
29. *Ibid.*, 426-27. With Browne's death the Chair of History and Political Science remained vacant until 1892, when John Hanson Thomas McPherson, who held a Ph.D. degree from John Hopkins University, accepted the position.
30. *Scroll of Phi Delta Theta,* VII (May-June, 1883), 259. Additional information on Browne in the archives of Phi Delta Theta was supplied by R. E. Blackwell, Alumni Secretary, Oxford, Ohio, in a letter to E. M. Coulter. Aug. 3, 1965.

31. *Weekly Banner-Watchman* (Athens, Ga.), May 8, 1883 (3, 4).

32. See also Hull, *Historical Sketch of the University of Georgia,* 118.

33. Vouchers 23, 30, 33; Journal FF, 54-61. Records of the Settlement of the Browne Estate. See also *Atlanta Constitution,* April 29, 1883 (3, 1). The total Browne tends to divide into two parts—the Browne in public operation, bold and aggressive in support of his well-known principles, optimistic and forward-looking; but the Browne in his private correspondence, often despondent and bordering on weakness, as he commented on his miserable health and poverty, ready to accept charity from his dearest friends. Although the inventory of his estate would seem to indicate that his possessions placed him far from poverty, yet when the estate was liquidated, it did not get him out of debt. If there had been a possibility of securing a fair market price for the items sold, his estate might have left a surplus.

34. The wills are on file in the Records of the Settlement of the Browne Estate.

35. "Wm. M. Browne decd. Proceedings to Probate Will in Solemn Form. Filed Aug. 4, 1884"; Minutes, 1878-1885, p. 420, *ibid.*

36. *Ibid.*

37. Journal FF, 54-61, *ibid.*

38. Journal HH, 538, *ibid.*

39. Journal FF, 54-61; Journal HH, 538, 541; Proceedings; Sale Bill, 1883, *ibid.*

40. Will Record D, 447-48, *ibid.* See also *Weekly Banner - Watchman,* (Athens, Ga.), Jan. 15, 1884 (3, 3).

41. James Jackson, Atlanta, Jan. 9, 1883 [1884], to Jefferson Davis, in Jefferson Davis Letters, in Confederate Museum, Richmond. Undoubtedly when Browne made this will, he expected soon to follow his wife to the grave—not expecting to live long enough to carry out his wife's desire that she be buried in Athens.

42. *Ibid.*

43. Proceedings, "Renunciation of James Jackson & Jefferson Davis as Exers of Wm. M. Browne desd," Records of the Settlement of Browne Estate.

44. Journal HH, 538, 541, 542; Return, 1886; Vouchers 9, 11; Proceedings; Minutes, 1878-1885, p. 439, all *ibid.* See also *Weekly Banner-Watchman* (Athens, Ga.), May 8, 1883 (3, 5); Jan. 29, 1884 (4, 5); March 11, 1884 (1, 5).

APPENDIX I

1. April 29, 1883 (3, 1).

2. *Weekly Georgian* (Athens, Ga.), Jan. 4, 1876 (2, 2); *Weekly Banner-Watchman* (Athens, Ga.), March 11, 1884 (1, 5); *Atlanta Constitution,* April 29, 1883 (3, 1).

3. *Strolls about Athens during the Early Seventies* (n.p., n.d.), p. 40.

4. *Weekly Georgian* (Athens, Ga), Jan. 4, 1876 (2, 2).

5. *Historical Sketch of the University of Georgia,* 118.

6. Minutes of the Faculty, University of Georgia, 1881-1889, p. 114.

7. Tuck, *Four Years at the University of Georgia,* 127.

8. *Southern Farm and Home,* II (Nov., 1870), 35.

9. Ezra J. Warner, *Generals in Gray. Lives of the Confederate Commanders* (Baton Rogue, 1959), 368, n. 74.

10. Quoted in *Southern Farm and Home,* III (Nov., 1871), 29.

11. *Diary,* 170.

12. John O'Hart, *Irish Pedigrees: or, The Origin and Stem of the Irish Nation* (2 vols.; New York, 1923), I, 851.

13. For instance, Patrick, *Jefferson Davis and his Cabinet,* 101; Mark Mayo Boatner, III, *The Civil War Dictionary* (New York, 1959), 92.

14. The mistake was started probably by Joseph T. Derry in his *Georgia,* VI, 400. Among those writers re-

peating this error were William J. Northern, ed., *Men of Mark in Georgia* . . . (7 vols.; Atlanta, 1907-

1912), III, 289-90, and Boatner, III, *The Civil War Dictionary* (New York, 1959), 92.

APPENDIX II

1. See James Morton Callahan, *The Diplomatic History of the Southern Confederacy* (Baltimore, 1901), 11-24.

2. 1872, (1, 2-3).

3. Owsley, *King Cotton Diplomacy,* consult index.

4. Copy in Pickett Papers, III, 10055-10059. Col. H. B. Fant of the National Archives located this letter and generously supplied a transcript.

5. For short sketches of Henningsen, see Lonn, *Foreigners in the Confederacy,* 189-90; B. Estvan, *War Pictures from the South* (New York, 1863), 342-44; Laurence Greene, *The Filibuster. The Career of William Walker* (Indianapolis, 1937), consult index.

6. Copy in Pickett Papers, III, 10065-10073. Col. H. B. Fant of the National Archives located this letter and generously supplied a transcript.

❧ Bibliography ❧

I. BOOKS

Appletons' Annual Cyclopaedia and Register of Important Events of the Year 1881. . . . N.s. VI (whole series XXI). New York: D. Appleton and Company, 1889.

Appletons' Annual Cyclopaedia and Register of Important Events of the Year 1882. . . . N.s. VII (whole series XXII). New York: D. Appleton and Company, 1889.

Biographical Directory of the American Congress, 1774-1927. Washington, D. C.: Government Printing Office, 1928.

Black, Chauncey F., ed. *Essays and Speeches of Jeremiah S. Black, With a Biographical Sketch.* New York: D. Appleton and Company, 1885.

Boatner, Mark Mayo III. *The Civil War Dictionary.* New York: David McKay Company, Inc., 1959.

Boykin, Samuel, ed. *A Memorial Volume of the Hon. Howell Cobb of Georgia.* Philadelphia: J. B. Lippincott and Company, 1870.

[Buchanan, James.] *Mr. Buchanan's Administration on the Eve of the Revolution.* New York: D. Appleton and Company, 1866.

Callahan, James Morton. *The Diplomatic History of the Southern Confederacy.* ("The Albert Shaw Lectures on Diplomatic History," 1900.) Baltimore: The Johns Hopkins Press, 1901.

Chesnut, Mary Boykin. *A Diary from Dixie,* ed. Ben Ames Williams. Boston: Houghton Mifflin Company, 1949.

Cobb, Mary McKinley. *Swallow Flights.* Atlanta: Oglethorpe University Press, 1929.

Congressional Globe: Containing the Debates and Proceedings of the First Session of the Thirty-Sixth Congress: also, of the Special Session of the Senate. Washington, D. C.: Printed at the Office of John C. Rives, 1860. Pt. I, 1859-1860.

"The Covode Investigation." No. 648 of *Reports of Committees of the House of Representatives, Made during the First Session of the Thirty-Sixth Congress, 1859-1860.* Serial No. 1071. 5 vols. Washington, D.C.: Thomas H. Ford, Printer, 1860.

Curtis, George Ticknor. *Life of James Buchanan, Fifteenth President of the United States.* 2 vols. New York: Harper and Brothers, 1883.

Derry, Joseph T. *Georgia.* Vol. VI of Clement A. Evans, ed. *Confederate Military History.* Atlanta; Confederate Publishing Company, 1899.

Estvàn, B. *War Pictures of the South.* New York: D. Appleton and Company, 1863.

Greeley, Horace and John F. Cleveland. *A Political Text-Book for 1860.* New York: Tribune Association, 1860.

Greene, Laurence. *The Filibuster. The Career of William Walker.* Indianapolis: The Bobbs-Merrill Company, 1937.

Hesseltine, William B. *Confederate Leaders in the New South.* Baton Rouge: Louisiana State University Press, 1950.

Hughes, Nathaniel Chairs, Jr. *General William J. Hardee, Old Reliable.* Baton Rouge: Louisiana State University Press, 1965.

Hull, Augustus Longstreet. *Annals of Athens, Georgia, 1801-1901.* Athens: Banner Job Office, 1906

Hull, Augustus Longstreet. *A Historical Sketch of the University of Georgia.* Atlanta: The Foote & Davies Co., 1894.

Johnson, Allen and Dumas Malone, eds. *Dictionary of American Biography.* (Authors Edition). New York: Charles Scribner's Sons, 1937.

Jones, Charles C., Jr. *A Roster of General Officers, Heads of Departments, Senators, Representatives, Military Organizations, &c., &c., in Confederate Service during the War Between the States.* Richmond: Southern Historical Society, 1876.

Jones, Charles C., Jr. *The Siege of Savannah in December, 1864, and the Confederate Operations in Georgia and the Third Military District in South Carolina during General Sherman's March from Atlanta to the Sea.* 2 vols. Albany, N. Y.: Joel Munsell, 1874.

Jones, J. B. *A Rebel War Clerk's Diary at the Confederate States Capital,* ed. Howard Swiggett. 2 vols. New York: Old Hickory Bookshop, 1935.

Journal of the Congress of the Confederate States of America, 1861-1865. 7 vols. Washington: Government Printing Office, 1904-1905.

King, Horatio. *Turning on the Light. A Dispassionate Survey of President Buchanan's Administration, from 1860 to its Close.* . . . Philadelphia: J. B. Lippincott Company, 1895.

Klein, Philip Shriver. *President James Buchanan, A Biography.* University Park, Pa.: The Pennsylvania University Press, 1962.

Lonn, Ella. *Foreigners in the Confederacy.* Chapel Hill: University of North Carolina Press, 1940.

Moore, Albert Burton. *Conscription and Conflict in the Confederacy.* New York: The Macmillan Company, 1924.

Moore, John Bassett, ed. *The Works of James Buchanan, Comprising his Speeches, State Papers, and Private Correspondence.* 12 vols. Philadelphia: J. B. Lippincott Company, 1908-1911.

Nevins, Allan and Milton Halsey Thomas, eds. *The Diary of George Templeton Strong.* 4 vols. New York: The Macmillan Company, 1952.

Nichols, Roy Franklin. *The Disruption of American Democracy.* New York: The Macmillan Company, 1948.

Northen, William J., ed. *Men of Mark in Georgia.* . . . 7 vols. Atlanta: A. B. Caldwell, 1907-1912.

Official Records of the Union and Confederate Navies in the War of the Rebellion. 30 vols. and index. Washington: Government Printing Office, 1894-1927.

O'Hart, John. *Irish Pedigrees; or, The Origin and Stem of the Irish Nation.* 2 vols. New York: Murphy & McCarthy, 1923.

Owsley, Frank Lawrence. *King Cotton Diplomacy. Foreign Relations of the Confederate States of America,* rev. Harriet Chappell Owsley. 2nd ed. Chicago: The University of Chicago Press, 1959.

"Pardons by the President." No. 16 of *Executive Documents . . . of the House of Representatives during the Second Session of the Fortieth Congress, 1867-'68.* 20 vols. Washington: Government Printing Office, 1868.

Patrick, Rembert W. *Jefferson Davis and his Cabinet.* Baton Rouge: Louisiana State University Press, 1961.

Phillips, Ulrich Bonnell, ed. *The Correspondence of Robert Toombs, Alexander H. Stephens, and Howell Cobb.* Vol. II of *Annual Report of the American Historical Association for the Year 1911.* Washington: [Government Printing Office?], 1913.

"Public Printing." No. 205 of *Reports of Committees of the Senate of the United States for the First Session of the Thirty-Sixth Congress.* Serial No. 1040. 2 vols. Washington, D. C.: George W. Bowman, Printer, 1860.

"Public Printing." No. 249 of *Reports of Committees of the House of Representatives, Made during the First Session of the Thirty-Sixth Congress:1859-'60.* Serial No. 1068. 5 vols. Washington, D. C.: Thomas H. Ford, Printer, 1860.

Quinn, Rev. D. A. *Heroes and Heroines, or Reminiscences of the Yellow Fever Epidemic that Afflicted the City of Memphis during the Autumn Months of 1873, 1878, and 1879, to which is Added a Graphic Description of Missionary Life in Eastern Arkansas.* Providence, R. I.: E. L. Freeman and Son, 1887.

Ranck, James Byrne. *Albert Gallatin Brown, Radical Southern Nationalist.* New York: D. Appleton-Century Company, 1937.

Richardson, James D., comp. *A Compilation of the Messages and Papers of the Confederacy, Including the Diplomatic Correspondence, 1861-1865.* 2 vols. Nashville, Tenn.: United States Publishing Company, 1905.

Richardson, James D., comp. *A Compilation of the Messages and Papers of the Presidents, 1789-1897.* 11 vols. Washington, D. C.: Published by Authority of Congress, 1899.

Rowland, Dunbar, ed. *Jefferson Davis, Constitutionalist. His Letters, Papers, and Speeches.* 10 vols. Jackson, Miss.: Mississippi Department of Archives and History, 1923.

Russell, William Howard. *My Diary North and South.* Boston: T. O. H. P. Burnham, 1863.

Sanger, George P., ed. *Statutes at Large, Treaties and Proclamations, of the United States of America from December 5, 1859 to March 3, 1863. . . .* Boston: Little, Brown and Company, 1865. Vol. XII.

Statutes at Large of the Confederate States of America, Passed at the First Session of the Second Congress; 1864. Richmond: R. M. Smith, Printer to the Congress, 1864.

Stegeman, John F. *These Men She Gave. Civil War Diary of Athens, Georgia.* Athens: University of Georgia Press, 1964.

Strode, Hudson. *Jefferson Davis, American Patriot, 1808-1861.* New York: Harcourt, Brace and Company, 1955.

————. *Jefferson Davis, Confederate President.* New York: Harcourt, Brace and Company, 1959.

Tuck, Henry C. *Four Years at the University of Georgia, 1877-1881.* Athens, Ga.: Published by the author, 1938.

War of the Rebellion: A Compilation of the Official Records of the Union and Confederate Armies. 127 books and index. Washington, D. C.: Government Printing Office, 1880-1901.

Warner, Ezra J. *Generals in Gray, Lives of the Confederate Commanders.* Baton Rouge: Louisiana State University Press, 1959.

Winston, Robert W. *High Stakes and Hair Triggers. The Life of Jefferson Davis.* New York: Henry Holt and Company, 1930.

II. MANUSCRIPTS

Adjutant General File: Letters Received, 1860-1865. Department of Archives and History, Atlanta, Georgia.

Adjutant General's Letter Book, Nos. 24, 26, 27. Department of Archives and History, Atlanta, Georgia.

S.L.M. Barlow Papers. Henry E. Huntington Library, San Marino, California.

Colonel David C. Barrow Papers. University of Georgia General Library, Athens, Georgia.

Jeremiah S. Black Papers. Manuscript Division, Library of Congress, Washington, D. C.

John W. Bonner Collection. In possession of John W. Bonner, Athens, Georgia.

William Montague Browne Amnesty Papers. Record Group No. 94, National Archives, Washington, D. C.

William Montague Browne letter to Col. J. S. Preston. Manuscript Collection, New-York Historical Society Library, New York City.

"Wm. M. Browne, War Department Letters Received, 420-B, 1863." Microcopy 437, Rolls 82, 94, 95, 109, 144, National Archives, Washington, D. C.

James Buchanan Papers. Historical Society of Pennsylvania Library, Philadelphia, Pennsylvania.

Cobb, Erwin, Lamar Collection. University of Georgia General Library, Athens, Georgia.

Howell Cobb Letter Book, 1863-1865. University of Georgia General Library, Athens, Georgia.

Howell Cobb Papers. University of Georgia General Library, Athens, Georgia.

Thomas R. R. Cobb Papers (typed copies). University of Georgia General Library, Athens, Georgia.

Compiled Service Records of Confederate General and Staff Officers and Non Regimental Enlisted Men. Microcopy 331, Roll 37, National Archives, Washington, D. C.

Jefferson Davis Letters. Confederate Museum, Richmond, Virginia.

Jefferson Davis Papers. Duke University General Library, Durham, North Carolina.

Jefferson Davis Papers. Louisiana Historical Association Collection, Manuscript Division, Tulane University Library, New Orleans, Louisiana.

Deed Record, A, V, W. Office of Oglethorpe County Clerk of Court, Lexington, Georgia.

Deed Record W, X, Y, AA. Office of Clarke County Clerk of Court, Athens, Georgia.

"8th Census 1860 [Population], District of Columbia: Georgetown, City of Washington, 1-890, No. 101." Microcopy, National Archives, Washington, D. C.

"1st Battalion Cavalry, Local Defence — Va. Formerly Known as 'Browne's Reconnaisance Corps' and as 'Browne's Cavalry Battalion.' " Microcopy 324, Roll 15, National Archives, Washington, D. C.

Georgia Governor's Letter Book, 1861-1865. Department of Archives and History, Atlanta, Georgia.

Governor's Office File: Letters to Gov. Brown, 1860-1865. Department of Archives and History, Atlanta, Georgia.

Felix Hargrett Collection. University of Georgia General Library, Athens, Georgia.

"Mrs. Burton Harrison's Scrap Book, 1859-1909." Burton Harrison Collection, Manuscript Division, Library of Congress, Washington, D. C.

Joseph Holt Papers. Manuscript Division, Library of Congress, Washington, D. C.

Charles C. Jones, Jr., Letter Book. 1870-1872, 1876, 1877. Duke University General Library, Durham, North Carolina.

Charles C. Jones, Jr., Papers, 1866-1877. Duke University General Library, Durham, North Carolina.

Charles C. Jones, Jr., "Siege and Evacuation of Savannah, Georgia in December 1864 . . . Illustrated." University of Georgia General Library, Athens, Georgia. See Jones, Jr. below under division IV. Pamphlets and Periodicals.

Horatio King Papers. Manuscript Division, Library of Congress, Washington, D. C.

Patrick Hues Mell Collection. University of Georgia General Library, Athens, Georgia.

Minutes of the Board of Trustees, University of Georgia (title varies), 1858-1877, 1878-1886. University of Georgia General Library, Athens, Georgia.

Minutes of the Faculty, University of Georgia (title varies), 1850-1873, 1873-1881, 1881-1889. University of Georgia General Library, Athens, Georgia.

Minutes of the Superior Court, Vol. 22 (1864-1868) and Vol. 24 (1870-1871). Office of the Clarke County Clerk of Court, Athens, Georgia.

Miscellaneous letters. In possession of E. M. Coulter, Athens, Georgia.

William L. Mitchell Collection. In possession of E. M. Coulter, Athens, Georgia.

Mortgage Record, Liens. Office of Oglethorpe County Clerk of Court, Lexington, Georgia.

John G. Nicolay Papers. Manuscript Division, Library of Congress, Washington, D. C.

Frederick Law Olmsted Papers. Manuscript Division, Library of Congress, Washington, D. C.

Personal Papers—Miscellaneous. Box STER-STY, Folder "Stuart, W. Ac. 3240, 1 Letter to, from Wm. M. ———? [Browne]," Manuscript Division, Library of Congress, Washington, D. C.

Pickett Papers of Confederate States of America Collection. Manuscript Division, Library of Congress, Washington, D. C.

Keith Read Collection. Emory University General Library, Atlanta, Georgia.

Records of the Department of State. Domestic Letters, 53: 250, National Archives, Washington, D. C.

Records of the Settlement of the William M. Browne Estate. Office of Clarke County Ordinary, Athens, Georgia.

> These records consist of a mass of unarranged papers, including "Inventory and Appraisment. Estate of Gen. Wm. M. Browne," "Proceedings to Probate Will in Solemn Form," "Return of Howell Cobb Administration with Will Annexed of W. M. Browne, deceased," "Sale Bill Property of Wm. M. Browne, deceased, May 12th 1883," "Sale Bill of Personal Property Est. Gen. Wm. M. Browne decd., Feb. 20, 1886," "Vouchers of Howell Cobb, Admr. Genl. Wm. M. Browne, deceased. Return of 1886." Also Journal FF, Record of Inventory and Appraisments; Journal HH, Record of Returns; Minutes, 1878-1885; Will Book, D.

Register of Letters Received. Quartermaster General, Ch. 5, Vol. VII, National Archives, Washington, D. C.

Alexander H. Stephens Papers. Duke University General Library, Durham, North Carolina.

Superior Court Record, Writs, Vol. XXX (1861-1872). Office of Clarke County Clerk of Court, Athens, Georgia.

Trustee Correspondence, University of Georgia, 1866-1891. University of Georgia General Library, Athens, Georgia.

III. NEWSPAPERS

Atlanta Constitution, 1870, 1883.

Atlanta Journal, 1883.

Campaign Constitution (Washington, D. C.), 1860.

Chronicle and Constitutionalist (Augusta, Ga.), 1883.

Constitution (Washington, D. C.), 1859-1861.

Daily Constitutionalist (Augusta, Ga.), 1866.

Daily National Intelligencer (Washington, D. C.), 1860.

Louisville (Ky.) *Daily Courier,* 1866-1868.

Memphis Daily Appeal, 1872, 1873.

Montgomery Weekly Advertiser, 1861.

Montgomery Weekly Mail, 1861.

New-York Daily Tribune, 1861.

New York Journal of Commerce, 1854-1859.

Northeast Georgian (Athens, Ga.), 1872-1876. Title varies as simply *Georgian* and *Weekly Georgian.*

Savannah Morning News, 1883.

Southern Banner (Athens, Ga.), 1861-1864, 1866, 1868-1872, 1878, 1881. Title varies as simply *Banner.*

Southern Watchman (Athens, Ga.), 1866-1871.

Weekly Banner-Watchman (Athens, Ga.), 1883, 1884, 1887.

Weekly Georgian (Athens, Ga.), 1875-1877.

Weekly Montgomery Confederation, 1861.

World (New York), 1868-1869.

IV. PAMPHLETS AND PERIODICALS

Banner of the South and Plantation Journal (Augusta, Ga.), I (1870).

Brooks, Robert Preston, ed. "Howell Cobb Papers," in *Georgia Historical Quarterly,* VI (1922).

Catalogue of the University of Georgia (title varies), 1875, 1877, 1878, 1879, 1880.

Coulter, E. Merton. "Slavery and Freedom in Athens, Georgia, 1860-1866," in *Georgia Historical Quarterly,* XLIX (Sept., 1965).

Harper's Weekly. A Journal of Civilization (New York), XXXIII, No. 1701 (July 27, 1889).

Illustrated London News, XXXVII (July-Dec., 1860).

Jones, Charles C., Jr. *Siege and Evacuation of Savannah, Georgia, in De-*

cember 1864. An Address Delivered before the Confederate Survivors' Association, in Augusta, Georgia, . . . on Memorial Day, April 26th, 1890. Augusta, Ga.: Chronicle Publishing Company, 1890. This is a pamphlet of 30 pages bound into a large book with binder's title: *Siege and Evacuation of Savannah, Georgia in December 1864 . . . Illustrated,* enlarged by including many holograph letters, pictures, clippings, etc. In University of Georgia Library.

Morris, Sylvanus. *Strolls about Athens during the Early Seventies.* N.p., n.d.

"Mrs. Elizabeth Church Robb—An Obituary," in *Georgia Historical Quarterly,* XLVIII (1964), 471-473.

Scroll of Phi Delta Theta, VII (May-June, 1883).

Southern Cultivator. A Practical and Scientific Magazine for the Plantation, the Garden and the Family Circle (Athens, Ga.), XXVIII (1870).

Southern Farm and Home. A Magazine of Agriculture, Manufactures and Domestic Economy (Macon, Ga.; Memphis, Tenn.), I-IV (1869-1873).

≫ Index ≪

"John Plowhandles," frequent correspondent of *Southern Farm and Home,* 197

Johnson, Andrew, praised by Browne, 137

Johnson, Herschel V., nominated for vice-presidency, 43; votes against confirmation of Browne's brigadier generalship, 120

Johnson, James, signs Browne's pardon, 125

Johnston, Albert Sidney, liked by Browne, 135

Johnston, Richard Malcolm, supposed addressee of Browne letter, 117; coauthor of life of Alexander H. Stephens, 268

Johnston, William Preston, on Davis' military staff, 100; witnesses Browne's will, 262; bequest by Browne, 263

"Johnston" letter, by Browne, 117

Jones, C. C., Jr., comments on Sherman's capture of Savannah, 116-17; borrows books from University Library, 241; offered position by University, 241; regrets Browne's ill health, 256

Jones, John B., caustic critic of Browne and of others, 82, 104, 119

Jones, William, agricultural editor, 190

Jones, W. L., agricultural editor, 190

Journey in the Seaboard Slave States, 39

Julian, George W., Browne comments on, 163

J. W. Burke and Company, newspaper proprietors, 161; publish *Southern Farm and Home,* 189

Kansas dispute, 12

Kelley, William D., Browne comments on, 162

Kenelworth ivy, 133

Kentucky, trade promoted by Browne, 157-58; aids suffering South, 157

Kilpatrick, Judson, attempts to capture Richmond, 100; on march through Georgia, 116

King, Horatio, attacks Browne and *Constitution,* 50-51, 69-71, 73; defends Buchanan, 284 (n. 40)

King James I, 1

Lady Blake, author, Browne's estimate, 213

Lady Napier, in Washington, 30

Lamar, L. Q. C., quoted, 208

Land Grant Act, 207, 234

Landscaping, promoted by Browne, 245

Lane, Harriet, White House hostess, 33-34; on Bedford Springs holiday, 36; visits *Great Eastern,* 37

Lane, Joseph, nominated for vice-presidency in Charleston Convention, 42; in 1860 campaign and election, 45, 46, 47, 49, 50

Lanier Hotel, Macon residence of Browne, 225

Lawton, Alexander R., Savannah resident, 156

Lecky, Edward Hartpole, author, Browne's estimate, 218

Lecompton Democrats, 12, 13

Lee, G. W. Custis, in defense of Richmond, 100; praised by Browne, 135; elected to professorship in University of Georgia, 229; does not accept, 229; picture of owned by Browne, 254; bequest by Browne, 263

Lee, Robert E., Browne's comments on, 135, 142

Lewis, David W., agricultural official, 205

Liberal Republicans, 177

"Liberty Hall," Crawfordsville, Ga., home of Alexander H. Stephens, 230

Life Insurance, 193-94, 199, 208-209

Life of Alexander H. Stephens, by William Hand Browne and Richard Malcolm Johnston, 268

Lightning rods, Browne's advice, 200

Lincoln, Abraham, Browne comments on, 49, 51-52, 66, 91

Lincoln, Mary Todd (Mrs. Abraham), comments on, 88

Lincoln's Gettysburg Address, answered prospectively by Browne, 55-56

Lippincott's, Browne's estimate, 222-23

Lipscomb, Andrew A., Chancellor of University of Georgia, 129; picture of owned by Browne, 254

Lochrane, A. O., in Georgia Reconstruction, 167

London Star, quoted, 57

Longstreet, Augustus Baldwin, letter on slavery, 10

Lord Byron, in Byron controversy, 217

Lord Lytton (Bulwer-Lytton), author, Browne's editorial on, 195; estimate as an author, 211

Lord Morpeth, 3; joke on how he was addressed, 89